The digital writer

Sean Morey

FOUNTAINHEAD
PRESS

Our green initiatives include:

Electronic Products
We deliver products in non-paper form whenever possible. This includes pdf downloadables, flash drives, & CDs.

Electronic Samples
We use Xample, a new electronic sampling system. Instructor samples are sent via a personalized web page that links to pdf downloads.

FSC Certified Printers
All of our printers are certified by the Forest Service Council which promotes environmentally and socially responsible management of the world's forests. This program allows consumer groups, individual consumers, and businesses to work together hand-in-hand to promote responsible use of the world's forests as a renewable and sustainable resource.

Recycled Paper
Most of our products are printed on a minimum of 30% post-consumer waste recycled paper.

Support of Green Causes
When we do print, we donate a portion of our revenue to green causes. Listed below are a few of the organizations that have received donations from Fountainhead Press. We welcome your feedback and suggestions for contributions, as we are always searching for worthy initiatives.
Rainforest 2 Reef
Environmental Working Group

Design: Susan Moore
Developmental Editor: Amy Salisbury-Werhane

For information, please call or write:
1-800-586-0330
Fountainhead Press
Southlake, TX 76092
Web Site: www.fountainheadpress.com
E-mail: customerservice@fountainheadpress.com

ISBN Print Edition: 978-1-68036-354-8

ISBN Digital Edition: 978-1-68036-193-3

Printed in the United States of America

This one's for Fisher.

Acknowledgments

This book began with a lunch conversation with Felix Frazier about the state of the academic publishing industry and how to teach digital media in a way that also used digital media, incorporating the technology into the design of the pedagogical materials. Rather than simply produce an e-book made up of scanned pages with a few annotated tools, Felix had the vision and foresight to push this project and think bigger. I offer Felix my sincere and deepest gratitude for this and for his faith and diligence in working through this project, helping me to keep aiming for the larger goal, and for believing in this project from that first conversation.

This book is also very much a product of the ideas that it espouses, and one of those is certainly the collaborative nature of writing. Although this book's cover displays only one name, it's more accurate to say that it was composed by many writers, some of which will never read the book and only know that they granted an image and signed a permissions form. Some nonhuman (and human) contributors will read this book not knowing they helped write it. Of course, others contributed consciously and painstakingly, especially Amy Salisbury-Werhane, Susan Moore, Shelley Smith, and the rest of the Fountainhead Press production team. Without their expertise, guidance, and thoughtful comments this book would never have reached production. I also want to thank Scott Timian for his patience to work through this project and his steadfast determination in seeing this book's development from start to finish, and everyone at Fountainhead Press for their enthusiasm and encouragement. Thanks also to Clay Arnold, who helped germinate some of the original ideas for this project.

Thanks to all my students who show me new things, give me fresh perspective, and constantly make me grow as a teacher.

Finally, I want to thank friends and family. Of friends, John Tinnell, Aaron Beveridge, and Caroline Stone have helped me rethink what writing with new media technologies can mean and the effects it can produce. Many thanks go to Greg Ulmer—even though this book may not completely execute an electrate logic, it breathes with an electrate spirit. And especially, I thank Sid Dobrin, who has given me invaluable advice about writing books and let me steal some of his ideas (OK, all of them). Of family, you have become too numerous to list, but you know who you are—I thank all of you. Most importantly, though, my deepest gratitude goes to Aubrey, Sofia, and Fisher for hanging in there with me and making this project worthwhile.

Preface to Instructors

When I first began teaching, I was fortunate to be in a graduate program that stressed not only the analysis of digital texts but also their production. In other words, I learned that we as writing teachers—broadly construed—shouldn't just teach students how to interpret film, websites, online video, blogs, brand marks, and other digital and visual media, but we should also teach them how to *make* such media, so they can become producers of digital texts and not just consumers of digital media.

Such is the impetus for this book. *The Digital Writer* is an attempt to combine both the hermeneutical strengths found in other books on digital writing as well as the pedagogical instruction to teach students how to make these texts for themselves. While students using this text might not create their own Internet start-up, receive recognition at a film festival, or become the latest blogging sensation, they will begin to understand how to interpret, plan, compose, revise, and disseminate digital texts that can solve problems in their daily lives, whether it's standing out on a job search by creating a video résumé, learning the best social media practices, or creating a video essay to bring attention to an important cause in their community. While they will certainly be able to use these skills toward other writing courses in their university careers, this book looks beyond the university, to where students engage with digital media outside of the classroom.

Both inside and outside the classroom, the definition of "writing" continues to expand to include non-alphabetic print modalities. Both inside and outside the academic curriculum, students need to know how to manipulate images in a photo editor, edit video, mix text and image, and choose the best online media for a rhetorical situation. Most of the time, students already compose these texts through tweets, wall posts, emails, and YouTube. However, they don't always write these rhetorically, according to a thorough reading of audience and the rhetorical environment. They don't always choose the best genre, medium, and design to fit this environment. This book addresses a rhetorical process for creating and reading digital texts, walking students through the process from traditional rhetorical questions, to ones specific for digital writing.

Many classes that teach digital writing do so in a very narrow sense, and worse, sometimes create a dichotomy between "writing" with words and making texts with visuals and other media, which provide just another kind of writing. Often writing with new technologies focuses mainly on either the technology, or reading digital texts produced by the technology. However, few classes, and even fewer textbooks, focus on both analyzing digital works *and* producing them. Producing works of digital writing, or writing through digital media (which also includes alphabetic print), is of central importance for today's students who must be able to read the visuals they see around them every day, make sense of what they see, and relate them to their own lives. However, to be truly rhetorical and participate in a democratic society, students must also be able to produce such digital images and video; they need a visual rhetoric in addition to a literate one. They need to be able to write and think in images and not just in words.

This textbook separates digital writing from literacy because, stemming from the work of Gregory L. Ulmer, the typical digital writing texts that a student will encounter do not operate (wholly) based on a literate logic, but on what Ulmer calls electracy, a post-literate language apparatus that is emerging in the current multi-media saturated environment. Succinctly, Ulmer states that "electracy is to the digital internet what literacy is to print." Electracy is different than literacy because it incorporates the chief psychological component that alphabetic text is unequipped to handle—emotion. Part of the critical analysis that the visual rhetoric of digital texts should attend to is the emotional response (and what that entails for community interpretation and action) that visually-based and interactive digital texts evoke. Except for *Internet Invention*, Ulmer's textbook designed for upper-division hypermedia courses, no other textbook on digital writing exists that teaches from an electrate perspective.

However, there are traditional writing elements that a digital writing text should address. *The Digital Writer* covers these different design principles but does so in a culturally responsible way that looks at the rhetorical reasons for why such design principles should be used and how they should be used ethically. Students learn to read common digital texts that exist in the public sphere, what these texts try to argue, and how students can make use of such design principles for their own rhetorical purposes.

To accomplish all of this, *The Digital Writer* incorporates some specific features to help both you and the student create and study digital texts. Features of this book include

Focus on Digital Media as Writing

Many textbooks will attempt to fit digital writing into a print-based paradigm. However, doing so can be reductive, limiting how students understand and compose digital texts. For example, a video résumé is not just a reading of a list of accomplishments to a video camera. Instead, it is a genre that uses the logic of video editing, such as cuts, montage, lighting, and other elements not found in a print résumé. By taking a terminological approach that breaks teaching digital writing out of a traditional writing frame while still situating it within a tradition of writing, *The Digital Writer* helps students create and engage with digital writing more creatively. For example, although much of the terminology in the book might be new to students—such as electracy, montage, or puncept—terms such as these help students focus on writing practices specific to mediums other than alphabetic writing and provide them more tools when producing texts in different digital media.

Video Tutorials

Several of the assignments in *The Digital Writer* are best completed by using media production software such as photo and video editors. To help you better understand how to use and teach these platforms, this book includes links to video tutorials that show the basics and some advanced techniques toward making the texts required of the various assignments. You can also share these links with your students, providing them with ready-made pedagogical aids. In addition, this book also offers a list of common programs found on most computer systems, as well as a list of software available for free online.

In-Depth Analysis

Although *The Digital Writer* stresses digital production, it also walks students through examples and case studies on which they can model their own texts. Such analysis includes how the text might be composed, how it functions rhetorically, or larger social impacts that might concern its production or reception. You can also use these examples as models for the analysis of other, similar examples, helping students learn to read digital texts before attempting to write their own. For example, chapter 4 provides a thorough look at the Waste Isolation Pilot Plant and how they account for audiences that may not exist for 10,000 years. While students probably won't have to consider this kind of audience, this in-depth analysis helps them to think through those audiences that will read their documents.

Fresh (and Classic) Examples

The Digital Writer uses contemporary examples of photographs, advertisements, videos, artwork, and other visuals to appeal to students (such as the use of memes or music videos as examples). However, the book also injects some classic examples from time to time, but avoids the overused iconic images found in many visual readers. When such images do appear, they do so to offer a new perspective or history of the image not found in other textbooks. Moreover, the examples are selected to be interesting, edgy, and sometimes humorous to students, helping them engage more aesthetically, emotionally, creatively, and critically.

Hyperlinked Examples

Most of the examples in *The Digital Writer* include an online component made accessible through Google Goggles, a Quick Reference code, or a hyperlink. Using a smartphone, tablet, or a computer with Internet connection, students can "click" on a photo, podcast, or video still and view (or listen) to the example. This feature makes the print book more interactive, and allows you to teach digital writing *with* digital writing, even if your classroom isn't equipped with computers for every student.

Adaptable Assignments

Since there might be some technologies or software that you or your students don't have access to, most of the assignments in *The Digital Writer* can be adapted as traditional writing assignments, composed with traditional writing technologies (pencil and paper), or written within a word processor. For example, a video résumé can be adapted to a visual résumé, or a video essay can be scripted as a more traditional, written research report. Even if you don't have all the digital tools discussed in this text, your students can still analyze digital texts, write about them, and learn how to compose them in other modalities.

Preface to Students

Imagine living during a time when the only people who wrote were the sons of kings or pharaohs. Or, imagine living in a society that had just learned of the alphabet and was coming to terms with how to use it in their daily lives. You probably don't often think about how alien a technology writing can seem, for Western cultural traditions have incorporated, developed, and improved upon writing for over 2,500 years. However, writing was once a strange, magical technology, made more natural to us over time by its evolution, most notably from the ancient Greeks who gave the alphabet vowels and started to invent practices for writing, such as concepts, proofs, or definitions (before writing, there were no definitions, at least not the kind found in a dictionary).

Writing is no longer just the domain and privilege of the highest classes of a society; you probably write on a daily basis and were taught to read and write as soon as you were able (although, unfortunately, not everyone is taught to read and write). Yet, a writer today finds herself in another time of transition with strange writings that go beyond the alphabet. Never before have so many writing technologies been invented and introduced in such a short span of time. While the Greeks inherited the alphabet from the Phoenicians, and used a few basic writing tools to make letters, the past few years have seen an amazing proliferation in the ways that writers communicate and make not only letters but all kinds of meaning with all kinds of marks.

Writers make and upload millions of hours of videos to YouTube, a service only started in 2005. Writers unleash a barrage of tweets on Twitter, launched in 2006. Facebook, only slightly older, appeared in 2004. And Google, which seems to be everywhere, offering every kind of service including writing platforms like Blogger, first searched the Internet in 1998. The most recent of Google's projects, Google Glass, affords a method to write and read "in the air" as it provides a mobile augmented reality platform, so that as one goes about his or her daily activities, one can instantly write texts, send tweets, snap photos, or shoot video from a pair of wearable glasses. And speaking of devices, Apple's iPhone, already released in multiple generations, first became available only in 2007.

Whenever a new writing technology comes along, a society has to invent how to use it. Although you probably take alphabetic writing for granted, Aristotle—an ancient Greek philosopher—lived when the technology of the alphabet was still new and tried to determine the rules for how writing should work, developing theories that eventually produced mathematics, science, and literature. In short, Aristotle helped develop *literacy*. Gregory L. Ulmer, a modern-day media scholar, has identified the current era of digital writing as *electracy*, a word that combines the shared component of writing across media—*electricity*—and the *trace*, a term for the marks an author leaves as he or she writes with digital technologies (electricity + trace = electracy). As Ulmer writes, "electracy is to the digital internet what literacy is to print." If an author writes letters to make words, he or she writes with electricity to make hypertext, images, video, and all the other kinds of texts made with computers, smartphones, video cameras, and other devices.

As modern-day Aristotles living amongst new writing technologies, Ulmer believes that we need to investigate and write digitally. Given all the technologies that allow us to compose digital texts—texts that use images, videos, hyperlinks, and other forms of writing in addition to the alphabet—we must develop and learn how writing in this new communication environment is different from writing with the written word. Today's writers live in an era unlike any other, and what it means "to write" is changing on a daily basis.

Although writing nearly 50 years ago, the educational advice from another media scholar, Marshall McLuhan, still rings true:

> Would it not seem natural and necessary that the young be provided with at least as much training of perception in this graphic and photographic world as they get in the typographic? In fact, they need more training in graphics… (*Understanding Media* 230)

While digital writing in an age of electracy is more than just simply learning the tools, *The Digital Writer* starts (or continues) you down the path of how to write with digital technologies and logics, realizing that the path continues to shift. This text may be difficult at times, asking you to engage with new writing tools and terminology that you might not have encountered before. However, by the end of the book, you'll be able to produce your own digital texts, to write both graphically and typographically, and to know the reasons and logic behind your compositions. As culture continues to shift from literacy to electracy, you'll find that knowing how to make these kinds of texts and knowing how to contend with new writing technologies will be essential, for everyday holds the potential that writing will never again be the same.

Chapter Descriptions

Chapter 1: Digital Writing

Chapter 1 provides an introduction to digital writing, discusses how it's different from "analog" writing, and includes the background you'll need as you progress through the text. Ultimately, no matter which specific outputs you make, all of these assignments will require you to make a variety of connections between different parts of images, between text and image, between image and environment, and between different kinds of digital media. The rest of the chapter descriptions appear below.

Chapter 2: Digital Rhetoric

While digital writing has its own kind of rhetoric, many traditional rhetorical techniques can still be useful when reading and writing in digital environments. This chapter will provide some basic characteristics of digital rhetoric, but also connect digital rhetoric with classical rhetoric, demonstrating a continuity between the present and the past. The chapter will cover the rhetorical appeals of *logos, pathos, ethos*, and *kairos*, and will examine and illustrate each appeal using both print and digital examples. While you may have learned these terms in other writing classes, this chapter will both refresh your memory and refresh your understanding within a visual context.

Chapter 3: Digital Argument

While you've probably learned how to craft arguments in other writing classes, creating an argument through digital writing can be a bit different. However, even though you'll be working with text, images, video, sound, and writing technologies other than a traditional word processor, these media can still be used to craft arguments that you might usually associate with traditional essays. In this chapter, you will learn how to write your own arguments and how arguments function across different digital media.

Chapter 4: Digital Analysis

As stated above, this text's primary goal is to have you making your own digital texts for your own purposes. However, an understanding of how to "read" or view these texts in a rhetorical context can help make you a better designer and producer of digital texts. Chapter 4 will look at a variety of different kinds of digital texts and provide tools for how to approach their analysis, looking for the argumentative features in each. While the chapter is not an exhaustive rehearsal of all the possible readings a digital text may have, it will help you think rhetorically about different kinds of arguments based in digital media.

Chapter 5: Digital Audiences

Most of the decisions you make when writing will revolve around your understanding of what your audience wants, expects, likes, dislikes, and will find persuasive. Determining these preferences requires a careful analysis of your audience, and you must screen them before writing. However, especially with digital texts, audiences can also be actors who interact with your texts. Moreover, the ultimate goal of any rhetorical communication is to get your audience to act (or not act) in a particular way. However, with digital writing, your audience may not even be human, such as search engine robots that scour the web on behalf of search engines such as Google or Bing. This chapter will offer instruction on how to research and analyze your multiple audiences, and how to design different digital media to maximize their activity during and after engaging with your digital texts.

Chapter 6: Digital Research

While you've probably conducted research to write a paper for another composition class, other kinds of research are often necessary when composing a piece of digital writing. In addition to reviewing traditional research methods, this chapter will explain some other research practices you'll need to consider in the pre-production phase of your writing. This research might include investigating the history of a particular visual element you want to include in a design, the best software to complete a particular effect, or who holds the copyright on a piece of media you want to integrate into a video project. This chapter will cover some basics for you to consider before fully launching into design and production.

Chapter 7: Digital Genres and Modes

Although any text could be converted into a digital text, some texts are more digitally native than others. For instance, an image created wholly in Photoshop might be considered a true digital image while a painting that's merely scanned might be considered just a digital copy. While this book mostly avoids these distinctions, this chapter covers particular genres of digital texts that usually can't be created offline and scanned online, such as webpages, digital videos, social media, blogs, and other digital genres. In addition, this chapter discusses modes, or the purposes why we write, such as to inform, explain, or describe, purposes that persist no matter which genres we use.

Chapter 8: Digital Images

Since many digital texts include digital images, you should be able to create and edit this type of digital media. This chapter introduces you to four facets of digital images: the technologies of digital images, the categories of digital images, the rhetorics of digital images, and the ethics of using digital images.

Chapter 9: Digital Video

In addition to digital images, many digital texts include digital videos, you should be able to create and edit this type of digital media, even if the videos lack the full-scale production of a film company. While this chapter discusses some of the technical elements of making digital videos, it also covers the writing that goes into making a video, the rhetorical construction of videos, and how to incorporate them into their digital texts.

Chapter 10: Digital Editing

One of the most important parts in the process of any piece of writing is the step of editing and revising. This chapter will cover techniques that will help during the revising process for digital modes such as image and video, as well as traditional writing, since all of these media are intertwined during the production process. While digital writing requires its own set of specific practices when revising, some basic underlying principles govern all types of revision, and here you'll learn both.

Chapter 11: Digital Delivery

The Greek orator Demosthenes once claimed that delivery was the most important aspect of rhetoric. How you say something can be as important as what you say, and this chapter explains different considerations for how to deliver your digital productions, whether it be as simple as on which site to start a blog, different places to upload videos for particular audiences, or even something as complex as Search Engine Optimization for blogs so that audiences can more easily find them.

Table of Contents

The DIGITAL Writer

Digital Writing

In the film *The Matrix* (Figure 1.1), the protagonist, named Neo (played by Keanu Reeves), comes to learn that the world he inhabits is not made of matter that he can touch and hold, but rather it is one of illusion, a virtual reality made up of digital codes that only seems to be real. As the story unfolds, Neo no longer sees the illusion, but the actual strings of code, the binary code of 1s and 0s that create every structure, every image, and every word. His entire world is written with digital codes, and he can only defeat his enemies once he learns to master the digital world that surrounds him. He does this by becoming a digital writer.

Credit: Everett Collection

Figure 1.1
Neo from *The Matrix*, or "the one," learns to see his whole world as strings of digital codes.

Becoming Digital

You might not live in a world controlled by machines, but you must still learn how to master the digital technologies you interact with on a daily basis. Although the buildings, vehicles, appliances, clothes, and other objects you encounter aren't made *of* digital writing, they are made *with* digital writing. Many of the daily objects you encounter require complex computer software programs to design them, computer algorithms to run the machinery that makes them,

Credit: Konstantin Von Wedelstaedt

Figure 1.2
How many kinds of digital codes do you think it takes to deliver a package?

and digital writing programs to create their instruction manuals. Even if an object isn't designed with a computer, such as an ear of corn, digital writing at some point intersects with that corn's growth and production, such as the tractor harvester that collects it or the transportation logistics that get it to the grocery store (Figure 1.2).

While Neo is a fictional character, Thomas Suarez is not. Suarez writes code for real, and he was just 12 years old when he taught himself how to code and build iPhone apps. Eventually, he started a school coding club and taught other kids how to build apps for themselves, helping them all become digital writers (Figure 1.3).

However, digital writing appeared long before computer algorithms and codes. Digital, in one sense, simply means larger wholes that can be broken into discrete parts and rearranged elsewhere, as opposed to analog, which are wholes that cannot be broken apart (and still function). An MP3 file can be broken into smaller

Credit: *TEDx*

Figure 1.3
Suarez wasn't interested in just playing video games; he wanted to make them as well.

units, transferred across the world, and then reassembled into the same song. You cannot do this with a record. If you break the record into pieces, you might be able to glue it back together again, but the sounds won't be exactly the same as they were before.

In the same way, the alphabet provides a digital code. With only 26 symbols, you can create millions of words and rearrange them in any conceivable order to create existing words or even new words. The digital nature of the alphabet allows you to remember only 26 symbols you can rearrange to make up any word, rather than individual symbols for each object, action, or idea you may want to name.

Of course, another meaning of "digital" refers not to the writing itself, but the means of writing: your fingers (this is what "digit" originally meant in Latin). Whether pressing cuneiform into clay tablets, inking hieroglyphics onto papyrus, chiseling letters into marble, typing text with a typewriter or a keyboard, or gesturing words onto a touch screen or in the air for a motion sensor, you typically rely upon the digits of your hands to write with. For those who no longer have the use of their hands, other means of writing exist, such as voice-to-text programs. However, you predominantly use your digits to write, especially the thumbs, when texting from a smartphone. When you write digitally, you do so in more ways than one.

To think of a "digital writer" is to consider all these ways of writing digitally, and you can probably think of many other ways that writing is digital. In fact, nearly all writing you do is connected to digital writing in some way, from the smartphones you use to send text messages, to the laptops you take to school, the electronic pens you use to sign a credit card purchase, or the news you might follow on television.

Building

Link

Stop for a minute. In a group, write down a list of all the digital writing technologies you used since you got up this morning. Now, next to this list, create a second list that identifies the last writing you did without the use of digital technologies. Discuss these examples, particularly the nondigital writing. Is there a sense that even these nondigital writing technologies are still digital?

Engine

Search

How would you define "digital writing"? What instruments or tools do you associate with digital writing? In what locations would you expect digital writing to occur? How might you describe digital writing to your parents or grandparents? What tasks, jobs, or careers do you most associate with digital writing? Create your own definition, and compare it with the definitions that follow.

Defining Digital Writing

Even if you wrote with a pencil and paper and sent your messages via carrier pigeons, a whole network of international collaboration, commerce, and transport has been synchronized with digital technologies in order to make that pencil and paper (and perhaps breed and raise the carrier pigeon). When you write, you are interconnected with digital networks through digital writing; you are in the matrix. In a very real sense, you were born into a digital world with doctors and nurses who used digital writing technologies. If the first photo taken of you wasn't a digital sonogram, then it was most likely taken with a digital camera. You are a digital writer in more ways than one. Like Neo in *The Matrix*, once you realize the digital nature of all writing, once you see the world around you as it "really" is, you have an advantage by understanding the larger interconnectedness of writing and technology. You will more effectively use current digital writing technologies, but also you will adapt more easily to new writing technologies. For the purposes of this book, the term "digital writing"—as well as "digital writer"—mainly requires you to consider particular aspects (none of which involve knowing kung fu).

Requires electronic technology

This aspect may seem pretty obvious, but consider the many devices available for writing. While previous cultures may have adopted very few tools and media for writing—consider the ancient Babylonians who mainly used clay and a stylus to create cuneiform tablets—you have computers, smartphones, tablets, digital cameras, electronic pens, graphic design programs, presentation software programs, and many means available for writing digital texts. Moreover, "analog" texts composed on paper with ink or pencil can be digitized through optical scanners or digital snapshots.

Makes use of the Internet

While technically you can compose a digital text without being connected to the Internet, to be a truly savvy digital writer, you'll need to make use of the many digital writing tools available online. Resources and storage made available through cloud computing provide free or inexpensive ways to produce texts and can impact the kind of hardware you purchase or use. In addition, because many of your digital texts will be delivered through the Internet—not only through email but also through social media websites such as Facebook, YouTube, LinkedIn, and many others—you will need to consider how online delivery and reception influences how you create the text. Chapter 11 will delve more deeply into the topic of digital delivery.

Relies on multiple codes

As discussed above, the alphabet itself provides a code for writing a visible form of spoken language. However, digital writing combines the alphabet with many other kinds of codes to create digital texts. For instance, Hypertext Markup Language (HTML) is the main code used to build websites. This code includes letters from the alphabet, but these letters no longer mean the same thing. The HTML tag <b> doesn't refer to the sound "b," but to the text property "bold," something seen and not heard. When you change a photograph from color to black and white in a photo editor, you're using an algorithmic code to enact the transition. Some codes, such as the QR code in Figure 1.4, may not use letters at all. Even if you don't know the many codes that make a software program work, you're still writing with them. Although you may not need to know all these codes to be a digital writer, having an awareness of them can help you consider the possibilities and limitations of constructing a particular text.

Uses digital images

Just like the relationship between digital writing and the Internet, you could compose digital texts without using any images at all. However, you've probably noticed that most digital texts, from professional websites to social media platforms, make heavy use of digital images. In fact, you might also compose digital texts that are only digital images, such as through Tumblr or Instagram. Even digital writing that is primarily text-based, such as email and SMS messages, often are used to send digital images in addition to alphabetic text. Because of the ease and prevalence of composing with images in online environments, your audience will expect to see images alongside text, and you should always think of digital writing as also writing with images.

Operates in more than one medium or genre

Professional writers are often required to be able to write a variety of documents, such as proposals, manuals, instructions, memos, letters, emails, reports, and many other genres. Your role as a digital writer is similar, for in addition to these document genres, you should be able to design websites, manage social media campaigns, create digital images, produce videos, and write other kinds of digital texts. In addition, the content for one medium or genre must often be adapted to others. For instance, a video advertisement might need to be converted to a radio spot, or a print document may need to be altered and turned into a web-based document. As a digital writer, when composing a document, you should ask yourself what other media or genres you might need to write toward.

Requires research

Just like any kind of writing, digital writing requires research when composing a document. However, the kinds of resources may vary from those you would use for a traditional print-based document. For instance, while you may use digital databases, such as Wikipedia or Google Scholar, to get you started with any kind of writing assignment, a digital text that includes images, videos, audio, and other media may require you to use digital resources, such as an image search, YouTube, Internet Movie Database (IMDb), or the Internet Archive. As with any reference source, you must be able to discern between trustworthy and untrustworthy digital research resources and know how to cite them. Chapter 6 will look at this topic in more detail.

Communicates in a social environment

A print-based document may be sent to a few people, or even distributed widely as a flyer or brochure, but doing so can be costly and often time consuming. By contrast, digital texts can be sent to one recipient or a million viewers with a few mouse clicks and within a few seconds. While the recipient of a print document may make copies and send them to others, she could do this much quicker if the document was in a digital format. Overall, writing and disseminating digital texts becomes a much more social activity for many digital writing genres, such as blogs, social media platforms, and other venues that encourage audience feedback and participation. As a digital writer, you need to be keenly aware of where your document may end up and how it might be reappropriated. While you can't account for every potential audience, you should at least consider the negative consequences of placing a particular text online.

Makes use of rhetorical devices

Usually, when you're writing for an external audience, you have some goal in mind: You want to persuade the reader to accept you into a graduate program or to give you a job; you might want to persuade your member of congress to vote yes or no on a particular bill; you might want to make people aware that your band is playing downtown this weekend. Whatever the purpose, you'll use rhetoric to help persuade your audience they should take a certain action. Digital writing is no different and requires careful attention to the rhetorical techniques found in traditional kinds of writing, such as *logos*, *pathos*, *ethos*, and *kairos*. However, digital writing requires more consideration of the medium, genre, and design of these texts. To help you consider the rhetorical situation when writing digital texts, this book will introduce you to the rhetorical tetrahedron discussed later in this chapter.

Has digital audiences

As discussed above, digital writing has an audience that interacts with your documents much more socially and interactively than with print-based forms of writing. This interaction through digital tools and technologies makes your audience into digital versions that often appear to you as digital codes and through identities such as avatars. Thus, you and your audience come to know about one another in ways specific to digital technologies because any of you can perform a Google search on one another or look up one another on Facebook. However, when considering your audience for digital texts, you also must consider the nonhuman readers of your documents, such as search engine robots that stand between you and your human readers. Digital writing must take into account these digital audiences as well as your final readers.

Rhetorical Continuities

Although digital writing makes use of new rhetorical techniques, some continuities with older rhetorical traditions still remain. For example, digital arguments are still arguments: They make a claim.

As discussed more in Chapter 3, a claim (also called a thesis statement) makes an argument to establish a position about the world, usually toward some purpose. A simple description about digital and nondigital writing technologies is not an argument. However, making a claim that one kind of technology is better than the other because of its use value is an argument, or at least begins an argument. The purpose might be to persuade the reader he should adopt one kind of technology over the other. In the assignment at the end of this chapter, you will be asked to write a report, and evaluate (make a claim about) digital versus nondigital forms of writing.

Remains in a constant state of revision

You may have heard the phrase, "Writing is never finished, only abandoned." This maxim suggests that a writer could revise and revise and revise a document, but deadlines or other constraints ultimately mean she has to stop at some point and distribute the document to her audience. You may experience this feeling every time you turn in an essay for class. Given the finality of print—and the expense of printing new editions—authors of print-based works cannot return to their works often to revise them if they want to. However, if this maxim holds true for print documents, it's even truer for digital writing—

at least, the first part of the saying. With digital writing, the writing is never finished, for it's much easier to revise hypertext in a digital medium than it is to change a printed document. In addition, audiences of websites, such as blogs, expect updated content on a regular basis, requiring you to return to digital writing. Moreover, because search robots are constantly changing how and where your online document might appear to a search engine—and thus to human readers—your document is constantly changing in the ways it interacts with audiences and the Internet as a whole. Even if you ultimately stop working on a digital text, it's never finished, and never totally abandoned.

Although you'll learn about many more aspects of digital writing that will be covered in this book, these are the major themes you'll most commonly encounter as you compose and analyze digital texts.

 DIGITAL Connections

For more on how humans are becoming more digital, check out the BBC's podcast series "Digital Human" by Aleks Krotoski.

www.bbc.co.uk/programmes/b01n7094

Defining "Text" and "Writing"

Digital writing makes use of not just words, but images, sounds, code, and other forms of "texts." Toward a more comprehensive understanding of the kind of texts that digital writing produces, this book will refer to a "text" not simply as a text that uses alphabetic writing, but any kind of artifact produced by humans. Thus, a film, painting, sculpture, clothing, building, website, text message, video, song—virtually any object—can be read as a text. For instance, you might think of an airplane as a vehicle rather than a text, but as soon as that airplane has a paint job and a logo, it becomes a symbol and more than just a means to travel. As soon as that airplane includes more legroom than another, it makes an argument for why you should fly in it versus in its competitor. Text can be seen, it can be heard, and it can be felt through textures and patterns, such as braille or larger seats. While we might say a food-based text such as a cake can also be smelled and tasted, this textbook doesn't cover these senses, although they certainly contribute to how you compose and interpret such texts.

In addition, this textbook uses the term "writing" to describe any action that produces a text. Thus, writing might refer to composing a traditional essay, but it also might refer to making a video or editing computer code. When the textbook uses the term, "alphabetic writing," it's specifically referring to writing that uses the alphabet to make words.

Rhetorical Links: Classical Greece to the Digital Globe

You have probably heard this term before, but what is "rhetoric" anyway? The answer depends on whom you ask. Many people, upon hearing the word rhetoric, equate the term with descriptions such as "hot air," "empty," "lacking substance," or "overblown." Such descriptions paint rhetoric in a negative light, that suggests rhetoric may make words "pretty" at best, but "manipulative" at worst.

However, rhetoric might be better understood according to some of the definitions below. These people understood rhetoric not as a devious tool, but as a necessary method for making an argument. In fact, any time you try to argue a point, you're using rhetoric to help you do so.

> **Aristotle**: Rhetoric is "the faculty of discovering in any particular case all of the available means of persuasion."
>
> **Cicero**: "Rhetoric is one great art composed of five lesser arts: inventio, dispositio, elocutio, memoria, and pronunciatio." Rhetoric is "speech designed to persuade."
>
> **Quintilian**: "Rhetoric is the art of speaking well" or ". . . good man speaking well."
>
> **Francis Bacon:** "Rhetoric is the application of reason to imagination for the better moving of the will."
>
> **I. A. Richards:** "Rhetoric is the study of misunderstandings and their remedies."
>
> **Erika Lindemann:** "Rhetoric is a form of reasoning about probabilities, based on assumptions people share as members of a community."

> **Philip Johnson:** "Rhetoric is the art of framing an argument so that it can be appreciated by an audience."
>
> **Andrea Lunsford:** "Rhetoric is the art, practice, and study of human communication."
>
> **Sidney I. Dobrin:** "Rhetoric, quite simply, is how we use language to communicate—to persuade, to inform, to narrate, to remember, or to do any number of the things we use language to do."
>
> **Kenneth Burke:** "Rhetoric [is] the manipulation of men's beliefs for political ends...the basic function of rhetoric [is] the use of words by human agents to form attitudes or to induce actions in other human agents."

As this last definition from Kenneth Burke implies, it's important to understand that rhetoric itself can be an act, and a person making an argument is taking an action. Theodore Roosevelt has stated that "Rhetoric is a poor substitute for action, and we have trusted only to rhetoric. If we are really to be a great nation, we must not merely talk; we must act big."

What Roosevelt misunderstands is that rhetoric *is* action, that his words *create* action. Without rhetoric, he could not persuade the nation to become great.

Plato and Aristotle

Most of our Western tradition of rhetoric and philosophy originates from classical Greece (508-322 BCE), particularly from the figures of Socrates, Plato, and Aristotle, and we can still trace many rhetorical and philosophical terms and principles back to this trio.

Although he helped develop literate concepts, Socrates himself did not read or write. Still, he was able to think in abstract ways that most could only do through the tools and technologies of reading and writing, and so it is sometimes said that Socrates was the only man able to do literacy in his head alone. Luckily, Socrates's student, Plato, recorded many of Socrates's dialogues, giving us an idea of what Socrates thought and taught his students. Of course, Plato filtered these dialogues based on his own ideas and perceptions, and he would take these teachings and tutor his own students, forming the Academy, one of the first schools and a predecessor to the modern university.

Plato understood rhetoric as persuasion but felt that rhetoric needed to be tied to dialectic, a method of dialogue identified by Simon Blackburn as "the process of eliciting the truth by means of questions aimed at opening out what is already implicitly known, or at exposing the contradictions and muddles of an opponent's position." Here, rhetoric as dialectic works as philosophy, trying to uncover the truth as flaws and inconsistencies are identified and stripped away. Rhetoric, then, is not only about persuasion but also about uncovering the truth. For Plato, however, this "truth" was "Truth" with a capital "T"; he believed there were universal Truths that existed in heaven and could be discovered only through philosophy. One couldn't uncover this Truth through observing the world, for the world was an imperfect reflection of the real Truths that existed in heaven. Only by engaging in dialectic could Truth be revealed.

Many of Plato's ideas about rhetoric work against the Sophists, teachers of rhetoric who would travel from city to city and recruit students whom they would teach for a fee. Sophists typically taught logic, analysis of language and thought, and how to develop and form arguments. In general, Sophists taught there was no universal truth that existed outside of man, but that our words and discourse shape the world. Thus, any use of rhetoric seeks not to uncover some universal state of being but is rather used toward the particular context and circumstances surrounding the issue, including its application toward concepts of morality and immorality. Because they were looking for particular, situational truths (little "t") instead of universal Truths (big "T"), Plato accused the Sophists of offering weaker or "worse" forms of rhetoric that misled an audience, making a weaker argument seem stronger than it was.

In his dialogue the *Gorgias*, Plato works against these Sophistic ideas and attacks rhetoric when it is separated from dialectic; in other words, he attacks rhetoric when it's not used with dialectic to uncover Truths. Throughout the dialogue, Plato and his fellow participants attempt to define rhetoric, with Plato offering that "…one part of it would be flattery, I suppose, and shameful public harangue, while the other—that of getting the souls of the citizens to be as good as possible and of striving valiantly to say what is best, whether the audience will find it more pleasant or more unpleasant—is something admirable. But you've never seen this type of oratory…" Alone, Plato identifies rhetoric as mere flattery, simply trying to win the audience regardless of the truth, and this is the most common form, because he feels one has never seen orators trying to use rhetoric to get "the souls of the citizens to be as good as possible." As such, he argues this is a bad, immoral use of rhetoric. Rhetoric used for good must be tied to philosophy so that it will have a moral compass to help guide its proper use. The only way to get at this truth is through discussion with others in order to gain knowledge of each other's souls, which is dialectic.

In another of Plato's dialogues, the *Phaedrus*, Plato attacks writing because—unlike a person—a piece of writing itself cannot answer questions, cannot be tailored to specific audiences, and cannot defend itself. In other words, writing cannot engage in dialectic conversation, so the reader cannot interrogate the writing's "soul" and know if it uses rhetoric for good or bad purposes. Writing, therefore, cannot be used as a method for uncovering Truth.

For Aristotle, a student of Plato, the dialectic method is also one of persuasion, but he splits rhetoric from dialectic so rhetoric has a more applied, practical dimension while reserving dialectic for theoretical inquiry and seeking essential truths. In other words, the application of the dialectic took place in courts or the assembly when a practical decision must be made, and not when attempting to think about universal truths.

This practical dimension of rhetoric was important because of Greece's democratic government. Within a democratic country of laws, we rarely settle disputes and misunderstandings through violence (although, unfortunately, this sometimes happens). Rhetoric is one of the primary ways we settle these disputes. Aristotle realized this within his own context of a fledgling Greek democracy and understood that rhetoric was an important means to communicate effectively, a skill that was now needed by all citizens to participate in government. In his text *Rhetoric*, Aristotle wrote:

> *Again, it is absurd to hold that a man ought to be ashamed of being unable to defend himself with his limbs, but not of being unable to defend himself with speech and reason, when the use of rational speech is more distinctive of a human being than the use of his limbs. And if it be objected that one who uses such power of speech unjustly might do great harm, that is a charge which may be made in common against all good things except virtue, and above all against the things that are most useful, as strength, health, wealth, generalship. A man can confer the greatest of benefits by a right use of these, and inflict the greatest of injuries by using them wrongly.*

In other words, rhetorical power is just as important (if not more so) as physical power, and just as you shouldn't use physical force for ill gains, neither should you employ rhetoric for unethical purposes. As with any other skill or tool, you should be proud of the ability to create savvy, rhetorically sound arguments to persuade an audience of your point of view.

Aristotle composed a treatise on rhetoric in order to identify those parts or elements of rhetoric that seemed to be most successful and useful. While Aristotle does think those who use rhetoric should be moral, he offers that the main goal of rhetoric should be to persuade an audience, and much of his advice focuses on how to invent arguments that will best convince an audience. In his work, *Rhetoric*, Aristotle gives us the concepts of *logos, ethos,* and *pathos*, as well as the canons of rhetoric—invention, arrangement, style, memory, and delivery—that you will learn more about throughout this text.

While this text is more concerned with giving you practical techniques and tools for rhetorical practice in your daily lives, and not helping you to uncover big truths, some aspects of digital writing do bring up some of the issues Plato was concerned about. For instance, even though you might be separated from your audience by thousands of miles, digital writing tools allow you to engage in rhetorical dialogue in ways that older media don't allow. You can literally be face to face with your audience via Skype, or you can converse through microblogging or SMS messaging in real time. The instantaneous response of digital writing platforms allows for rhetorical engagements to happen at a rapid pace, and for rhetors and audiences to refine their statements and uncover "truth," whatever that might mean for each participant.

Modes and Forms of Rhetoric

Although Plato and Aristotle wrote about rhetoric 2,500 years ago, many of their insights still resonate today. This text attempts to make some of these connections explicit in the Rhetorical Continuities sections. However, as you read the text, consider for yourself how new, emerging forms of digital rhetorics connect back to these ancient ideas.

Building

Link

In a group, discuss how you understood the term "rhetoric" before starting this chapter. Had you only understood the term negatively, such as "empty rhetoric," or had you previously studied rhetoric as a means to communicate and build arguments? Draft a report based on your discussion, and share it with the class.

Engine

Search

Based on the understanding of rhetoric presented so far, when was the last time you used rhetoric and what was the context? Were you successful, or did you fail to persuade your audience? Write a short report of this experience, and share it with the class.

Another important consideration of rhetoric is that it doesn't occur only in writing with words, or alphabetic writing, but in other modes of writing as well, and in all the technologies used for writing. As Aristotle states above, rhetoric includes "all" the available means of persuasion, and sometimes these means include other forms of writing than just words and text. Images, physical objects, movies, television, and music can all be used rhetorically. A film, such as Disney's *Wall-E*, can try to warn us of a possible future should we use up all of Earth's resources. A powerful photograph can make audiences rethink an issue and start political change. A blog can be created in order to more quickly spread an issue important to its author.

Figure 1.5
The very shape of the Washington Monument is itself rhetorical.

The buildings and monuments around us are rhetorical. The Washington Monument uses the shape of the obelisk, which can be read as tall, strong, straight, and upright, all values that the designer hoped to associate with George Washington and the United States in general. The shape of the monument makes an argument for how you should remember Washington, and the choice of the monument's shape is one of the "means of persuasion" used to do this. The Washington National Monument Society, who drafted the first proposal for the monument, understood the monument's rhetorical impact very well:

It is proposed that the contemplated monument shall be like him in whose honor it is to be constructed, unparalleled in the world, and commensurate with the gratitude, liberality, and patriotism of the people by whom it is to be erected...[It] should blend stupendousness with elegance, and be of such magnitude and beauty as to be an object of pride to the American people, and of admiration to all who see it. Its material is intended to be wholly American, and to be of marble and granite brought from each state, that each state may participate in the glory of contributing material as well as in funds to its construction.

By including stone from each state, the monument, as seen in Figure 1.5, makes a rhetorical gesture that the states were all connected through Washington and his leadership during the American Revolution.

The *logos* for your favorite sports teams are also rhetorical, especially those that use a fierce, menacing animal. For instance, the Florida Panthers NHL hockey team partially chose the Florida panther as a logo because, as the former team manager stated, the Florida panther "is the quickest striking of all cats. Hopefully, that's how we will be on the ice." However, the former team owner, Wayne Huizenga, also selected the Florida Panther because of the animal's endangered status, helping to communicate the panther's plight across the country. This logo choice in Figure 1.6 was rhetorical and was used to help spread an environmental message as well as make his hockey team seem tough.

Credit: NHL, Florida Panthers

Figure 1.6
The Florida panther was chosen as a mascot because it conveys an argument about the quickness and ferocity of the Florida Panthers NHL hockey team. However, this choice also makes an argument that the Florida Panthers team cares about the plight of the endangered Florida panther.

Other sports teams use logos to connect with ideas or citizens of a region. The New England Patriots are appealing to the revolutionary spirit of the Boston area and their patriotism. The Miami Heat connects with South Florida's hot temperatures, but also the threat that their opponents might get "burned." Fans in these local areas identify with this message, helping to persuade them to support the team and see themselves as part of a larger group. And what is the action to which the authors hope this rhetorical strategy ultimately leads? Ticket and merchandise sales. One action begets another.

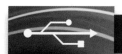 **DIGITAL Connections**

Top Gun Boosting Service Sign-ups

By Mark Evje

SAN DIEGO—Regulations prohibit the Navy from promoting the hit movie *Top Gun* in its recruitment efforts, but the film extolling the service's best fighter jocks apparently has become a valuable tool . . . in some parts of the Southwest anyway.

As Chapter 3 will discuss in more detail, movies can also use rhetoric to make a point or create an argument, even if this argument is implied and not immediately obvious. Moreover, sometimes an organization or movement can use a movie as rhetorical evidence to help them take an action.

When the film opened in May, recruiters in some cities manned tables outside movie houses during *Top Gun* premieres to answer questions from would-be flyboys emerging with a new-found need for speed from an F-14 warplane.

Navy recruiting officials say they didn't keep track of that operation's success, but they have noticed more inquiries than usual about the naval aviation officer candidate program since the movie's release.

They don't think it's a coincidence.

"Two groups I can identify (as having increased interest) are individuals who have applied in the past and were turned down or dropped out of Aviation Officers Training School, and individuals who are approaching the maximum age limit (to apply)," said Lt. Ray Gray, head of the officer programs department in Los Angeles.

In 1986, the movie *Top Gun*, starring Tom Cruise, was released in theaters. The film portrays the psychological struggles of one of the country's best naval aviators as he comes to terms with personal and professional difficulties, ultimately overcoming them. Because of the positive portrayal of the U.S. Navy and the excitement of flying Navy aircraft, the real-life U.S. Navy saw a dramatic increase in recruitment numbers, even setting up recruiting tables outside of movie theaters. Consider Mark Evje's article "*Top Gun* Boosting Service Sign-ups" originally published in the *Los Angeles Times*.

"There seems to have been a big rush in those categories that I have to attribute to the movie. I've asked several of these individuals if they've seen the movie and if that's why they came down to talk to us again and they've said 'yes'.

"On the other end of the spectrum, we've seen a general increase in interest in young men who don't yet qualify for the program, and I have to attribute that to *Top Gun* also."

Lt. Sandy Stairs, the Navy's representative while the film was in production, said Navy regulations prohibit the service from "selectively endorsing or appearing to endorse a commercial product," like the movie, even though it favorably portrays the Navy and could aid in recruiting.

"Some recruiters have said to me that a lot of young high school graduates said they've seen the movie and would like to sign up for naval aviation, but we don't actively go out and say, 'Go see the movie.' We're not in the business of promoting the movie, we're in the business of recruiting people," Stairs said.

But Lt. Cmdr. Laura Marlowe, officer in charge of recruiting for the naval officer program in Arizona and San Diego, Riverside, and San Bernardino counties, said her recruiters in Phoenix have received twice as many calls as usual about the aviation program in the last month.

"They couldn't specifically say it was a direct result of *Top Gun*, but they suspect it probably had a lot to do with it because when they would talk to applicants, about 90 percent said they had seen the movie," Marlowe said.

"Maybe it hadn't made them call in, but they'd been thinking about (joining the Navy) and this was just the kicker that put them over the line," Marlowe said.

> The high-adrenaline aerial fight scenes, high-tech jets, and patriotic overtones all provide rhetorical appeals to help persuade audiences of the honor and valor of serving as a naval aviator, even if the movie's ultimate goal is to entertain and earn ticket sales. Although it didn't directly promote the movie, the U.S. Navy was able to capitalize on the rhetorical messages implied within the movie and use these messages toward other actions, such as signing up new recruits.

As you'll read more in Chapter 2 (and throughout the book), digital rhetoric uses many forms of rhetoric but also incorporates digital practices that other kinds of writing do not allow. For instance, the act of making text into a hyperlink is a rhetorical choice that signals to readers they should click on the hyperlink, that doing so is in their best interest to learn more. Creating a hyperlink is an act meant to produce another act. Incorporating a YouTube clip into a blog post can help provide an example to your audience, helping them to better understand your point and hopefully act in the way you desire. Using a hashtag in a Twitter post suggests to the audience your message is part of a broader conversation, rhetorically situating the tweet within a larger argument. All of these choices can improve the chances of persuading your audience, and that's all rhetoric really is, whether in an oral speech, a written essay, or a Facebook post.

Building

As you've probably noticed, blockbuster films often are used to sell products by linking a soft drink, snack, or restaurant with the movies' releases. In this way, the companies that produce the affiliated products are attempting to use the movies as a way to convince viewers to buy their goods. However, what other ways do you think movies can be used rhetorically? With a partner, find examples of how movies can be incorporated into other texts, or used as examples in arguments, to help illustrate or argue a point. Write down your examples, and share them with the class.

Engine

Analyze the top trending Twitter hashtags. What kind of tweets are these tags linked to? Why do you think the authors are incorporating these tags? What rhetorical advantage do you think they gain (how does it help their attempt at communicating)? Write a summary of your findings, and share them with the class.

From Literacy to Electracy: Writing Technologies

The examples of digital rhetoric listed above require a specific technology: digital applications—such as a word processor or a photo editor—and the digital Internet. Up until now, traditional forms of rhetoric usually involved techniques developed for speech (orality) or for writing with the alphabet (literacy). While you still continue to use literate techniques and technologies when forming arguments, you must begin to think beyond this literate frame when using digital technologies, for digital writing tools can do a lot more than those that developed literacy.

For instance, when you think about writing, you might imagine sitting at a desk with paper and pencil, typing a document on your computer for class, or writing on your blog. You might also envision the different situations in which you write. You probably write notes for class, scribble a list for the store, jot down a phone number, or post a message for a roommate. You write in a variety of contexts every day, whether within formal academic settings or toward informal, everyday tasks.

And while all these situations call for writing, do you ever use images to supplement or replace writing? Do you create shopping lists with images of what you plan to buy, or jot a diagram to help you remember a concept from class? Do you take a picture of a new contact when you add her to your phone's address book?

In some respect, the first question posed above is misleading. You always use images when you write, for that's what writing is—images used as representations for aural words. In essence, this is what the alphabet is—a set of images for the basic sounds you use to say those words. The "words" you're reading right now are not "words" exactly, but images of words. Whenever you write, you write with images.

Writing with the images of the alphabet—what this book will call alphabetic writing—has existed for roughly 2,500 years in various incarnations of alphabets. However, its logic system, how you use these systems of images, has been evolving slowly during that time. Many cite the ancient Greeks as the first culture that really analyzed how writing could be used and developed, especially the figures of Socrates, Plato, and Aristotle (Figure 1.7).

For example, the concept of giving an object a "definition" didn't always exist and had to be invented as a literate practice. The ability to write the essence of a thing (its definition), and commit it to an image, provided one of the first early inventions of what writing could create. Eventually, dividing the "things" of the world into particular definitions produced the natural sciences. Even though natural historians still argue about how to divide animals, plants, rocks, or planets into different categories, they still use definitions to accomplish their work.

Figure 1.7
Socrates, Plato, and Aristotle helped determine how you use alphabetic writing nearly 2,500 years later.

Rhetoric and electracy

In general, the term "literacy" refers to the ability to use alphabetic writing, which denotes mastery in both reading and writing with letters. This ability includes not only skill at making the letters, but also understanding the logic and practices that make them work to build words, sentences, paragraphs, pages, and books, as well as arguments, proofs, concepts, and definitions. Reading or writing a book is certainly one aspect of literacy, but a literate person also can use inductive or deductive logic, make and break apart an argument, understand a fallacy, or organize information into a logical system.

Writing, however, continues to evolve and society is moving into a postliterate age that uses other kinds of writing tools, practices, and logics. Since the invention of photography in the 1800s, the image has come into prominence as a mode of recording experience, prompting scholars such as W. J. T. Mitchell to call the current age the "pictorial turn."

Credit: Mack Male

Figure 1.8
Before the photographer ever takes the actual photo, she has to make a lot of choices, such as camera angle, subject positioning, lighting, what to include in the frame, and what to leave out.

However, composing an image doesn't stop once you "take" a picture. These photographs are often incorporated into other media, and new images are composed. Taking a photograph, as Roland Barthes describes, is not simply an act of "recording" what's in front of the lens, but a rhetorical process. The photographer chooses what elements of a photo should remain in the frame, what elements receive the focus or most prominence, how the people or object should be positioned, or whether the person or object should even be aware his/her/its photograph is being taken (Figure 1.8).

Many of your own photos probably end up on social media sites. In this way, you compose images and then compose with images, just as you compose with images of words when you write a paper. And after you take a picture, you often revise it, using a photo editor to remove distortions or crop a photo to focus on a particular element.

While this textbook is partly constructed with alphabetic writing, and at times discusses alphabetic writing, it is mostly focused on writing with the image, both the skills and logics necessary to do so. Such skill sets are not inherently literate, but what Gregory L. Ulmer refers to as "electrate," the skill sets needed to effectively communicate within a digital media environment. As a supplement to the literate skills you've already developed, this text looks at electracy (sometimes referred to as "digital literacy" or "media literacy").

Why use the term "electracy" over ones such as "digital literacy?" As Jan Holmevik explains:

> What has happened during the process of the digitization of writing is that it has escaped its traditional forms and arenas, and thus the literate apparatus as conceived by the ancient Greeks is no longer sufficient to account for all its forms and permutations. Therefore, writing can no longer be a privileged form of expression now that so many other expressive forms exist in the digital space. (Inter/vention, p. 5)

In other words, because "literacy" refers specifically to alphabetic writing, terms such as "digital literacies" are no longer sufficient to explain and account for the many innovative and creative ways people are using digital writing. In fact, a term like "literacy" limits the ways you can think about digital writing since it tries to frame it in terms of older writing technologies and logics.

Electrate skills and emerging technologies

Such logic and skill sets don't just appear from nothing but have to be invented. While someone invented the automobile (or horseless carriage) and probably had the idea that it would be used for transportation, many other practices and purposes for the car were invented since the invention of the actual technology. You don't just use automobiles for transportation, but also for fun, relaxation, or sport. The rules for driving had to be invented, as well as making sure people knew the rules (thus, driver's licenses) and techniques for making sure cars kept working (changing the oil, checking tire pressure, filling it with fuel). Being "literate" in the automobile entails more than just building a car and more than just driving one.

The same process occurred with writing. But just as the ancient Greeks began the invention process for literacy, someone needs to invent the logic and practices of electracy. Who is currently developing electrate skill sets? To the extent that people as individuals have adopted digital technologies, all users of these technologies invent new practices and uses every day, whether or not these practices catch on and become used by everyone else. For example, people are inventing uses for the emerging technology of augmented reality, which overlays digital information onto physical spaces, to display information in museum exhibits, create new kinds of mobile games, display repair instructions to astronauts, train medical doctors, and help consumers see how furniture will look in their homes, with new practices being developed every day (Figure 1.9). Eventually, such practices will become institutionalized and their uses become widespread. Regarding these practices, another question arises: Which institutions have spread the most usage practices of an emerging electracy?

Credit: Mr3641

Figure 1.9
Emerging writing technologies, such as augmented reality, need people to invent how to use them.

Ulmer cites the institution of "entertainment" as the dominant producer of electrate practices, which can be widely understood as the products of Hollywood movies, but also the smaller units of media entertainment, including video games, graphic novels, and photography. In addition, advertising and marketing adopt the logic of cinema and make advertisements entertaining, humorous, sad, and ironic, and give them other narrative techniques to hook a viewer and make them part of a product's "story."

The underlying principle of these entertainment practices is that they don't necessarily appeal to a person's conscious literate logic of analysis, but to their emotions. Such logic is based in aesthetics, or what the viewer likes. If a viewer doesn't like the "look" of a design, then chances are he will have a negative reaction to whatever the design is trying to argue, whether or not he agrees with the "literate" message the design is trying to communicate.

The electrate skill set this text will present, then, is one of design and aesthetics, and how these aspects of writing can be used toward rhetorical goals in digital environments. This text will present general design aesthetics that most beginning arts classes might teach, such as courses in photography, painting, or web design. However, this text will place these practices under the larger umbrella of "writing," because these are all ways to produce a mark, to create visible (and sometimes audible) ways of communicating through the digital Internet, even if some of those visuals become printed and distributed in hard copy.

Electracy, although postliterate, is also parallel to literacy. Literacy is useful and will always exist alongside electracy (just as people still use oral modes, such as the church recital, theatrical plays, and political debates). Part of learning electrate skill sets is also learning how alphabetic writing adapts, integrates, and supports certain practices of visual communication. Throughout the examples and assignments in this text, you will still need to rely on literate modes of analysis and composition and apply them to understanding and creating more electrate modes of writing. Authors will use the practices that they're best at as a way to build and develop new ones.

Building

Link

In a group, discuss when you use images as a substitute for alphabetic writing, such as with shopping lists, diagrams, directions, a color, or other information. Do you feel the image is more effective than writing something out? Is it quicker? Write down your examples, and share them with the class.

Engine

Search

Research the term "electracy," and find a scholarly article that uses this term. Write a brief report on the article, including its main ideas and purpose, and share it with the class.

Building Links Across Rhetorical Tools

The "rhetorical triangle," is a diagram meant to help students learn about the different rhetorical elements at play when communicating with an audience.

Figure 1.10 offers one version of the rhetorical triangle that focuses on the different people involved when communicating. The three vertices represent the writer, audience, and message. Together, these three elements make up the major parts of any rhetorical exchange.

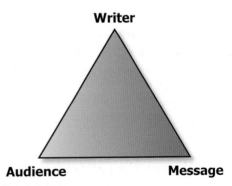

Figure 1.10
The rhetorical triangle showing writer, audience, and message

The point labeled, "writer," represents not simply the person writing, but those aspects of the person that affect her or his rhetorical appeal, such as her character, credibility as a speaker, eloquence in delivery, style of writing, choice of examples, and other rhetorical choices she might make.

The "audience" makes up another point of the rhetorical triangle. The audience has its own beliefs, values, expectations, and experiences the author must consider when crafting an argument. Failure to ask these questions when designing a text can lead you to make poor rhetorical choices and fail to convince your audience. Even worse, you might offend them and make it harder to communicate with them in the future.

The last point represents the actual "message" or the subject of a text, including its information, claims, style, examples, evidence, and structure. Reading a text for these aspects of its message can help you identify an ethical argument from one that is unethical, "good" rhetoric from "bad" rhetoric, and can also help you identify where the argument is weak due to lack of evidence or information about the subject. Asking these questions can also help you strengthen your own writing by helping you to become aware of how you've constructed your text.

While this triangle can be useful for thinking about how different rhetorical elements interact when communicating, it provides a very static way of understanding how communication works. The act of making an argument doesn't occur in a two-dimensional world, but one in which people, things, events, and time all affect the larger situation. The argument you might make at one point in time could completely change five minutes later. The simplicity of the rhetorical triangle can't take this complexity into account.

Credit: © Fountainhead Press

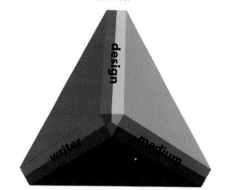

Figure 1.11
The rhetorical tetrahedron
youtu.be/QM996yemH5o

As an alternative, this book suggests a three-dimensional version called the rhetorical tetrahedron (Figure 1.11). A tetrahedron is a three-dimensional shape made up of four triangles. This model incorporates the traditional labels of writer, audience, and message but also adds three other elements that are important to digital writing, a kind of writing that goes beyond writing on paper. These elements are medium, design, and genre.

As you can see in Figure 1.11, instead of placing these six aspects on the points of the tetrahedron, this book places them on the edges. A point only represents a single number, while the edge can represent a continuum. Rather than considering just a single audience, the edge labeled, "audience," suggests you consider all the possible audiences that might read a particular work, for in a world with Facebook and Twitter, documents can quickly circulate beyond your intended audience. Rarely does a document find a single audience, and often an author must consider everyone that will encounter the document. This includes not only human audiences, but also nonhuman ones, such as search engine robots, bits of code that search the web on behalf of search engines like Google or Bing and categorize this information to optimize a user's search results. You may never directly encounter these invisible audiences, but if you post a document online, these audiences will eventually find it.

Of course, the rhetorical tetrahedron also helps you analyze other works of digital writing. You can use the same six elements to ask questions of the message itself, of the writer of the work, its intended audience, why a particular medium was chosen, how it was designed, and why a particular genre was selected. These questions can help you understand digital texts as you encounter them on a daily basis.

Building Link

As a class, leave the classroom and explore campus for 15 minutes. Look for as many kinds of writing as you can find, and note the medium, design, and genre in which the writing appears. You might even snap pictures of each example with your smartphone, especially if you have difficulty identifying these aspects. After 15 minutes, return to class and share your examples. Discuss why you think each example of writing was created in a certain medium, was designed in its current form, and why a particular genre was used.

Engine Search

Research the history of the rhetorical triangle. When did it first become widely used as an educational aid to study rhetoric? How has it changed throughout the years? Write a report based on your research, and share it with the class.

Writing Digitally: Medium, Design, and Genre

For writing traditional essays, the questions of medium, design, and genre are usually pretty simple. Most often, the medium is 8.5" x 11" white paper, the design consists of double-spaced 12 pt. Times New Roman font, and the genre is a five-paragraph essay, short response, or term paper.

When writing digitally, the number of choices you have for each of these explodes. For a medium, should you choose paper? Video? A website? A podcast? A blog? How will the design of your website, video, or blog look when you're not simply limited to font selection and margin size? And should you present your work as an essay? A short documentary? The tetrahedron represents these aspects of writing, helping you to remember to take them into account as you compose in digital modes.

As the old cliché states, "It's not what you say, but how you say it." This "how" relates to these three aspects. As already discussed, aesthetics play an important role in rhetoric. If an audience "likes" what they see or hear, then the audience is more inclined to act in the way the writer is requesting. The design of a composition (and this includes something as "literate" as an essay for class) can be as important as the content of its message. Instead of separating the design (form) from content, consider them integral and always interrelated.

As part of the design, the genre plays an important role in how the piece communicates to an audience. Should you create the design as a flyer or brochure, or make it interactive as a website or online video? Does the audience expect the information to appear in a certain form, such as an email, memo, or letter? If so, these expectations limit the choices you have. The genre you choose will influence how you design the visual composition, and your ideas for a design will likewise influence what genres you feel will best fit your overall message.

The design and genre come together in the medium you choose. The proposal genre can appear in the medium of paper, but it also can appear via a website or video. An essay also can appear in a different medium than you're probably used to, and your instructor may have you complete the video essay assignment in Chapter 9. Much of your choice in medium will depend upon your audience's expectations about standard pairings of genre and medium, or limitations your audience may have in using different media. While you should be creative in thinking about new ways to mix the two, if your audience does not have the resources to play a video proposal sent to them on DVD, they will never see your design nor receive your message. Whenever you're considering design, genre, and medium, you often have to consider all of them together simultaneously, just as you do writer, audience, and message.

The sliding continuum along the edge of the tetrahedron allows you to visualize the flux of possibilities that may exist when you're working on a document with others. Likewise, a range of mediums, designs, and genres may be selected from, and a single point ignores this diverse range.

Moreover, many texts are not written by a single writer, but instead have many collaborators that contribute to a piece of writing, whether it's a simple memo or something more complex like a website.

As a three-dimensional object, the tetrahedron also moves in space and time to represent the shifting nature of a rhetorical situation. In Chapter 2, you'll learn about *kairos*, the timing of rhetoric, an often neglected component that helps you to think about the "right" moment for speaking or writing. *Kairos* is an important element the traditional two-dimensional rhetorical triangles leave out. Furthermore, *kairos* is especially important in digital writing because the Internet allows the delivery of a document at a moment's whim, and as Figure 1.12 demonstrates, once a document is on the web, there are no "take-backs."

Credit: Ad Council

THE DECISION'S OUT OF YOUR HANDS NOW.

Figure 1.12
Remember to "think before you post" images or other documents to the Internet, because once you hit send, it's "out of your hands."

youtu.be/oPZZu7reBEs

"The Medium Is the Message"

"The medium is the message." This famous quote from media scholar Marshall McLuhan suggests the medium becomes a message in itself, no matter what the content (Figure 1.13). One of his examples for this was the light bulb (a different kind of medium than you're probably used to thinking about). By itself, the light bulb emits light, and it doesn't matter what that light is used for. This light can be used to do anything from working on your car to watching a football game at night. The important feature is not what you do with the light bulb, but that the light bulb allows you to alter how you conduct your life. The important message is that you can do anything at night because of the medium of the light bulb and not the particular activity (content) you choose.

Credit: John Reeves

Figure 1.13
Marshall McLuhan argues that "the medium is the message."

Beyond the light bulb, McLuhan was interested in how all media affect human lives, from print to television. Given the new devices being released every day in your own time, you might consider other media, from smartphones to tablets, as media that have their own messages, no matter what content the user is viewing or interacting with. The fact that the user can interact with

Figure 1.14
Sergey Brin, wearing Google Glass.

what they see on a touchscreen has become a message in its own right, but one often masked by the content.

The choice of medium, then, becomes an important part of an author's *ethos* and reflects on the author's character. What if Sergey Brin, the co-founder of Google, started using an old Polaroid camera to take pictures instead of his recent project, Google Glass (Figure 1.14)? You would probably ask why the leader of one of the biggest computer software companies and one of the leading computer innovators is using technology that is more than 60 years old. Doesn't he have something better available, and doesn't he know how to use it? In fact, he does, and he uses Google Glass to post pictures and video instantly to his Google+ page.

Focus on Production: Theory and Praxis

This text will analyze—and ask you to analyze—a variety of digital compositions to reveal how they function rhetorically. These analytical dissections can help you recognize persuasive elements in the texts you see around you every day. However, this analysis is mainly focused on the production of your own texts. While it is important to know how to "read" an image, this text's ultimate goal is for you to be able to produce your own digital writings for a variety of purposes, audiences, contexts, and rhetorical situations.

As you encounter sections in the text that analyze an image or video, the analysis will suggest ways you can use similar techniques within your own works. Use these examples as relays or models to construct your own digital writings. Remember, however, that yours will be much different given that you will have a different rhetorical situation. The basic principles in the example, however, will be applicable to all of your works.

Focus on Environment: Images and the Outside World

When this text discusses "environment," it's referring to more than just the natural environment. For instance, this text will often discuss the environmental effects of using different kinds of media. However, "environment" also refers to the larger rhetorical environment in which you might see, make, or place an image. This larger visual environment will most likely contain many other images, whether this is a public bulletin board where you might place a flyer, or a website that has a variety of images, videos, and texts (Figure 1.15). Each chapter will consider some of these environmental aspects you should be aware of when taking a particular step in the production process (Figure 1.16).

Figure 1.15
After Hurricane Katrina struck New Orleans, many residents of the city temporarily moved to Houston for shelter. During the natural disaster, many families were separated, and bulletin boards such as this one provided a location to place notes. This bulletin board provides just one example of how environment, in many senses of the word, influences writing.

Figure 1.16
Unlike more "natural" writing technologies, such as paper and pencils, electronic writing tools can poison the environment if not disposed of properly. However, they are usually just tossed into landfills without thinking about the toxic effects.

KEY Terms

alphabet	*kairos*
analog	literacy
Aristotle	medium
audience	message
augmented reality	Plato
code	QR code
dialectic	rhetoric
digital	rhetorical tetrahedron
digital writing	rhetorical triangle
electracy	technology
environment	text
genre	writer
image	writing
Internet	

Comparative Research Report

Locate an example of writing you consider to be "traditional" or "nondigital" and one you consider to be "digital writing" that makes use of some of the criteria listed above. Write a report that compares and contrasts the two pieces of writing. How do the two pieces of writing differ from each other? How are they similar?

The length of the assignment should be decided by your instructor.

Also, because the examples for this assignment can vary widely, check in with your instructor to make sure your selections meet the goals of your class.

From DIGITAL Writers

Pencil vs. Computer: Study Asks If It Makes a Difference on Tests

By Pamela Mendels

Later this month, about 150 fourth graders in the Wellesley, Mass. public school system are scheduled to spend two hours or so in classrooms monitored by exam proctors as they complete the essay portion of a state standardized test.

It may sound like another nerve-racking exercise in high-stakes testing, but in this case, the students, some of whom will do their writing on computers, others with old-fashioned paper and pencil, can breathe easy. This is one test that won't count for them.

> Pamela Mendels is a senior editor at *The Wallace Foundation* and has regularly contributed to *The New York Times*. Most of her writing covers government, censorship, and civil rights issues. As an example of an essay that compares and contrasts two pieces of writing technology, consider this article by Mendels, who takes a look at how computers might affect taking tests.

Rather, the mock-exam session is part of a study going on in Wellesley these days to take a look at a cyber-age question: Should school officials start exchanging No. 2 pencils for keyboards when they give essay examinations to an emerging generation of computer-savvy students?

It is a question crying out for an answer, says Matthew King, superintendent of Wellesley schools and a person who far prefers the computer to handwriting.

"If I were given a written test in which I had to use a pencil, I'd be in big trouble," said King, who oversees an affluent suburban Boston school district of about 3,800 students. "If that's true for me, I can imagine what it would be like for young people who are making more use, at younger ages, of computers for writing."

The study, which is being financed by the Massachusetts Department of Education and will take a look at eighth and 10th graders, too, comes at a time when schools are feeling the impact of two major trends in education, study researchers said.

One is the push to get technology into schools and students onto computers. In some cases this has led teachers to encourage students, especially those for whom writing and drafting with a pencil is awkward, to use computers for composition instead.

The other trend is increased emphasis on testing to see if students meet minimum state academic standards. Today, about 48 states have such exams and increasingly the tests are becoming serious business, determining things like whether students are promoted to the next grade or whether schools are performing adequately.

In Massachusetts, for example, members of the high school class of 2003 will become the first in that state required to pass the Massachusetts Comprehensive Assessment System Test, better known as MCAS, in order to receive a high school diploma.

It is common for these state tests to have an essay section, but rare for them to be given with anything other than a pencil. The potential problem, therefore, researchers suspect, is that the technology trend and the test trend could be colliding, at least for young people who routinely use computers for writing.

When handed a pencil and notebook for a high-stakes test, these computer-trained students, who are used to the speed and ease of word-processing software, could end up turning in essays far inferior to what they are capable of producing at a keyboard, researchers say.

Indeed, two studies he has helped conduct since 1997 have found some evidence that students used to keyboarding are working at a disadvantage on pencil-and-paper tests, said Michael K. Russell, the main researcher on the Wellesley study. Russell is a professor and senior research fellow for the National Board on Educational Testing and Public Policy at Boston College.

Russell and Thomas J. Pilati, director of libraries and educational technologies for Wellesley schools, want to see if there is a similar result in the study in Wellesley. The researchers also hope to explore what questions are raised when students are allowed to use computers for test-taking.

Already, they have uncovered some problems.

One, is that if students are given the option—pencil or computer—they can't be counted on to make the wisest decision. In one of the previous studies, Russell said, some students said they preferred to use computers even though they were slow typists and might have fared better in longhand. Perhaps they were attracted by the novelty of using a computer or by the idea that technology is fun, he said. In any case, "If you give kids a choice, a lot are going to make the wrong choice," he said.

Russell saw another potential problem when older Wellesley students participated in the study last month. Some computer-equipped students with access to printers wanted to print out rough drafts of their essays, revise them on paper and complete the revisions on the computer screen.

To anyone who regularly uses a word-processing program for composition this way of writing seems only natural. But imagine the headaches for school officials who bend over backward to try to prevent cheating on exams.

"This introduces security problems," Russell said. "You have noise, you lose control. It complicates the whole testing environment."

Whatever the results of the study, Robert A. Schaeffer, public education director of The National Center for Fair & Open Testing, a Cambridge, Mass.-based advocacy group, said the research is an important step in examining possible inequities in test-giving in the age of the computer.

"We need to make sure that the way we are having people respond on those tests is, in fact, a level playing field," he said.

STUDENT Example

Keeli Fricks wrote this essay for one of my classes. It describes the history of the QWERTY keyboard as well as the origins of the word and reference.

April 29, 2012

Professor Sean Morey

English 460

The Computer Keyboard

"QWERTY" is an awkward yet familiar word and has appeared in print, according to the Oxford English Dictionary, at least since 1929 and has been used as an adjective or a noun to describe a particular keyboard layout (QWERTY). The word QWERTY is rather unique in that the meaning of the word is self-explanatory to those familiar with modern typing, and in that the word is often written in capital letters. Q, W, E, R, T, and Y are the first six letters of the modern computer keyboard that is the standard for many countries with Latin-based languages, as well as others. This seemingly random arrangement of letters, as seen on the computer keyboards across the world, can be traced back to the typewriter which is the world's first popular typing machine. In spite of that fact that many argue that the QWERTY keyboard is not the best keyboard for people to have persisted in using, it is so firmly embedded in technology and society that it has survived relatively unchanged for well over a century.

The keyboards of original typewriters were arranged as might seem logical, that is, alphabetically. The problem with this logical system was, oddly enough, its efficiency. The ease of use of these keyboards and the resulting typing speeds caused the keys of the typewriter to jam often. Alternatives to the straightforward alphabetical arrangements were proposed, and thus the QWERTY keyboard was born. The QWERTY layout was designed to place the most commonly used letters, which in English are E, A, R, I, O, and T, as far apart on the machine as possible (Oxford) in order to slow down typing and minimize the frequency of jams. Five of the six most commonly used letters are on the top of the row and not on the home row of the keyboard, which further slows the fluidity of typing as well as the typing speed. The relative success of this system, combined with its prevalence, has been enough to ensure that the QWERTY keyboard has remained in use for more than a century of technological revolution without undergoing any major changes or renovations. It was already firmly enough embedded as a letter arrangement for typing technologies that as computers advanced, the QWERTY keyboard became the standard keyboard for the modern computer as well.

As with the case of every new technology throughout history, old technologies and old media are required in order to use or to explain the new technology or media. This was certainly the case with the computer keyboard and the typewriter. ENIAC, the first computer, was made in 1946. It used teletype, which combined typewriters and keypunches to input data. It was not until 1964 that a computer was released that had a visual display terminal. This visual display, the early computer screen, vastly facilitated the communicative ease and capabilities of the computers (Das). These display terminals encouraged the use and integration of an electronic keyboard for the input of information. By the late-1970s electronic keyboards were accepted as the standard accompaniment to a computer. These retained the format of what was nearly a century-old QWERTY keyboard format which then continued to be used through the development of the personal computer and other writing technologies, such as cellular phones.

There are several different types of keyboards on the market to offer competition to the traditional QWERTY format for those users who feel that the technological advances that have occurred since 1874 warrant a change in the layout of the keyboard. One of the more popular alternatives is the Dvorak keyboard. The Dvorak keyboard was patented in 1932 and claims that 70% of the typing on their keyboard takes place in the home row whereas less than 32% of typing occurs in the home how in QWERTY keyboards (This is True).

A study at the Assistive Technology Research Institute at Misericordia University suggests that the reason few studies exist that show any true benefits of the Dvorak keyboard is due to the prevalence of finding subjects who are not thoroughly biased toward the QWERTY keyboard already (Anson).

Typewriters and computers no longer retain their dominion over QWERTY keyboards. This letter layout can now be utilized to write on smartphones, which have risen in popularity, pocket dictionaries, and even e-readers such as the Kindle. As technology becomes more pervasive in our own lives, so does the impractical, ubiquitous QWERTY keyboard. Although more practical alternatives have been presented, none of these keyboard formats have gained much popularity, and all are dwarfed by the shadow of the QWERTY. Whether the keyboard can be tapped on a touch-screen, rolled up, or is attached to the computer, it is almost undoubtedly a QWERTY keyboard and, barring a major revolution of pragmatic typists, it is not likely to go out of style any time soon.

Works Cited

Anson, Denis, Christa Eck, James King, Regina Mooney, Christopher Sansom, Bryan Wilkerson, and Daniel Wychulis. "Efficacy of Alternate Keyboard Configurations: Dvorak vs. Reverse-QWERTY." *Assistive Technology Research Institute at Miseracordia University,* Miseracordia University, 2004, atri.misericordia.edu/Papers/Dvorak.php.

Cassingham, Randy. "The Dvorak Keyboard." *This is True,* This is True, Inc, 2009, www.thisistrue.com/blog-the_dvorak_keyboard.html.

"Typing Through Time: Keyboard History." *Blog Page, DasKeyboard,* 2011, www.daskeyboard.com/blog/typing-through-time-the-history-of-the-keyboard/.

"Which Letters in the Alphabet are Used Most Often?" Oxford Dictionaries, Oxford UP, 2012, www.oxforddictionaries.com/us/words/which-letters-are-used-most.

"QWERTY." *Oxford Dictionaries,* Oxford UP, 2016, www.oxforddictionaries.com/us/definition/american_english/qwerty?q=QWERTY.

CHAPTER 2

Digital Rhetoric

Hector Cruz, a photographer in Clarkesville, Tennessee, wanted to support his wife's breastfeeding of their newborn daughter. Although he wanted to attend breastfeeding classes and learn with her, he was often turned away from these all-female groups, sometimes for good reasons. However, he felt helpless to support his wife. In response, he began taking photographs of new dads "breastfeeding" their infants (Figure 2.1).

Although photography might be considered "visual rhetoric," most cameras are now digital, and most photos are digitally editable. In addition, the methods Cruz used to communicate his message were digital, circulating the photos online, reaching audiences in places distant from his Clarkesville home, and using social media to help his campaign go viral.

Credit: CNN

Figure 2.1
Hector Cruz employed digital rhetoric, whether he knew it or not.
http://www.cnn.com/videos/
us/2014/04/02/pkg-breastfeeding-
dad-campaign.wsmv/video/playlists/
breastfeeding-controversies/

Whenever you make a claim, you make a statement that can be argued. And whenever you start to build that argument around the claim, you employ rhetoric. Although there are many ways to define rhetoric, as Chapter 1 shows, you can simply state that rhetoric refers to all the tools you can use when trying to craft an argument and convince someone of your perspective, or persuade someone to take an action. Remember, rather than being something negative, rhetoric helps you communicate in daily life.

Cruz was just a humble dad in Tennessee who had a claim to make, and through the use of digital rhetoric he was able to reach and convince a much larger audience than he would have been able to do otherwise.

Most of what you'll create and analyze from this textbook can be considered digital rhetoric, a branch of rhetoric that refers to how a writer uses digital writing technologies and practices to persuade audiences through the use of images, graphics, video, Internet connectivity, and other digital media.

Rhetorical Continuities

You should remember from Chapter 1 that even though digital writing makes use of new rhetorical techniques, some continuities with older rhetorical traditions still remain. For example, digital arguments are still arguments; they make a claim. This claim may be explicit, with clear reasons and evidence, or it might be implicit, making the readers fill in this information for themselves. Digital writing still makes a claim when trying to persuade a reader. It just does so through digital means and methods.

Building

Link

With a partner, discuss whether you think all rhetoric today is digital, or if some nondigital forms of rhetoric still persist. In other words, can you still argue without at some point resorting to digital technologies? Make a list of these examples, and share them with the class.

Engine

Search

Like the Cruz story above, find another example in which someone uses digital rhetoric to help make his or her argument. Share the example with the class and explain how you think it qualifies as both "digital" and "rhetoric." In other words, how does the example use digital writing in order to help persuade an audience?

Defining Digital Rhetoric

Because almost all of the writing you currently compose is done through some sort of digital technology, you might say that all of your arguments employ some sort of digital rhetoric whenever you try to persuade someone. If you were making a micro-argument through Twitter, you might employ hashtags to focus the argument toward a specific audience. If you maintain a blog, you might supplement text with digital images and hyperlinks to help make your points. Building on the definition of digital writing from the first chapter, we might define digital rhetoric as having these attributes.

Uses electronic technologies

As a digital writer, you will obviously use electronic technologies to create your texts. However, which technologies you use can be a rhetorical choice in itself. Should you use a blogging platform to reach an audience, or will they respond better to an email or text message? While previous cultures may have adopted very few tools and media for writing—consider the ancient Babylonians who mainly used clay and a stylus to create cuneiform tablets—you have computers, smartphones, tablets, digital cameras, electronic pens, graphic design programs, presentation software, and many more means available for writing digital texts. Your audience will respond to each of these technologies in a different way, and you should consider how each technology helps or hurts your argument.

Attends to human and nonhuman audiences

While most of your audience will be human, audiences of digital texts can also include web browsers and search engine robots that scour the web on behalf of search engines such as Google or Bing. In order to employ digital rhetoric effectively, you must research and analyze your multiple audiences and know how to design different texts to maximize their activity with online digital audiences.

Uses multiple codes

In order to reach these multiple audiences, digital rhetoric combines the alphabet with many other kinds of codes to create digital texts. Some codes, such as a QR code, may not use letters at all. While the words, images, and sounds provide one kind of code for your human readers, digital rhetoric also relies on writing and coding for these nonhuman readers discussed above, such as web robots and other computer algorithms that read hypertext and HTML differently. While your primary audience is likely to be an actual person, the software that codes digital technologies also plays a role and must be considered as a rhetorical participant.

Uses digital images

You've probably noticed that most digital texts, from professional websites to social media platforms, make heavy use of digital images. You probably even fill your SMS text messages with snapshots or emojis if you're not posting images directly to YouTube, Vine, or Instagram. Although you can certainly create digital compositions that don't include visuals, digital images can provide rhetorical effectiveness by capturing the attention of your reader or showing information that might be difficult for words to describe. In addition, your audience will likely expect to see some visual representation or example of what you discuss through text. As a digital rhetor, you should consider how digital images can enhance the persuasiveness of your text, and how you might edit those images for effective use.

Makes use of interactivity

While all forms of rhetoric are interactive, for the very act of listening and thinking about an argument is interactive, digital technologies make this interaction more immediate and robust. Digital tools, such as comments, the ability to easily share materials, and the ability to remix existing texts for one's own purposes, make digital writing much more interactive. As a digital writer, you should pay attention to how an audience will interact with your document and whether or not such interaction helps your rhetorical purpose.

Leverages circulation

Although messages have always been circulated by listeners, circulation becomes instantaneous and is multiplied through digital technologies. Instead of making photocopies and handing them out one person at a time, you can now send a message instantly to millions of readers. Digital rhetoric leverages this capability to not only reach an initial audience, but also to encourage that audience to further spread your message through forwards, retweets, shares, and other tools that promote the spreading of digital writing.

Focuses on *kairos*

Because of the ability for instantaneous communication through digital technologies, the timing of a message is more important than ever. For example, marketing researchers have pinpointed the best time of the day to tweet about a product based on peak Twitter usage. As a digital writer, you must pay attention to the time and place in which you present your argument.

Highlights design, medium, and genre

Digital rhetoric includes traditional aspects of the rhetorical tetrahedron, such as writer, audience, and message. However, because digital writing often takes such visually rich forms in a variety of layouts and platforms, it becomes even more important to focus on the design, medium, and genre of a digital text and how each of these can be used to help persuade the audience.

Forms of digital rhetoric

In addition to the basic principles of digital rhetoric presented above, digital rhetoric also takes some specific forms and uses techniques not available to traditional print forms of writing. While not exhaustive, these forms discuss some basic tools that can be used to enhance the rhetorical effectiveness of a digital text.

Comments

Many websites, blogs, and other social media platforms provide the means for viewers and readers to leave comments. The comments may be directed at the authors of the site or to other commentators. Comments allow a level of participation not readily available in nondigital writing. This participation allows new readers to learn about your site, granting it more exposure, but some comments might hurt your site overall. Comments are discussed more in Chapter 7.

Search Engine Optimization

When you write in a digital environment, you must consider not only human audiences, but also digital audiences, especially algorithms and web robots that might "read" your writing. In order for web robots to better find and index your writing on search engines such as Google and Bing, you need to develop writing and coding strategies called Search Engine Optimization, or SEO. These practices are covered more extensively in Chapter 5.

Rhetorical velocity

You've probably heard the term "going viral." This occurs when users rapidly share the same video, image, story, or other piece of digital writing, causing it to spread like a virus through the Internet. This phenomenon doesn't have to occur accidentally, but it can be used rhetorically.

Jim Ridolfo and Dànielle Nicole DeVoss have theorized a practice they call "rhetorical velocity" through which a rhetor anticipates how her audience will make use of a particular text or document to further her own purposes. This rhetorical practice is discussed more in Chapter 5.

Hyperlinks

The success of the Internet has partially been due to hyperlinks, text and images that can be linked to other digital texts and can create unique paths from one location to another. What you choose to link and where you choose to lead your viewer can be rhetorical decisions that affect how they read and respond to your text. When you compose a digital text, you should consider how hyperlinks can help you make your argument. Chapter 7 discusses these strategies in more detail.

Tagging

Just as hyperlinks can be used rhetorically, so can tags that you apply to blog posts, tweets, images, and other digital texts. For instance, as mentioned above, tags can help organize your material into logical relationships so your reader can more easily navigate your text and argument. Tags also can relate your argument to others, giving the reader a sense of the larger conversation in which you're engaged. Tags and tagging will be covered more in Chapter 7.

Remix

One of the most common practices of digital writing is reusing existing works to create new ones. This practice is often called remixing. While remixing isn't new, it has become much easier and more prevalent given the digital transformation of media, making the operations of cut and paste more convenient. Remix will be discussed more in Chapter 6.

Avatar

If you have a Facebook, Twitter, or LinkedIn account, or you play *World of Warcraft* or are on Second Life, then you probably have some sort of profile pic or image that you use to associate with your accounts. In general terms, this image can be referred to as an avatar, which makes up the totality of your online persona. How you choose to construct your avatar can have important implications for your *ethos* as a writer, affecting how your readers respond to you. Chapter 7 will provide more details about these considerations when you build an avatar identity.

Building

Link

Research the different kinds of codes that are typically used to construct online texts such as webpages (HTML, CSS, and XML are just a few). What is unique about each kind of code you find? What purpose does each serve? Might there be a rhetorical reason to choose one code over another?

Engine

Search

Find three examples in which a writer has used digital technologies to help circulate his or her text. Was this circulation accidental, or do you think the writer intended and hoped that his or her audience would spread the message? Share your examples and thoughts with the class.

The Rhetorical Triangle: *Logos, Ethos,* and *Pathos*

While digital media have their own kind of rhetoric, these rhetorical techniques build upon more traditional rhetorical techniques that can still be useful when reading and writing digital texts. This section will provide an overview of basic rhetorical techniques but reframe their concepts for use in the rest of the text.

In Chapter 1, you looked at the rhetorical triangle, made up of points for writer, audience, and message. In addition to this configuration, you can also label the three points of the triangle with the three basic appeals of rhetoric: *logos, ethos,* and *pathos.* These appeals represent rhetorical choices you can make, choices that change as the rhetorical situation changes. The following rhetorical elements will help you think about how to make different kinds of rhetorical appeals, as well as how to avoid some pitfalls that might hurt the content and delivery of your message.

Logos

Logos is a Greek term that translates to "word" and is usually understood as the "logic" of your argument. For instance, when writing a research paper, you would most likely include definitions, evidence, deductive or inductive reasoning, or examples to support your points.

These elements typically provide the logical reasons why a reader should accept your perspective. This kind of logic is usually based on facts, precedence, descriptions, empirical observations, computation, and other evidence not necessarily based on emotion. *Logos* is the persuasionary tactic of Spock in *Star Trek.* Spock argues with logical appeals, but he can also be convinced with logical appeals.

Credit: © International Shark Attack File, Florida Museum of Natural History, University of Florida

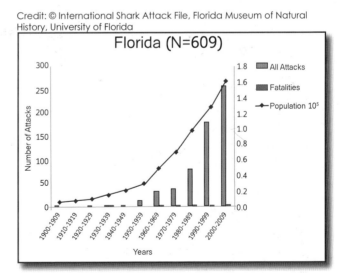

Figure 2.2
Graph comparing shark attacks with population growth over the past century.

The graph in Figure 2.2 shows the relationship between shark attacks and population in the state of Florida. The trend indicates that as human population increases, so do the occurrences of shark attacks. The logical relationship that the graph attempts to show is that sharks aren't attacking more swimmers because they're aggressive and out to eat people, but as more people enter the water and encounter sharks, more possibilities exist for human and shark interaction.

The organization that produced this graphic—the International Shark Attack File—also points out that your chance of being killed in a shark attack is 1 in 3,748,067. Comparatively, your chance of dying from a car accident is 1 in 84. These graphs and statistics attempt to persuade viewers of the site through logical, scientific means. As Spock might say, the fear of being killed by a shark is . . . illogical.

Logos also includes the arrangement, organization, and internal consistency of a document. For example, if you were:

▪ creating a documentary about a historical event, the retelling would be much more logical if you followed a chronological sequence.

▪ designing a video tutorial to teach someone how to edit a video in Apple's iMovie, then placing each step in sequential order would be important; otherwise, the tutorial would be worthless.

▪ writing a legal brief to a judge about your client who is accused of armed robbery, instead of using synonyms such as weapon, handgun, gun, or pistol, the brief would make more logical sense if you refer to the weapon consistently, using only one term.

Besides using words logically, digital images, texts, and symbols can be used logically to show *logos* as well. Figure 2.3 depicts

Credit: Six Flags Over Texas

Figure 2.3
This map of Six Flags Over Texas clusters information by theme and use of color.

the map you might use if you visited Six Flags. Note how similar information is clustered together based on the theme of each different section of the park so the audience can easily find popular rides and locations. Also, notice how the map uses color in a logical way: Each theme has a different color so it can be located more easily on the map. If you look at other kinds of maps, such as a road atlas or political map, you'll notice a logical use of color.

On the home page for Clemson University (Figure 2.4), information is arranged logically by audience. Each major link on the navigation menu provides further links to information that is relevant to particular readers. It wouldn't make much sense to include information on how to donate money (in the Alumni section) within the Prospective Students section. On a sports news site like ESPN.com, you wouldn't expect to find hockey scores in the football section; this would defy audience expectations.

Credit: Clemson University

Figure 2.4
Clemson University's home page organizes its information by audience.

If you're entering (or starting) a conversation on Twitter, hashtags provide a way to organize information by topics so that your audience knows logically which category with which to associate your tweets.

Consider carefully not only the particular evidence you use to create an argument, but also how you arrange and present that evidence.

Building

Look at television commercials from cell phone providers (such as Sprint, Verizon, AT&T, T-Mobile, or Alltel). What's the claim of the commercial—what does it attempt to argue? How does each commercial use *logos* to create its argument and support this claim? Do the commercials use statistics? Do they use comparison and contrast? Do they use color to create organization or associations within the commercial? For each provider, list as many strategies as you can, and provide your findings to the class.

Link

Engine

Search

As mentioned above, the use of hashtags on Twitter can provide a useful way of organizing information, creating a reference point for readers. Select four or five Twitter accounts, and study how the authors use hashtags. Do you feel they make good use of hashtags? Do they overuse hashtags so their tweets fall under too many categories? Do they neglect to use hashtags at all? Consider the rhetorical reasoning they might have used (or not used) employing hashtags, and share your findings with the class.

Ethos

Ethos refers to the audience's trust in the author of a document. An audience typically believes an author—or has trust in his or her argument—when he or she has some expertise or special knowledge about a subject.

For instance, if you had a question about how to build a house, you would probably trust the information given to you by an architect or construction contractor rather than an English professor. The contractor has expert knowledge and experience to suggest that her advice will help you complete the project successfully.

If you want to know the weather forecast, you would trust a meteorologist more than a cardiologist. On the other hand, you would trust the cardiologist to diagnose your heart health over the meteorologist. When creating your own texts, you should use sources you feel will persuade the audience— sources the audience will trust. You've probably used such sources in other research papers; these same principles of *ethos* apply to digital texts as well.

Ethos might be present from the outset, or reveal itself during the unfolding of a piece of writing, video, or other kind of communicative event. If you've watched the weather segment of the local television news station, you'll often hear or see that the channel's meteorologist has some sort of certification or approval from a national organization (Figure 2.5). This statement is an attempt to give credentials to the meteorologist so viewers know they can trust the forecaster.

Credit: American Meteorological Service

Figure 2.5 According to the American Meteorological Service, "The AMS Seal of Approval was launched in 1957 as a way to recognize on-air meteorologists for their sound delivery of weather information to the general public. Among radio and television meteorologists, the AMS Seal of Approval is sought as a mark of distinction." Having the seal can enhance a meteorologist's *ethos*.

Audiences also tend to trust information from those who are impartial and have nothing to gain from an argument. For instance, if a city investigated whether a new football stadium for the local NFL team would raise money for the community, the city would probably trust independent experts in city planning and economics rather than the owner of the team who has a clear vested interest in building the stadium. While the owner may care whether the whole community benefits or not, the audience knows he will personally benefit. The meteorologist wants to create an accurate forecast to keep her job, but she gains nothing if the weather consists of sun or snow.

However, sometimes this kind of information isn't given up front. Perhaps, through conversations with your English professor, you learn that he has built his own house and has lots of advice to give you, advice that a professional contractor might not think of. While you would still trust someone in building construction more, the fact that your professor is also a do-it-yourselfer might convince you that he has unique insights that an expert might not. In this case, the speaker's *ethos* develops and convinces you despite your initial hesitation at taking his advice. Of course, the presence of *ethos* doesn't necessarily mean that an audience will agree with the author's perspective, but *ethos* makes it more likely that the audience will believe what the author communicates and take him or her more seriously.

One common means of creating *ethos* is through the use of celebrity endorsements. If one wants a good basketball shoe, what better shoe than that of a famous basketball player like Michael Jordan? His credibility is so well established that other famous basketball players wear his shoes, such as Dwyane Wade, even though Jordan has been retired for many years. This endorsement from current players further increases the credibility of Jordan and his shoes.

Credit: Nike, Inc.

Figure 2.6 provides the background of how Nike designed Jordan shoes for Dwayne Wade, Carmelo Anthony, and Chris Paul. While the video uses a lot of logical arguments about foot movement, materials, and athlete needs, it also relies on Wade, Anthony, and Paul as the users of the product to attest to its benefits. Because the audience

Figure 2.6
New Team Jordan Signature Shoes: Celebrities and designers add their credibility to Nike's discussion of these shoes.
www.youtube.com/watch?v=grGSpZoGaRg

knows these players are great—they have proven their *ethos* on the court—they're more inclined to trust them.

Logically, the audience might know these celebrities are paid a lot of money to endorse and use these products, but they can still be influenced by who delivers the message. In order to provide balance to the players' voices, the video also interviews the shoe designers themselves. These designers do not use the shoes as the players do, but because they are most likely material engineers of some sort, they provide a different kind of credibility (mostly based on arguments of *logos*) for why they should be trusted by the audience.

In certain digital texts, such as social media applications, other elements can indicate credibility. The number of followers a Facebook, YouTube, or Twitter user has can suggest that she or he is not only "genuine," but that if others like this account, you might as well. Online reviews also help to establish *ethos*, not only for particular products, but also for particular comments or posts in blogs, forums, or other online venues.

Finally, a writer loses credibility if her writing contains grammatical errors or factual mistakes. When establishing your own *ethos*, it's critical that you check your sources, proofread your writing, and polish your documents as much as possible. This advice pertains to written texts and also to images, videos, and any digital texts you might produce. Of course, in microblogging and SMS messages, shorthand and abbreviations are often acceptable.

DIGITAL Connections

Why 'Ethos Brands' Like Ben & Jerry's and TOMS Shoes Need to Improve Their Storytelling

By Kath Hipwell

Sweat shops, childhood obesity, looking after our planet, fair trade, animal testing, children having shoes to wear to school: these are all issues that most people will engage with on an emotional level and which are popularly debated topics in current affairs.

Ethos is often about developing your own story as a speaker. Consider this article from Kath Hipwell published on campaignlive.co.uk, in which she discusses the importance of storytelling when creating positive *ethos*.

These are also stories that *ethos* brands have at their disposal and which should have a ready-made audience.

Brands can learn a lot from broadcasters on how to attract audiences with gripping and compelling content. Someone who learnt these lessons first hand is Paul Lindley, founder of the hugely successful baby food brand Ella's Kitchen, and previously deputy managing director of Nickelodeon. He poured what he learnt at Nickelodeon—'put the consumer first, think like a child, get parents on board'—into the *ethos* of his brand: making healthy food that's also fun for babies and kids.

So has he translated his knowledge into gripping content for his brand, which champions this heartfelt belief?

Ella's Kitchen has made a smattering of 'product demo' films such as a 'Baby Thrill-O-Meter' which shows screen tested tots testing different food flavours and providing endearing facial expressions along the way.

Doting parents are also invited to upload films of their suspiciously clean offspring consuming Ella's food to YouTube and have a 'clever expert' assess whether they are enjoying it or not.

So far, so healthy and wholesome, but not a whole lot of fun. Given the founder's insight into broadcasters' formula for attractive and compelling content, and a founding *ethos* that is also a huge conversation point amongst many new parents, it feels like there is a lot more they could be doing.

TOMS Shoes is another brand with a fantastic founding story.

Eight years ago Blake Mycoskie was travelling in Argentina and saw that the village children he had befriended didn't have shoes to protect their feet. He was moved to help and set up TOMS Shoes on the principle that he would match every pair of shoes he sells with a new pair for a child that needs them.

One for One. Sounds like a great premise for a film. And there are films, on YouTube of course, packed with uplifting images of children around the world being fitted with their TOMS shoes, but lacking any real sense of the narrative and emotional impact that this brilliant story could have.

Ben & Jerry's have been vocal in their condemnation of brands who focus on profit above the 'common good'. They are proud to be a 'values-led business' and believe these values lead them to decisions others would deem too risky. They famously celebrated the legalisation of same sex marriages in Vermont by re-naming their Chubby Hubby flavour Hubby Hubby for a month. They are rightly proud of their *ethos* and share it in a short film to promote their 'free cone day', an annual event since their first anniversary in 1979.

The film was moderately interesting but I'd have rather had a free cone. Unfortunately, another promisingly entitled film, 'Peace Love and Ice Cream' was about as entertaining as the bit when you're waiting for your Ben & Jerry's to warm up from the freezer.

Chipotle is the poster child for this kind of content.

Its *ethos* is so strong and central to the brand that it has rarely needed to make traditional advertising, rather communicating its beliefs through branded content and games that audiences choose to interact with—in their millions.

There are some amazing stories to be told by brands that live by their values and Chipotle proves that worthy beliefs can be communicated through content in a way that is charming, funny, and not at all worthy.

Brands can bring a genuinely interesting, different and often quite a personal angle to the values they champion and I think audiences would be inspired by the same *ethos* that established these brands in the first place.

Building

Link

Choose a well-known person (from government, business, entertainment, or academia) who uses at least three different social media sites, such as Facebook, LinkedIn, Twitter, or YouTube. How does the writer craft his or her *ethos* on each site? Is the *ethos* similar across sites, or does each site present a different *ethos*? Does the writer include any information that might hurt his or her *ethos*? Draft a report of your findings, and share them with the class.

Search Engine

Research the top 10 YouTube channels that have the most subscribers. Who maintains these channels? Individuals? Organizations or corporations? Do you feel the number of subscribers actually lends *ethos* to these channels and their owners, or do you think such numbers are rhetorically unimportant? What do you think is gained and lost by having such a high number of subscribers? Write a brief report with your findings, and share it with the class.

Pathos

Often, someone's state of mind, or mood, plays an important role in how he receives a particular message. If you're angry, you often respond to information differently than if you're calm. If you lost your dog and needed help persuading an audience to help you find her, you would have a much better chance if you were able to elicit the emotions of sorrow or panic, helping the audience to share your own emotions. This would help place the audience in a sympathetic state of mind that would make them more receptive, increasing the likelihood they would help you search the neighborhood. *Pathos* names this emotional appeal made within a text and can be a very powerful rhetorical tool to help your reader understand your point of view.

Pathos is also an appeal to one's identity, in which most people have an emotional investment. Typically, politicians use the language of patriotism as a way to appeal to a collective sense of what it means to be a member of a certain country, and that language plays to an emotional connection *with* the country. Patriotic language often uses code words or phrases that many people identify with and feel identifies them. For example, Americans are "hard-working" or "independent." Within this discourse, the speaker places herself within the group she is addressing so the audience identifies her as "one of us" and is more likely to accept her message.

In addition, the politician is also trying to flatter the audience, making listeners like the speaker more, perhaps by saying that as Americans they must be "hard-working" and "independent," so they identify with and believe these descriptions about themselves. The audience develops a more positive reaction to the politician who makes the compliment.

You can also summon the experiences of the audience and discuss the emotional connections the audience has to those experiences. If you were trying to persuade someone to donate money to help Haiti after its earthquake, you might cite another disaster your audience has experienced more directly (such as a hurricane or tornado), evoking a shared sense of pity or fear between the people of Haiti and themselves. As another example, consider this excerpt from Dr. Martin Luther King, Jr.'s "I Have A Dream" speech:

> *I am not unmindful that some of you have come here out of great trials and tribulations. Some of you have come fresh from narrow jail cells. And some of you have come from areas where your quest—quest for freedom left you battered by the storms of persecution and staggered by the winds of police brutality. You have been the veterans of creative suffering. Continue to work with the faith that unearned suffering is redemptive. Go back to Mississippi, go back to Alabama, go back to South Carolina, go back to Georgia, go back to Louisiana, go back to the slums and ghettos of our northern cities, knowing that somehow this situation can and will be changed.*

Here, Dr. King describes the shared struggles of his listeners and their self-interest in obtaining civil rights. He creates an image of "trials and tribulations" to remind his audience of the emotional pain they've undergone to reach this point, creating an emotional connection that he uses to rally them to keep fighting. Note also how he flatters his audience, calling them the "veterans of creative suffering."

Pathos can also be used to induce the audience to feel an emotion toward a particular person or group. However, you should do this, strangely enough, logically. For instance, certain categories are typically associated with certain

Figure 2.7
Although these fish logically fall into the categories of "predator" and "prey," emotionally, audiences usually root for the "little guy," or in this case, the "little fish."

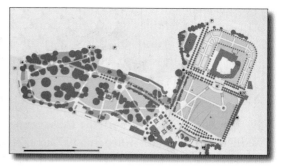

Figure 2.8
While a detailed plan of a park can make a logical appeal, you'd more effectively create *pathos* if you used an image that helped to show how the audience's children might play and enjoy the park once it's built.

emotions. "Predators" might make us fearful, while "prey" evokes sympathy, making the audience feel sorry for the animal being hunted (Figure 2.7). The categories are logical constructions, but you can use them in this way to create emotion.

For example, if you want to create positive emotions about a new park that the city wants to build, you might describe the project by depicting a scene of children playing in the park rather than simply telling the audience, "You should be happy about this park" (Figure 2.8). Because most people typically dislike bullies, the writer might frame an adversary as being a bully, providing a clear category the audience can be angry with (again, this can be done easily in digital platforms that allow tagging). Most of *pathos* involves using a story or image that taps into the values of listeners, making the audience imagine the author's emotion as their own. Use creative images to create a scene that summons these emotions.

Advertisements often use *pathos* to appeal to emotions. Figure 2.9 shows a commercial for the American Society for the Prevention of Cruelty to Animals (ASPCA). This commercial makes use of images of wounded animals to elicit two emotional reactions: sympathy for the abused animals and anger toward those who would commit such acts. In addition to the images, the commercial uses the popular yet somber song "Angel," by Sarah McLachlan, to connect the animals with the positive connotations the audience might usually associate with angels. The ad also uses an appeal from Sarah McLachlan herself, providing a celebrity spokesperson to help persuade the audience they should support the ASCPA.

However, as indicated by the meme in Figure 2.10, sometimes an appeal can be too good and turn people away. Many view the ASCPA

Credit: © ASPCA

Figure 2.9
This public service announcement uses a song to elicit *pathos* and a celebrity to create *ethos*.
www.youtube.com/watch?v=YliPZ0p0SNQ

Credit: quickmeme

HI MY NAME'S SARAH MCLACHLAN

I'M ABOUT TO RUIN YOUR DAY

Figure 2.10
Sometimes, an appeal can be too strong for a viewer to take.

commercials as too sad, making them want to turn the commercials off rather than watch them. Because the images from the commercial are highly memorable, and because the short commercial can be posted easily on YouTube, this genre can be remixed easily into other digital texts and used for other purposes.

Figure 2.11
QR code for an image search of vintage Camel ads

Cigarette advertisements have used many appeals throughout the decades. Figure 2.11 provides a QR code for an image search for "vintage cigarette ads," that often appeal to *ethos*. Many of these vintage ads included taglines stating something like "More doctors smoke Camels than any other cigarette," encouraging the viewer to believe that one should trust the doctor regarding the best brand of cigarette to smoke.

Figure 2.12
This cigarette ad attempts to evoke the mood of "cool," and changing the "c" to a "k" isn't fooling anyone.

Of course, more recent ads have used emotional appeals, specifically in the guise of "Joe Camel," the cigarette-smoking camel developed by the tobacco company R. J. Reynolds. Joe Camel is depicted in a variety of leisure activities, from playing pool to riding motorcycles, appearing cool and "smooth." These ads do not make a logical appeal, but an emotional one, attempting to coerce the viewer into buying not only a cigarette but also the state of mind. This state of mind varies depending on the ad, but Joe Camel and other cigarette ads mostly promote the mood of "cool" (Figure 2.12).

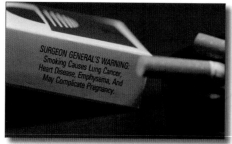

Figure 2.13
The surgeons general's cigarette warning uses facts to appeal to its audience.

Credit: fda.gov

Figure 2.14
New cigarette ads try to appeal to *pathos* (emotion) more than *logos* (reason).

To counter the "cool" mood of tobacco use, the United States Food and Drug Administration (FDA) attempted to create a counter mood in a set of new warning labels to be placed on cigarette packaging. Rather than the standard "surgeon general's warning" (Figure 2.13), the new packaging displays more graphic examples of what can happen to those who smoke. Figure 2.14, an example of one of these ads, compares a healthy set of lungs with those exhibiting damage from smoking cigarettes. The FDA (Figure 2.15) hopes that these ads strike a more emotional appeal (*pathos*) than the current warning, which simply states the facts about the damage smoking can cause (*logos*).

Credit: fda.gov   Credit: Anti-Smoking PSA/CDC

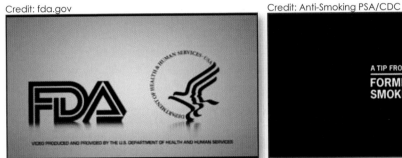

Figure 2.15
FDA announcement unveiling the new cigarette warning ads
www.youtube.com/watch?v=ps0ASyGjXXo

Figure 2.16
Testimonies from former smokers are effective, but are they too effective?
www.youtube.com/watch?v=EyVLKHEqTu0

Like the ASPCA public service announcements, many viewers feel these new antismoking warnings are too sad or grotesque, especially the television commercials that are a part of this public service announcement campaign (Figure 2.16). You should consider if your own appeals will grab your audience's attention or shock them so much they tune out your argument.

Rhetorical Continuities

The point of *pathos* isn't to solely elicit emotions in your audience. Whether spoken, written, or image-based, the most effective arguments are usually those that have elements of all three rhetorical appeals: *logos*, *ethos*, and *pathos*. You don't want your audience acting on emotion alone, but in conjunction with *logos* and *ethos*; all three should be directed toward some desired outcome, the reason for your writing.

DIGITAL Connections

Pathos in Advertising

By Molly Peel

Consider this article published with Maus Media Group by Molly Peel, who discusses the use of *pathos* by Beats by Dr. Dre.

One of the first things you learn in any speech class is the importance of *pathos. Pathos* is one of the main three rhetorical strategies in persuasive speaking, along with *ethos* and *logos*. Each device represents a necessary part of persuasive speaking: credibility (*ethos*), reason (*logos*) and emotion (*pathos*). Of the three, *pathos* is the most powerful. It can be seen in Dr. King's "I Have a Dream" speech, in the romantic declarations of every chick-flick, and, oddly enough, in Beats by Dre's latest commercial, "The Game Before the Game."

www.youtube.com/watch?v=v_i3Lcjli84

It begins with soccer player Neymar da Silva Santos Jr. receiving an inspirational phone call from his father before a match, then goes on to show other prominent professionals preparing for their matches—walking into the locker room, doing warm-up exercises, repeating pre-match superstitions, putting on their uniforms, and taping various injuries—and of course, they're doing this while listening to music with their Beats headphones. There are also brief flashes of fans from across the world partaking in their own pre-match superstitions interspersed throughout the ad, like a Dutch man putting on orange wooden shoes, a woman painting her face with her team's colors, a group of guys having drinks at the pub, and Serena Williams painting her nails to look like American flags.

This strategy is brilliant. Instead of beating the viewer over the head with their product, they fit it seamlessly, organically into the background of these powerful and emotional scenes. There are few things that get people from around the world emotionally involved as much as soccer does—even if you have no interest in soccer, you can't get through this commercial without getting goosebumps.

A commercial like this is pure *pathos*. Instead of trying to justify why you should buy their headphones, they make you want to by showing how vital they are to your favorite soccer players' pre-match warm-ups.

Of course, other rhetorical devices can be useful when advertising your product or service too. But if you want to get customers who will love your brand, rather than just like it or need it, consider *pathos*.

Building

Link

View the video about the new cigarette warning labels in Figure 2.15. How do the officials who are interviewed talk about the new labels? In other words, how do they frame the selection of the images in terms of *pathos*, *logos*, or *ethos*? Why do you think they discuss the new labels as they do? Research opposition to the new ads, and analyze how this opposition makes its own arguments as well. Report your findings to the class.

Engine

Search

Revisit the hashtags you looked at earlier. In addition to creating logical categories, how do you think these tags create emotional connections or responses from viewers? Are some of the hashtags humorous? Offensive? Thought provoking? Write a short report that discusses how these hashtags might be considered an appeal to *pathos*, and share your findings with the class.

Rhetorical Timing: *Kairos*

Timing is also an important rhetorical element to consider, which can be identified in the Greek concept of *kairos*.

This concept will help you think about how to make different kinds of rhetorical appeals in the right time and place (again, you might think of this as the argument's "setting"), as well as how to avoid some pitfalls that might hurt the content and delivery of your message.

The ancient Greeks used two words to denote two different kinds of time. The word *chronos* refers to chronological time (the word "chronological" comes from *chronos*). This kind of time describes sequential happenings, annual and daily cycles often recognized as making up "time."

However, they also used the word *kairos*, which refers to a particular moment in time that has some special significance. While *chronos* can be measured

Figure 2.17
This fresco painting by Francesco Salviati depicts the idea of *kairos* as a mythical figure. What do you think his physical attributes say about the concept of *kairos*?

quantitatively by a watch, *kairos* is more qualitative, measured not by a device but by intuition and foresight (Figure 2.17).

As an analogy, if a football team is in position to win a game with a field goal, the players on the field often will wait to score in order to run as much time off the clock as possible. Usually, the coach will call a time out with only a few seconds left, so the other team will not have time to get the ball back and score. Here, the coach is choosing the best, most effective moment to call a time out to help win the game. The kicker might miss the field goal, but if he makes it, the other team won't have a chance to win (Figure 2.18).

Within rhetoric, *kairos* signifies the best, most strategic moment in which one should communicate. If one communicates too early, before an audience is prepared to hear an argument, or too late, when the argument is no longer necessary or valid, then the rhetor has not utilized the kairotic moment to make the best case.

In a political campaign, for instance, a candidate might wait until the week before the election to present his or her most effective evidence against his or her opponent. Waiting to reveal this evidence allows the politician to make it fresh in the voters' minds as they enter the voting booths. This opportune moment would give the candidate being attacked less time to respond, and not enough time could elapse before voting day to help voters forget.

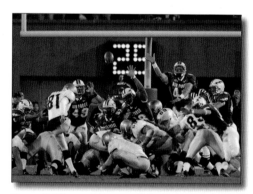

Figure 2.18
Navy waited until four seconds left to kick this field goal, winning the game against Air Force.

Many politicians called for gun reform after the mass shootings at Sandy Hook Elementary School in 2012 (Figure 2.19). This terrible tragedy put the issue of gun availability in the country's mind. The period after the shootings was the most kairotic moment in which to advocate gun control, right after the event showed everyone what could happen if the wrong person got a gun. If politicians had advanced gun control before the shooting, the issue would not have received much media coverage as other issues were more pressing. However, if too much time passed after this event, then the pain and heartache would fade from memory, making the issue feel less

Credit: VOA Video

Figure 2.19
The shootings at Sandy Hook Elementary School provided a kairotic moment to discuss gun control.
www.youtube.com/watch?v=gAmr-A-F8K8

important than during the immediate aftermath. In other words, the mood would have changed. *Kairos*, then, is partly about capturing the audience during a particular emotion.

DIGITAL Connections

Comment on "Words that Zing" by Colleen Jones

By Stewart McCoy

Kairos is really about *when* you communicate a message, so *kairos* is more concerned with Web interactions such as those encountered during a user flow for an e-commerce checkout, a tutorial, subscription process, Web app interaction, search apps, or office apps. An example of what I mean is when a new user logs into Google Docs for the first time

> As related to digital writing, *kairos* can become even more important, as many interactions are in real-time and require precise timing to connect with the audience. Consider Stewart McCoy's response to Colleen Jones's essay on *kairos*, "Words that Zing," published in *A List Apart*.

and they are presented with a pop-up box offering an optional tour. That first login is a kairotic moment where Google can educate its new users about how they'll benefit from using the application. Another example would be when a user is buying flowers on FTD.com and during the check-out process is presented the option of adding a gift card or a box of chocolates to their order before submitting their payment information.

Building

Link

Kairos doesn't exist alone, but combines with the other appeals of *logos*, *ethos*, and *pathos*. For instance, *pathos* can be used to stir the emotions of the audience around a particular event, but choosing to use this appeal at the right time is *kairotic*. Even the timing for when *pathos* might be used within a speech uses *kairos*, for a speaker may save her most rousing and emotional point for the end, when the audience will remember it the best. With a partner, locate an example of where you think an author combines *kairos* with the other rhetorical appeals of *logos*, *ethos*, and *pathos*. How does the writer choose the best moment to use one of these other appeals? Write a brief report of your example and findings, and share them with the class.

Engine

Search

Examine a typical news website and the role that *kairos* might play in posting news stories. How does the site try to make use of *kairos*? Does the site try to present news at an opportune time, or simply as it happens? Make sure you consider all the facets of news it presents, from news stories to editorials to blogs.

KEY Terms

avatar	*logos*
chronos	*pathos*
comments	QR (Quick Response) codes
digital rhetoric	remix
ethos	rhetorical velocity
hashtag	Search Engine Optimization
hyperlinks	(SEO)
kairos	tagging

Digital Rhetoric Report

This chapter looks at a variety of ways rhetoric can be digital, as well as some more traditional rhetorical appeals that exist in all texts. However, since the concept of "digital rhetoric" is fairly new, many scholars and researchers continue to debate about exactly what digital rhetoric *is* as well as develop new rhetorical techniques for digital technologies.

For this assignment, conduct your own research that builds upon the definitions and techniques that would fall under the term "digital rhetoric." What do other scholars say about "digital rhetoric"? How do they suggest digital technologies can be used to persuade an audience? Are there other disciplines, such as online marketing, that have developed strategies that could be called "rhetorical"?

You can compose this report in electronic or print format, but check with your instructor. She or he will also inform you of the required length and number of sources required. However, if you do produce a print document, consider incorporating digital elements within the text, such as QR codes, especially if you refer to web-based examples such as websites or online videos.

From DIGITAL Writers

Digital Rhetoric: Toward an Integrated Theory

By James Zappen

The concept of a digital rhetoric is at once exciting and troublesome. It is exciting because it holds promise of opening new vistas of opportunity for rhetorical studies and troublesome because it reveals the difficulties and the challenges of adapting a rhetorical tradition more than 2,000 years old to the conditions and constraints of the new digital media.

> As an example of an essay that attempts to define digital rhetoric, consider this article published in *Technical Communication Quarterly* by James Zappen. Compare and contrast his definition with what you've learned already.

Explorations of this concept show how traditional rhetorical strategies function in digital spaces and suggest how these strategies are being reconceived and reconfigured within these spaces (Fogg; Gurak, *Persuasion*; Warnick; Welch). Studies of the new digital media explore their basic characteristics, affordances, and constraints (Fagerjord; Gurak,

> Zappen is a professor of communications and media at Rensselaer Polytechnic Institute, where he researches and writes about contemporary rhetoric, digital rhetoric, and intercultural education.

Cyberliteracy; Manovich), their opportunities for creating individual identities (Johnson-Eilola; Miller; Turkle), and their potential for building social communities (Arnold, Gibbs, and Wright; Blanchard; Matei and Ball-Rokeach; Quan-Haase and Wellman). Collectively, these studies suggest how traditional rhetoric might be extended and transformed into a comprehensive theory of digital rhetoric and how such a theory might contribute to the larger body of rhetorical theory and criticism and the rhetoric of science and technology in particular.

STRATEGIES OF SELF-EXPRESSION AND COLLABORATION

Studies of digital rhetoric help to explain how traditional rhetorical strategies of persuasion function and how they are being reconfigured in digital spaces. Laura J. Gurak shows how strategies of persuasion based upon Aristotle's notions of *ethos*, *pathos*, and *logos* function to motivate action and belief in the online debates about Lotus MarketPlace and the Clipper Chip (*Persuasion*). In the case of Lotus MarketPlace, for example, the product—a CD-ROM database of direct-mail marketing information about American consumers—raised issues related to personal privacy, provoked strong protests via newsgroups and e-mail, and, as a consequence, was never placed on the market (19–31). According to Gurak, the protests were based upon a highly emotive and often inflammatory *ethos*; in contrast, Lotus' response was based upon a hard-facts corporate *logos*, which was both untimely and inadequate to the situation and thereby ensured the failure of the product (85–91, 93–96, 114–24). B. J. Fogg shows how the computer itself (and its associated software) functions as a persuasive technology: as a tool when, for example, it simplifies processes or customizes information; as a medium when it simulates cause-and-effect processes, environments, or objects; and as a social actor through a variety of physical, psychological, linguistic, and social cues (23–120). Fogg is particularly interested in how computers as persuasive technologies (hence captology) achieve credibility (*ethos*) and in the ethics of various kinds of persuasive appeals, including appeals to the emotions (*pathos*) (5, 121–81, 211–39).

Barbara Warnick similarly explores the uses of persuasion in digital media, especially digital texts, but she also observes the potential of these media to extend and transform traditional notions of rhetoric as persuasion. Describing attempts to attract women to the Internet and the World Wide Web in the late 1990s, for example, she notes the failure of persuasive appeals in traditional print media and in cybergrrl narratives (so-named because the "cybergrrls" were seeking to distinguish themselves from the "girls" depicted in Internet pornography), which she claims were "elitist and hierarchically motivated" (71–82). In contrast, she notes the success of Web-based alternatives to mainstream media, including e-zines, which offered a variety of forums for self-expression and new modes of interacting with others—"welcoming places where invitational discourse becomes truly inviting" (82–86). Again, describing Web-based political parody in the 2000 presidential campaign, she notes their success as persuasion, effected, however, through a heteroglossic cacophony of voices, offering opportunities for reader participation and interactivity and achieving unity of purpose not through direct appeals or explicit arguments, but through a web of reciprocal links and intertextual references (87–113). Kathleen E. Welch likewise observes the potential of digital media to transform traditional notions of persuasion when she observes characteristics of both oral and print media in the new "electric rhetoric," which she claims can be both additive and subordinate, aggregative and analytic, redundant and copious, agonistic and collaborative or participatory, situational and abstract (106, 108, 184–86). I have sought to contribute to this discussion in my epilogue to *The Rebirth of Dialogue*, where I argue that dialogue—conceived not as a mode of persuasion, but as a testing of one's own ideas, a contesting of others' ideas, and a collaborative creating of ideas—is possible in any medium: oral, print, digital (146–61). Collectively, these studies are challenging the view that associates rhetoric exclusively with persuasion, a view that has persisted for more than two millennia.

CHARACTERISTICS, AFFORDANCES, CONSTRAINTS

Studies of the new digital media explain some of the basic characteristics of communication in digital spaces and some of their attendant difficulties. Such basic characteristics function as both affordances and constraints and so help to explain how the new media support and enable the transformation of the old rhetoric of persuasion into a new digital rhetoric that encourages self-expression, participation, and creative collaboration. Gurak identifies some of these basic characteristics—speed, reach, anonymity, and interactivity—and explains how they function as both affordances and constraints (*Cyberliteracy* 29–46). Speed encourages an oral and casual style, but it also encourages redundant and repetitive postings (30–33). Reach permits communication among multiple participants in an array of media and thus the development of communities of interest on a global scale; however, it does not include the benefits of gatekeeping (33–37). Anonymity encourages experiments in self and gender identities, but it also problematizes notions of authorship and ownership and encourages "flaming"—the hostile expression of strong emotions (38–43). Interactivity permits closer access to other people with increased opportunities for discussion and feedback, but it also permits increased opportunities for intrusions upon personal privacy (44–46).

These characteristics accord with our everyday experiences with digital communication technologies but raise some difficulties upon closer scrutiny. Thus, Lev Manovich, for example, questions whether terms such as "digital" and "interactivity" have any real meaning. Manovich finds in the new media characteristics of numerical representation, modularity, automation, variability, and transcoding (27–48). Because new media are digitally coded assemblages of discrete components (numerically represented and modular), they enable creation of media objects at low and high levels, from the most simple photo and text manipulations to the most advanced Artificial Intelligence (AI) applications (automation) (27–36). For the same reasons, they can appear in different versions (variability) so that a media database, for example, can produce an almost infinite variety of end-user objects, which can be customized for different users, manipulated through hyperlinks, periodically updated, and scaled upon demand (33–45).

Finally, new media can also be translated from one layer to another (transcoding)—from a computer layer to a cultural layer—so that the media database, for example, becomes a cultural form in its own right (45–48). Given these characteristics, Manovich questions the use of the term "digital," which can refer to analog-to-digital conversion, common representational code, or numerical representation, only the last having any relevance to the other characteristics (52).

Similarly, he questions the use of the term "interactivity" since it states only the most basic fact about computer structures and operations and is therefore, without further qualification, simply redundant (55–56). Anders Fagerjord accepts these key characteristics as a point of departure, but he emphasizes their communicative aspect and observes the tendency of the modularized and variable components of Web media to come together in a process that he calls "rhetorical convergence" (306–13, 318). Fagerjord uses the term "rhetorical" to emphasize both the Web author's choices of topics, arguments, sequences, and words and the reader's processes of selection and semiosis—noting, however, that we have barely begun to describe and catalog these choices and these processes (307, 313). How, then, should we understand the relationship between author and reader, and how should we understand the processes by which authors and readers work together to achieve self-expression or creative collaboration?

THE FORMATION OF IDENTITIES AND COMMUNITIES

Studies of the new digital media also explore some of the purposes and outcomes of communication in digital spaces: not only persuasion for the purpose of moving audiences to action or belief, but also self-expression for the purpose of exploring individual and group identities and participation and creative collaboration for the purpose of building communities of shared interest. Warnick's analyses, cited above, show how the new media—"symbolic action as carried out through visual images, specialized argots, hypertext patterns"— are used to form identity and community (12, 15). Other analyses explore the processes of forming identities and communities as complex interactions, both online and offline, between ourselves and others, thus providing context and meaning for the term "interactivity."

Sherry Turkle explains the processes of identity formation as interactions among multiple versions of our online selves and between these and our real selves: "As players participate [in Multiple-User Domains, or MUDs], they become authors not only of text, but of themselves, constructing new selves through social interaction.

"One player says, 'You are the character, and you are not the character, both at the same time.' Another says, 'You are who you pretend to be.' MUDs provide worlds for anonymous social interaction in which one can play a role as close to or as far away from one's 'real self' as one chooses" (11–12). But these interactions between ourselves and others are not entirely of our own choosing. In some online environments, such as hypertext environments, these interactions encompass not only our selves as authors, but also our own and others' selves as readers. As Johndan Johnson-Eilola points out, "a hypertext not only invites readers to participate in making the text, but forces them to do so, requiring both readers and writers to become 'co-learners'" (145).

Such processes of identity formation through social interaction are reminiscent of the traditional rhetorical concept of *ethos*. As Carolyn R. Miller observes, identity formation as the creation of human character is closely associated with Aristotle's understanding of *ethos* as "more than our knowledge of someone's prior reputation but…also, importantly, a product of the ongoing performance itself, made on the fly, in the course of interaction" (269). But what is the nature of this interaction? Surely it is something more than an interaction between speaker and audience in the traditional sense but, rather, a complex negotiation between various versions of our online and our real selves, between our many representations of our selves and our listeners and readers, and, not least (as Manovich suggests), between our many selves and the computer structures and operations through which we represent these selves to others.

Similarly, the formation of communities of shared interest is an outcome of processes of interactions, both online and offline, between ourselves and others. Numerous studies have documented the close connection between online and offline communities. Anabel Quan-Haase and Barry Wellman, for example, observe a reciprocal relationship between online and offline communities and a net increase in social ties: "Rather than weakening other forms of community, those who are more active offline are more active online—and vice versa" (320). Similarly, Sorin Matei and Sandra J. Ball-Rokeach claim a "the more, the more" relationship between online and offline communities, and they also claim that this relationship holds across differences in gender, income, age, education, and ethnicity (406, 420). As a graphic illustration of this relationship, Michael Arnold, Martin R. Gibbs, and Philippa Wright offer a comment by a participant at a social gathering (with free food and alcohol) held by developers promoting new homes with intranet connectivity in a suburb of Melbourne, Australia: "Yes, an intranet is all very well, but do we still get free beer and a barbeque?" (187–88, 193).

IMPLICATIONS FOR RHETORICAL STUDIES

Digital rhetoric is thus an amalgam of more-or-less discrete components rather than a complete and integrated theory in its own right. These discrete components nonetheless provide at least a partial outline for such a theory, which has potential to contribute to the larger body of rhetorical theory and criticism and the rhetoric of science and technology in particular. Suppose, for example, that scientific inquiry were situated within the context of digital spaces with the characteristics and potential outcomes and the strategies of self-expression, participation, and collaboration that we now associate with these spaces. What kind of rhetoric of science would we find within these spaces? What is the potential of Internet2 (http://www.internet2.edu) to foster creative collaborations, to promote the development of scientific communities, and to produce new ideas and significant research results? What is the potential of digital discussion spaces such as Slashdot (http://slashdot.org, especially the

Science section) to cultivate interest, disseminate information, and encourage discussion on current issues in science and technology among both scientists and nonscientists? A theory of digital rhetoric that recognizes how the traditional rhetoric of persuasion is being transformed in digital spaces invites such questions and thus offers new opportunities for inquiry in rhetorical theory and criticism and an expanded vision of what the rhetoric of science and technology might become within the next decade and beyond.

Works Cited

Arnold, Michael, Martin R. Gibbs, and Philippa Wright. "Intranets and Local Community: 'Yes, an intranet is all very well, but do we still get free beer and a barbeque?'" *Communities and Technologies: Proceedings of the First International Conference on Communities and Technologies: C&T 2003*, edited by Marleen Huysman, Etienne Wenger, and Volker Wulf, Kluwer, 2003, pp. 185–204.

Blanchard, Anita. "Blogs as Virtual Communities: Identifying a Sense of Community in the Julie/Julia Project." *Into the Blogosphere: Rhetoric, Community, and Culture of Weblogs*, edited by Laura Gurak, Smiljana Antonijevic, Laurie Johnson, Clancy Ratliff, and Jessica Reyman, University of Minnesota 14 Dec. 2004, blog.lib.umn.edu/blogosphere.

Fagerjord, Anders. "Rhetorical Convergence: Studying Web Media." *Digital Media Revisited: Theoretical and Conceptual Innovation in Digital Domains*, edited by Gunnar Liestøl, Andrew Morrison, and Terje Rasmussen, MIT P, 2003, pp. 293–325.

Fogg, B. J. *Persuasive Technology: Using Computers to Change What We Think and Do*. Morgan Kaufmann Series in Interactive Technologies, Morgan, 2003.

Gurak, Laura J. *Cyberliteracy: Navigating the Internet with Awareness*. Yale UP, 2001.

———. *Persuasion and Privacy in Cyberspace: The Online Protests over Lotus MarketPlace and the Clipper Chip*. Yale UP, 1997.

Johnson-Eilola, Johndan. *Nostalgic Angels: Rearticulating Hypertext Writing. New Directions in Computers and Composition Studies*. Ablex, 1997.

Manovich, Lev. *The Language of New Media*. Leonardo, MIT P, 2001.

Matei, Sorin, and Sandra J. Ball-Rokeach. "Belonging in Geographic, Ethnic, and Internet Spaces." *The Internet in Everyday Life*, edited by Barry Wellman and Caroline Haythornthwaite, Information Age Series, Blackwell, 2002, pp. 404–27.

Miller, Carolyn R. "Writing in a Culture of Simulation: *Ethos* Online." *The Semiotics of Writing: Transdisciplinary Perspectives on the Technology of Writing*, edited by Patrick Coppock, Semiotic and Cognitive Studies, Brepols, 2001, pp. 253–79.

Quan-Haase, Anabel, and Barry Wellman, with James C. Witte and Keith N. Hampton. "Capitalizing on the Net: Social Contact, Civic Engagement, and Sense of Community." *The Internet in Everyday Life*, edited by Barry Wellman and Caroline Haythornthwaite, Information Age Series, Blackwell, 2002, pp. 291–324.

Turkle, Sherry. *Life on the Screen: Identity in the Age of the Internet*. Simon, 1995.

Warnick, Barbara. *Critical Literacy in a Digital Era: Technology, Rhetoric, and the Public Interest*. Erlbaum, 2002.

Welch, Kathleen E. *Electric Rhetoric: Classical Rhetoric, Oralism, and a New Literacy*. Digital Communication, MIT P, 1999.

Zappen, James P. *The Rebirth of Dialogue: Bakhtin, Socrates, and the Rhetorical Tradition*. SUNY P, 2004.

STUDENT Example

Today we see people striving not to be left behind the fast-growing digital universe. While the traditional roots of rhetoric are still appealing, we must think about how they can be applied to social networks, blogs, vlogs, and whatever new stream of information and networking that has been invented during the reading of this webpage. Today's rhetoric is, after all, a digital rhetoric. Digital rhetoric encompasses rhetoric that has adapted to the general public's standards of being appealed to and persuaded in our growing digital world.

JohnKarlo Velazquez is a student from Borough of Manhattan Community College at John Jay College. He is a computer and information systems major.

Digital Rhetoric for a Digital World

By JohnKarlo Velazquez

Foundations

The foundation of rhetoric has not needed to change for us to understand digital rhetoric. This foundation can be studied in the writings of the famous philosopher of ancient Greece, Aristotle. Aristotle (as reviewed by the YouTube video, "Using the Rhetorical Triangle and Rhetorical Appeals," by YouTube's David Wright) wrote about the rhetorical triangle in which there is an author, an audience, and a text. This has not changed with digital rhetoric; the only exception is that the text may now come in the form of video or audio. There is still a piece written or created by an author for an audience to appeal to or persuade them. The same goes with Aristotle's view on *logos*, *ethos*, and *pathos*. These tools that authors use in their work to connect with their audience are still deployed in digital spaces.

Design and Persuasion

The most obvious aspect of digital rhetoric today is visual persuasion or persuasive design. This encompasses strategic applications related to rhetorical principles that result in the organization and customization of what the audience sees. Before digital rhetoric, visual persuasion would have been related to art works like sculptures and paintings; today we find this most commonly in relation to web designs. In an interview with Andrew Chak, "Guiding Users with Persuasive Design: An Interview with Andrew Chak" by Christine Perfetti, Chak responds that "To be successful, sites must go beyond usability by focusing on

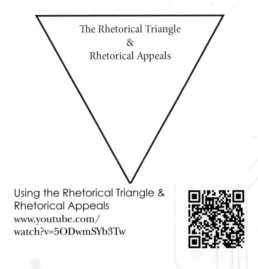

The Rhetorical Triangle & Rhetorical Appeals

Using the Rhetorical Triangle & Rhetorical Appeals
www.youtube.com/
watch?v=5ODwmSYb3Tw

persuasive design. They must motivate users by taking advantage of persuasive tactics that will make them take action. The most persuasive websites focus on making users feel comfortable about making decisions and helping them act on them." Chak is speaking about the simple task of making a website user-friendly as a form of persuasion to encourage readers to continue exploring the website. This could easily be interpreted as one of Aristotle's rhetorical terms of *pathos* where we see an appeal to the audience's emotions of comfort. This new application of a rhetorical term in a digital world is a prime example of digital rhetoric.

A more specific example of persuasive design in digital cultures is the relatively recent Facebook redesigns. Facebook has redesigned its layout almost annually to ensure a user-friendly website that will appeal to the audiences and encourage them to frequent the website. During each of these updates, Facebook boosted their creditability by assuring their users that this was an improvement to make Facebook easier. Now while some may have disliked or had trouble adjusting, the amount of Facebook users only increased.

New Age Rhetoric Is Here

Digital rhetoric is new age rhetoric. We experience it every day with everything, especially with everyone having a personal page on the web. Social networks like Facebook, Instagram, Vine, blogs, and vlogs represent rhetoric in our growing, instant, visually stimulated, tech-savvy digital generation. Digital rhetoric is the remake of old tools to appeal to and persuade the people of today and tomorrow.

CHAPTER 3

Digital Arguments

In 2014, an audio recording that contained racist comments made by Donald Sterling—former owner of the Los Angeles Clippers professional basketball team—was released by the celebrity gossip blog *TMZ*. After the audio recording's release, many people posted videos in response to Sterling's comments. While some of these responses were from celebrities, such as Lil Wayne and Snoop Dogg, many more came from ordinary citizens who felt the need to express why they felt Sterling was wrong and how he should be punished by the NBA. YouTube, as a digital platform, allowed anyone with a digital camera to quickly deliver his or her argument to the world.

Although not all of the video responses to Sterling's comments are "good" arguments, they still use traditional argumentative strategies. While other writing classes teach how to create arguments through traditional, alphabetic forms of writing, creating an argument through digital writing can be a bit different. However, even though you'll be working with text, images, video, sound, and writing technologies other than a traditional word processor, these media can still be used to craft arguments you might usually associate with traditional essays. Such arguments don't need to be explicit but can be designed in a way that their arguments are implicit within a narrative and not overtly stated (Figure 3.1). In this chapter, you will learn how to write your own arguments and how arguments function across different digital media.

Credit: Carsten Tolkmit

Figure 3.1
Words aren't the only way to make arguments.

When you're developing an argument, the rhetorical elements *logos*, *ethos*, *pathos*, and *kairos* will be very useful. Consider these four rhetorical appeals and how you might incorporate them into your arguments. Also remember that factors such as the writer, message, audience, design, medium, and genre also affect your argument. For instance, an audience might respond more positively to one design or medium over another, and so these choices also should influence how you construct and deliver your argument.

Elements of an Argument

When first developing an argument, you should consider some of the essentials almost every argument makes use of. This section will discuss those essential elements, as well as how to develop a claim and the ideas that will support that claim.

Essential components

At the very least, an argument should include the following elements: an arguable topic, a claim or thesis statement, valid reasons, credible evidence, opposing arguments, a clearly defined audience, and a conclusion. Each of these elements work together to produce an argument that is not only well supported but also justifiable to present.

Arguable topic

In order for an argument to occur, the topic must be debatable from at least two perspectives. Generally, established, observable facts such as the effect of gravity on the Earth aren't debatable. You could try to argue that a rock dropped from a building wouldn't fall to the ground, but you would probably have little evidence to support your claim. Thus, you must have good reasons why your position should be heard.

Claim or thesis statement

To make an argument is to establish a claim about the world, usually toward some purpose. A simple description about the facilities at two hospitals is not an argument. However, making a claim that one hospital is better than the other because of these facilities is an argument, or at least the beginning of an argument. The purpose might be to convince readers they should visit one hospital over the other if they want the best treatment.

Valid reasons

If you don't have a good reason for making your argument, then the audience might not take it seriously. For example, the argument about the best hospital could have life and death reasons associated with the choice. Often, you can get at your reasons by following your major claim with "because." You should choose this hospital "because your life might depend on it." If the audience doesn't think your reason for arguing is valid, they might not pay attention.

Credible evidence

In order to convince your audience of your claim, you need evidence to support that claim. You might argue that "If you're sick, you should go to Hospital A over Hospital B because your life might depend on it. Hospital A has the most advanced equipment, the best-trained doctors, and a lower death rate than Hospital B." These three pieces of evidence help support your claim and reason.

Opposing arguments

Rather than ignoring the arguments the opposing side might use, it's best to acknowledge them and then explain why they are either wrong, insignificant, or insufficient. For example, the opposing side might argue that Hospital B has faster ambulance times than Hospital A. If you have researched your topic well, you might know the difference in average ambulance response times is only 26 seconds. Given all the other positive attributes that Hospital A has, you should acknowledge this fact but then point out that it's an insignificant amount of time given the quality of care a patient will receive upon reaching Hospital A.

Audience

This audience may simply be the person you're arguing with, or it may consist of all your Twitter followers. The important point to remember about audiences is that they have their own history, assumptions, expectations, and attitudes about the topic you might be arguing about. Learn as much as you can about your audience as you prepare your argument and adjust what you write to meet this audience's needs.

Conclusion

The conclusion should reiterate the claim and reason, but also tell the audience exactly what you'd like them to do next. Tell the audience the action they should take, and remind them what's at stake if they don't.

Developing a claim with a thesis statement

Although your claim might be implicit (see below), your audience should have some idea what you're trying to argue. Thus, early in your argument you should state what you're trying to persuade your audience about—often called a thesis statement. A thesis statement typically looks like this:

> The U.S. Congress should pass a nationwide law that makes texting and driving illegal. The danger is too great to let individual states decide.

Here, the issue is texting while driving, and the claim declares what should be done about the issue as well as a reason for the claim. However, you should also consider your purpose and audience when making the claim. If your audience was simply your friend, you might revise the claim to state:

> You should not text while driving. You might get into an accident.

Because your friend has no individual power to pass laws, only the power to control her own behavior, the context of your claim shifts. Your claim about this issue might further shift if you were writing a letter to phone companies:

> Samsung should make phones that block texting when in a moving vehicle. Texting while driving makes a driver 23 times more likely to crash.

Obviously, this last one needs work, because opposing arguments might ask the question "What if the person texting is just a passenger?" However, you can see how the specifics of the claim shift depending upon the audience and the purpose. The purpose of the first claim was not to get a law passed, but to stop the dangerous habit of texting while driving—a purpose that was pursued through other claims with other audiences.

Developing supporting ideas

Although you may know what you want to argue about, you sometimes need to spend time developing ideas to build the topic into a full-fledged argument. The following techniques can be used to help think about and develop your ideas toward your intended purpose and audience.

Read

Although writing and reading are different activities, reading about your topic can help you generate ideas and think about your topic in ways you might not have considered. You will, of course, read much about your topic when conducting research, and this is usually the first step in developing ideas.

Question

Think about your topic by asking specific questions from a variety of perspectives. In the hospital example above, you might think about what you would value in a particular hospital, what experts value in a hospital, and what patients from a variety of demographics each value. For instance, the needs of the elderly are much different from those of children, and a hospital might serve one demographic better than the other. Question what makes a good hospital in general, and then ask what makes a good hospital for your particular audience. This kind of interrogation will help you develop those ideas you need to consider for your argument.

Discuss

Sometimes, you need answers to questions that reading alone can't provide. In this case, discuss your ideas and questions with others. What do these individuals value in relation to your argument? What are their expectations, background, and prior knowledge? You can use their answers to help you generate reasons and evidence for your claim that can appeal to different kinds of audiences.

Search

Sometimes looking at visuals related to your topic can help you develop ideas. You might perform a Google search on "hospitals" that would provide images to help you think about the different facets of a hospital. You might visit a hospital to see one up close. You might also watch television shows or movies that focus on your topic, as these shows might raise questions you'll need to consider. As you look, pay attention to the details and take notes; often, these notes will help you generate writing.

Write

Often the act of writing spurs thinking and leads to other writing. Consider these writing strategies that can help you develop ideas.

- **Brainstorming**: This method simply asks you to come up with as many ideas as possible about your topic or problem you want to address. For instance, you might place as many key words as you can about your topic together on a page to help you see how each word relates to the others. These relationships might spark more ideas, eventually producing a general outline you then need to fill. The important part to remember is to write down whatever comes to mind, even if it seems crazy at first. Some of the most creative ideas came about by putting together things no one else had even considered.

- **Freewriting**: A step beyond basic brainstorming, freewriting asks you to write thoughts not just as words, but as more complete sentences. Of course, these sentences don't have to make sense at first, for freewriting isn't always about what first comes out. Simply sitting down and freewriting, no matter what comes out, can help you get into the mood of writing, eventually producing a word or phrase that gives you an idea. The most important action is just to write and fill the blank page with words. To better facilitate freewriting, you might also set yourself a time limit. For example, no matter what comes out, write for 15 minutes, not stopping until the time is up.

- **Drafting**: More substantial than brainstorming or freewriting, drafting requires you to committ more thought and effort in order to develop a more complete idea. In other words, rather than dealing with the nuts and bolts of an idea, drafting is the act of putting those ideas from brainstorming and freewriting together in order to see what takes shape.

- **Doodling**: Although you might consider doodling to be a trivial activity done out of boredom, doodling and drawing actually help the imagination develop ideas or flesh out and refine ones you might already have. Sometimes, putting ideas into images instead of words can help shift your perspective and generate new thoughts.

Building

Link

With a partner, choose a recent issue (besides the current debate around texting while driving). Develop at least five claims about this topic from a variety of perspectives and/or audiences. For each claim, develop reasons to support it, as well as three examples of evidence. Share these claims with the class, and discuss how each might be strengthened and which audience each claim most likely targets.

Engine

Search

Locate an editorial in your local newspaper or one found online. Examine the argument in terms of the elements above. What claim does the author make? What reason does he or she provide? What evidence is offered to support the claim? What opposing arguments are given, if any? Write a brief report of your examination, and share it with the class.

Explicit Arguments

Before turning to narrative arguments that are more prominent in digital media, you should revisit the basic structure of traditional, explicit arguments you may be more accustomed to writing. While written arguments can be implicit—not directly stating what the reader should think—advanced writing classes usually ask you to write explicit arguments that state a claim and provide support for why the reader should adopt your point of view.

As discussed above, most arguments break down into three basic parts: a claim, reasons, and evidence. The first part of any argument is to make a claim. For instance, you might claim that vegetarianism is a better diet than one that includes animal meat. However, a claim is not enough by itself—you also must provide reasons why the audience should believe your claim. In order to accomplish this, you might state reasons such as: "A plant-based diet prevents more diseases"; "Plants are packed with more nutrients"; or "A plant-based diet reduces animal suffering and cruelty."

Figure 3.2
"Eat More Kale" is a claim but has no explicit reasons or evidence.

Figure 3.3
This bumper sticker also makes a claim without explicit reasons or evidence.

However, just as a claim needs reasons to support it, these reasons need supporting evidence (Figures 3.2 and 3.3). You might then cite scientific studies that show reduced cancer rates in vegetarians, state findings that green leafy vegetables have more protein by weight than meat, or demonstrate how plant-based foods are less acidic than meat and thus reduce inflammation and increase general health. Such evidence makes it more likely that your audience will accept your overall argument, depending on the credibility (*ethos*) of whom you cite. You should also include possible counterarguments in order to refute them. Many advocates against a plant-based diet suggest humans have canines and evolved to eat meat. However, humans also have other organs they no longer use, such as the appendix, and so you might dismiss this counterargument by suggesting that the canines are also no longer needed.

In this example, *logos*, *pathos*, and *ethos* play a big part in your argument. If you're citing scientific studies, you're mainly appealing to *logos* (the scientific logic of the study) and *ethos* (the credibility of the scientists conducting the studies). Of course, you can also appeal to *pathos*, perhaps appealing to the emotions the audience might have toward the animals, which suffer so that humans can consume them. As always, you have to know your audience and which appeals might work best. One audience member might balk at emotional appeals but appreciate a more scientific approach.

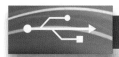

DIGITAL Connections

How Political Ads Can Elect a President

By Julian Zelizer

Last week, American Crossroads, Karl Rove's nonprofit operation that was highly effective in 2010, launched a blistering ad charging that President Barack Obama has failed to help American families.

A woman described as the mother of two grown children without jobs says to the camera, "I supported President Obama because he spoke so beautifully. He promised change. But things changed for the worse."

Obama also found himself in the middle of a controversy when Cory Booker, the popular Democratic mayor of Newark, New Jersey, criticized a spot that had attacked Mitt Romney's work at Bain Capital. It had been paid for by the Obama campaign.

Television spots are the medium through which the modern campaign is fought. The success or failure of the candidates at producing effective advertisements could have a huge influence on the outcome in November.

Each side of the campaign will spend inordinate amounts of money to pay for 30-second advertisements—which will also be spread through the Internet—that seek to define the message of the campaign of 2012 and the terms of the fight.

> Toward an argument about digital writing itself, in an opinion piece for *CNN*, history and public affairs professor Julian Zelizer discusses the role of media in presidential elections.
>
> In this piece, written before the 2012 presidential election, Zelizer argues that television has come to dominate how Americans choose a political candidate (Figure 3.4). Read over his argument and pay attention to the reasons and kinds of evidence he provides.

Credit: Carsten Pete Souza

Figure 3.4
Barack Obama effectively uses television to reach his many audiences.

"Television is no gimmick," said Roger Ailes, Richard Nixon's campaign consultant, in 1968, "and nobody will ever be elected to major office again without presenting themselves well on it."

Ailes was right. Since 1952, when television had become a regular part of many American homes, the campaign spot has become a defining feature of modern politics.

Figure 3.5
Dwight D. Eisenhower won his election through the use of television commercials.

According to The Living Room Candidate, an outstanding site that allows viewers to see many of these commercials, military hero Dwight Eisenhower (Figure 3.5) launched a presidential campaign spot based on the advice of advertising executive Rosser Reeves who thought this was the best way to reach the electorate.

Democrat Adlai Stevenson was disgusted by the use of commercials. "The idea that you can merchandise candidates for high office like breakfast cereal," he famously quipped, "is the ultimate indignity to the democratic process." Eisenhower won.

Like it or not, spots have dominated campaigns. Although there have been tremendous variations in the kinds of spots Americans have seen, there have been several consistent types that politicians have used that we are likely to see in the coming months.

The first is the character assassination spot. These are the ads in which candidates exploit a perceived weakness of their opponent, highlight this weakness and use it through the spot to shape how voters perceive them. The most infamous of all was the Daisy ad in 1964: Lyndon Johnson's campaign broadcast a spot featuring a little girl picking petals off a flower until viewers saw a mushroom cloud in her eye.

> Zelizer's claim is relatively easy to locate in this article: the best use of television by Obama or Romney will determine the outcome of the presidential election. What reasons does Zelizer provide for this claim? In several places, he states that television spots have become the primary medium through which candidates express their views and wage their campaign and that a huge amount of money is spent on these spots. As part of his rhetorical strategy, Zelizer incorporates the expert opinion of Richard Nixon's former campaign consultant, Roger Ailes.

The point was to take fears that Barry Goldwater was a reckless hawk on military matters and craft them into a shocking image that could scare people into believing he would launch a nuclear war.

Another famous example came in 2004, when George Bush's campaign broadcast an ad featuring Massachusetts Sen. John Kerry windsailing, moving in different directions. After going over a series of issues on which Kerry had switched his position, the narrator says, "John Kerry: whichever way the wind blows."

The ad played off perceptions that Kerry lacked core principles and sold this as the essence of his character. A more vicious ad in that campaign came from an independent group that featured veterans questioning Kerry's war record during Vietnam. The ad gave rise to the term "swift-boating" in modern campaigns.

Another type is the issue-based spot, which highlights a particular area of controversy that does not play well for the opposition or which triggers a debate about a subject that will raise problems for opponents.

Figure 3.6
Dwight D. Eisenhower argues that voting for his opponent will result in "high prices."

www.livingroomcandidate.org/commercials/1952/high-prices

One of the first ads by Eisenhower, called "High Prices," featured him answering questions to average citizens (who were filmed separately though it looked like they were addressing him), many of which revolved around the cost of living and inflation (Figure 3.6).

President Richard Nixon broadcast a powerful ad in 1972 that featured plastic soldiers being wiped off the table as a way to raise fears about defense budget cuts taking place under the Democratic Congress and which would accelerate if Sen. George McGovern was in the White House.

In 1988, campaign guru Lee Atwater filmed the "Willie Horton" ad, which revolved around a felon furlough program in Massachusetts when Michael Dukakis was governor, to talk about law and order.

There are also the guilt by association spots through which candidates try to tie an opponent to an unpopular figure or events through the power of image. In 2008, Barack Obama ran an ad that showed Republican John McCain embracing the unpopular George W. Bush repeatedly. In one of Richard Nixon's ads in 1968, the camera showed images of Vice President Hubert Humphrey juxtaposed with the chaotic Democratic Convention in 1968 where anti-war protesters clashed with the city police in Chicago's Grant Park. No words were needed.

The final spot is a very different kind, the candidate-boast spot. It is usually simple and direct, literally an advertisement for the person who is running. Jimmy Carter broadcast a very effective example in 1976, when he talked about his personal story in Georgia and used his own upbringing as the most important characteristic of the campaign. "1976. Across our land," the narrator says, "a new beginning is under way, led by a man whose roots are founded in the American tradition."

Ronald Reagan's campaign featured "Morning in America" in 1984 which highlighted the revival of the economy, and emphasized that the nation would be strong (Figure 3.7). "Under the leadership of President

With the reasons for his claim established, Zelizer goes on to offer a variety of evidence to support these reasons, primarily focusing on iconic and memorable examples of how the use of television helped or hurt various campaigns. Throughout, he balances *logos* and *ethos*, providing logical evidence to support his claim from the words of credible sources that have experience in politics. In order to avoid angering a reader through a particular bias (a negative aspect of *pathos*), Zelizer further balances his argument with sources from Democratic and Republican presidential candidates. These examples offer precedence for the modern-day television campaign spots and how their use has steadily grown until they have become a necessity.

Figure 3.7
Ronald Reagan told a positive story about his presidency is his "Morning in America" commercial.
www.youtube.com/watch?v=_fy-uhxiXcE

Reagan, our country is prouder and stronger and better." In 1996, Bill Clinton's campaign spoke about his being a bridge to the future.

This year both campaigns will likely draw on all of these kinds of spots to sell their message. They will be the subject of debate and play an important role in shaping the perceptions that voters have of each candidate.

Obama and Romney will need to be careful that the spots they broadcast, or which independent groups broadcast for them, don't backfire on them rather than their opponents, and they will need to make sure to convey enough positive messages along with the negative. But the candidate that pulls off the best ad campaign will vastly improve his odds of winning the White House in November.

Rhetorical Continuities

While some texts are more difficult to read than others, most literate writing can easily be examined in this way to identify the claim, reasons, and evidence that make up an explicit argument, and you should make use of this kind of close examination when reading and composing any kind of text. However, as discussed later in this chapter, developing an argument in a visual medium requires different strategies.

Building

Link

Locate (a) a written opinion piece, (b) an opinion delivered through video, and (c) an opinion delivered through radio (via recorded podcast). Compare and contrast how each argument is constructed differently for each medium. Do all arguments clearly state the claim and make the argument explicit? Do some use different kinds of evidence? How is each similar? Compile your findings into a report, and share them with the class.

Search

Engine

Locate a paper from another class in which you composed an explicit argument with a claim, reasons, and evidence. Create a script or storyboard for how you would turn this paper into a video that presented the same explicit argument. Would you simply read the text to a video camera, or add visuals to replace textual descriptions? How would you adjust rhetorical appeals such as *logos* or *pathos*? Share your storyboard with the class, and discuss what changes you made and why. If you have time, consider making the actual video.

Implicit Arguments

Unlike explicit arguments, which directly state a claim, implicit arguments use more indirect means of persuasion to place an idea into the viewer's mind. For example, the photograph in Figure 3.8 depicts a naked infant breastfeeding.

Credit: Tabula Rosa, 2004. Adbusters

Figure 3.8
The organization Adbusters is trying to make an argument with this image.

This infant's skin is covered with tattoos of many well-known corporations and entertainment companies. This image doesn't make an explicit claim but attempts to plant some message into the viewer's mind, making an implied argument. You might deduce that the creator of the image wants the viewer to consider how such companies affect a person, even from birth, or how corporations dominate a person's life and own him or her as much as he or she owns their products. Whatever idea you come away with, the fact that you come away with an idea at all proves the image's implied argument was successful. Even without a claim, reasons, and evidence, such implied messages make the audience think and come to conclusions themselves, which can be an even more powerful form of persuasion, since the audience develops the answer on its own.

In May 2012, New York City Mayor Michael Bloomberg pushed for a city ordinance that banned food service establishments—such as restaurants or street venders—from selling sugary soft drinks larger than 16 ounces (Figure 3.9).

Credit: Chang W. Lee/*The New York Times*

Figure 3.9
To make a visual argument, New York City Mayor Michael Bloomberg presented the different sizes of soda cups juxtaposed by sugar cubes showing how much sugar is in each size soda.

His motivation was to decrease obesity—which he claimed was causing more than 5,000 deaths a year in the city—by limiting the amount of soda a person could order at any one time. When a skeptic of his proposal pointed out that a customer could simply buy two 16-ounce drinks, thus bypassing the supposed intent of the law to limit soda consumption, Bloomberg commented that the proposed ban was

> [. . .] purely education. It forces you to see the difference, in the case of the two different sized cups... The public does act when they get the information. And all we're doing here is saying, "If you want to order 32 ounces of soda, in a restaurant that we supervise, this restaurant must give you two 16-ounce glasses."

While Bloomberg's justification of the soda ban is explicit, his ultimate goal is to make an implicit argument when someone orders a drink (or two). Bloomberg's two different size cups create a visual argument, showing the customer the difference between one or two cups, an argument that he justifies with scientific studies (*logos*) about consumer behavior, but which isn't provided to customers at the time they order their drink(s):

> The proposed ban forces you to see the difference in the case of the two different size cups and you can decide. We're not taking away anybody's rights at all to do anything. All we're doing is forcing you to recognize that you're drinking an enormous amount of sugar.

Bloomberg doesn't want to convince his audience with a direct, explicit argument about soda but simply to make an implied, visual argument about how much sugar they might be drinking and to get his audience to further consider how that sugar might be affecting their bodies. Bloomberg simply aims to plant an idea. But this example shows that although implied arguments aren't direct, they can be forceful, and even forced upon a viewer.

When you compose your own visual arguments that use implicit means of persuasion, you might use various kinds of appeals such as *logos*, *pathos*, and *ethos*, and you might include some sort of evidence or reasons for what your visual is suggesting. In other words, you can use some of the tactics found in explicit arguments, but you're not tied to using all or any of them. Sometimes placing *logos* in a visual helps, but it's not necessary; you simply need to get your audience to consider your point of view. Of course, the better you do that, the more persuasive you will be in convincing the audience that your point of view is the best one.

Building

Link

Compose a list of video games you have either played or are familiar with. For each game on the list, determine if the game is trying to make an implicit argument about something. Note any implicit messages for each video game on your list. Does the game provide any reasons or evidence for its implicit argument? Make your own claim about how the video game makes an argument. Include reasons and evidence, and share your argument with the class.

Engine

Search

Through YouTube or another video search engine, try to find Michael Bloomberg's press conference in which he announces his plan to ban restaurants from selling sugary soft drinks in sizes larger than 16 ounces. In this press conference, determine if Bloomberg makes an explicit or implicit argument about this ban. If explicit, locate the various components of his argument, including claims, reasons, and evidence. If implicit, how does he try to convey this idea to his audience? Compare the argument he makes in the press conference to what he later tells reporters, such as in the statements above. Is he actually making multiple kinds of arguments between selling the idea of the ban to the public and the argument that New Yorkers need to reduce their sugar intake? Write a claim based on your finding and share it with the class.

Argument and the Rhetorical Situation

While the rhetorical appeals provide a way to understand the major choices and appeals when writing, there are a few other elements you should consider. Before you begin to write, you should evaluate the rhetorical situation in which you find yourself, such as your reason for writing and the purpose of the document. Also, although they were discussed in Chapter 1, techniques for analyzing the audience are also detailed below, since they are such an important part of understanding your reason, purpose, and rhetorical strategies. This section will point out some of the elements you'll need to figure out before fully committing to a final draft of a design, whether that design is visual and based in digital media, or simply a standard written assignment.

Exigency

Most writing starts with an exigency, a term that refers to the reason one writes. For example, a teacher assigns a writing task, so you have to write for class. Perhaps you have to remember what to get from the store and need to write a list to make sure you don't forget anything. Exigency also can refer to some imperfection in the world that compels you to write, such as a vote by your congressional representative you don't agree with, prompting you to write him a letter expressing your disapproval. Exigency simply refers to this reason or situation that requires you to write.

Figure 3.10
An unfortunate exigency has prompted someone to make this flyer.

For instance, if your dog runs away, this situation prompts you to write a flyer to inform others that you've lost your dog (Figure 3.10). Such an exigency could possibly have many different writing strategies to solve the problem that demands writing as a solution. You'll have to carefully consider the entire situation and determine what audiences you're trying to reach, what outcomes you desire, and the best medium in which to convey your message.

Figure 3.11
This AT&T ad shows how writing technologies can work together to solve problems quicker.

In this example, the situation requires that you communicate to the public to solve the problem of finding your dog. Since the dog is probably still nearby in the neighborhood (or nearby neighborhoods), you might devise a strategy that delivers your message locally. You could possibly solve the problem by making phone calls, but a flyer is probably more efficient. Of course, with digital writing, traditional flyers, phones, and other technologies work together as seen in Figure 3.11.

Here are some additional examples of exigencies for writing.

- You need to create original diagrams and graphs to supplement the text of a scientific research paper.

- Your college is offering travel support to attend an undergraduate research conference in your field, and you need to write a proposal in order to apply.

- You're a computer science major who has been asked to develop a series of how-to videos about designing simple smartphone apps.

- You've been selected to attend a study abroad program in China for your major, and you need to create a flyer to seek Chinese language tutoring to learn as much about the language and culture before you go.

- You need to develop a social media networking plan in order to maximize job opportunities and connections upon graduation.

- You plan to apply to graduate schools and need to write a statement of purpose and revise an old paper for your writing sample.

- You've decided to start your own business to make money during college and you need to design a logo.

Each of these examples has a very different reason for writing and will require different kinds of writing to solve each problem. The exigency may seem obvious and not really worthy of thorough investigation. However, fully understanding how the writing situation developed can help you plan a rhetorical course of action and determine the best path for your message.

For instance, suppose you're a philosophy major applying for travel support against all the other undergraduates at your school. You learn from your friend, a history major, that she has applied for the travel award three times, and has been rejected every year. You further learn that those approving the award are primarily from scientific backgrounds and don't always understand the kind of work the humanities contributes and how this kind of research measures up against work done in the fields of science, technology, engineering, and mathematics. Based on this knowledge, you know you have to research what kind of evidence might convince this audience about the kind of research done in your major and how it will help benefit you and the university if you were to attend. Alternatively, you might draft a letter that asks for more representation on the committee from humanities departments, or decide your time might be better spent looking for more favorable funding opportunities. Knowing the bigger picture behind the immediate reason—the larger ecology of exigency—can help you craft a more effective and efficient argument and get that argument heard.

Remember that exigency influences not just those documents written with traditional text but also those written within digital formats, including images, whether such digital texts include web content, a new brand mark, or a music video. The release of a new movie often requires its marketing and promotion. This problem is often solved in part with commercials, movie posters, a website, and a social media campaign.

Building

Link

Choose a website such as Facebook, YouTube, or Twitter. Research the background of the site, and find or conjecture on the exigency (or exigencies) that caused the founders to create the site. What problem did the site solve?

Engine

Search

In 2011, the Miami Marlins, a professional baseball team, changed the team's visual identity, including the brand mark and team colors. Using this example (or your own), research the situation and determine the exigency for this change. Why were new colors and a brand mark needed? Again, what problems did the design change solve?

Purposes and outcomes

After you consider the exigency, you should identify the purpose and outcome you want to achieve. A Facebook post letting people know you've lost your dog informs them of your situation, but informing may not have been your purpose. Instead, you probably want to inform *and* persuade the reader to take some action. Your purpose is to persuade the reader to act by letting you know if he or she has seen your dog.

Part of thinking about your purpose for writing, then, is to consider what outcomes you want to achieve. Do you simply want your audience to be aware of some sort of information? Do you want your readers to have a better understanding of something they might already be aware of? Do you want the audience to perform some action after reading your document? These are all different outcomes that require different strategies and involve different purposes from the outset.

When assessing your purpose, examine the outcome the document is meant to achieve and the practical ways the document fulfills that outcome. If you create a flyer to inform people about a local issue, what elements must it contain so a reader can make use of it? Is this document's purpose to contain all the information the reader needs to know or only pique his interest so he can learn more? If the latter, then the document's purpose isn't just to inform, but to propose that he seek out more information on the topic. For the flyer to be successful, you should include a website URL or a phone number so the reader can make use of the interest your flyer generated and act accordingly. Typically, a document will have at least one or more purposes:

- **inform:** convey information to a reader he or she might be unaware of
- **define:** convey the characteristics of something the audience needs to better understand
- **explain:** convey how to go about a particular action or engage in a process, how a past action has unfolded, or how a future action will unfold
- **propose:** convey a particular outcome that you want the audience to make, whether this is an action or simply a decision

A well-written flyer advertising a lost dog would exhibit all of these different purposes. For example, it would inform the audience that a dog has been lost and define different aspects about the dog, such as its breed, color, size, name, and other important features. The flyer would also explain how the reader should proceed should she find the dog, such as giving her a phone number to contact. Finally, the flyer should propose an action to the audience, such as contacting the owner. Notice that not all of these purposes need to be presented as "written" text—you might "define" the pet by offering a picture that shows what it looks like (Figure 3.12).

Consider also that your purpose for writing may not be your audience's purpose for reading and reacting to a document. While *you* care about the dog you've lost, your audience may not.

Figure 3.12
This flyer uses multiple photos, places important information in a different font color, describes where the dog was last seen, and includes contact information. The flyer also includes other important information, such as the dog's deafness and friendliness.

However, you might persuade them to act by offering a reward for their help, hoping that the audience will be moved to act based on financial compensation if not simply wanting to do a good deed. When creating an argument, be aware of the multiple purposes in a document, considering not only your own reasons for writing but also your audience's reasons for responding.

Building

Link

Recall memorable television commercials you've seen or find ones on Internet video sites such as YouTube. Watch the commercials and list the many purposes involved. For instance, what was the purpose of the company that sponsored the commercial? What outcome does the commercial try to achieve? What strategies does the commercial use (i.e., does it inform, define, explain, propose)? Finally, what purposes do you think the audience might have for acting upon the commercial?

Engine

Search

Locate a Facebook page for a commercial or nonprofit organization. What's the purpose of this page? To inform, define, explain, or propose? Can you think of other purposes that the organization might have for creating and communicating with a Facebook page? Draft a short report, and share your findings with the class.

Audience

As discussed above, you need to clarify your purpose when creating a document, and the outcomes you wish to happen. However, you also must consider your audience's needs to ensure they can fulfill their own purpose after reading your document.

Even if a neighbor wants to start looking for your lost pet, she may not be able to if you fail to include a photo or description of the dog; she wouldn't know which dog to look for. Also, if you simply include the breed of the dog, such as "border collie," the audience may not know the physical features of this breed and be equally lost and unable to help. If you don't include any contact information, then even if the reader found the dog, he wouldn't be able to let you know the good news, and he may be forced to take the dog to the local animal shelter instead. To avoid these undesirable outcomes, you need to anticipate these needs and clarify your intended audience when planning any text. To meet audience needs, examine how they might interact with a document according to the guidelines below.

Analyzing multiple audiences

When you write, you must typically account for multiple audiences who may view your documents. Each of these audiences may have a different reason for reading and be accustomed to reading on different kinds of devices, and you need to consider how to address their reasons and needs.

Several strategies allow you to adapt your writing for these audiences. First, you might tailor your document toward a very narrow, specific audience. For example, if you were writing a software book about Hypertext Markup Language (HTML), you might focus on an audience of computer science students who would have extensive background with computers and coding, and you could leave out a lot of information that a novice would need to understand.

On the other end of the spectrum, you might write the same book very broadly, such as the *For Dummies* series, which provides enough information for a person with any experience level to learn. The computer science majors would probably roll their eyes at a lot of the language and information in this book, but they could still use it (just not as efficiently). Focusing on your audience is an important step when planning to write.

Also, you must consider the secondary and tertiary audiences that read your writing and account for their needs as well. For example, you are the primary audience for your course's syllabus. You use the syllabus to understand the course policies, learn which books to purchase, and see what assignments are required and when they're due. Your purpose when reading the document is to learn about the class.

However, your instructor probably also has secondary and tertiary audiences that she or he must consider. Many of the course policies are most likely dictated by university policy. Your instructor needs to make sure these policies are present and will satisfy a reader from the university's compliance department. Sometimes specific course requirements are dictated by the state legislature, so the instructor must consider this possible audience.

You also should consider the access that multiple audiences have to your writing. If you were to place a document on the World Wide Web, are you intending

Figure 3.13
Many television viewers have a negative attitude toward most television commercials.

for anyone to be able to read and understand it, or only a certain group or demographic? Of course, you should realize that even if you only aim your writing toward a smaller group, most anyone can gain access to it, so you should make sure the contents are not sensitive.

Analyzing audience expectations

Different audiences will expect different things from a document. As the syllabus example above demonstrates, students will expect certain information to be in a syllabus, while university officials will look for other information to be present.

As another example, consider a television program. The typical viewer only cares about the actual content of the show, and not usually the commercials. In fact, she or he may change the channel during the commercials and watch a different show (Figure 3.13). However, the sponsors that pay for commercials will want to make sure their ads actually air during the breaks and may hire someone to watch all the commercials and make sure their ads appear. In other situations, both viewers and sponsors might expect and seek out good commercials during certain events, such as the Super Bowl.

Audiences also have different attitudes about what they view and read: positive, negative, and neutral. If you're watching a machinima on YouTube, such as *Red vs. Blue*, you're probably familiar with the video game *Halo*, engaged in the material, and have a positive attitude when initially viewing fan-based clips. In this case, the creator of the video does not anticipate any hostility toward his or her message (Figure 3.14).

Credit: Rooster Teeth Productions

Figure 3.14
Most of the audience members of *Red vs. Blue* machinima probably have a positive attitude toward the clips.

If you see a political advertisement from a political party you disagree with, however, you would probably approach this ad with a negative attitude. If you were the advertisement's intended audience, the creators of the ad would need to find rhetorical ways to overcome that negative attitude to convince you of their point of view.

Finally, if you have no particular attitude toward the author or content, perhaps it is a documentary about penguins, then the filmmaker would simply need to show you her point of view by presenting the benefits of her particular message. She doesn't have to overcome a negative attitude, just show you why the documentary is important and why you should pay attention.

In each of these examples, your audience's expectations and attitudes will determine how you craft your message, design your document, and what rhetorical techniques you'll need to use.

Analyzing audience use

Imagine opening up a road atlas and trying to find an alternative route around a serious accident on the highway. Typically, you would expect to find a map of the country or state that includes road names, distances, points of interest, and other features that would help you navigate via automobile.

What if, instead, you found maps that included the political information for each state, county, and city—which areas voted Democrat or Republican, or how different areas responded to political issues? Most likely, this particular map would be useless to you, and you would be stuck in traffic for several hours. In addition to the expectations audiences have, they also have different uses for documents. This political map might make sense when discussing politics, but not while traveling. Likewise, the road atlas wouldn't do much good to navigate a state park, which requires more detail and includes roads and trails not normally accessible by cars (Figure 3.15).

The environment in which audiences use a map may be much different as well. An atlas usually has very large pages that can contain enough detail while making reading easy for the driver (or passenger) in a moving vehicle (Figure 3.16). A hiker in the woods doesn't usually need this large a map—in fact, a smaller, more compact map might be ideal. The hiker might also appreciate a map printed on waterproof paper in case it rains or he accidently drops it in a lake or stream. How you plan and design a map for use in a car would be very different from a map you would design for use in the woods of a state park.

Figure 3.15
A road atlas doesn't do much good once the road ends.

Figure 3.16
Using an atlas in a cramped car is much different than using it in other environments.

Figure 2.4, the screenshot of Clemson University's home page you looked at in Chapter 2, demonstrates sensitivity to multiple audiences, audience expectations, and audience use. If you look at the menu (you can also actively use the site at www.clemson.edu), you can see that it's divided by the multiple audiences Clemson expects to use the site: students, faculty/staff, alumni, and partners.

Each of these audiences has different needs and expectations of the site, and will use it differently. Prospective students need to learn about application procedures, tuition rates, information about the university, and academic programs. Current students will need to find the academic calendar, schedule of classes, community information, and Blackboard access. Faculty will expect links to their class rolls, human resources information, and other administrative content that affects them. As you go online and explore the other links, you'll see that each section of the menu specifically tailors its information for a particular audience, anticipating what they'll need and how they will use the site.

Beware of unintended audiences

Remember that these guidelines primarily help you target your *intended* audiences. As briefly discussed in Chapter 1 and as you'll read more fully throughout the rest of the book, digital technologies make the delivery to *only* your intended audience nearly impossible. When nearly any kind of document can be forwarded through email, or posted on someone else's website, Facebook page, or Twitter profile, you never really know who your final audience will be (Figure 3.17). While you might think such worries don't affect you (for you're probably not a celebrity, government official, or top secret agent), even the wrong phrasing in an email can turn into a piece of evidence in a court of law.

Credit: Lance Armstrong

Figure 3.17
Lance Armstrong probably regrets tweeting this photo of him lying next to his Tour de France jerseys. Only a few months later he would admit to doping (bad *kairos*?), and Oprah Winfrey showed the image during her television interview with Armstrong.

For example, many of the internal memos sent between the football staff and administration of Penn State University eventually became public during the hearings for Jerry Sandusky, who was accused and found guilty of sexually abusing children. Once the documents were made public through legal proceedings, they then appeared online, on TV, and in many other outlets. While you might think it was right that such documents came to light, you might feel differently about your own documents you'd like to keep from ESPN, CNN, and other media organizations. Keep in mind, then, that any document can reappear in other contexts and have possible negative effects. Be careful, very careful, with the kinds of documents you distribute online.

Building

Link

Search engine robots provide other (nonhuman) audiences that find documents on the web for search engines. Search Engine Optimization (SEO) is a practice that attempts to maximize the possibility that a search robot will find a particular site and index it so it appears as high as possible in a search result. Research search robots, SEO, and some of the practices used by marketers to write for these invisible audiences. Prepare a research report with your findings, and present it to your instructor.

Engine

Search

Prepare six definitions of the term "web robot" for the following audiences, keeping in mind how the definition might change depending on the prior knowledge, expertise, and needs of the audience.

- computer scientist
- website developer
- online marketer
- attorney
- high school student
- fifth grade student

How does your definition change for each of these audiences? What details might some need to know that others don't? Share and discuss your definitions with the class.

Logical fallacies

Logical fallacies are rhetorical faults that can occur in any kind of writing and often affect *logos*, the logical argument you're trying to make. These fallacies can affect the soundness of your evidence, and—if noticed—affect how your audience responds to your argument and you as an author. Fallacies in *logos* can also affect your *ethos*. For these reasons, rhetorical textbooks often advise against making these fallacies. However, logical fallacies can still significantly affect emotion, appealing to *pathos*.

Credit: Zach Weiner

Figure 3.18
"Your face" is never a good reason to support an argument.

Ad hominem

This fallacy attempts to discredit the speaker's argument by attacking the speaker's character (Figure 3.18). For example: "The president's policies won't work because he's a socialist." Rather than debating the merits of the president's actual policies, the author attempts to attack the president's person, switching the debate from the substance of the policies to the president's perceived character (something that would also have to be proven rather than just claimed).

Begging the question

In this fallacy, rather than proving a particular question and reaching a conclusion, an author assumes the conclusion and incorporates it into a claim. For example: "Irresponsible teenagers should not be allowed to drink alcohol before the age of 21." Rather than making an argument that teenagers are irresponsible, which would prove the claim they should not be allowed to drink earlier than age 21, the author inserts that conclusion within the claim by using the word "irresponsible," assuming the conclusion and bypassing the question that really needs to be answered.

Circular argument

A circular argument restates the claim as evidence of its proof, rather than developing logical reasons to support the claim (Figure 3.19). For example: "LeBron James is a good basketball player because he plays basketball well."

In this case, the evidence just rephrases the initial claim and doesn't actually add any evidence to support it. Instead, the author might focus on James's statistics, work ethic, knowledge of the game, or other qualities that good basketball players typically have.

Either/or

This fallacy reduces an argument to only two possible options when many are probably available (Figure 3.20). For example: "We can either stop all fishing or all the fish will become extinct." While some fish stocks are becoming significantly depleted, others are not, so a combination of different regulations could allow for some fishing to occur without destroying the populations of all fish. Also, there are different kinds of fishing that affect populations differently. For example, many game fish are caught but immediately released back into the sea, which affects their populations much differently than food fish such as tuna. The choice is much more nuanced than just an either/or.

Figure 3.19
Circular reasoning doesn't really work—logically at least.

Figure 3.20
Benjamin Franklin's famous cartoon actually presents an either/or fallacy.

Genetic fallacy

When one assumes that a person's origins determine his or her character, one commits a genetic fallacy. For example: "Even though the presidential candidate was born in the United States, his parents were not, so he must not be American enough to run the country." Where the candidate's parents were born does not logically equate to how "American" the candidate is. This type of fallacy also pertains to the origins of objects and ideas. For example: "The new policy in favor of universal health care is stupid because a democrat came up with it." In this case, the speaker is creating his opinion of the idea based upon his opinion of the political party that advocates it, when the two are not innately connected. This fallacy also can pertain to the "genetics" of the speaker as well, and how he or she incorrectly interprets data based on its origin. For example: "My parents told me that dinosaurs never really existed, so I don't care what paleontologists say."

Hasty generalization

This fallacy occurs when one reaches a conclusion without considering all the evidence, sometimes due to preexisting bias. For example: "All terrorists plotting against the United States are Muslim extremists." Such a statement could come from a knee-jerk reaction based on the sole case of the World Trade Center attacks. However, many terrorists in the United States are not Muslim, such as Timothy McVeigh, who bombed the Alfred P. Murrah Federal Building in Oklahoma City, or Eric Rudolph, who committed a series of bombings, most notably the Olympic Park during the 1996 Olympics in Atlanta, Georgia.

Moral equivalence

This fallacy attempts to equate acts or atrocities that are not equal in their severity. For example: "I get paid so little, I feel like a modern-day slave." Unlike the employee, who actually receives a paycheck and has the choice to leave the job, slaves had neither pay nor choice, and so this is not an equivalent comparison. Moral equivalencies may also invoke prior acts to excuse new ones. For example: "Our administration has recently used torture to get information, but so have our enemies." Here, the fallacy is claiming that because their enemies commit torturous acts, it's OK for the administration to do so as well. Just because torture has been used in the past or by others does not mean it's all right to use it in the future.

Post hoc, ergo propter hoc

This Latin phrase translates to "after this, therefore because of this," which identifies a fallacy in cause and effect relationships between two actions or events. This fallacy makes the assumption that if Y happened after X, then X must have caused Y. For example: "After downloading and installing a program from the Internet, your computer crashes. You assume that the program must be faulty and caused the crash." Without more evidence, you can't assume that just because the computer crashed after you installed the new program the program caused the crash. The computer may have had other problems and the timing is just coincidence.

Red herring

A "red herring" occurs when a speaker attempts to divert the conversation by introducing a tangent line of thought to avoid discussing the main issues at stake. For example: "Oil consumption may be leading to climate change, but how will we run our cars and maintain our economy if we don't use oil?" In this example, the speaker is attempting to shift the debate from climate change itself to the economic issues of oil consumption. While these issues are interconnected, it is still important to discuss the workings and dynamics of the atmospheric conditions and not just cast them aside.

Slippery slope

In this fallacy, an argument is made that if a particular action or event occurs, then an unwanted consequence will inevitably follow. For example: "If we let homosexuals marry, then what's to stop someone from polygamous marriage or marrying his or her horse?" Letting humans marry is not the same thing as letting humans and animals marry, and one does not logically lead to the other.

Straw man

Just as a man built with straw is easy to destroy, a straw man fallacy indicates when a speaker attempts to reduce an opponent's argument so that it seems weak or flimsy, thereby making it easier to defeat rhetorically (Figure 3.21). For example: "Anyone who favors gun control hates freedom." One can advocate for gun control and still support freedom. However, by reducing the argument to such a simplistic motive, and by eliminating the nuanced debate that accompanies the arguments for gun control, the speaker diminishes the argument to a minimalistic phrase that's easy to side with.

Figure 3.21
Sometimes saying a statement is "just rhetoric" makes a straw man out of both the speaker and rhetoric. This statement reducing someone's argument to "just rhetoric" is itself rhetorical.

Building

Link

With a partner, visit YouTube and try to find television commercials that demonstrate each of the fallacies listed above. Examine these commercials and argue whether you think each fallacy was committed intentionally or accidentally. Support your claim with reasons and evidence. Present your findings to the class.

Engine

Search

Through an image search, find cartoons, diagrams, or other visuals that represent each of the fallacies listed above. Create either a blog or digital scrapbook of these examples, and share them with the class.

KEY Terms

ad hominem
audience
begging the question
circular argument
claim
either/or
ethos
evidence
exigency
explicit argument
genetic fallacy
hasty generalization
implicit argument

kairos
logical fallacy
logos
moral equivalence
outcome
pathos
post hoc, ergo propter hoc
purpose
reasons
red herring
slippery slope
straw man

YouTube Response

Chances are you've probably visited the website YouTube and viewed videos (especially after reading this chapter). In fact, you may have even posted your own. One of YouTube's strengths is the relative ease by which anyone can post a video. With this ease also comes the ease of responding to other users' videos with your own, typically called, simply, a "video response."

For this activity, you will create your own video responding to another. Take your time choosing a video; it should be one that interests you but that also calls you to make an argumentative response. For instance, if you're interested in fishing, you may respond to a user's video that shows the person mishandling a fish before releasing it, arguing that (1) the person should handle the fish better to help it survive, and (2) poor handling through video promotes and suggests to other anglers that such poor technique is OK.

You might also respond to more commercial videos posted online. In 2012, the country music artist Brad Paisley released a song called "Accidental Racist" (Figure 3.22). The lyrics to this song caused a bit of controversy at the time of its release, prompting an opportunity to respond to the video through one's own video (Figure 3.23). If you were affected by this song, you might compose a video attacking or defending it, depending on your point of view.

Figure 3.22
This song by Brad Paisley sparked a bit of controversy.

www.youtube.com/watch?v=QPl-Ss-iJLo

Figure 3.23
Corey Guyton offers his response to "Accidental Racist."

www.youtube.com/watch?v=aRJ6XANlHV0

Although your instructor will provide you with more specific guidelines for your YouTube response, the overall project should:

- last two to three minutes in length;
- provide a thesis or claim with reasons and evidence;
- include a short research report about the topic;
- include tags, descriptions, hyperlinks, and other features to help audiences find and use the video;
- include an outline or script; and
- include a one-page memo detailing the argument you hoped to make, and noting your intended audience.

Rather than just cobbling a video together, take serious care during the prewriting phase of this project to make sure it comes together in a clear, coherent, and professional manner. While the quality of the video and audio will depend on the available resources you have in your class or on campus, the quality of the video's content depends on the amount of time and effort you put into its research and preparation. As a general process, consider the following steps toward completing your video response.

Choose a topic: A video response, like a written response, first requires that you choose your topic—that you determine what you'd like to produce your video about. As with other kinds of writing, find a topic (i.e., YouTube video) that interests you, one that calls you to write.

Research your topic: As with any writing assignment, much of the work comes before you start writing. If you're focusing on a video about a local environmental issue, research not only the perspectives of the video but also the context and history of the environmental problem discussed in the video. If the issue concerns drilling for oil offshore, you should research the history of oil drilling, its problems and benefits, so you have a better understanding of the issue as a whole.

Plan and draft: Before turning on the webcam or picking up the camera, plan your initial components and the structure of your argument. This plan can include writing an essay first—making sure you have a claim, reasons, and evidence—or it can offer a more basic outline of the argument and the major scenes and visuals you hope to include. Once you clarify the main points for yourself, you can start to think more visually.

Create a storyboard: Your video may simply be you responding via a webcam. However, you might also include other graphics if you have access to a video editor such as iMovie. If you plan on making a more elaborate response, once you've completed a script, create a storyboard that depicts each shot. The storyboard will be invaluable as both a conceptual tool—helping you to see your video before you actually assemble and edit it—as well as an organizational tool, providing a framework for visually arranging your script and making sure you account for all the shots you might need.

Create a shot list and gather footage: Once you have a script of your response, you can create a shot list. This list will provide an important resource to ensure you gather all of the video footage or images you might want to include. When producing the video, try to gather this footage as early as possible, as editing will be more time consuming than you may realize and is often the longest part of the process.

Add narration: Although your project may not require it, you may want to add voice-over narration to your video to comment on the footage or images or to maintain the argumentative arc. If you've adequately planned for your video response, you have already written this narration in your script. Like your shooting list, create a list of sounds you plan to use, including narration, and create these audio files before starting the revision process.

Create a rough cut: After you have gathered your footage and recorded any narration you'll need, use your storyboards as a guide to assemble your clips into a single rough cut of your video essay. Try to complete as much of the video as possible so you will have a better idea of how you might revise the piece.

Revise, edit, proof: Once you have a rough cut, you can begin revising. As discussed in this chapter, start with the large-scale changes first. Notice where the gaps in argument occur, which shots and scenes look bad, and which look bad when sequenced together. If you're simply recording yourself via a webcam, review the footage and note any problems. You may want to go back and rerecord your argument to eliminate any errors. Once you've accomplished the revision, you can begin to edit transitions and other elements before performing a final proof. Ask your peers to review your work as well, since they can offer input on problems you might not notice.

Save and distribute: As you work, save your video file often. Once you've finished, consider what file format you'll need to distribute it in. If you record straight to YouTube, or if your video editor has a preset button to upload to YouTube, distribution is easy. If you're uploading to YouTube from a stand-alone file, you might consider MPEG, AVI, MOV, or other formats that use less memory. However, YouTube can accept a wide array of video file formats, including HD formats. Whatever distribution method you plan, research what file formats are acceptable and research the specifics of those file formats. While your video might look good in the video editor, it can look lousy if you save it in the wrong format.

From DIGITAL Writers

Taylor Swift video, "22"

www.youtube.com/
watch?v=AgFeZr5ptV8

Conan O'Brien's response to "22"

www.youtube.com/
watch?v=cjpLE6ueL7s

Conan O'Brien is a writer and comedian whose show, *Conan,* appears on TBS. He also earned a double major in English and history from Harvard University.

As an example of a video response on YouTube, consider this response from O'Brien to Taylor Swift's music video "22." Note the claim that O'Brien starts out with and how he incorporates examples and evidence to support the claim.

STUDENT Example

"Today's child is bewildered
when he enters
the 19th century environment
that still characterizes
the educational establishment
where information is scarce
but ordered and structured
by fragmented, classified patterns
subjects, and schedules."
- Marshall McLuhan 1967

Michael Wesch's video "A
Vision of Students Today"

www.youtube.com/
watch?v=dGCJ46vyR9o

Video Response by
Thompson Roberts

www.youtube.com/
watch?v=ZoPlBYkBnD0

Now, watch this video and
response student example.
Thompson Roberts responds to
Michael Wesch's video, "A Vision
of Students Today." Again, noting
the claim in the response, notice
how Roberts supports his initial
conclusions.

CHAPTER 4

Digital Analysis

For 15 years, scientists who analyzed HIV structures have been baffled by a particular problem. They needed to understand an enzyme, the Mason-Pfizer monkey virus (M-PMV) retroviral protease, in order to work toward a cure for the disease. Given this roadblock, researchers experimented by giving the problem to a group of computer gamers within a crowdsourcing computer game called Foldit, which allows users to map, create, and interact with 3-D structures. By analyzing the three-dimensional structure the way they would analyze a 3-D gaming environment, these gamers were able to model the enzyme and solve the problem in less than three weeks. Very few of these gamers had any background in biochemistry. However, they all had skill at analyzing digital texts and digital environments.

As mentioned in the preface, this text's primary goal is to have you making your own digital texts for your own rhetorical purposes. However, an understanding of how to "read" or view other people's digital writing from rhetorical perspectives can help make you a better author of your own digital productions. As you've seen already, a digital writer does not only use alphabetic writing but also incorporates images, video, sound, and other media when composing text. Not every text will have all of these media, but the digital writer must know how and when to use multimedia when appropriate, and he or she must be able to recognize how other texts were created. In other words, while reading is not the same activity as writing, they influence each other and are interconnected, and being a better reader can make you a better writer, even if you're writing with words, images, sounds, and video.

This chapter will look at a variety of different kinds of visual texts and provide tools for how to analyze them, pointing out the argumentative features in each example. While the chapter is not an exhaustive rehearsal of all the possible readings a text may have, it will help you think rhetorically about different kinds of digital arguments.

The following strategies for reading digital texts closely follow some of the elements you'll use to construct digital texts, especially those discussed in Chapter 2 on rhetoric, Chapter 5 on audience, and Chapter 6 on genres. Because Chapters 5 and 6 provide an extensive overview of analyzing audiences and genres, this chapter will primarily focus on the rhetorical aspects examined in the previous chapter, although it will touch on some basic design questions you should ask about any digital text.

When reading a text, you can use the rhetorical triangle as a starting place to ask questions about the text, analyzing those questions (and answers) about the writer, audience, and message. You can also consider other elements shown on the rhetorical tetrahedron, such as design, medium, and genre, as well as *kairos*. In other words, use these tools as a rubric or guide when both reading and writing.

Critical Thinking and Analyzing Rhetorical Features

You have probably heard the term "critical thinking." If you're like me, you might have even thought that all thinking is critical, so what's special about critical thinking? Likewise, you might equate analysis with the act of looking. However, these terms focus both of these faculties toward specific goals. In short, to think critically about a text is to question every aspect of it in order to understand how it was constructed, who constructed it, and why.

- Why did the writer include a certain example as evidence?
- Why did the writer use this typeface?
- Why did the writer include this image?
- What audience is the writer trying to reach?
- What makes the writer believable?

This list of questions can go on, but the important point is that you, as a critical thinker, dig into a text and interrogate it. To think critically, then, is to actively engage with a text rather than taking it for granted, primarily by taking it apart and looking at its individual components. This "taking apart" is the process of analysis. Once you have analyzed all the pieces, you can then put them back together again, see the whole, and make a judgment about how the text works and whether it works well. The rest of the chapter will help you determine the most important parts of a text to analyze, guiding your critical thinking about a text.

Building

Link

With a partner, choose a text. In addition to the questions listed above, write down as many questions you can think to ask about the text. Share this list of questions with the class, noting which ones you asked that no one else considered.

Engine

Search

Research what other kinds of "thinking" exist besides critical thinking. How is critical thinking different from these other modes of thought? How are they similar? How can they be combined to get a better picture of the world around you?

Writer and purpose

When analyzing a text, knowledge about the writer of a work can help you determine the exigency and purpose of a text. For these reasons, the writer should be one of the first elements of the rhetorical triangle you examine when analyzing a text. Behind every kind of writing is at least one writer who created it, and while a text can be read and understood without knowing the writer's identity, the originator of a text can help explain much about it. For example, much of ancient Egyptian art depicts stories of Egypt's pharaohs. While these rulers didn't write Egyptian art and hieroglyphics by their own hand, they did sanction their creation and probably had very important reasons for doing so (Figure 4.1).

Figure 4.1
Egyptian pharaohs often required scribes to write for them. In this wall painting, a scribe is recording deliveries for the pharaoh.

In the context of the Egyptian empire, a pharaoh needed to keep his or her kingdom united by ensuring that subjects remained loyal and enemies didn't attack. These concerns provide the exigency for the large amount of artwork on Egyptian buildings for the purpose of propaganda, a kind of political art designed to influence an audience to think a particular way (usually in support of the rulers). The Egyptian pharaohs needed their subjects to respect and fear them (lest some ambitious individual try to overthrow him or her and take over) and make any enemies think twice before attacking. Any art depicting the pharaohs should be full of praise and exaggerate their feats.

Figure 4.2 depicts a wall carving inside one of the Abu Simbel temples that shows the pharaoh Ramesses II fighting in the Battle of Kadesh. From this relief, the audience understands that Ramesses gained a great victory, forcing his enemy—the Hittites—to agree to a truce. However, documents found in the Hittite capital Boğazköy claim that the Hittites were the true victor. The writer of the document can determine a great deal about the exigency, purpose, and ultimate message of a particular text.

Figure 4.2
Wall carving of Ramesses II, located inside one of the Abu Simbel temples.

Such propaganda by the ancient Egyptians can teach a lot about text authorship in the modern age. While Ramesses might have commissioned the images on his temples, he did not do the actual carving. Those who did carve the stone surfaces worked collaboratively, sometimes over many years or generations. Of course, these craftsmen receive little credit for their writings.

Rhetorical Continuities

Like the walls on Ramesses's monuments, many digital texts you see around you are not attributed to the "writer" who actually creates it. Typically, a graphic, poster, billboard, film, and even book are not written by a single person but by a team of specialists. Twitter messages and Facebook pages of companies and celebrities are often managed by PR firms. Graphic designers might determine how an image should look, but experts in computer drafting might actually create the final version in Photoshop. Often, a single individual doesn't decide on the final version of a design, but instead a committee decides, voting to make a final decision.

Finally, like Ramesses, a company may provide the motivation and basic narrative that needs to be told and leave it to others (either in-house or contracted technical writers or graphic designers) to create the finished piece. Typically, you may never know the writers of these messages, such as company websites, blogs, brand marks, or advertisements, unless you were to conduct background research and find out. When you're trying to read a visual text and want to consider how the writer affects your analysis, you might have to dig a little deeper to find out the writer's identity (or, of course, identities).

When you attempt to identify the author of a text, you often have to make a decision about what level of authorship is important. This level of detail about the writer will help you better identify the writer's intentions for creating a text, but to research this information you'll have to isolate the level of authorship you feel is most important to your reading. For instance, is it more important to consider the sponsor of the work, or the individual(s) who physically created it? Your own motivations for looking at a work will help you answer these questions.

Building

Link

Through an online search, locate the credits from a video game you enjoy playing or are familiar with. For example, search for *"Halo 2* end credits" (Figure 4.3). Analyze how the video game represents its authors. What terms does it use? Are any of these terms similar to those used in other genres, such as books, movies, or music? Which ones are different? How would you ascribe authorship to this video game as a whole? Present your findings and thoughts to the class for further discussion.

Figure 4.3
How does *Halo 2* credit its writers?

www.youtube.com/
watch?v=7hrzCWPl0Ag

Engine

Search

Analyze a logo from a company whose products you frequently use or like (perhaps such as Apple, Nike, Coca-Cola, etc.). Research the origins of their brand mark, and map the various kinds of writers who worked to produce these marks. If possible, try to identify the individuals who created the brand marks, and if different, the artists who took that design and produced the first renderings.

Audience

Besides the writer, you should analyze the writer's message for the writer's intended audience. You usually never write for a totally general audience, but instead imagine a specific, intended audience. In order to determine what this intended audience is for the writer of a particular work, you'll have to do just as much (if not more) research into the writer and his or her message. The following prompts provide some specific issues to address as you begin your research.

Beliefs and values

What were the beliefs and values of the writer's audience? Did they most likely believe in a particular religion, form of government, or worldview? Did they value community or individualism? Freedom or slavery? Competition or cooperation? By analyzing these beliefs and values, you will be able to learn what audience had to be persuaded, and you can analyze the message for signs that the writer understood how to appeal to the audience's beliefs and values.

Expectations

What did the writer's audience most likely want? In other words, what problem did the writer try to address, and based on your research, did the writer's argument help solve that problem in a way the audience accepted? If the argument did not meet the audience's expectations, why do you think this is? You can also research what kind of medium, design, or genre the audience might have expected from the writer. An audience reading a writer's message on a blog article for the magazine *U.S. News & World Report* would expect a much different message than if reading a blog for *People* magazine (Figure 4.4). The first magazine covers politics and world affairs, while the second mainly explores celebrity life. Such expectations can tell you much about the writer's audience.

Figure 4.4
The magazine for which an author writes will determine the audience he or she reaches.

Experiences

What was daily life like for the writer's audience? Did they live during a productive, booming period of civilization, or was their life poor and full of hardships? Or, did their experience change from one condition to another? Was there a major war going on at the time, or some other significant event? Does the writer seem to be targeting a specific segment of his or her community, such as a specific class or industry? For instance, the Federal Emergency Management Agency's advertisement in Figure 4.5 displays a flooded street and a hardware store. This ad clearly targets small business owners, which is also evident in the ad's text. However, because of the flooded street, this ad also targets those business owners near rivers and oceans, or those subject to hurricanes, and not necessarily those subject to other disasters such as earthquakes. If you research the ad's creation, you'll learn that the advertisement was created a few months before hurricane season started in the United States. Understanding the daily routine of the writer's audience, or how that routine became interrupted, can help you make more sense of the writer's message.

Credit: FEMA

Figure 4.5
The Federal Emergency Management Agency would like to help keep small business owners from going underwater.

www.fema.gov/medialibrary/media_records/12398

Medium

In what medium did the audience receive the writer's message? The writer's choice of print, television, or radio most likely affected the audience's reception of the message. Different audiences use media differently and read different kinds of media, and someone who reads a newspaper might expect a different writing style than someone who reads a blog, even if the topic and content are generally the same in each. By researching this information, you can gather clues about the audience the writer most likely intended to reach. Try to determine if the medium of the message played a significant role in how the audience responded to the message.

Building

Link

Analyze a variety of online advertisements from a single company, preferably marketing the same product (such as a soft drink company). How do you think the ads are designed to appeal to different audiences? Are the words different? Do the ads use different celebrities or models? Does the use of color change? Are the ads animated or in video form? On what website does each ad appear? Try to anticipate the different audiences each ad is meant to reach. Write your findings in a brief report, and share them with the class.

Engine

Analyze various commercials for products you buy. Does the commercial contain any clues to its intended audience, such as language, setting, actors, or other elements? Whom do you think this commercial is targeting? What makes you believe so? Do you feel that you, as a buyer of this product, are represented as one of those intended audience members, or do you think the commercial doesn't reach you even though you buy the product? If this is the case, how might the company alter the commercial with you in mind as the intended audience member? Record your thoughts, and share them with the class.

Message

When looking at "message" on the rhetorical triangle, some of the questions you might ask about the message are the context and subject that inform how an audience understands the message. Researching the context of an image can provide important information about a text, including what the message is actually about. As you saw with the example of Ramesses's propaganda, a text always exists within a historical moment and is created to meet certain needs of a particular time and place (even if this time is a potential, future time, such as letting your descendants know how great you were). Without knowing anything about that image's context, it's difficult to determine the subject of the work (the Battle of Kadesh), as well as other questions, such as why the image was constructed, how, when, or by whom.

Analyzing the context can provide important clues for reading an image. You cannot know what an image is really "about" unless you know this larger historical context in which it appeared (or appears currently), and so the subject and context are always intertwined. Since images often offer less evidence about their context than alphabetic writing, you'll have to look for other clues to provide details.

You've already examined how knowledge of the writer and audience can provide information for reading an image. In addition to these elements, you also can research the larger historical context, which includes not only who created the image and whom it was created for, but also when the text was created, in what part of the world, the perceptions or attitudes of the audience at the time, as well as how that audience originally received the image.

Credit: Agent001

Credit: Christian Görmer

Figure 4.6
The Physical Impossibility of Death in the Mind of Someone Living by Damien Hirst

Figure 4.7
Damien Hirst

Figure 4.6 shows an artwork titled *The Physical Impossibility of Death in the Mind of Someone Living* by Damien Hirst (Figure 4.7). The facts you can easily learn from a simple web search include data such as its materials (tiger shark, glass, steel, 5 percent formaldehyde solution), dimensions (2170 x 5420 x 1800 mm), the date of its creation (1991), and the person who funded the artwork (Charles Saatchi).

From just this information, more questions arise, such as Hirst's background and how he got the tiger shark. Hirst was a British artist and became associated with the art movement Britart, or Young British Artists, a group who were known for creating art that had shock value, was composed of throwaway materials, and had an attitude that Kate Bush writes was "both oppositional and entrepreneurial." Knowing this, you can clearly see the shock value of the tiger shark, as well as the simple materials of glass and steel, which are not especially valuable in their own right.

In addition, besides the motivation and purpose behind getting a shark that is large enough to scare and eat people, the idea that a dead shark carcass can be considered "throwaway" is controversial.

How did audiences respond to the artwork? As with many works of art, Hirst's piece elicited mixed responses. Upon the artwork's visit to the New York Metropolitan Museum of Art in 2007, Roberta Smith writes:

> *Will the shark attract a new audience to the Met? Maybe. Is it worth the trip? Definitely. Mr. Hirst's detractors accuse him of being a Conceptual artist, with the implication (misguided even*

for most genuine Conceptual art) that you don't need to see the work in person. Mr. Hirst often aims to fry the mind (and misses more than he hits), but he does so by setting up direct, often visceral experiences, of which the shark remains the most out-standing.

In keeping with the piece's title, the shark is simultaneously life and death incarnate in a way you don't quite grasp until you see it, suspended and silent, in its tank. It gives the innately demonic urge to live a demonic, deathlike form.

Smith finds that despite the artwork being "conceptual" rather than aesthetic, it is definitely worth seeing, and the artwork will leave the viewer with a "visceral experience." Others, however, did not see the same value in the artwork and criticized it as contributing to the decline of British art, or simply refused to recognize a dead shark encased in a tank of formaldehyde as art at all.

However, despite concerns about the artwork's status as art, others question the attainment of the shark itself. Some critics (many from outside the art circle) chastised Hirst for killing a shark specifically for this project rather than using a shark that was already dead. Organizations such as People for the Ethical Treatment of Animals have condemned Hirst's work that involves killing animals, and artist Bill Gusky writes:

The shark in Damien Hirst's Conceptual piece The Physical Impossibility of Death in the Mind of Someone Living—*a spectacular fourteen-footer— was caught and killed in Australia specifically for this work.*

It doesn't get much more sickening than this.

Almost as if to match Mr. Hirst's and Charles Saatchi's moral character, the original shark has slipped into an advanced and irretrievable state of decay, rotting so terribly that its tiny sheltered world became dark and murky with the sickness of it. Those standing outside and looking in could only marvel at the stench from which they were protected by a thin wall of unimaginable wealth.

So now they've killed another shark. This majestic and most unlucky victim is fully thirteen feet long.

Given the title of the work, Hirst's subject was much larger and more complex than just a dead shark: the psychological interaction that occurs when one sees a dead animal. While this interaction might have occurred subconsciously, for many viewers, the subject was simply the shark itself and the concept of "shock." When researching a particular image, then, the larger context in which it originally appeared can tell you a great deal about the work itself. Given that much of the shock around Hirst's artwork developed because he killed a shark to make it, you can deduce that his audience values living animals more than killing them to create a new artwork. Of course, the context covered here is only a fraction of all the information that might be important to reading this particular image. Current events, the political leaders at the time, and other coincidences also can affect how one reads a text.

Building

Choose a famous painting or photograph. Analyze the photograph according to some of the suggestions above, including who created it, why it was created, the historical context around its creation, and how audiences typically view the image now. Write your findings in a brief report, and share them with the class.

Link

Engine

One of the symbols used regularly in daily Twitter interactions is the # symbol, typically when identifying a conversation or topic in Twitter messages. Research the history of the # symbol and how it evolved into its current uses (for instance, while Twitter calls it a "hashtag," other contexts refer to it as the "pound" symbol; why?). Compose a report detailing your findings, and share them with the class.

Search

Analyzing Rhetorical Appeals

Another way to analyze texts is based on the classical appeals included in the rhetorical triangle: *logos*, *ethos*, and *pathos*. As discussed in previous chapters, the rhetorical triangle can be modified to study these rhetorical appeals by placing them at the three points of the triangle. While you can use the rhetorical triangle to construct an argument, you can also use it to read arguments you find in a variety of texts. When you need to evaluate digital writing, use the rhetorical triangle according to each of the appeals below as a mode of analysis when looking at any text. In addition, you can think of a tetrahedron, a three-dimensional representation of a triangle, when considering the ways texts exist in three-dimensional space in a variety of designs, mediums, and genres, and how they exist in a specific time (*kairos*). Take these rhetorical elements into account when you analyze rhetorical arguments.

Logos

Logos, as you remember, is an appeal to the reader based on logical claims. When looking at a digital text from this point of view, you want to examine how a text attempts to convince the reader by making a reasoned argument.

DIGITAL Connections

Global Warming? Not Always

By Martin P. Hoerling

Boulder, Colo. — California is now in the midst of the third year of one of its worst droughts on record. As our planet gradually warms from our rampant burning of fossil fuels, it's only natural to wonder what role climate change has played in California's troubles.

The answer is this: At present, the scientific evidence does not support an argument that the drought there is appreciably linked to human-induced climate change.

Often, logical appeals take the form of facts, comparing and contrasting objects or courses of action, cause-and-effect analysis, statistics, and well-reasoned assumptions based on observable phenomena or shared cultural values.

For instance, in this editorial from *The New York Times*, Martin P. Hoerling argues that some weather and environmental effects aren't necessarily caused by the most obvious suspects.

The drought has many attributes of historical droughts over that region—in particular, a lack of storms and rainfall that would normally arrive from the Pacific Ocean with considerable frequency. It resembles the droughts that afflicted the state in 1976 and 1977. Those years were at least as dry as the last two years have been for the state as a whole.

[...]

What's different this time, however, is that the demand for water has greatly increased in the state, and it may very well be that the current stress created by the failed rains is more severe than for similar rainfall deficits 40 years ago. It is at least intuitive that growth patterns, population increases and the rising value of the state's agricultural sector have increased.

[...]

Other indicators and aspects of rainfall behavior could also be conducive to drought. These include the gap between rainy days, the intensity of rains when they do occur and the effects of warming temperatures in California and for the planet as a whole. Even if the average seasonal rainfall isn't changing, changes in these other factors could alter the risk of drought. What is the evidence there?

One way of accounting for the combined effects of rainfall and temperature on drought is to examine soil moisture. Long-term soil moisture observations are not readily available, but have been estimated using sophisticated models. The 2012 report on extreme events by the Intergovernmental Panel on Climate Change examined the evidence for regional changes in soil moisture since 1950, and made the following assessment for western North America:

"No overall or slight decrease in dryness since 1950; large variability; large drought of the 1930s dominates."

The team of 42 scientists who made that assessment assigned it a rating of "medium confidence" that they were correct. The report also assessed the scientific evidence for how drought over western North America will change in the 21st century, finding an "inconsistent signal in consecutive dry days and soil moisture changes."

A 2013 report by the I.P.C.C. reaffirmed that finding and concluded: "Recent long-term droughts in western North America cannot definitively be shown to lie outside the very large envelope of natural precipitation variability in this region, particularly given new evidence of the history of high-magnitude natural drought and pluvial episodes suggested by paleo-climatic reconstructions."

Thus, the scientific evidence does not support an argument that human-induced climate change has played any appreciable role in the current California drought.

But that is not to say that a warmer climate cannot and will not act to decrease soil moisture and amplify the severity of future naturally occurring

To make his point, Hoerling compares the drought to historical trends, points out the increase in demand for water from an increase in human population, includes analysis of soil moisture, discusses changes in precipitation patterns, and cites scientific evidence.

droughts. It simply reminds us that the current drought, like its ancestors, continues to be strongly driven by shifts in the location of storm tracks that may or may not deliver rains to the narrow strip of the West Coast.

Of course *logos* usually doesn't exist alone, and you could probably make the case that *ethos* and *pathos* also appear in texts. However, on the surface at least, *logos* is one of the more prevalent appeals in Hoerling's article.

Building

Link

Logos comes from the ancient Greek word for "word." Appeals to *logos* are based in thinking with the word, typically analytical thought. With a partner, look through a variety of company brand marks. Do you think any of these brand marks attempt to use the rhetorical appeal of *logos* to make a connection with the audience? Which elements suggest this? How might a company's brand mark connect with the meaning of *logos* based in its early meaning as "word"? Report your findings to the class.

Engine

Search

Analyze an advertisement for your favorite food. What kinds of appeals to *logos* does this advertisement make? What kinds of evidence does it provide? If the ad doesn't seem to appeal to *logos*, what logical claims would you include in the ad in order to persuade readers to eat the food? Share your ideas with the class.

Ethos

You also can analyze a text based on the writer's *ethos*, or his or her credibility as an author. You'll want to know what qualifications the writer has to make the statements he or she does. What is the writer's background and experience? Is the writer presenting his or her argument for good reasons, or does the writer have a secret ulterior motive? Basically, is this someone you can trust?

The *ethos* of two writers already discussed, Ramesses and Martin P. Hoerling, differ quite radically. Because Hoerling is a research meterologist who specializes in climate dynamics at the Earth System Research Laboratory of the National Oceanic and Atmospheric Administration, he has the background to back up his claims and the motivation of a scientist who explains with the facts. He can't present just any data to support his argument, but information that is grounded in observable scientific data. While Hoerling cites historical data to help make his claim (*logos*), he is an authority figure based on his education and expertise (*ethos*), and therefore qualified to speak on the topic of climate change. Because he doesn't seem to have any other motives, such as selling a good or service, you would typically trust him more than someone who was trying to get something from you.

Ramesses, on the other hand, was the pharaoh of Egypt and could write whatever he wanted. His status as ruler doesn't necessarily make his statements more truthful but instead probably makes them more suspect. As you've already seen, both Ramesses's texts and those found at the Hittite capital, Boğazköy, claim victory at the Battle of Kadesh. Most historians believe Ramesses was able to force a truce (he was losing badly for much of the battle), and so neither civilization truly won. Given that the very purpose of the carving inside the Abu Simbel temple is selfish, a piece of propaganda aimed at keeping Ramesses's empire together with him as ruler, you can definitely question whether his motives for writing were as independent as Hoerling's and decide that he's not entirely trustworthy as a writer (or, at least, as the sponsor of the carvings).

Rhetorical Continuities

Besides a writer's credentials, other structural and formal elements can affect how you read a writer's *ethos* within a text. Audiences often find fault with a writer who makes spelling or grammatical mistakes in his writing, and his *ethos* as a writer often diminishes for his readers. You can make the same assessment of digital works. Does the text seem well designed, making good use of elements such as color, white space, typeface, and other design choices? Or is the text hastily composed, sloppy, and look amateurish? Would you say, "that text looks like it was created by a professional," or would you remark that "my five-year-old niece could compose something better than that"? Many digital texts you encounter are professionally created, but many are not. Because digital texts are often created quickly and with less editorial supervision (such as blog posts, online articles, tweets, status updates, etc.), or are sent from smartphones or tablets that often facilitate errors in typing because of small virtual keyboards, mistakes are probably more likely to occur. These simple mistakes can make the audience question the creator's *ethos* (Figure 4.8).

Figure 4.8
Based on this rusty sign, would you trust this body shop to repair your car?

When analyzing a text for *ethos*, then, consider these facets of the writer's credibility. Is the writer credentialed to make the claims she or he does? If not, does she use supporting evidence that is credentialed? Does the writer seem to respect his or her reader, or does he treat the reader condescendingly? Does the writer use any of the logical fallacies discussed in Chapter 3 that would make the audience question how well he or she understands the argument? Finally, does the writer craft a well-written or well-designed text, or does the text look unorganized and difficult to read? These questions will help you begin to make sense of the writer's *ethos* when reading a text.

Building

Link

Analyze a variety of articles from Wikipedia. How does each article attempt to establish *ethos*? What kinds of sources do they site? Are these sources credible? Is the article free of major mechanical and grammatical errors? In addition to looking at the articles, research how Wikipedia works, and the role of moderators in the site. Finally, look through the same (or similar) entries in a print encyclopedia (or an online version of a print encyclopedia). How does this version create *ethos*? Does it establish *ethos* in the same way as Wikipedia, or does it use a different approach? Record your results, and share them with the class.

Engine

Search

In the previous section (on *logos*), you found advertisements for your favorite food. Look back at these advertisements, and analyze how they use *ethos* to supplement their argument. Do they use celebrities, famous chefs, or perhaps endorsements from nutrition or health organizations? What elements appear that suggest you can trust the claims they make? Do you believe in these claims? Why or why not? Record your ideas, and share them with the class.

Pathos

In many cases, images that make an argument will use appeals to *pathos*, as you've already seen with examples of cigarette ads in Chapter 2. Images appeal to the parts of the brain that respond emotionally to visual stimuli. While alphabetic text can certainly produce emotional responses, the images and videos used in digital writing can do it more quickly and with greater force. Reading *pathos* in the visual elements of a digital text becomes an important skill in order to understand more systematically how these images are attempting to reach a viewer.

The "Donating Blood" section for the website of the American Red Cross uses several techniques to appeal to the audience's emotions, particularly through the stories of those who have already given blood. For instance, one donor states that:

> I am a Red Cross blood donor that won't give up. I tried to give blood when I was 18, but was declined in both my junior and senior high school years. Once I got to college, I was deferred again. I was finally able to give blood and have given twice. I love donating blood. The thought of being able to help save three people's lives every time I go makes me feel like a better person.

Another writes:

> I lost both of my parents in a short period of time. My dad needed blood transfusions during several surgeries and when my mom was battling cancer the chemo made her so weak she needed transfusions twice. I was so thankful then that they were able to get the life sustaining blood they needed and thankful to the unknown people who had donated. Now I do my part to help. I ask myself, "If not me, then who?"

These stories provide inspiring and heartbreaking accounts that attempt to persuade the reader through the emotion of these events. Once the reader donates blood, she is invited to share her own story, adding another appeal to *pathos* and also making her feel as if she is a member of a larger community. The first reason the Red Cross lists for donating blood: "It feels great to donate!"

Digital texts that feature images can also use *pathos*. Figure 4.9 displays an advertisement to encourage riders to wear their helmets while on a bicycle, motorcycle, or other open-air vehicle. Here, the message relies mostly on the fear of receiving a significant brain injury, one that could require lifelong care or possibly death. While the text also attempts to use logical arguments, citing statistics of how many people injure themselves each year from not wearing helmets, the ad's predominant appeal is toward *pathos*, creating an emotional response to make

Credit: Ogilvy & Mather Vietnam

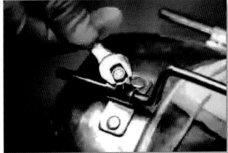

Figure 4.9
Note how this ad uses *pathos* to persuade you to wear a helmet.
https://www.youtube.com/watch?v=7TpWG2GD20c

people reconsider their actions and protect their heads out on the roads. The appeal is sometimes called a "fear" appeal, because it plays on readers' fears of what might happen if they do not act on the message.

Credit: Don't mess with Texas®

Figure 4.10
If you litter, you mess with Texas. Don't do it.

Credit: Greenpeace/Lowe AG, Switzerland

Figure 4.12
This Greenpeace ad appeals to a sense of being a citizen of the world.

Credit: James Montgomery Flag

Figure 4.11
This advertisement clearly calls for the patriot in you to "wake up."

Often, texts can appeal to shared values, which usually include a sense of community, either in the regions where audiences live, a country as a whole (patriotism), or in a global context. Figures 4.10, 4.11, and 4.12 offer an example of each of these.

Figure 4.10 is a website for "Don't mess with Texas," aimed at keeping people from littering in the Lone Star State. While their ads offer many logical arguments about not littering, their main message is one based on local pride—and the warning of a veiled threat as in the popular saying "Don't mess with Texas" (this campaign also uses the pun of "mess" to provide a bit of humor to the ads).

Figure 4.11 appeals to a national audience. This advertisement from World War I attempted to persuade Americans to join in the war effort. The female figure is depicted as "Miss America," asleep to the war being fought overseas.

Figure 4.12 goes beyond the national and appeals to the global citizen. This ad for Greenpeace shows not a school of fish but a school of litter flowing through the seas. This image might produce feelings of shame, pity, or sadness, or appeal to the idea that humans need to be more responsible with their trash disposal.

It is not aimed at any particular body of water but oceans in general, something everyone shares in one way or another.

When analyzing an image for its emotional appeals, think specifically about the particular kinds of emotions it appeals to (fear, love, anger) and which desires it taps into (social acceptance, adventure, sex). This strategy will help you then determine the kinds of audiences the image is attempting to reach and can give you ideas about how to compose your own images toward your own audiences.

Building

Link

Look back at the company brand marks you selected to research regarding their *logos*. Do any of these brand marks have an emotional component? If not, can you think of brand marks that do? Do they appeal to your desires for adventure, social status, or patriotism? Are the brand marks that create an emotional connection from newer companies or long-established companies? Discuss why you think the brand marks create an emotional connection, and share the results with the class.

Engine

Search

In the last two sections, you analyzed advertisements for your favorite food, considering their appeals to *logos* and *ethos*. How do ads for this same food create appeals toward *pathos*? Do they create a sense of nostalgia? Do they present you with an appeal toward social acceptance? Adventure? Do they make you hungry, and would you consider hunger a type of emotion? Record your findings, and share them with the class.

Kairos

You also can analyze an image for its timing—when it was placed within a particular moment. As discussed in Chapter 2, *kairos* identifies the best rhetorical moment to help make a particular argument. When analyzing a particular image, you might ask some of the following questions to help you determine why the author created the text at a particular moment or opportunity.

1. What's in the text that relates to other local, national, or global events?

2. Is there a pressing need to communicate that cannot wait until a later time?

3. Is there a certain mood or atmosphere the image attempts to tap into?

Kairos is very prevalent in all the traditional writing you already do. For instance, when you submit a class paper usually depends upon a deadline. Once the deadline passes, the most opportune moment for writing has passed. Of course, this is an easy example with a clear time in which to act. Other situations might be fuzzier. If you miss that deadline, then you might write an email to your professor explaining why the paper was late. When is the most opportune moment to send this email? If you know you'll be late, should you send the email before the due date? Should you send it immediately after the due date? Typically, you probably wouldn't send the email a month later. What timing do you think your professor would prefer?

DIGITAL Connections

Why Putin Doesn't Respect Us

By Thomas L. Friedman

Just as we've turned the coverage of politics into sports, we're doing the same with geopolitics. There is much nonsense being written about how Vladimir Putin showed how he is "tougher" than Barack Obama and how Obama now needs to demonstrate his manhood. This is how great powers get drawn into the politics of small tribes and end up in great wars that end badly for everyone. We vastly exaggerate Putin's strength—so does he—and we vastly underestimate our own strength, and ability to weaken him through nonmilitary means.

Let's start with Putin. Any man who actually believes, as Putin has said, that the breakup of the Soviet Union was "the greatest geopolitical catastrophe" of the 20th century is caught up in a dangerous fantasy that can't end well for him or his people. The Soviet Union

Newspaper op-eds usually make good use of *kairos* by addressing a situation at the right moment. For instance, on March 4, 2014, Thomas L. Friedman wrote this op-ed during the beginning of the confrontation between Russia, Ukraine, and the United States over the Crimean peninsula. He uses this moment not to discuss the right course of action about Crimea, but to comment on Putin's lack of respect for the United States, and the "larger trend" that Putin seems to be pursuing. If he had written this article six months earlier, it wouldn't have received as much attention, and viewers might have been wondering why *The New York Times* had published it. However, because he seizes the moment when the country of Russia and its president, Putin, is in the public consciousness, he has a much more aware and receptive audience.

died because Communism could not provide rising standards of living, and its collapse actually unleashed boundless human energy all across Eastern Europe and Russia. A wise Putin would have redesigned Russia so its vast human talent could take advantage of all that energy. He would be fighting today to get Russia into the European Union, not to keep Ukraine out. But that is not who Putin is and never will be. He is guilty of the soft bigotry of low expectations toward his people and prefers to turn Russia into a mafia-run petro-state—all the better to steal from.

So Putin is now fighting human nature among his own young people and his neighbors—who both want more E.U. and less Putinism. To put it in market terms, Putin is long oil and short history. He has made himself steadily richer and Russia steadily more reliant on natural resources rather than its human ones. History will not be kind to him—especially if energy prices ever collapse.

So spare me the Putin-body-slammed-Obama prattle. This isn't All-Star Wrestling. The fact that Putin has seized Crimea, a Russian-speaking zone of Ukraine, once part of Russia, where many of the citizens prefer to be part of Russia and where Russia has a major naval base, is not like taking Poland. I support economic and diplomatic sanctions to punish Russia for its violation of international norms and making clear that harsher sanctions, even military aid for Kiev, would ensue should Putin try to bite off more of Ukraine. But we need to remember that that little corner of the world is always going to mean more, much more, to Putin than to us, and we should refrain from making threats on which we're not going to deliver.

What disturbs me about Crimea is the larger trend it fits into, that Putinism used to just be a threat to Russia but is now becoming a threat to global stability. I opposed expanding NATO toward Russia after the Cold War, when Russia was at its most democratic and least threatening. It remains one of the dumbest things we've ever done and, of course, laid the groundwork for Putin's rise.

For a long time, Putin has exploited the humiliation and anti-Western attitudes NATO expansion triggered to gain popularity, but this seems to have become so fundamental to his domestic politics that it has locked him into a zero-sum relationship with the West that makes it hard to see how we collaborate with him in more serious trouble spots, like Syria or Iran. President Bashar al-Assad of Syria is engaged in monstrous, genocidal behavior that also threatens the stability of the Middle East. But Putin stands by him. At least half the people of Ukraine long to be part of Europe, but he treated that understandable desire as a NATO plot and quickly resorted to force.

I don't want to go to war with Putin, but it is time we expose his real weakness and our real strength. That, though, requires a long-term strategy—not just fulminating on *Meet the Press*. It requires going after the twin pillars of his regime: oil and gas. Just as the oil glut of the 1980s, partly engineered by the Saudis, brought down global oil prices to a level that helped collapse Soviet Communism, we could do the same today to Putinism by putting the right long-term policies in place. That is by investing in the facilities to liquefy and export our natural gas bounty (provided it is extracted at the highest environmental standards) and making Europe, which gets 30 percent of its gas from Russia, more dependent on us instead. I'd also raise our gasoline tax, put in place a carbon tax and a national renewable energy portfolio standard—all of which would also help lower the global oil price (and make us stronger, with cleaner air, less oil dependence and more innovation).

You want to frighten Putin? Just announce those steps. But you know the story, the tough guys in Washington who want to take on Putin would rather ask 1 percent of Americans—the military and their families—to make the ultimate sacrifice than have all of us make a small sacrifice in the form of tiny energy price increases. Those tough guys who thump their chests in Congress but run for the hills if you ask them to vote for a 10-cent increase in the gasoline tax that would actually boost our leverage, they'll never rise to this challenge. We'll do anything to expose Putin's weakness; anything that isn't hard. And you wonder why Putin holds us in contempt?

Kairos also appears in other kinds of writing. Figure 4.13 depicts an advertisement for relief after Hurricane Sandy struck the east coast of the United States. To achieve maximum effectiveness—or to seize the opportune moment—this ad needed to appear shortly after the hurricane struck. If the ad appeared too late, then many people may have forgotten about this disaster, or another disaster may have created other exigencies.

You also might look at uprisings in Africa and the Middle East during the spring of 2011 as examples of seizing the kairotic moment. For the protestors, the most opportune moment to send Twitter messages about the situation was during the protests, to let media outlets know what was happening so the outside world could support their efforts (Figure 4.14). To make such tweets well before the peak of the protests or well after any of the regimes were overthrown would not have had the intended impact or reaction. Writers must make use of *kairos* during this short window of time before it closes.

Figure 4.15 displays a modified "Apple" advertisement from a group called "Freedom From Porn" located in San Francisco, California. If you were to ask how *kairos* relates to this image, or why the writers might have posted the image when they did, you could search for events that occurred during the same time period.

Because the group seems to be juxtaposing the iPad and pornography for some rhetorical purpose, you also might ask if any events that involved Apple products occurred in San Francisco during this time, such as an iPad or other Apple product release. Researching these questions, you would discover that Apple did not release any major product, but the Apple Worldwide Developers Conference, a meeting of Apple developers, did take place in San Francisco during this time. The creators of the ad clearly timed its delivery to correspond to this meeting and to make sure the developers attending the conference got the message.

Figure 4.13
This advertisement from the Ad Council asks for donations and lets the audience know their contributions are "hard at work" toward medicine, water, and construction.

Figure 4.14
An Egyptian protestor in Cairo's Tahrir Square with a flyer that refers to social media's role in the 2011 Egyptian Revolution

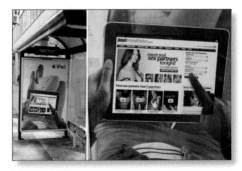

Figure 4.15
The group "Freedom From Porn" waited until the Apple Worldwide Developers Conference to spread their ads protesting Apple's policies on pornography.

Building

Visit a news website. Analyze the opinion pieces and determine how each meets a kairotic opportunity. Do you think any of these opinions appear too late or too early for a particular conversation? For example, discussions about women's right to vote would probably be too late, since this debate occurred nearly 100 years ago. However, there may be authors who write about arguments you feel have been settled long ago. What new exigency occurs to make the timing of these pieces appropriate? How does the website use social media and other digital writing platforms to spread this opinion? Write your results in a report, and share them with the class.

Engine

In the last three sections, you analyzed advertisements for your favorite food, considering their appeals to *logos, ethos,* and *pathos*. How do ads for this same food tap into *kairos*? Do they enter into a conversation that is already going on about particular dietary fads, health advice, or concerns about food safety? Do they relate to current events at the time of their release, such as sporting events or holidays? Consider some of these factors, think of your own, and research how the writers might have used *kairos*. Compose your results in a report, and share them with the class.

Analyzing Argument

Finally, you should also consider the argument itself that the writer is attempting to make, as well as how she or he makes that argument. Digital writing makes use of both written and visual arguments that make use of some of the same strategies, such as argument by analogy, definition, comparison and contrast, as well as stating claims and reasons. While the visual arguments found in digital texts often don't have the space (or if a video, time) to develop an argument the way a traditional essay does, you can still look for some of these features when analyzing digital texts.

Claims, reasons, evidence

In traditional forms of writing, arguments are composed by making a claim and then supporting it with reasons and evidence. These argumentative elements also may be present in digital texts that are primarily visual, although sometimes hidden from view. To investigate a visual text and uncover these elements, you can start by asking yourself the following questions.

What is the main claim of the text?

Of the main parts that compose an argument, a text will usually have some sort of claim. Although not in complete sentences, you can probably easily interpret the claim in Figure 4.16, an advertisement for Chick-fil-A restaurants. The text above the image of the cows, which reads "Go De-Calf This Mornin," indicates by juxtaposition that the ad refers to "de-calf" as "without cow," and thus eating chicken. Here the text anchors the meaning of the image.

Figure 4.17 provides another example of how text can anchor the claim of the image. In this ad, the model, Patrick Ribbsaeter, appears chained, and the written text reads "Wild animals don't belong in chains: keep elephants out of zoos." Here, the main claim appears in the second line, "keep elephants out of zoos," with the first part, "wild animals don't belong in chains" as a reason for the claim.

However, some texts may make claims while not using any written text (or very little written text) to provide a specific meaning. Figure 4.18 displays a clump of rainforest in the shape of a set of lungs. In the right lung, loggers are clear-cutting the forest, destroying the lower lobe. The text at the bottom, "before it's too late," doesn't provide a claim, but instead provides support for the claim, which may be something like "the rainforests are the lungs of the earth, and we need to protect them," which then may be coupled with "before it's too late." The use of visual metaphor is an effective and powerful way to quickly make a claim without resorting to the use of text. The downside, of course, is that your readers might misinterpret your metaphor without any text to guide them.

Figure 4.16
Despite very little text, this Chick-fil-A ad still makes an argument.

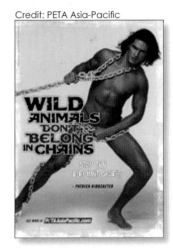

Figure 4.17
This ad makes a very direct claim. What role does the visual play?

Figure 4.18
If you had to interpret this ad's argument, how would you phrase it?

What reasons support the claim?

Figure 4.19 shows Paul McCartney, one of the Beatles, in an ad promoting vegetarianism. While the most prominent text "I am Paul McCartney, and I am a Vegetarian," is most likely the main claim and could be continued into "and you should be a vegetarian, too," the main reason for this argument is provided in the anecdote in the upper right-hand corner of the image where McCartney tells of the time he caught a fish and realized "that his life was as important to him as mine is to me." In this example, the reason for becoming a vegetarian relates to the consciousness of animals. While this reason can be debated further, it provides some indication of why one might want to accept the main claim.

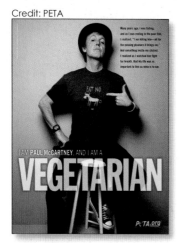

Credit: PETA

Figure 4.19
This ad provides a very explicit reason to back up its claim.

Credit: Clay Bennett

Figure 4.20
This cartoon only uses two words. How would you phrase its argument?

Many texts, however, do not provide explicit reasons for a claim, and instead leave it to the audience to fill in those reasons themselves. Figure 4.20 depicts a stork labeled as "resources" carrying ten children to their expectant families. This image provides an analogy for overpopulation and the strain it will have on Earth's finite resources. However, this image doesn't state that overpopulation is bad or why it is bad. Instead, the audience is left to fill in the unstated reasons or realize that the image is suggesting that overpopulation is bad, because it puts undue strain on resources and will send them (like the stork) crashing to the ground. Because the audience knows it needs resources to survive, the cartoon doesn't have to provide that reason; the audience provides it on its own.

What evidence backs the text's reasoning?

Although reasons for a claim are often missing from visual texts, authors do include evidence on occasion. Figure 4.21 depicts an advertisement against human trafficking. Its main claim is "Human trafficking is more active than ever. YOU can help." The writer does not state the reasons why this is a problem. He or she probably assumes that the audience will think that "of course we shouldn't traffic in human beings."

While the author doesn't provide reasons for this problem, the author does provide evidence about the statistics of victims: "99 percent of victims are not rescued." Should one be taken and find oneself in this situation, chances are the abductee will never be seen again, making this statistic very powerful. When creating your own texts, especially when incorporating images, you might choose to be selective about what evidence you provide because you have little space to do so. Also, since readers prefer smaller chunks of text when reading online, you should also be selective when using written text, offering your most powerful reasons. Choose claims/evidence you think will most impact your readers and get their attention.

Credit: thea21campaign.org

Figure 4.21
This ad uses a powerful statistic as evidence.

Does the text provide any counterarguments?

As discussed previously, most visual texts don't have the space to provide a full-fledged argument you might typically think of when writing a paper. In this literate context, you are often taught you should address counterarguments to your claim and then discuss how they aren't applicable or are otherwise wrong. Figure 4.22 uses its main title to provide one of the counterarguments to global warming before then explaining how this statement is incorrect. This example is completely word-based with no image and is the exception that proves the general rule that most visual texts do not include this level of counterargument. However, you should still be conscious of them when analyzing a text, for they do occasionally appear.

Credit: Oxfam Great Britain

Figure 4.22
This ad provides a counterargument, but is all text. Do you find it effective?

While some of these claims may be literally "spelled out" through written text, many digital arguments are composed simply of images without text. Keep in mind that many of the arguments you're looking for may be implicit rather than explicit.

Building

Link

Choose a company that has a product for which they create print and television advertisements. After locating these ads and commercials, analyze and compare how the authors modify their use of claims, reasons, evidence, and counterarguments for each medium. For television commercials, does spoken dialogue substitute for written text? How much does the visual still play an important part? Record your findings, and share them with the class.

Engine

Search

Return to the advertisements for your favorite food. If possible, analyze the company's website for this food, and compare the information it contains with its advertisements (in as many media as you can locate). How does the company's argument (or construction of the argument) change from website to print ad to television commercial (and to other media)? Write a report of your analysis, and share it with the class.

Analyzing Design, Medium, and Genre

As discussed in Chapter 1, the rhetorical tetrahedron provides a model that accounts for design, medium, and genre in addition to writer, audience, and message. This section considers these first three elements, which you should analyze as you consider a digital text as a whole. Remember, just as all six of these rhetorical elements appear together in the rhetorical tetrahedron, they also exist and affect each other in real-world rhetorical situations. Although the following discussion isolates these elements, they're always affecting, and are affected by, the other rhetorical elements.

Design

What follows are a few design elements to consider when analyzing a text. Use this information to help you ask questions about visuals and investigate how they use different design characteristics.

Color

The use of color can help contribute to an argument by selecting hues associated with particular themes or emotions. Typically, the colors red, orange, and yellow stimulate the appetite, and so these colors often are used in food advertising. Figure 4.23 depicts an ad for McDonald's that uses red and yellow in this way. Of course, McDonald's was clever enough to compose its visual identity in red and yellow, so whenever one sees its logo or food packaging, the appetite has a greater chance of becoming excited.

Figure 4.23
This McDonald's building uses colors that appeal to your appetite.

However, these colors also signify caution, warning, and danger signs on technical documents and dangerous machinery, and of course, you commonly see red on stop signs.

The color green has been used extensively when creating messages with an environmental theme, but it also represents money, and so it may be found on a variety of advertisements promoting financial products. When analyzing a particular text, pay attention to the dominant colors that are present, and research the possible meanings of those colors. How do they influence the way you respond to a text?

Credit: Nick Moreau

Figure 4.24
This ad for Apple's iPod uses contrast to clearly show its product.

Color also can be used to contrast different information, making different design elements stand out. Figure 4.24, an advertisement for Apple's iPod, uses only three colors to establish high contrast, so the white iPod and headphones are clearly visible in the advertisement. Also, the font color is the same as that of the product in the ad, making it clear what the text refers to in the image.

Typeface

Like color, typeface can bolster an argument implicitly by creating a mood or atmosphere. For example, conservative, clean typefaces like **Helvetica** may suggest the idea of uniformity or convention. Typefaces such as **Comic Sans** may suggest a whimsical nature. Other typefaces, such as **Broadway**, literally invoke their namesake, such as the large marquis typeface that displays a Broadway production's title. A typeface such as **Futura** is intended to evoke the future.

Credit: Cancer Patients Aid Association/Touchstone Advertising

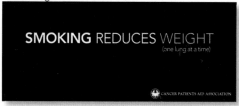

Figure 4.25
This ad uses typography to effectively "show" its argument.

Typefaces can provide personality or characteristics to text that say something beyond the words in which they're composed. In any text you're analyzing, determine which typefaces the text uses, and research the creation, intended use, and typical response to that typeface. In addition, other font characteristics can be used to contribute to an argument, such as Figure 4.25, which changes the font from bold to normal to thin in order to to reference a commonly cited alleged effect of smoking—weight loss—by suggesting lost weight through diseases such as lung cancer, an important part of the advertisement's message.

Layout

How a particular text is laid out will determine many other important elements, such as emphasis, balance, harmony, use of white space, and other design considerations. For any particular image, you might ask what elements the writer emphasizes over others. While you can probably tell which words an author wants to stand out based on font typography and font weight, you also should pay attention to which visual elements hold more importance than others.

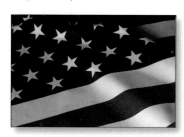

Figure 4.26
The stars, which represent the 50 states, are united by proximity.

For example, proximity offers one way to arrange a design's layout. The United States flag, for instance, uses proximity to group the stars together in one location, visually and metaphorically suggesting that they're together and thus "united" (Figure 4.26).

Credit: Red Cross/JWT, Shanghai, China

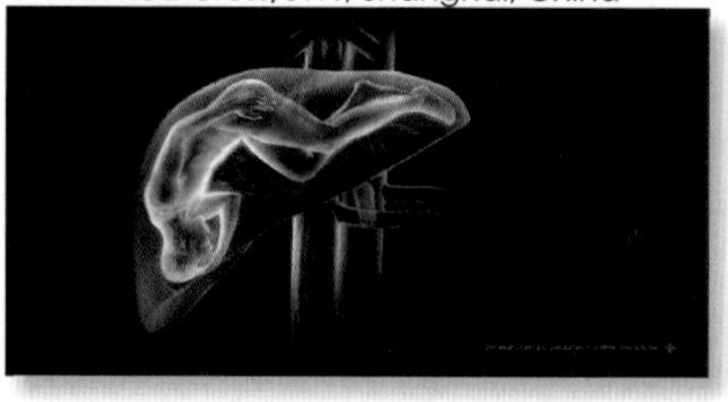

Figure 4.27
This image isolates the organ/man on a black background.

Figure 4.27 uses isolation by placing a figure in an organ against an empty black background, separating the joined figures from any other visual elements and making them the focal point of the public service announcement. This design also isolates the liver from the rest of the body, making the message clearer. How and where ele-

ments of a text are placed in relationship to each other can create rhetorical effect, drawing the reader's eyes to certain parts and helping to persuade the reader of a certain point, even if only by placing the reader in a particular mood or atmosphere regarding the message.

Building

Select an image that makes an argument using juxtaposition of both text and image. Using a photo editor, create different versions of the image by erasing the current text and recreating it (using the same words) by changing the typography. How does changing the typography change the atmosphere (and the message) of the image as a whole? Share your different versions of the image with the class, and discuss how you think the meaning changes for each.

Engine

As discussed in this section, food companies often select colors that appeal to the audience's appetite. Look back at the food advertisements you've collected for the previous assignments in this chapter. Analyze the colors of the ads, and note which ones use colors such as red, orange, or yellow. Do these colors appeal to you in these ads? Why or why not? What other colors are used? Do you find these colors attractive when considering a food product to eat, or do the colors make the food unappetizing? Write a brief report detailing the use of color in these ads, and share the results with the class.

Genre and medium

When analyzing a text, you should also examine the genre and medium in which it appears. These two rhetorical elements are very closely connected, and thus worth discussing together.

You're probably already familiar with genres and mediums as they occur in more traditional workplace or academic documents. For instance, the genre of a letter is more formal than that of an email. If you wanted to recommend a change to your boss or colleague, you might do so in the genre of a recommendation report rather than a laboratory report; these two documents obviously serve different functions for different audiences.

Visual documents too require carefully selected genres as well as the medium in which that genre takes its ultimate form. Such genres might include photographs, illustrations, maps, charts, graphs, paintings, commercials, websites, posters, or flyers. Any of these genres could appear in a variety of media, such as print/paper, audio, video, or an assortment of digital formats.

For example, you might ask if the image appears as a flyer, a poster, or a bill-board. Is the billboard paper-based or on an LCD display? Is the image painted on the side of a bus, making it a moving image, or does it appear electronically as a commercial, a website, or a commercial in a website? How the image is deliv-ered affects how the reader responds to it. A commercial placed on television can usually only be viewed once, unless the viewer has a digital video recorder and can rewind live television. Of course, the viewer might be equally inclined to fast-forward through the commercial. Online commercials, however, typi-cally can be viewed repeatedly, and also shared among friends, especially when posted on YouTube. This form of medium greatly increases the distribution of the typical commercial genre.

Some companies use the standard genre of the advertisement in some very interesting and creative media. Figure 4.28 is a photograph of an advertisement for Bounty paper towels. Here, the traditional product shot and tagline of the product is combined with a huge coffee cup that has been spilled on the side-walk. The overall message is delivered through the scale of the "mess" being made.

In figure 4.29, a billboard for the television program *Law & Order*, the image integrates with the building itself, so the police detective holds the building's light as if it were a light in the interrogation room.

Credit: Bounty/Publicis New York   Credit: Colenso BBDO, Auckland

Figure 4.28
This ad for Bounty paper towels makes the viewer interact with it, even when trying to avoid or ignore it.

Figure 4.29
This ad for *Law & Order* makes use of the existing physical space for a unique effect.

Finally, the poster in Figure 4.30 is specifically designed to be wrapped around a round column so that the message ("what goes around comes around") is actually enacted by the poster itself. If this poster were laid flat, or wrapped around a square column, it would lose its effectiveness.

Whenever you analyze a text, ask yourself "Why did the designer create the text in this genre?" and "Why did she create the text in this medium?" Some of the answers to these questions might be obvious. For example, if the text appears outdoors, the medium might need to be waterproof to withstand the elements. The medium may need to be a static medium that is not electronic (of course, some electronics are waterproofed to be placed outside). Placing an advertisement on a bus might help to increase exposure as it moves about a city. While a YouTube video isn't located outside where people can see it, placing a video in an online medium might actually garner more attention because people can share it more easily. Decisions about genre and medium are rhetorical choices meant to reach particular audiences and persuade them and are important considerations when analyzing a visual text.

Credit: bigantinternational.com

Figure 4.30
This ad, arguing for the United States to stop the wars in Iraq and Afghanistan, is designed specifically for this particular physical environment.

Building

Link

Walk through campus and take photographs of different visual texts. Analyze and discuss the genre and medium used for each text, and consider if you think the use is effective. Could the designer have chosen better options? What creative ways can you come up with to deliver the same message (using the examples above as models)? Share your examples and results with the class.

Engine

Search

Analyze a restaurant or fast food chain that you frequent. How does the company make use of different genres and designs to market and provide information about their products? Make a list of as many genres and media as you can (from menus to nutritional information and from websites to food containers). How does each provide a specific purpose or niche for making particular arguments about their product? How might they be modified or improved? Share your list and ideas with the class.

KEY Terms

analogy	evidence
analysis	genre
argument	medium
claim	reason
context	subject
critical thinking	symbol
design	writer

Analysis of a Digital Text

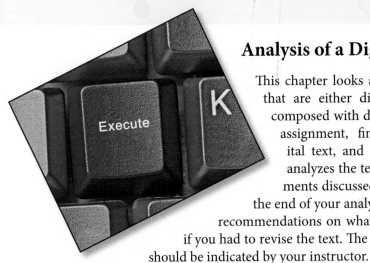

This chapter looks at a variety of texts that are either digital in nature, or composed with digital tools. For this assignment, find your own digital text, and write a report that analyzes the text based on the elements discussed in this chapter. At the end of your analysis, provide a list of recommendations on what you might change if you had to revise the text. The length of the report should be indicated by your instructor.

Examples of digital texts might include a website, an online advertisement, a video, an e-book, or a video game. You also might choose to analyze a printed text that was created with digital tools or one that incorporates digital interfaces such as Quick Reference codes (like those used in this book) or other web-based elements. In either case, make sure your instructor agrees that your choice fulfills the goal of this assignment and the goal of your class.

To get started, you might include the following elements in your analysis.

Writer
Who is the writer of the text? What is the writer's background? What does this information tell you about the text that might not be evident otherwise?

Purpose
What is the purpose of the text? What goal does it attempt to achieve, or what problem does it try to solve? Why was it written?

Audience
Who is the intended audience for this text? How will they use the text? How do they interact with the text? Is the text well designed for this audience and use?

Context and Subject
What is the context and subject of the text? What is the larger history of this subject and context, and how does this history affect the reading of this particular text?

Logos

What logical appeals does the text attempt to make to the reader? Are these appeals effective?

Ethos

What evidence does the text provide to suggest that the author is trustworthy and qualified to speak about the text's subject? Is this evidence effective?

Pathos

What emotional appeals does the text attempt to make to the reader? Are these appeals effective?

Kairos

Research when the text was created. Are there any historical events that coincide with the text's delivery date that would suggest the author created a timely argument? Note that a "historical event" doesn't necessarily mean something as publicized as a disaster or war, but it can be something more commonplace, such as a local election or sporting event.

Symbols and Analogies

Does the text use any symbols or analogies? If so, how recognizable are these elements? What is their history?

Claim, Reasons, and Evidence

Does the text make a specific claim, or is it only suggested? Does the text provide reasons for the audience to adopt its claim? Does it provide evidence to support these reasons?

Design

What design elements, such as color, typography, or layout does the text use to appeal to its readers or to help them make use of the text? Do you find the design effective in helping to achieve its purpose?

Genre and Medium

What genre does the author choose for the text, and what medium? Why do you think the author chose this particular genre or medium? Would a different choice have been better?

From DIGITAL Writers

There and Not Quite Back Again

Reviewed on PlayStation 4 and Xbox One

April 10, 2014

As an example of an analysis of a digital text, consider Steve Butts's review of the videogame *Lego The Hobbit* published on IGN.com.

Butts is Editor-in-Chief for IGN.com, an online resource that focuses on video gaming and entertainment media.

To the great surprise of no one, the Lego games are finally going there and, well, not quite back again in *Lego The Hobbit*. The game follows the first two films of the *Hobbit* movie trilogy, giving us a chance to lead Bilbo and company all the way from the comforts of Bag End to the dwarf home beneath the Lonely Mountain. It's a fun journey to be sure, but confusing at times, and not entirely satisfying.

An Unexpected Party

Lego The Hobbit clings to the series' standard combat and exploration, but, as usual, a handful of welcome twists make things a bit more interesting this time around. A few different rhythm-based challenges, an item creation system tied to resource collection, and the "find the missing piece" mini-game from February's *Lego Movie* game make *The Hobbit* more than just a button masher, although it is still mostly just that. Thankfully, the environmental challenges and enemies are sophisticated enough to keep the action engaging.

In comparison to the roster in last year's *Lego Marvel* game, many of the characters in the Hobbit feel like, at best, minor variations of each other. It certainly doesn't help that they all sort of look alike, and it can get a little confusing to tell the dwarves apart. But you'll need to pay attention, as each dwarf has one unique ability, like Bombur's ability to turn into a bouncing platform or Bofur's mining power, that needs to be applied to the narrowly scripted environmental challenges.

Chip the Glasses and Crack the Plates

The extended action sequences and sometimes slapstick humor of *The Hobbit* films make a good fit for a Lego game. Honestly, there's always been something a little disjointed about watching Cyclops wreck the X-Mansion or Luke Sky-walker destroy Yoda's house, but seeing the Dwarves go to town demolishing absolutely everything in Bag End or Rivendell makes perfect sense. When you see them literally start smashing Bilbo's cupboards and Elrond's tables, it just feels right. From the plate juggling in Bilbo's kitchen to the golden toilets in Smaug's hoard, there are also loads of humorous little touches that keep the charm going.

Lego The Hobbit also looks beautiful. The settings are very convincing, with loads of little details and plenty of suitably moody lighting. The world is filled with fantastic creatures and monsters, and developer Traveller's Tales has done a great job adapting the giant eagles, goblin kings, and dragons to the standard Lego models. The only real problem with the graphics is that the more realistic color palette and sheer density of some of the scenes can make it very difficult to see who you are or what you're doing. The sometimes inconsistent camera angles don't help things much. More than once, I just found myself just attacking and jumping at random in the hopes that I would eventually figure out where I was.

To Dungeons Deep and Caverns Old

The main story clocks in at about six hours, but there's much more to do and see in the world once you've completed the main missions. Each mission unlocks events around the map, and you'll be able to spend hours digging into the recipes, errands, and encounters around Middle-earth. A campfire system lets you change the time of day to open up new events, and you can always call on a giant eagle to get you from one end of the map to the other.

While most of the missions are fairly predictable, I was impressed with the Hobbit's take on the solo sections. For Riddles in the Dark, Bilbo's joined by a dazed goblin, for instance. There are also some tremendous set pieces where the characters are facing off against the dragon, or climbing up the body of a very active and very angry stone giant.

Unfortunately, the story sort of goes by in a flash. Last year's *Lego Marvel* showed what Traveller's Tales can do with an original story, so *The Hobbit's* abbreviated, sometimes scattered storytelling feels like a step back. There are narrative bits tying the missions together, but the whole game presumes that you already know the source material well enough to fill in the gaps yourself. (You probably do, but if you're playing with kids it might not be clear to them.) It's particularly troublesome to track the events between the spider attack and the dwarves' arrival at Lake Town. The game also ends where the second movie ends, which left me wanting more—and not in a good way.

The Verdict

Lego The Hobbit won't surprise fans of the Lego series, but the new gameplay systems add just enough complexity to keep things interesting. New events and mining opportunities make exploration of the open world almost as fun as the main missions. The storytelling presumes you already know the source material by heart, which means things are sometimes a bit disjointed, and the game, like the movies it's based on, ends at an awkward place. But like almost all the Lego games, this is a journey worth taking.

STUDENT Example

ENG675

Brian Gaines

Dr. Sean Morey

22 October 2012

> Brian Gaines earned a Master of Arts in professional communication from Clemson University and is currently a multimedia/web/graphic designer at Tri-County Technical College.

Gangnam Style: Content and Rhetorical Analysis

The YouTube video for *Gangnam Style*, by the K-pop artist Park Jae-Sang, better known by the stage name Psy, has reached 515,324,880 views at the time of this writing, and more than 7,000,000 views within the last 24 hours. This video, which was uploaded on July 15, 2012, has rapidly become the most viewed video in YouTube history (www.guinnessworldrecords.com/news/2012/9/gangnam-style-now-most-liked-video-in-YouTube-history-44977). To better understand the massive popularity of this video, some of the possible themes of this video must be identified and analyzed. Some of those themes include: the rise of the upper class in the Gangnam District of Seoul, South Korea; wealth as a means of control and status in the notion of knowledge/power among the "nouveau riche"; the parody of the popularity of Western culture in Asia; the parody of the newly wealthy in the Gangnam District; and, to a lesser extent, the objectification of women and men in the male gaze.

The Gangnam District in Seoul, South Korea, is one of 25 government districts that make up the Seoul Metropolitan Area. Gangnam is located south of Han River and as of the 2010 census, has a population of 527,641. Until the late 1970s, the area was one of the least developed areas of Seoul. As a result of intense development over the past 30 years, Gangnam has become the most affluent area of Seoul and South Korea as a whole. This economic and real estate boom to the region in the early 2000s has created a generation of newly wealthy individuals, much to the chagrin of the more traditional aristocracy who have historically resided north of the Han River. The new wealth has drawn the trendiest boutiques and clubs and a proliferation of plastic surgery clinics, but it has also provided access to something considered vital in modern South Korea: top-notch education in the form of prestigious private tutoring and prep schools. Gangnam households spend nearly four times more on education than the national average. In terms of Western culture, Gangnam District is the Korean equivalent of Beverly Hills, California.

This uprising of a newly wealthy class, or nouveau riche in Seoul, as in many cultures, presents an interesting dichotomy to the established wealth and power of the aristocracy. The newly wealthy alter their appearance through plastic surgery, exercise, and expensive, high-end fashion. This is in stark contrast to the more modest wealthy families who, through hard work or long established status, have remained in the upper echelons of society. This establishing of a new wealthy class, who have access to the best educational opportunities, a solid infrastructure, and who have the means to purchase imported high-end goods like luxury automobiles, challenges the notion of knowledge/power established by the more traditional elements of Korean society. This shift in power thus creates a tension among the aristocracy and the nouveau riche.

The song and subsequent video contain subtle clues that reinforce this claim of the newly wealthy. The lyrics of the song, while seemingly nonsensical, contain clues to the materialistic values of the nouveau riche.

***English Translation of* Gangnam Style:**
Oppa's Gangnam style
Gangnam style

A girl who is warm and graceful during the day
A classy girl who knows how to enjoy a cup of coffee
A girl whose heart gets hotter when night comes
A girl with that kind of twist

I'm a guy
A guy who is as warm as you during the day
A guy who downs his coffee before it cools down
A guy whose heart bursts when night comes
That kind of guy

Beautiful, loveable
Yes you, hey, yes you, hey
Beautiful, loveable
Yes you, hey, yes you, hey
Now let's go until the end

(Lyrics and translation courtesy of http://knowyourmeme.com/memes/gangnam-style)

The lyrics, in particular "A classy girl who knows how to enjoy a cup of coffee" can be inferred as a reference to the Western practice of Western women, in particular American women, frequenting coffee shops, such as Starbucks, and spending large amounts of money on coffee. According to Max Fisher's August 23, 2012, article in *The Atlantic*, "In Korea, there's a joke poking fun at women who eat 2,000-won (about $2) ramen for lunch and then spend 6,000 won on Starbucks coffee." They're called Doenjangnyeo, or "soybean paste women" for their propensity to scrimp on essentials so they can overspend on conspicuous luxuries, of which coffee is, believe it or not, one of the most common. "The number of coffee shops has gone up tremendously, particularly in Gangnam," Hong said. "Coffee shops have become the place where people go to be seen and spend ridiculous amounts of money." (www.theatlantic.com/international/archive/2012/08/gangnam-style-dissected-the-subversive-message-within-south-koreas-music-video-sensation/261462/#). This overindulgence in coffee can be construed as a symbol of status among the newly wealthy and probably not a practice of those accustomed to wealth.

Symbols of wealth appear throughout the video. At approximately :30, the COEX Tower (Figure 1) appears in the background. The COEX complex, operated by Coex Co. Ltd., contains a convention and exhibition center, a shopping mall, three luxury hotels, an urban airport terminal, a multiplex cinema, an aquarium, CoexArtium Theater, the Asia-Europe Meeting Tower, and the Seven Luck Casino. This complex serves as a center of business and commerce that serves upwards of 200,000 people daily. Even with the placement in the background, its positioning, looming over Psy, gives the structure salience, and reinforces the concept of the ideals that the newly wealthy of Gangnam hold dear.

Figure 1.
The COEX Tower, *Gangnam Style*, 2012.
From the source: www.youtube.com/watch?v=9bZkp7q19f0

The symbol of horses, which appears several times in the video, serves a two-fold purpose, commenting on both wealth and the type of woman Psy appears to be looking for. The appearance of what appears to be thoroughbred horses at :18 (Figure 2) are an allusion to the ownership of horses as a symbol of wealth in Western society. The apparent luxury of the stable and the shiny coats of the horses reinforce the claim of horse ownership as a status symbol. These symbols serve as a parody of the stereotype of the Asian obsessed with Western culture. By using these symbols, Psy is able to take ownership of the parody, and serves to parody the Gangnam District, as well.

Horses also appear in the form of a carousel, another icon of leisurely Western culture, and appeal to the pathos of living an extravagant lifestyle. The horse, in Korean culture, also makes appeals to pathos. People born during the year of the horse are said to be "skillful with money," popular, and enjoy crowds. Women born during the year of the horse are believed to be undesirable partners for marriage, due to their independence. Financial savvy, and a perceived independence for women, which could embody such traits as sexual promiscuity, can be another trait associated with the ethos of Western society.

Figure 2.
Horse Stables, *Gangnam Style*, 2012.
From the source: www.youtube.com/watch?v=9bZkp7q19f0

European luxury cars, most notably Mercedes-Benz, can be seen several times throughout the video. At 1:40, 2:43, and 3:50, these cars are featured prominently, much like in hip-hop and rap videos that have been popular since the mid-1980s in the United States and Europe. The Mercedes-Benz brand has long been lauded as a status symbol and as such plays into the *ethos* of the video.

The video also contains several parodies pertaining to the newly wealthy denizens of the Gangnam District. Psy, who himself grew up in the Gangnam District, appears to be the antithesis of the newly wealthy. He is portrayed as overweight, partying with senior citizens in buses, hanging out in semi-industrial areas, watching old men playing board games, attempting to romance beautiful women on public transportation, and dancing in a parking garage. This is all in direct contrast to the image of someone from Gangnam, the affluent, thin, young jet setter with a largely disposable income. A closer look at the video also shows women walking backward wearing large brimmed hats. This common practice in Southeast Asia is usually performed by women of working and poor classes, to aid in keeping their skin light, an indicator of wealth and privilege in Asia. Tanned skin in Asian culture is a sure indication of someone who is a laborer or farmer who works outside for long hours (Figures 3 and 4).

Figure 3.
Women Walking Backward, *Gangnam Style*, 2012.
From the source: www.youtube.com/watch?v=9bZkp7q19f0

Figure 4.
Brian Gaines, Vietnamese Rice Paddy Worker, 2010. ©2010 Brian Gaines.

The parody continues in the scene where Psy is seen walking with two models. While the three of them are dressed in expensive clothing with wind in their hair (a parody of a fashion shoot), the three of them are then bombarded by garbage and a white substance that could either be foam or confetti. This serves as a commentary on disposable Western culture and fashion, and a nod to a "grunge" style such as gutter punk or heroin chic (Figure 5).

Figure 5.
Psy and Models in Garbage, *Gangnam Style*, 2012.
From the source: www.youtube.com/watch?v=9bZkp7q19f0

The male gaze, in regard to objectifying women as well as men, is also quite prevalent in this video. In several scenes, Psy is seen trying to engage beautiful Asian women, most of whom are scantily clad, have light skin, and hair that is made to look more Caucasian. Additionally, Psy is seen in several scenes wearing a towel in a sauna as a woman would, cuddling with a large male, and both of them are admiring a half-naked tattooed man. In another scene, Psy is dancing provocatively with an androgynous person in a yellow suit. In an adjacent scene, an elevator door opens to a man dressed in shorts and a cowboy hat pelvic thrusting over Psy's head. While this isn't overtly homosexual, it appears as if it is a parody of the perceived loose sexual morals of Westerners as opposed to the more reserved Asian culture. It also somewhat parodies the reluctant acceptance of queer culture into the mainstream.

In these scenes, Psy also parodies Orientalism by holding Asian women who appear to want to look more Caucasian as an object of exoticism and desire, in much the same fashion as an American or European male would. Also, by engaging in Orientalism, Psy is challenging the notion of knowledge/power from a Eurocentric perspective as well as parodying a centuries-old practice.

While popular culture is teeming with disposable hits, misses, and moments of complete enigma, every so often a brilliantly scathing satire of that culture slips into the mainstream. With *Gangnam Style,* Psy has managed to execute that satire from a rhetorical perspective on multiple levels.

Works Cited

Fisher, Max. "Gangnam Style, Dissected: The Subversive Message Within South Korea's Music Video Sensation." *The Atlantic,* August 23, 2012, www.theatlantic.com/international/archive/2012/08/gangnam-style-dissected-the-subversive-message-within-south-koreas-music-video-sensation/261462/.

Klug, Foster and YouKyung Lee. "What is the meaning behind 'Gangnam Style' video?" *Chicago Sun-Times,* September 19, 2012, www.suntimes.com/news/world/15243653-418/story.html.

"Korean Zodiac - Animal Signs." *Customs and Traditions,* K4E Consulting, 2012, www.korea-4expats.com/article-zodiac-animals-signs-sibijisin.html.

Marrs, Meghan. "Top 25 Most Popular *YouTube* Videos Of All Time: What Makes A Video Go Viral?" *Business2Community,* October 12, 2012, http://www.business2community.com/social-media/top-25-most-popular-youtube-videos-of-all-time-what-makes-a-video-go-viral-0296832#w7kGGG1hEqepczvZ.99.

Psy, "Gangnam Style". *YouTube,* 2012. Google, Inc, www.youtube.com/watch?v=9bZkp7q19f0.

CHAPTER 5

Digital Audiences

Nicholas Douglas, a 16-year-old student in Port St. Lucie, Florida, noticed some suspicious activity near his campus locker. When he checked out his locker, he found that his iPhone had been stolen. Without any leads, the police could do nothing. Later that day, sitting with his cousin and sister, both of whom had their computers on, Douglas decided to search Facebook for traces of his stolen phone. He visited a Facebook page for a local trading service (similar to Craigslist), recognized one of the persons who had snooped around his locker, and contacted the suspect through his friend's account. When the number that called him back was his own, he knew he had the right guy and set up a sting with the aid of his school's resource officer.

While this scenario may sound more like a detective story than a rhetorical encounter, Douglas made a few clever decisions. He recognized that if the thief was stealing iPhones, he or she might be fairly tech savvy. Thus, his "audience" might be online somewhere trying to sell the stolen goods. He also realized he could use other people's avatars (his friend's) in order to mask his own identity and fool his audience, convincing him to meet in a public place. Douglas was quickly able to make use of the digital writing tools he had nearby, analyze the situation, and persuade his audience to act in the way that he wished.

The ultimate goal of any rhetorical communication is to get your audience to act (or not act) in a particular way. However, especially with digital texts, audiences also can be actors who interact with your texts in ways that go beyond simply responding to the text itself, and you should account for the possible ways this interaction occurs. In addition, your audience may not even be human. They may include search engine robots that scour the web on behalf of search engines such as Google or Bing. This chapter will offer guidance on how to research and analyze your multiple audiences and how to design different texts to maximize their activity with online, digital audiences.

Most of the decisions you make when writing will revolve around your understanding of what your audience wants, expects, likes, dislikes, and will find persuasive. Determining these preferences requires a careful analysis of your audience, and you must screen them before writing. Thinking about how the audience might act in response to other rhetorical elements such *logos, ethos,* and *pathos* is a good way to start.

Accounting for Audience

Although Chapter 3 provides a much more detailed discussion about how you should account for audience when developing an argument, this section reiterates some of the important points and recasts them from a digital perspective. As discussed throughout the book, it is important to consider how your audience will react to your text. To ensure they take the intended action you wish them to take, it's best to identify your primary audiences. However, digital writing sometimes requires you to write for multiple audiences in tandem with your primary audience.

Primary and secondary audiences

Your primary audience is who you want to communicate with directly. This is the audience that will take the most direct interest in your writing, that will act on the requests you make, and the one you most need to persuade and account for as you develop your argument. However, although your primary audience will be the one to act upon your writing, secondary audiences might also take an interest in your writing and help you indirectly persuade your primary audience. For example, if you wanted your campus to protect an environmentally sensitive area on campus from further development, you would probably write directly to the university's president or another administrator. However, secondary audiences, such as other concerned students, faculty, local environmental groups, or other stakeholders, might help you persuade the primary audience if they also have the opportunity to hear your appeal. In other words, by also accounting for and arguing toward the secondary audience, you can help your chances of persuading the primary audience.

With digital writing technologies, this distinction between primary and secondary audience can become blurred. As discussed later in the chapter, you sometimes have to account for nonhuman audiences such as search engine robots. Although your primary audience is a human audience, search engine robots are often the first to "read" your writing, indexing it for search engines so it will appear in search engine results, which helps you reach the primary audience. When thinking about the practices of search engine optimization below, you should consider how both humans and nonhumans become a primary audience.

Tertiary audience

Beyond primary and secondary audiences, other readers might come across your document and take notice. Although this third audience might not take direct action or offer advice, they might still make a judgment upon you as a writer based on your writing. For instance, if you create a YouTube response for your instructor based on the assignment in this book, your primary audience would probably be the author of the original YouTube video, with the secondary audience those who follow this author and could chime in with comments. However, other audience members who happen to come across the video through other searches would make up this third audience. They may have no direct stake in your argument, but still form a judgment based on your response. Thus, although any immediate writing might not be directed at them, this tertiary audience could become a primary or secondary audience in the future, and so you want to make sure your writing reflects well upon your *ethos*.

Social audience

Although messages have always been circulated by listeners, circulation becomes instantaneous and is multiplied through digital technologies. Instead of making photocopies and handing them out one person at a time, you can now send a message instantly to millions of readers. Digital rhetoric leverages this capability to not only reach an initial audience, but also to encourage that audience to further spread your message through forwards, retweets, shares, and other tools that promote the spreading of digital writing.

Because of the presence of social media, we might say that everyone is a tertiary audience member. But moreover, they are also social audiences, reading, responding to, commenting on, and retweeting what you write. Because of this interactivity and the ability for one of your texts to quickly circulate, you should consider how such an audience might help you reach primary and secondary audiences. Even though a social audience may neither be able to take direct action, nor directly influence the primary audience, they can still spread your text and create interest, which will help secondary audiences notice your writing. As a digital writer, you need to be keenly aware of where your document may end up, and how it might be reappropriated. While you can't account for every potential audience, you should at least consider the negative consequences of placing a particular text online.

Selecting Elements for a Text

When you write digitally, especially when you combine images with words, you can think of writing as selecting from a database of material from which you choose elements, combine them, and make something new. How these different parts relate affects how the audience will respond to the overall text. As an analogy, you might consider the way a director selects actors for a movie production. To screen actors for a film is—in some ways—to literally screen them by placing them on film and seeing how they appear on the screen (Figure 5.1). How do they look? How do they move? How do they relate to other actors on a flat, two-dimensional medium? Just as you should user-test your designs before posting them online, directors want to see how an actor will test before casting him.

Credit: Everett Collection

Figure 5.1
This was a successful screen test for Henry Thomas for the movie E.T.

www.youtube.com/
watch?v=VzCeOqBFu6w&list=PLF0548378A4359F2B

Credit: Everett
Collection

Credit: Everett Collection

Figure 5.2
Can you imagine Lance Henriksen as the terminator?

Figure 5.3
Of course, Arnold Schwarzenegger got the part.

Just think how different some well-known movies might be with a different cast. For example, in the film, *The Terminator*, director James Cameron originally considered Lance Henriksen for the lead role (Figure 5.2). However, after Arnold Schwarzenegger read for the part of Kyle Reese, Cameron decided to "revise" his choices, placing Schwarzenegger in the title role (Figure 5.3). Henriksen was cast as a minor character and still appeared in the film, but the movie would have been much different without Schwarzenegger as the overbuilt, intimidating presence, not to mention his signature line, "I'll be back." Luckily, most elements in your text, like actors for roles, are digital, that is, interchangeable and rearrangeable, allowing you to be flexible as you write.

If you're a fan of the *Indiana Jones* movies, you might think that Harrison Ford is the perfect choice to play Indiana; however, he wasn't the first choice. George Lucas originally considered Tom Selleck to play the part (Figure 5.4). Selleck auditioned for the role but had already signed a contract to play Thomas Magnum in the television series, *Magnum P.I.*, when Lucas offered him the role. CBS, who created *Magnum P.I.*, wouldn't release Selleck from his contract, and because of this contractual conflict, Lucas and Steven Spielberg selected Ford for the part (Figure 5.5). You may find that contractual or legal conflicts, such as copyright issues around already existing media, force you to choose elements in a text that aren't your first choice. However, if you think creatively about what your audience really needs, you can usually overcome such constraints.

Credit: Everett Collection

Credit: Everett Collection

Figure 5.4
Tom Selleck in Hawaii to shoot *Magnum P.I.*

Figure 5.5
Now in his 70s, Harrison Ford still has what it takes to play Indiana Jones.

This analogy of film casting can be useful in thinking about how to "cast" your own production, even if it doesn't consist of live humans. Instead, your "actors" become the different digital elements that you include in the design—from images, to typefaces, to medium, to environment—all of which have to fit and work together for a text to be effective and act on your behalf toward your target audience.

You might select visual elements based on whether they "look" right for the role. For instance, you might use a certain typography because it looks right for a title or header, or because it fits a certain persona you're trying to capture for the tone of the text, or you may choose an image because its colors fit the color scheme of the design. If the image doesn't look quite right, you can use a digital photo editor (instead of makeup) to augment it.

You might think of an actor's performance as reflecting the versatility of a particular textual element. A particular element might look like it fits naturally and conveys a particular message in one setting, but if the design of that text changes or is converted from one kind of genre (flyer) to another (video), will the element have the same effect?

Rhetorical Continuities

In terms of writing, an author's "voice" often becomes synonymous with an author's "style." You can also look for this kind of voice-as-style in digital texts. If you analyze a design as a whole, does it have an overall style, a voice, which transcends the individual parts? Do the textual elements have a particular voice or tone that matches the message you want to send? Even though an email often doesn't make the same use of images and visual elements as a website or blog post might, the format and layout (placing elements into discreet sections, using headers or bullet points) tells the audience about your organizational skills and attention to detail.

Finally, getting a second opinion—either through peer review or by having someone you trust analyze your writing—is important when deciding on how to screen individual elements for your overall project. Some elements might not work the way you see it, or some may be unnecessary and actually detract from the goal and purpose of your design. Since, hopefully, lots of eyes will fall upon your text, you want to make sure you solicit feedback from lots of people before making your design public.

Building

Link

Choose two or three movies you love to watch in which the main character is iconic (such as Arnold Schwarzenegger as the Terminator). Analyze why you think the actor is a good choice for the role. Now, for each movie, recast the main character of the film with other actors. How would the movie change? How do you think audiences would react to the main character? How does the actor embody rhetorical appeals such as *logos, ethos, pathos,* or even *kairos*? Write a thesis statement that makes the claim for your choice of actor, and include reasons and evidence for why you think this actor should be cast in the role. Share your casting ideas with the class, and discuss how they would react to such a change and if they're persuaded by your argument.

Engine

Search

Think of a fictional work you've read lately. If you had to cast the various characters for a movie, whom would you consider? Why? How would you consider the traits mentioned here, such as chemistry, looks, performance, and voice? Would you use well-known actors, or do you have people in your own life (who are not celebrities) that you would cast instead? Create a casting list, and for each character state your claim, reasons, and evidence for why a director might choose each actor. Share your suggestions with the class.

Future Audiences

Usually, you think about a future audience when writing. You also write for an imagined audience, an audience you try to predict will be like your actual audience. While these two audiences differ in many ways, some audiences are more futuristic and imaginary than others. The following examples provide some insights toward screening audiences you will probably never meet and toward thinking about how your designs will need to operate long into the future to affect those audiences.

This first example uses writing for a world that would no longer be digital. According to a report by the U.S. National Academy of Sciences, current stores of nuclear waste could take as long as three million years to decay to normal levels. Because of this danger, the world's nuclear waste must be safely stored to shield humans from the radiation emitted from spent fuel rods and other forms of used nuclear materials. Even when safely stored, humans must be warned of the potential dangers at these storage sites, for the waste stored in them can pose danger for tens to hundreds of thousands of years.

Since humans have existed for much less time than it takes nuclear waste to decay, no one knows what languages, cultures, or even physical features will exist at that time. Governments and scientists have to design technical documentation that can warn future audiences about the impending threats, warning them not to enter waste facilities. This task is quite difficult. As an analogy, consider how you would tackle trying to read the inscriptions on the Egyptian pyramids if you were the first to find them. While you might have unleashed the curse of King Tutankhamen, future archaeologists might unleash something much worse.

Such future warnings are already being designed and created, but this rhetorical situation raises certain questions about future audiences that may be unan-

DIGITAL Connections

New Symbol Launched to Warn Public About Radiation Dangers

Press release by the IAEA

With radiating waves, a skull and crossbones, and a running person, a new ionizing radiation warning symbol is being introduced to supplement the traditional international symbol for radiation, the three cornered trefoil.

The new symbol is being launched today by the IAEA and the International Organization for Standardization (ISO) to help reduce needless deaths and serious injuries from accidental exposure to large radioactive sources. It will serve as a supplementary warning to the trefoil, which has no intuitive meaning and little recognition beyond those educated in its significance.

The new symbol is aimed at alerting anyone, anywhere to the potential dangers of being close to a large source of ionizing radiation, the result of a five-year project conducted in 11 countries

The long-standing international sign for radiation appears in Figure 5.6. While this warning sign is an elegant symbol, it doesn't offer much other context. In an attempt to update it, the International Atomic Energy Agency (IAEA) revised the warning to the one in Figure 5.7. The IAEA describes it in this Digital Connections.

From this description, you can see how thoroughly the IAEA attempted to account for audience when designing the new warning label. Its target audience is literally anyone and everyone, and the research the organization conducted reflects this.

Figure 5.6
Original radiation warning sign outside the Chernobyl accident site

Credit: International Atomic Energy Agency

Figure 5.7
New radiation warning sign

around the world. The symbol was tested with different population groups—mixed ages, varying educational backgrounds, male and female—to ensure that its message of "danger—stay away" was crystal clear and understood by all.

The new symbol, developed by human factor experts, graphic artists, and radiation protection experts, was tested by the Gallup Institute on a total of 1,650 individuals in Brazil, Mexico, Morocco, Kenya, Saudi Arabia, China, India, Thailand, Poland, Ukraine and the United States.

 **DIGITAL Connections**

Building a Better Radiation Warning Symbol

By John Brownlee

> John Brownlee, writing for *Wired* magazine, discusses the problem of the new warning that could occur despite extensive user testing by the IAEA.

The old radiation symbol was certainly a timeless masterpiece of paranoid Cold War aesthetics, but it only makes sense if you already know what it means. If confronted with the relic of such a symbol on the side of a barrel of toxic ooze that has been dug-up a hundred thousand years from now, how would the super-intelligent space monkeys of the future know it was a danger to them? The radiation warning symbol would tell them nothing: our simian descendants would crack open that container with an industrial sized can opener and start smearing the fluorescent toxic waste through their hair like styling gel.

To prevent this, the International Atomic Energy Agency is launching a new symbol, which they hope more clearly spells out the threat to those who don't already know what a radiation symbol means. But what is that threat? According to the new symbol, it's when a blowing fan causes a gigantic skull to chase a man into the side of an equilateral triangle, which then probably knocks him cold.

There's a lot of weirdo problems with this symbol, the biggest one being that it still uses the original radiation symbol without any sense of context.

You want to warn people a hundred thousand years in the future that there's dangerous radioactive elements about? All you need is two panels stenciled on the side of every barrel of nuclear sludge (Figure 5.8). In panel one, a monkey wearing a space suit and with a throbbing, exposed brain levers open a barrel of sludge. From the sun in the background of the panel, you can tell it's early morning. And in panel two, the monkey is just a skeleton standing in a sloughed-off puddle of his own melted skin at midnight, silently screaming before the open background. An arrow leads readers in the intended direction of the comic. Who's going to mistake that warning sign?

Credit: Ben Crum

Figure 5.8
You shouldn't monkey around with radiation.

Credit: U.S. Dept. of Energy

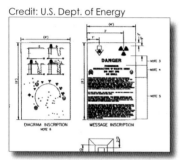

Figure 5.9
The plans for these larger markers include inscribing them in seven languages.

In addition to the new symbol, some locations, such as the Waste Isolation Pilot Plant (WIPP) in Carlsbad, New Mexico, will include 25-foot tall granite markers located around the WIPP facility, engraved with a message in seven languages: English, Spanish, French, Russian, Chinese, Arabic, and Navajo (Figure 5.9). Even if several of these languages become extinct or radically altered, future audiences will hopefully be able to make sense of the text should they still use any of the other seven languages.

In addition to these monument-size markers, the WIPP facility also will include 9-inch clay markers buried throughout the site, information rooms at the surface and underground, as well as radar reflectors and magnets, so future detection technologies should be able to tell that something strange is located at the site (Figure 5.10).

To tackle this problem, WIPP uses a variety of branding strategies, including different kinds of markers, several languages, and other techniques to get the

Credit: U.S. Dept. of Energy

⚠ DANGER ☢
POISONOUS RADIOACTIVE
WASTE HERE
DO NOT DIG OR DRILL

Figure 5.10
These 9-inch clay markers will be buried throughout the site.

audience's attention and ensure the message is understood. Similarly, companies often create many different kinds of advertisements, in diverse languages, using focus groups and test screenings to make sure the ad resonates with each kind of audience. Even though the WIPP location isn't trying to sell a product, many of its problems and tactics relate to those used by marketing companies. Of course, any brand message can fail, and only time (a lot of time) will tell if the WIPP site and IAEA are successful in their strategy.

KLM, Inc., a management consulting company, frames the radioactivity communication problem in terms of branding:

> *If there ever was a brand challenge, this could be it. How can we communicate the mortal, and almost unending, danger of radioactive waste across all present and future cultures and civilizations and possibly, even to nonhuman alien beings from outer space?*

These examples are important for you to consider because digital texts, more so than written documents, can potentially last much longer, circulate more widely, and be received by more audiences. This means you should thoroughly consider all your possible audiences when designing and composing a digital text. While you might not consciously compose for an audience that will live 10,000 years from now, it's quite possible that such audiences will be able to search some future database or digital museum for ancient Facebook posts or digital documents, some of which might be yours. You might not care what they think about your writing, but maybe you should. However, future audiences just one, five, or ten years in the future could have significant meaning for your job, relationship, or other aspects of your life. Keep the future audiences of your digital texts in mind.

Building

Link

Revisit the nuclear waste example above. Research more into this issue and what particular audiences the IAEA or WIPP considered. Can you think of any potential audience members that they neglected? Can you think of alternative ways to reach these audiences? Argue why you think IAEA or WIPP should consider another audience that they neglected. Remember to support your claim with reasons and evidence.

Search

Engine

Using the information in this example, as well as the research you conducted in the Link Building prompt above, design your own warning symbol for the nuclear waste site and a strategy for branding the WIPP location. How would it differ from the current WIPP strategy and IAEA symbol already in use? How would it accommodate audiences better than the current strategy? Make a claim based on your analysis, and support it with reasons and evidence.

Extraterrestrial Audiences

The nuclear waste example could apply to alien visitors as well. How would you warn these E.T.s to stay away from radioactive dump sites so they don't accidently unleash an intergalactic disaster? Moreover, if future cultures can't recognize current symbols or languages, how would a being from another planet? While this hypothetical audience might seem far-fetched, many attempts have been made to create messages for this audience. While you might never have to construct a text for aliens, thinking about such a task can help you consider earthly audiences in a more sophisticated way.

Figure 5.11
Carl Sagan, pictured here, helped to create the Pioneer 10 plaque.

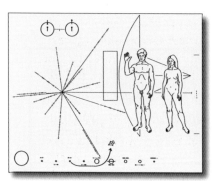

Figure 5.12
Pioneer 10 plaque designed by Carl Sagan and Frank Drake with the artwork by Linda Salzman Sagan

In 1972, the National Aeronautic and Space Administration (NASA) planned to launch the Pioneer 10 spacecraft (and, a year later, the Pioneer 11), which would be the first human-built object to leave the solar system.

In case an alien species intercepted the spacecraft, journalist Eric Burgess suggested that the Pioneer should carry some sort of message to inform the aliens about the spacecraft's origins.

Burgess approached Carl Sagan, who had previously discussed ways humans might communicate with extraterrestrials, and NASA agreed to let Sagan design a message to be attached to the Pioneer 10 (Sagan's wife at the time, Linda Salzman Sagan, created the artwork for the design).

Sagan chose to create a visual message in the form of a metal plaque (see Figures 5.11 and 5.12). Given the limited space, he could only convey limited information, and selected details he thought his audience might want to know. First, he included basic scientific facts he figured any intelligent, space-going life form would already know, such as the most abundant element in the universe, hydrogen, and its atomic properties (top-left corner).

The large, line-based schematic on the left indicates the position of the sun in relation to the center of the Milky Way galaxy, as well as fourteen other pulsar stars. Portraying this many pulsars provides a way to ensure the aliens can triangulate the origin of the spacecraft, even if some pulsars are missing, much as the multiple languages used at the WIPP location allow for cross-referencing of different languages.

The longest line that extends to the right represents the sun. Note how this line reaches toward the proximity of the human diagrams, helping to establish a line of trajectory to the creators of the spacecraft. To help ensure that aliens can find Pioneer 10's point of origin, Sagan also included a diagram of the solar system, noting the trajectory of the spacecraft from the third planet from the sun, Earth.

Of course, now that Pluto is no longer a "planet," one should hope that any aliens don't count from the outside of the solar system, otherwise they might deduce the spacecraft was launched from Venus. Aliens, like many human cultures, might read from right to left instead of left to right, or they may try to read the plaque upside down. In addition, when the plaque first appeared publicly, *Scientific American* pointed out that the arrow-based symbol derives from arrows used for hunting and warfare. If an extraterrestrial audience never invented such tools, they would be unclear the arrow represents direction and movement. Then again, all of this assumes that they categorize "planet" the same way humans do, or that they even reason with "categories" at all.

Finally, a diagram of human beings appears on the right side of the plaque. This diagram offers a nude perspective with most of the anatomical features of both a male and female. While many humans had negative reactions to depicting these figures in the nude, this choice probably makes sense to beings who might not use clothing.

Sagan also designed the male to provide the typical gesture of a wave. Of course, Sagan had no idea how an alien race might interpret this gesture; they might find that it offers a sign of aggression. However, Sagan also wanted to show that humans have limbs that can be articulated, as well as an opposable thumb. Behind the diagram of the humans is a line drawing of the Pioneer 10 spacecraft itself, drawn to scale to provide a way for aliens to determine the approximate size of earthlings.

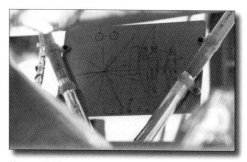

Figure 5.13
The Pioneer 10 plaque was mounted so that it faced into the space probe.

You also might think about the constraints between balancing environment with audience, especially considering that most devices that read digital texts don't do very well in harsh conditions. As you can see in Figure 5.13, NASA decided to place the plaque facing toward the spacecraft. Given the amount of small space debris Pioneer 10 might encounter, this orientation helps protect the message from being destroyed. In addition, the material of the plaque was made of gold-anodized aluminum to minimize corrosion (since gold does not rust). Hopefully, the aliens that intercept the spacecraft will eventually remove the plaque and notice the image (even if they notice with senses other than sight). However, they might also miss it, or assume the piece of metal is blank on both sides.

Building Link

Research and analyze later plaques that were designed for spacecraft launched after Pioneer 10, such as the Voyager, which contained a golden "record." How and why did NASA change the design? What modern ways of extraterrestrial communication are being used, if any? How have these designs and media changed? Which seem the most probable of being decoded by an alien race? Write a brief essay that argues which design you think seems the best, and make sure to support your claim with reasons and evidence.

Search Engine

Assume that you're an alien from another planet who just landed on Earth. As you explore, you find a dime on the surface of the planet. Since you have no preexisting knowledge of the planet's cultures or languages, and thus can't decode the writing, what kind of information can you deduce from the other features of the dime? Analyze the possible options, and create a list of possible meanings or assumptions about humans, and share them with the class.

Transnational Audiences

While you will probably never have to write for audiences that will exist 10,000 years from now, nor extraterrestrials, you do have to consider the various ways in which audiences that do not share your language or culture might view your digital texts. Figure 5.14 demonstrates a simple failure to communicate with a transnational audience. This image provides visual instructions on how to remove fallen rocks from a railroad track for South African miners who could not read alphabetic text.

Credit: William Horton, *Technical Communication*. Copyright © 1993 by Society for Technical Communication (STC).

Figure 5.14
While English speakers read this graphic from left to right, other cultures may read it from right to left.

At first glance, the image provides a pretty clear set of instructions. In frame one, the miner finds a rock; in frame two, the miner picks up the rock; in frame three, the miner carts the rock away. For the miners, the image also provides a pretty clear set of instructions. In frame one, cart a rock to the tracks; in frame two, set the rock on the tracks; in frame three, leave the rock on the tracks. As you've probably concluded, the South African miners read the image from right to left (as many cultures read), and thus for them the instructions meant the opposite of what they were intended to convey by the image's creator. A simple user test or conversation with some of the miners might have avoided this error, but the designer failed to screen his audience properly.

Building

Link

Analyze various traffic signs used in other countries. How well do these signs match with U.S. traffic signs? How do they differ? How might you read these signs differently than their intended meaning? Could accidents result from these misreadings? Write a short essay that makes a claim based on your findings. Remember to support your claim with reasons and evidence.

Engine

Search

Return to the traffic signs you analyzed in the prompt above. How do these signs make use of *pathos, ethos, logos,* or *kairos* to appeal to their readers? Do their shapes convey a particular appeal? Their colors? The typefaces? Using reasons and evidence as support, make an argument about how you think these traffic signs make use of rhetorical appeals.

It's easy to screen for a single, local transnational audience. When you're McDonald's, and serve 68 million customers a day with restaurants in 119 countries, user testing and accounting for these various audiences can be more difficult. To make their nutritional information more globalized so anyone could understand protein from carbohydrates, McDonald's attempted to create universal icons to represent each of these categories. The fast-food giant wanted to avoid any icons that might be ambiguous in meaning, especially meanings that might offend other cultures. To avoid these pitfalls, McDonald's teamed up with the marketing firm ENLASO to head the research. As Maxwell Hoffmann explains:

> McDonald's and ENLASO focused on five main nutrient visuals (calories, fat, carbohydrates, protein, salt) that would be used globally on packaging, and also designed and evaluated half a dozen supplemental nutrient visuals that might be needed in some locales. The team had to deal with four main challenges:
>
> 1. What visuals can communicate the desired nutrients?
> 2. Does the visual work in 109 countries without evoking negative or socially/politically inappropriate connotations?
> 3. Will the visual print or display well in all media, including packaging?
> 4. Does anyone else already own rights to the image that might prevent it from being used in this context?

Figure 5.15 depicts a screenshot from McDonald's nutritional information app that also shows the final icons that were agreed upon. However, several other icons were considered before these icons were selected.

For example, Figure 5.16 is one of the early icons that ENLASO tested. Take a moment and analyze the icon. What do you see? While McDonald's intended the image to represent grain or wheat, ENLASO ultimately classified it as an icon at high risk of being misinterpreted based on their market research. What did many respondents think it looked like?

A "scary alien" of course, such as that in Figure 5.17, which is the brand mark used for Dell's Alienware line of computers. Other ambiguous icons were also rejected. Many thought Figure 5.18 looked like either a slippery slope or the neck and head of a bird, perhaps signifying a bird sanctuary, while some users thought Figure 5.19 resembled a marijuana plant.

Other icons also confused transnational audiences. Besides calories, protein, fat, carbohydrates, and salt, McDonald's attempted to create icons for other nutritional information, such as calcium. Figure 5.20 depicts an original design of a bone, which makes sense when connected to calcium.

However, some users thought of dog bones or dog food when looking at the icon, which also has potentially insulting meanings in some Muslim cultures.

Credit: McDonald's

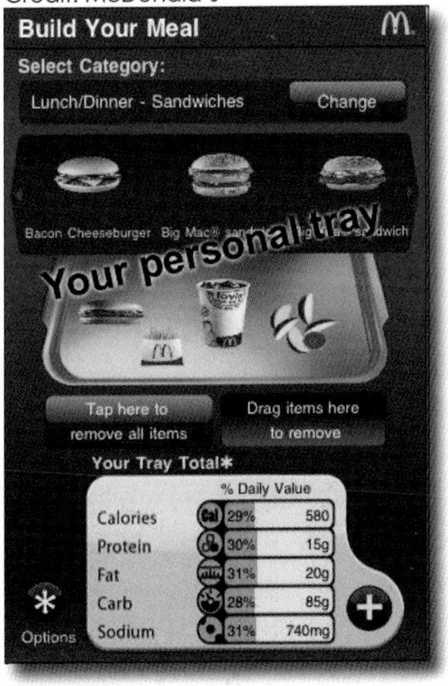

Figure 5.15
This McDonald's nutritional counter shows the final nutritional icons.

Figure 5.16
This early nutritional icon referring to "fiber" was widely interpreted as being an "alien."

ALIENWARE

Figure 5.17
If you look at Dell's Alienware brand mark, you can see why many saw Figure 5.16 as an alien.
Credit: Dell

Figure 5.18
This early nutritional icon for "fiber" was widely interpreted as being a "bird."

Figure 5.19
This early nutritional icon for "fiber" was widely interpreted as being a "marijuana plant."

Figure 5.20
While you might think of a "bone" as referring to calcium, not all audiences understood it this way.

Even if a design looks innocent at first, it might be perceived by audiences from other nations and cultures as unclear, or even worse, insulting. Do your best to research the cultures you're writing for, and when possible, get feedback from members of those cultures to avoid any negative reactions.

Building

Link

Create an icon for "candy" with transnational audiences in mind, similar to what McDonald's attempts in the example above. Consider how your icon uses rhetorical appeals, such as *logos*, *ethos*, or *pathos*, to reach your audience. After you've created the icon, analyze how different cultures think of candy. Some might consider candy to mean all kinds of sweets, while others have specific ideas of what a "candy" is. Also, think critically about what other objects your icon might resemble for these audiences. Once you've gathered this information, revise the icon to better reflect your research, and share both icons with the class.

Engine

Search

Suppose you work for a design firm and you're hired to create a company brand mark for a fish and aquarium shop that is opening stores in both the United States and China. How would you analyze your audience? What kinds of information would you gather to discern the differences between the two nations? Would you also have to consider cultural variance in each country as well? What kinds of design choices might you have to make so that each audience recognizes that the brand mark is for "pet" fish and not "food" fish? After you create the brand mark, how would you ensure the audience responds to it in a desirable way? Compile a research plan of what you think you would need to consider, and share this plan with the class.

Digital Audiences

Although the previous examples provide extreme possibilities for your audience, you'll most likely deal with more "earthly" readers of your texts. However, this doesn't mean that all of your audiences will be human. More and more, the audiences that read your digital texts are lines of computer code called "web robots." Human and nonhuman alike, both of these audiences will interact with your texts in ways not possible with printed documents, and you should be aware of how you might construct your texts in order to reach them and get your point across.

Audience as actors: rhetorical velocity

So far, this chapter has mainly considered how audiences use the texts that writers produce. In this sense, they become actors but usually as end users. However, audiences also can become actors that serve your rhetorical purposes. Jim Ridolfo and Dànielle Nicole DeVoss have theorized such a practice they call "rhetorical velocity" through which a rhetor anticipates how her audience will make use of a particular text or document to further her own purposes.

For instance, Ridolfo and DeVoss offer the example of an author disseminating a press release. Rather than this press release simply being read, the author anticipates that the audience will remix and remediate it into other texts, such as online or print news articles, blogs, or video content, whether live or recorded. In this way, the original audience doesn't just consume a text but reshapes and delivers this text to other audiences, who then may remix it again. The press release reaches a maximum velocity where as many people see it as possible, thanks to the actions of these audience-actors.

You might say that comedian Stephen Colbert practiced rhetorical velocity on his television show *The Colbert Report*. Occasionally, Colbert offered a "Green Screen Challenge," in which he filmed himself doing something in front of a green screen (used for special effects), and then distributed the video footage on his website (Figure 5.21). He challenged his audience to take that video footage and edit and remix it to create something new. His audience, who become authors, uploaded the new videos to his site, and he played them on the air, providing content for his show.

The band the Decemberists mimic this idea by asking fans to create their own music videos of the band playing their song "O Valencia!" in front of a green screen. This request was noted by Colbert, who, in gest, accused the Decemberists of stealing his idea and challenged them to a guitar duel, further using the original

Credit: Comedy Central/Viacom Entertainment Group

Figure 5.21
Stephen Colbert's Green Screen Challenge prompted audience participation that also produced content for the show.

Credit: Comedy Central/Viacom Entertainment Group

Figure 5.22
Colbert would reuse his Green Screen Challenge to create a "feud" with the band the Decemberists.

green screen idea to create new material for the show (Figure 5.22). The "Green Screen Challenge" creates a more nuanced relationship between author and audience that turns the audience into actors and the author into the audience.

Credit: Volkswagen/Deutsch, Inc.

Figure 5.23
This Volkswagen commercial was widely shared.
https://www.youtube.com/watch?v=Feq0ypUnv3k

Viral videos also exhibit some characteristics of rhetorical velocity. In 2011, Volkswagen released a Super Bowl advertisement in which a child dressed as Darth Vader attempts to use the Force to move objects (Figure 5.23). This video quickly spread across the Internet, and as the online advertising industry magazine *Advertising Age* states, "With 600 placements, the video is on pace to become one of the most-watched viral ads of all time."

The next year, Volkswagen created a trailer for its actual Super Bowl advertisement, generating buzz for a commercial as movie companies do for their films. While such advertisements do not necessarily invite users to manipulate and repost their works of media, the companies that produce them are hoping audiences will actively share the videos through YouTube, Facebook, and Twitter, spreading the commercials to a much wider audience.

Credit: Blendtec

Figure 5.24
Will it blend? This question has made it a popular meme.
www.youtube.com/watch?v=lAl28d6tbko

Finally, Internet memes also can integrate users and make them into actors. Some companies have begun to create their own memes, which circulate online. For instance, the company Blendtec, which makes blenders, created a meme called "Will It Blend?" in which they attempt to blend a variety of objects (Figure 5.24).

DIGITAL Connections

How to Effectively Market with Memes (Without Forcing It)

By Matthew Branson

Virgin Media opted to use an existing meme for their marketing and advertising campaigns. Recently, "Success Kid" has been spotted on their advertisements and website (Figure 5.25). This adorable, fist-pumping boy is a variant of a meme born on Flickr in 2007.

> Other companies, such as Virgin Media, incorporate existing memes created by others as a way to tap into the recognition of the meme. Consider this article from Matthew Branson from *BlueGlass Archive*.

Credit: Stephen Cannon

Tim just realised his parents get **HD channels** at no extra cost.

primesight

Figure 5.25
Virgin Media used a preexisting meme to sell its product.

Pros: Using "Success Kid," Virgin Media can tap into a new audience without alienating any of their other customers. If their users don't know about "Success Kid," they will simply see a cute mascot. If they do know about the meme, they could associate him with the brand and generate potentially risk-free traffic. Such a campaign requires significant research about your customers.

Cons: Without actively engaging in the meme's community and encouraging the growth of it, it could shorten the meme's lifespan and the source of free traffic. Eventually, the meme could lose popularity and leave Virgin Media looking for a new one.

Also, if the buzz behind the meme is not being properly tracked, things could take a turn for the worst if the meme were to change. Without seeing Virgin Media's results, it's impossible to tell whether or not this strategy will bring them long-term success. It

> In this case, the creator and subject of the photograph become actors in the design of an advertisement of which they are also a potential audience.

is still an interesting take on leveraging memes for marketing and paves the way for future companies.

[...]

FreeCreditReport.com's foray into the world of Internet memes came to an abrupt halt. In 2007, after being targeted by two major lawsuits, the company attempted to rebuild its brand by releasing online videos and commercials depicting people with poor credit being helped by its services.

Internet communities soon caught wind of the company's history, however, and began creating their own parody videos poking fun at the company's services (even the FTC joined in). These spread virally across the Internet, further damaging the brand. Since then, the company has had to refocus its efforts in other campaigns.

The moral of the story is that Internet memes can work both ways—for you or against you. It's very important to properly research any marketing campaign before starting it to minimize your chances of being labeled something you may not be able to hide from.

Building

Link

Visit www.knowyourmeme.com, and analyze the various memes on the site. Why do you think these memes gather audience attention and participation? What features do they all share? How does each meme invite participation beyond simply viewing the clip? How does each meme use rhetorical appeals, such as *logos*, *pathos*, or *ethos*, to help reach its audience? After you've analyzed these memes, develop a claim based on your answers to these questions. Make sure to include reasons and evidence for your claim.

Engine

Search

Consider your favorite Internet memes and viral videos. Analyze what they have in common. Why do you consider them worth watching? Why do you think others watch them? Have you shared any of these memes or videos online with friends? Why or why not? Write a short essay that argues your claims above, and make sure you include reasons and evidence to support these claims.

Nonhuman digital audiences

You may think your online audience consists of humans. Who else would be visiting your website or online documents? Those aliens mentioned earlier? Perhaps. More likely, though, your website is read by robots. No, not alien robots; instead, most web traffic is driven by nonhuman audiences such as search engines and web robots.

These robots scour the web looking for connections or associations between key words that search engine users enter, what kinds of search engine results they click on, and how such key words appear on other sites. Essentially, these robots try to make web searches more useful so when you search for something like "Internet memes" you get relevant content.

DIGITAL Connections

51 Percent of Total Online Traffic Is Non-Human

By Peter Murray

It probably is no surprise to most that much of online traffic isn't human. Hacker software, spam, or innocuous data collection from search engines all get their slice of the bandwidth pie. But what might surprise you is exactly how much bandwidth is consumed by humans versus non-humans. It's pretty much an even split.

> Consider this article by Peter Murray, published on singularity-hub.com. What are the rhetorical implications of more than half of web traffic being nonhuman?

Actually, a slight lead goes to the non-human, web-surfing robots.

According to a report by Internet security company, Incapsula, 51 percent of total online traffic is non-human. There's more bad news. Of the 51 percent, 20 percent of the traffic is accounted for by search engines, the other 31 percent are the bad bots.

Here's the breakdown:

- 49 percent human traffic, 51 percent non-human traffic

Non-human traffic:

- 5 percent hacking tools
- 2 percent comment spammers

- 5 percent "scrapers," software that posts the contents of your website to other websites, steals email addresses for spamming, or reverse engineers your website's pricing and business models

- 19 percent other sorts of spies that are competitive analyzers, sifting your website for key word and SEO (search engine optimization) data to help give them a competitive edge in climbing the search engine ladder

- 20 percent search engines and other benevolent bot traffic

The report was based on data compiled from 1,000 of Incapsula customer websites.

We always knew it was us against the machines. But until now the arms race had generally referred to virus versus anti-virus, malware versus anti-malware. Symantec wasn't warning us about the perils of non-human traffic. For web-based business owners though, that extra traffic can turn into lost business. TagMan recently reported that a delay of just one second in web page load time decreases page views by 11 percent, customer satisfaction by 16 percent, and conversions—the number of people who buy something divided by the number of visits—by 6.7 percent. Incapsula says it's easy enough to get around the hacker, scraper, and spam software, but that most website owners aren't equipped to spot the infiltrators.

We already knew that robots did some amazing things, now we learn that they're doing things we're not even aware of—at least not the extent. They're not alive, yet they're surfing the web more than we are. So who will win in the end, human or machine? Better monitoring tools—for free— would help. You can't get rid of the critters if you don't know they're there in the first place.

In relation to rhetorical velocity, you can make rhetorical use of nonhuman audiences. You can use search engine robots, writing so they index pages according to key words and help other audiences find your texts. For example, if you wanted to get search engine robots to index a site about apartments in your town, you would include key words in the HTML code such as "apartments," "rental units," "rental houses," or other terms you think a human audience would enter. Doing so becomes a means of reaching and persuading your audience to view your page.

While thinking about robots, you also have to screen your human audiences and how you think they'll search for your product or service. In addition, especially for this particular search, you should think about location. Because your apartments are probably in a fixed geographical area, you should include geographical key words within the site as well, such as the city in which the apartments are located, as well as the state (since many states have identical city names).

Such key words appear in several places. One of these locations is the <meta> information in the header of a website (Figure 5.26). This information is specifically targeted at web robots, and the human audience never sees it unless they right-click on a site and select "view source."

```
<meta name="robots" content="noodp, noydir" /><meta name="description" content="
Facebook is a social utility that connects people with friends and others who work,
study and live around them. People use Facebook to keep up with friends, upload an
unlimited number of photos, post links and videos, and learn more about the people they
meet." />
```

Figure 5.26
Nonhuman audiences, such as search engines, use metadata to index websites.

One of the other primary locations is within the page content itself, which is seen by both robots and humans. However, writing for each of these audiences requires a rhetorical and stylistic balance. Typically, the more times you include a key word such as "apartments" in a paragraph, the more a robot will think that the key word "apartment" is relevant to your page.

However, as you've probably learned from other writing classes, using the same word too many times in a sentence or paragraph does not meet most humans' stylistic preferences. For example, if you used the word "apartments" ten times in a single paragraph, the human audience would probably think your writing was too repetitive. While you might use synonyms to overcome this stylistic blunder, these synonyms can detract from how the web robot will view your page. Addressing both of these audiences is tricky, but you need to consider them simultaneously, for if the web robot doesn't think your site is relevant to a particular key word, then you'll never reach your final human audience.

 **DIGITAL Connections**

Are You Following a Bot?

By Andy Isaacson

One day last February, a Twitter user in California named Billy received a

In addition to simply posing as audiences, web robots sometimes become actors that respond to writing.

tweet from @JamesMTitus, identified in his profile as a "24-year-old dude" from Christchurch, New Zealand, who had the avatar of a tabby cat. "If you could bring one character to life from

Andy Isaacson, writing for *The Atlantic*, discusses this phenomenon.

your favorite book, who would it be?" @JamesMTitus asked. Billy tweeted back, "Jesus," to which @JamesMTitus replied: "honestly? no fracking way. ahahahhaa." Their exchange continued, and Billy began following @JamesMTitus. It probably never occurred to him that the Kiwi dude with an apparent love of cats was, in fact, a robot.

JamesMTitus was manufactured by cyber-security specialists in New Zealand participating in a two-week social-engineering experiment organized by the Web Ecology Project. Based in Boston, the group had conducted demographic analyses of Chatroulette and studies of Twitter networks during the recent Middle East protests. It was now interested in a question of particular concern to social-media experts and marketers: Is it possible not only to infiltrate social networks, but also to influence them on a large scale?

The group invited three teams to program "social bots"—fake identities—that could mimic human conversation on Twitter, and then picked 500 real users on the social network, the core of whom shared a fondness for cats. The Kiwis armed JamesMTitus with a database of generic responses ("Oh, that's very interesting, tell me more about that") and designed it to systematically test parts of the network for what tweets generated the most responses, and then to talk to the most responsive people.

Can one person controlling an identity, or a group of identities, really shape social architecture? Actually, yes. The Web Ecology Project's analysis of 2009's post-election protests in Iran revealed that only a handful of people accounted for most of the Twitter activity there. The attempt to steer large social groups toward a particular behavior or cause has long been the province of lobbyists, whose "astroturfing" seeks to camouflage their campaigns as genuine grassroots efforts, and company employees who pose on Internet message boards as unbiased consumers to tout their products. But social bots introduce new scale: they run off a server at practically no cost, and can reach thousands of people. The details that people reveal about their lives, in freely searchable tweets and blogs, offer bots a trove of personal information to work with. "The data coming off social networks allows for more-targeted social 'hacks' than ever before," says Tim Hwang, the director emeritus of the Web Ecology Project. And these hacks use "not just your interests, but your behavior."

A week after Hwang's experiment ended, Anonymous, a notorious hacker group, penetrated the e-mail accounts of the cyber-security firm HBGary Federal and revealed a solicitation of bids by the United States Air Force in June 2010 for "Persona Management Software"—a program that would enable the government to create multiple fake identities that trawl social-networking sites to collect data on real people and then use that data to gain credibility and to circulate propaganda. "We hadn't heard of anyone else doing this, but we assumed that it's got to be happening in a big way," says Hwang. His group has published the code for its experimental bots online, "to allow people to be aware of the problem and design countermeasures."

> Web robots can shape both social architecture, as well as the cyber-infrastructure of the Internet. As you can tell from this article, much of the material that these robots read involves a user's personal information. These robots then use this information for or against the user. While you probably won't build your own bot, you can learn how to write toward this audience and manipulate them to your rhetorical advantage.

The Web Ecology Project has started a spin-off group, called Pacific Social, to plan future experiments in social networking, like creating "connection-building" bots that bring together pro-democracy activists in a particular country, or ones that promote healthy habits. "There's a lot of potential for a lot of evil here," admits Hwang. "But there's also a lot of potential for a lot of good."

The practice of writing for these robots is called search engine optimization (SEO), briefly discussed in Chapter 2. Many complex practices of SEO exist and are constantly being invented, and no one knows the precise algorithms that search engine companies such as Google or Bing use to identify which sites get ranked higher than others. Although the audience is robotic and code-driven, writing for robots is a constantly shifting rhetorical situation, for search engine companies may change their algorithms at any time. If you don't think a computer-based algorithm can be both a significant audience and actor, consider the many online dating sites that help match potential partners or the *TEDx* Talk by Kevin Slavin in Figure 5.27. Toward a practice of basic SEO, which is essentially pitching an argument to an algorithm, the guidelines below offer some information and techniques to help you write for your robot audiences.

Figure 5.27
Kevin Slavin explains how algorithms shape the world.
www.youtube.com/watch?v=TDaFwnOiKVE

Understanding User Stats and Page Design

Rhetorically, page design matters, for it creates a sense of *ethos* that makes users trust the site and stay once they find it. This *ethos* drives the business of search engines and how to write for them.

A search engine's product is search results. Google's goal, put simply, is to give the audience the website that provides exactly what they're looking for in the top spot in the results. Google does not want spam in the results, nor does it want a harmful page in the results (such as one that might steal a user's identity or put a virus on his or her computer). Such results hurt the company's *ethos*, and the user would lose trust in Google.

Search engine companies have spent millions of dollars trying to write programs that can understand the syntax of the key word terms the user inputs. They want to know the user's goal—what the user is trying to achieve. If you put "Nike," into Google, the search engine wants to know if you are looking for information, the Nike corporate website, product reviews, or websites that sell Nike products. The search engine categorizes many terms based on what it thinks the user is looking for and yields different types of results based on this estimation.

Search engines are in a constant state of evolution, tweaking their algorithms so that their top results are increasingly the correct result. You might say, then, that Google is performing a constant rhetorical adjustment. But how does Google know if the correct result is displayed? The company tracks and keeps user statistics.

If searchers click on your link in the search engine results, go to your page, but decide it wasn't what they were looking for and bounce off the page (by hitting the back button), Google will count this against your page for that search term. Google has no way of knowing why the user bounced off. It could be because the page is not about the key word term, or that the user was looking for a page where she could buy something when your page is more informational, or because the page has really bad design. But when people bounce off, it counts against you and your web page's *ethos*. If lots of people bounce off (and the bounce rate is a higher percentage than those who stay at your site), your page will fall in the search rankings. Therefore, it's very important to establish that your web page is about the subject, is well designed, and is designed for web reading. Rhetorically, page design drives how people respond to your site, and search engines track that response. The more an audience trusts your information and remains on your page, human or robot, the more likely they'll accept your argument, and the better your web page will show in search results.

Key word research

Researching a key word is a part of the rhetorical analysis you should do when developing online texts and perhaps the most important step in SEO—and the one that is probably the most neglected. If you do not properly research and analyze the search volume for your subject (how many times a key word is searched for over a certain period), you are bound to head off in the wrong rhetorical direction. Before you begin optimizing, you need to determine which key word terms you are optimizing for.

- Never "guess" what the popular key word phrase will be, or its search volume. Often, users "dumb down" the syntax they enter into search engines and use key word phrases they would not use in their normal writing or speech. For instance, the key word combination "gainesville apartments" gets more than four times as much search volume as "gainesville florida apartments."

- You could probably come up with a list of more than 500 terms that people might use when searching for an apartment, but there is a short list of terms that will account for the majority of the search volume. These terms will be harder to compete for, but if you can come up high in the results, you will receive far more viewership.

- Since, at this point, you're probably not committed to an entire SEO campaign, you may be best served focusing on the long-tail terms: hundreds of low-traffic terms which, when aggregated, account for a large amount of traffic. This means you will need to greatly vary your text within the actual visible content on the page to include as many of these terms as possible.

- In order to gain the most traffic, your link should appear "above the fold" in the first page of the search results for the term (the fold refers to the bottom of the monitor, so users don't have to scroll down to see your link). Very few search users click to the second or third page of their search results.

- A page that is optimized for the term "apartments in Gainesville" may not necessarily rank well for the term "Gainesville apartments." You'll have to optimize the page separately for each of the terms you are focusing on.

- As always, you will need to determine the target audience: laypeople will use different key word terms than an expert—but there may be significantly less search volume for these technical terms.

Selecting key words

Once you have researched and analyzed how people search—and what they typically search for—you can build your key word list you can use when crafting a rhetorically effective page design.

- Begin by listing all of the related terms to your main key words. If you're writing an article on apartments, write down all of the words that relate to apartments. For example:

  apartments, apartment, housing, rental, home, dorm, flat, townhouse, loft, room, room for rent, one bedroom, pet friendly, apartment complex, for rent, rental, landlord, real estate, dorm, roommate, sublease, sublet

  If you're writing about a specific location, make a list of areas, states, counties, or cities that pertain to that area. Terms that are categories get the highest search volume. Users generally start their search wide and narrow it down from there.

- There are lots of free tools that allow you to research search volume, such as Google AdWords Keyword Planner (adwords.google.com/select/KeywordToolExternal) or goRank (www.gorank.com/analyze.php). These sites will help you identify how dense key words appear on your page, as well as the key words users input to search for a particular site. Find out the search volume for each of the terms and decide on which terms you want to focus on in your first round of SEO. For best results, you might focus on optimizing for the top ten terms first. If you're unsuccessful, go back and focus on the next most popular key words after the top ten.

Links

Both incoming and outgoing links affect your page. Incoming links (links on other pages that point to your page) have a very big impact. Google seems to think of incoming links in a similar way to "votes" or "likes." Again, rhetorically, this affects the *ethos* of the page's author. The text of the actual link (known as anchor text) is critically important, as is the subject of the original page and how it ranks for a term.

Link building is one of the most important (and difficult to manage) factors in SEO. If you can find a page that is about your subject that is listed in the Google search results and ranks well for the term, and you can get that page to link to your page, you will sometimes jump up in the search engine results. If and when you request a link, however, make sure you supply the owner of the other page with the exact text you want the link to read, using the key words you determined from your earlier research. In terms of *logos*, this helps the robot and human audiences clearly understand the subject of the link.

Title tags

If you "right click" on a web page and "view source," you can see the code that makes up the web page. Near the top of this code, you'll find a variety of <meta> tags, including the <title> tag (Figure 5.28).

```
<TITLE>Sean Morey, Sean W. Morey, Rhetoric and Composition,
New Media, Electracy</TITLE>
```

Figure 5.28
The <title> tag tells a search engine robot what a web page is about.

This information appears in the very top of the browser and is also looked at by Web robots. The <title> tag is one of the most important on-page SEO factors. Typically, you can include 70 characters within this tag—give or take—for the bigger search engines like Google. Search engines usually ignore characters beyond this amount. To reach this nonhuman audience, you should place important key words at the beginning of the tag.

Include both specific and categorical terms in this tag, and think wisely about how you include these terms because their placement affects both the ranking on search engines by web robots and actual click-throughs by human audiences. Remember that in most cases, the <title> tag is one of the biggest factors affecting your web page's ranking, and for your human reader it's also the bold, blue underlined text in the search engine results pages. This tag not only optimizes the page for a robot audience, but must also encourage an actual click by the human hand. In other words, a good <title> tag has to be written not only for a good ranking, but also for humans.

As has been expressed above, this is the real rhetorical problem of SEO—you are writing for two completely different audiences, which have very different needs. If you are writing about a company, you need your category term and the company name. All words used in the <title> tag must be used in the content of the page as well. For example, when optimizing for a company like Coca-Cola, you should include the top volume search term for your subject (such as soft drink, soda pop, etc.) and the company's name (Coca-Cola). You should also include a message to the user, who will read the <title> tag and think that the page sounds helpful and therefore click on it. For instance, "soft-drink | Enjoy the taste of Coca-Cola Classic, Diet Coke, and Coke Zero | The Coca-Cola Company." The <title> tag uses a combination of *logos* (what the page is about) as well as *ethos* (who is the author of this page) in order to help make an argument about the relevancy of the page.

File names

Just as you name your Word documents, you typically also name your individual web pages. While the most common "home" page for a website is "index.html," your other pages may be named with descriptors such as "contact.html" or "aboutus.html." How you name these pages affects how web robots index these pages, and you should use names that are relevant to both robot and human audiences. For example, a file name such as 0939201.html is pretty much meaningless to both humans and robots, while a file name titled "videoresume.html" conveys more information to both audiences. Consider file names as an appeal to *logos*, a logical rhetorical connection between what the audience is expecting and the actual content of the page.

Header tags

Often, you will organize your web pages with headers, just as you organize other kinds of documents such as letters, memos, reports, and various technical writing genres. On web pages, you code these headers using header tags, which are often written as <h1>, <h2>, <h3>, etc.

These header tags should be used like subtitles in the content of the page, and should be followed by paragraphs of visible text that use the same key words as in the headers.

For instance, in the earlier example of a website about apartments, the title might be "How to Find the Best Gainesville Apartments." The headers might then be "Cheap Apartments in Gainesville"; "Finding a Roommate in Gainesville"; and "How to Apply for Gainesville Apartments." Each of these header tags use key words that also appear in the title, and these key words should be repeated in the paragraph that follows each header. Don't repeat header tags (use only one <h1>, <h2>, <h3>, etc.), and the <h1> tag usually carries the most weight with web robots. Header tags should be stylized so they look like headers for the human reader, so use a larger, bolded font. As an appeal to *logos*, header tags help to logically structure the document so both humans and robots can find important sections.

Include key words in the main text

When composing the text the human user will read, you can insert key words into specific sentences in order to best write for web robots. Like headers, key words can be thought of as another appeal to *logos*.

- Use the top key word term (the one you chose to use in your title) in the first sentence of the first paragraph.

- Use that same key word term several times throughout the rest of the text (but no more than 1.5 to 2 percent of the text should be one single key word phrase). SEO experts often discuss finding the sweet spot in terms of key word density, so don't overdo it. Typically, you want between 2 and 7 percent of your text to be made up of all of the key word terms you researched earlier.

- Use variations of the key word term in the text: Gainesville apartments, apartments in Gainesville, Gainesville housing rentals. Not only does this replicate your key words for a robot audience, but it also creates stylistic variability for the human audience.

- Proximity matters. If you include the sentence "Gainesville apartments for rent are cheaper than you might think," Google will see the proximity of "cheaper" to "Gainesville apartments." The closer together the words are, the more likely you are to rank well for any given terms.

- Include key words at the beginning of a sentence.

- Bolding, italicizing, or underlining a key word may increase results.

- Write for a general human audience. Google and other search engines seem to like simple sentence structure.

Tag multimedia with key words

Images, video, and other kinds of multimedia often include an <alt> or <image title> tag in their code. You should include the key word terms in these tags for any multimedia you embed in the page content. These tags not only help web robots index the page, but they also help screen-reader software identify the content of the multimedia for blind users who must rely on textual descriptions to understand what the visual content is about.

Make it original

For each separate page on your website, make sure that each one includes original content. Google does not favorably rank websites that have two or three pages with the same information. If you're including a new page on the site, make sure it's unique. Although robots don't have emotions, you might think of them getting "bored" the way humans might if they see or hear the same information over and over again. Although perhaps far-fetched when it comes to these robots, you might consider originality as an appeal to *pathos*.

Revise

Just like any kind of writing, you should revise how you code your page for SEO as you develop new incoming links, new content, and gain new information about how people search for your site. If you don't rank high for your targeted search terms, keep changing your approach. Remember, however, that it takes time for web robots to reach your site and return, so several weeks may pass before you notice results.

Rhetorical Continuities

We often understand new writing technologies based on the ones that came before. As an example, when film was developed, it often relied on plays and books as source material before original screenplays were developed. The first written poems were simply spoken poems that were written down. Likewise, web page design often uses elements of familiar writing documents in order to assign their structure. For example, just as a written document has a title, headers, margins, footers, and other features, we often use these same terms when describing the parts of a web page. You might note, as you examine other digital genres, how similar terms are used across these different kinds of digital writing.

Building

Link

Look at the "page source" of a variety of websites. Compare how these sites use (or don't use) the SEO techniques mentioned above. Do they make good use of the <title> tag? Do they include key words in the page's main text? Do they include key words in the <alt> tags for images? Analyze the web pages for these features, and make an argument for how well each page writes for search engine robots. Include reasons and evidence to support your claim.

Engine

Search

Select a website not discussed in the Link Building prompt above. Engaging in the same analysis, write an SEO report on the site, noting what the site does well to write for nonhuman audiences, as well as what it does poorly. In an essay, argue for suggestions you think will help improve this aspect of the site. Make sure you include reasons and evidence to support this claim. After you've composed the report, share your findings with the class.

KEY Terms

casting	rhetorical velocity
file name	screening
future audience	search engine optimization
header tag	title tag
key word	transnational audience
link	web robots

Podcast

For this assignment, create an explicit or implicit argument and distribute it through a podcast. If explicit, make sure you incorporate a claim, reasons for that claim, and evidence. If your argument is implicit, consider how to win over your audience, such as by using anecdotes, presenting a fictional story, or by emotionally appealing to your listener.

A wide range of free audio programs can provide the basic software you need to make a podcast. Ideally, you will have access to a decent microphone, but some basic desktop computer microphones or webcam mics can be effective. While creating a podcast may seem simple beyond the initial technological setup, the following tips offer further suggestions to ensure your podcast sounds its best.

Make sure you revisit the rhetorical tetrahedron through your drafting and revising process.

Planning: Write a script or overall outline of what you plan to argue. This script will help keep you on track while recording and make sure your argument or story is the most logical or engaging. This script also can help you structure your claim, reasons, and evidence. Also, consider listening to podcasts created by others, such as the radio news organization National Public Radio. These podcasts can give you ideas about how to structure your own.

Testing, testing: Before recording your whole podcast, test your microphones and recording software a few times. Play back some of these test recordings and notice if the audio has too much static, too much background noise, too much hiss, too little volume, or if certain sounds like "p's" or "s's" stand out. If so, you might place a windscreen or "pop shield" in front of the mic to cut down on these sounds, or place a piece of paper between you and the microphone, testing this setup further to see if the sound improves. You can make some adjustments with an audio editor in postproduction, but it's best to record the sound as cleanly as possible before moving to postproduction.

Identity: While this principle is more important for a sustained, serial podcast, consider creating some sort of "identity" for your podcast. What does your podcast offer that others don't? What's your podcast's particular niche? You also might consider creating some sort of theme or catch phrase that's unique to your podcast.

Structure and organization: While you will hopefully organize and structure your podcast in the planning phase, make sure it has a coherent beginning, middle, and end, either as an explicit or implicit argument. Within this three-part structure, introduce what you're going to talk about, discuss it, and then restate what you just discussed or its conclusion. Since your audience can't go back and "read" what you said through audio easily, such structure helps them to remember.

Don't read: Although you should have a script or outline, try not to read the document when recording. You might read small sections of it, but try to sound spontaneous and free flowing. Reading from a script tends to dull the material, sound unnatural, and decrease emotion in the voice.

Length: Although variable, try to determine the appropriate length for your podcast. If too short, you won't be able to present a whole argument to the listener. However, if you create a podcast that is too long, the audience may stop listening, either from boredom or time constraints. Try to find a middle range—usually at least five minutes, but no more than 15 minutes.

Content: Since content is key, make sure you present something worth listening to. Why should an audience download your podcast? What does it have to offer? What will they learn? Will they be entertained? As always, you can't deliver your argument if your audience tunes out.

Review and revise: Just as you should ask your peers to review and comment on your written works, ask a classmate to listen to your podcast. Ask him where the content sounded dull, where he became confused, and if the audio quality detracted from the message. After you note his feedback, go back and revise or rerecord any material the reviewer found problematic.

Delivery: While you can electronically deliver your podcast in many ways, iTunes makes it simple to disseminate your podcast and allow anyone on the service to download it. Although you still have to host the podcast file on your own web space, iTunes allows many more people to find it by including it in its database. You can read more about submitting podcasts to iTunes here: www. apple.com/itunes/podcasts/specs.html.

From DIGITAL Writers

www.radiolab.org/story/312245-
rodney-versus-death/

As an example of a podcast, consider this episode from the podcast program *Radiolab*. What argument is the podcast trying to make? What kinds of evidence are presented? Research the program's sponsors and benefactors. Based on this information, who do you think the podcast's primary audience might be? How does the program's podcast cater to that audience? How does this topic or format fit radio in a way that it might not fit a more visual-based medium?

Radiolab is a radio-based program and podcast that examines the connections between science, philosophy, and human experience.

STUDENT Example

Informed Design by Kiera Prince

people.clemson.edu/~kieraw/
podcast.html

As a student podcast example, go to Kiera Prince's podcast, titled "Instructional Design." How is Prince's podcast structurally similar to the *Radiolab* podcast? Does she present similar evidence?

Prince produced this podcast while a student at Clemson University.

CHAPTER 6

Digital Research

Sitting in his high school biology class, then 15-year-old Jack Andraka was learning about antibodies and became interested in analytical methods using carbon nanotubes. Something clicked, and he realized this technology might be used to help diagnose pancreatic cancer, a disease that had claimed his good family friend. Poor early detection of this disease is one reason it is so deadly. He decided to do more research out of class. However, as a high school student, his access to lab resources and scientific research materials was meager com-

pared to that found in a research university. Undeterred, Andraka decided to start with "a teenager's two best friends: Google and Wikipedia." In addition to these sites, Andraka also used YouTube and free online journals to research his problem and eventually to invent a new test to catch pancreatic cancer in its early stages (Figure 6.1).

Figure 6.1
Jack Andraka developed a cancer test before he could legally drive.
www.ted.com/talks/jack_andraka_a_promising_test_for_pancreatic_cancer_from_a_teenager

As Andraka's case shows, the Internet can provide a wealth of information if you know where and how to look. As with any writing project, digital writing requires significant research to ensure your document has the best chance of reaching your desired audience with your intended message. Research not only helps you understand the nuances of your topic, but it also helps you evaluate different sources and points of view about your topic and better understand the audience that will read your message. However, compared with more traditional kinds of writing, additional kinds of research are often necessary when composing a text with digital media and technology.

Conducting research for digital texts is especially important because so many variables come into play. For instance, you must not only consider traditional elements, such as the audience you want to reach and the message you need to develop to reach that audience, but also what medium and genre will best fit the situation, and what design elements will most appeal to the audience. You might also need to research the environment in which the audience will read your message, and which technologies will best fit that environment. For instance, if you're designing a fish-identification card for fishing, you might research which kinds of paper are best for waterproof printing. You might also need to research what technology (text editor, photo editor, HTML editor) will best complete the message you wish to write.

Since you've reviewed many research topics in Chapter 3 (such as purpose, audience, and context), this chapter will explain the research practices you'll need to consider in the preproduction phase of your writing that are more specific to digital- and visual-based productions. This research includes investigating the history of a particular digital element you might want to include in a design, finding images through search engines, or researching the copyright owners of a piece of media you want to integrate into a project. This chapter will cover some basics for you to consider before fully launching into design and production.

Research Tools and Approaches

Research for digital writing can fall under two categories: research about a particular text, and research on where to find and gather texts. Well-researched projects will generally incorporate research from many types of sources and approaches. The following section discusses some general approaches to be aware of when researching a text for use in your projects, as well as some ways to find those texts.

Primary sources

When researching about a particular text, you should focus on primary sources written about a text. Primary sources provide original material about a text and provide the basis for other documents, and provide complete information that's not summarized or interpreted from another, secondary source. Primary sources allow you to read the source without another author mediating the material so you can come up with your own conclusion.

Secondary sources

However, it's often useful to examine what other authors say about a primary text, especially if these insights help you build your own argument about a text.

These secondary sources provide the opinions or evaluations of others about a primary text. As a researcher, you also need to evaluate and research these secondary sources. For instance, what is the author's perspective? What is the author's bias? What important information from the primary source does the author omit? Even when you're using secondary sources, you should have read and be familiar with the primary source.

Websites

Websites have many advantages as research sources because they're easy to use, the information can be copied or downloaded quickly, the material can be shared with others easily, and one source will often include hyperlinks to other information. However, websites often have little editorial oversight to make sure the information is accurate and reliable, online searches can return inappropriate results, and some sites charge money for their information.

Websites may be either primary or secondary sources. The material on NASA's website about a recent Mars landing will often present primary information about the landing, while a Wikipedia entry will summarize the landing by using the primary information from NASA's website. In this way, Wikipedia might present a good place to initially gather information about a text, but you should always go to the references at the bottom of the article and go to the primary source for deeper investigation. A blog post about the Mars landing might provide an interesting perspective, but this source should not be used to research the actual facts of the mission since blogs have less editorial oversight and are more prone to misinformation. For any source you use, always evaluate the credibility and reliability of the source and author before deciding to trust its material.

Databases

Often in the form of a website, databases can provide an index of information about images, videos, books, articles, news media, government documents, and other texts in a central, searchable location. Often, these databases are specific and geared toward a particular subject or audience. For instance, the Internet Movie Database (www.imdb.com) provides a database of every movie, actor, director, and other information related to film and television. If you needed a list of everyone who acted in a particular movie, this would be a great database resource. Google Scholar is another database that provides the ability to search a wide range of academic articles and books. These databases provide more credible information that's often reviewed by other professionals, as well as more specialized information that might not be available in more generalized sources such as a Wikipedia article. However, not all databases are free, as some require a registration fee to use. Check with your school's librarian, however, since most colleges and universities subscribe to a wide variety of databases for use by students and faculty.

Images and videos

Many digital texts incorporate images and videos, and so you may need to find these media for your own projects. When looking for images and videos, you will probably start with a Google Image search or a search for videos on YouTube. For these searches, the selection of good key words is important. Start broadly, and then refine as needed. If you were looking for an image of a burning building, you might simply put in "burning building," or "building fire." If that search turned up results that didn't meet your project, you might refine "building" into other key words such as skyscraper, house, church, meeting hall, or other building types. You might also use other descriptors such as the color of the building you want, its age, architectural style, camera angle, and other adjectives.

WIKIMEDIA COMMONS

Figure 6.2 Wikimedia Commons has a wide variety of images, many which fall under public domain.

In addition to image searches supported by search engines, you also can look at image-specific databases. Some of these include the image search engine Picsearch (picsearch.com), Getty Images (gettyimages.com), and AP Images (apimages.com). Of course, make sure you consider copyright laws when using databases that offer stock photography for a fee. The website Wikimedia Commons offers images that are in the public domain (Figure 6.2).

You can also look for images in the public domain through federal agencies such as NASA, as well as library websites that often scan and catalogue older, historical photos. The website archive.org also has a range of media in the public domain, including still images, texts, videos, audio, and even software. While you will most likely find many more sites, these should get you started.

Building

Create a list of as many image databases as you can find. Note which ones require payment for use, which ones offer their photos for free, and which require permissions. Once you've completed your list, share it with the class and merge it with the lists other groups produce.

Link

Engine

Search

Choose a photo you've taken with a digital camera. If you were going to assign key words to this image so it was easy to find through search engines, which key words would you choose? Shapes? Colors? Objects? Emotions? Analyze the image, and create a list of all the possible key words you might use, and rank them in order of importance. How did you decide upon these key words? How did you decide upon their ranking? Which search terms are denotative, and which are connotative? Write a report in which you make a claim for the terms you've chosen, and make sure to include reasons and evidence for your claim.

Textual Research: Wikipedia

Although visuals are important to digital writing, more text-based writing is important as well. Wikipedia, an online encyclopedia composed by anyone who wishes to contribute, is primarily text and hypertext. The few images per article that it does include are mostly for illustrative purposes, and the articles can be understood easily without any visual aids. Wikipedia provides numerous articles on millions of topics, and as of March 9, 2014, Wikipedia included 4,468,218 articles in English alone.

Because Wikipedia is so comprehensive, it provides a useful starting point for much of your research. However, you should never use it as a primary or secondary resource. Since Wikipedia is composed as a wiki with hypertext, almost anyone can edit it, and as you will read later, manipulate it just for fun. Thus, it's nearly impossible to determine how accurate the information is, or the trustworthiness of the authors. However, we can study Wikipedia as a product of digital writers and research how it is composed. Because it's so comprehensive, Wikipedia requires extensive research to create and maintain the site.

In general, Wikipedia is modeled on a traditional encyclopedia. Founders Jimmy Wales and Larry Sanger originally conceived of two encyclopedias, the first being called Nupedia, and focused more on a traditional encyclopedia that was controlled by experts. However, Wales and Sanger wanted to offer the public a free encyclopedia that could be used easily by everyone. In order to do this, they had to choose the best medium, and figure out how to make Nupedia more open. Since printing costs are expensive, the obvious choice for a free encyclopedia was to place it online. However, Wales and Sanger had to research the best options for doing this. Should the web-based encyclopedia be a typical website? A blog?

DIGITAL Connections

[Nupedia-l] Let's make a wiki

By Larry Sanger
Wed, 10 Jan 2001 12:50:32 -0800

Previous message: [Nupedia-l] Library and Information Science is active!
Next message: [Nupedia-l] Let's make a wiki
Messages sorted by: [date] [thread] [subject] [author]

> As Larry Sanger wrote in the Nupedia listserve at the time, he determined that the encyclopedia Nupedia should take the form of a wiki, which is an open, publically editable website.

No, this is not an indecent proposal. It's an idea to add a little feature to Nupedia. Jimmy Wales thinks that many people might find the idea objectionable, but I think not.

"Wiki," pronounced \wee'-kee\, derives from a Polynesian word, "wikiwiki," but what it means is a VERY open, VERY publicly-editable series of web pages. For example, I can start a page called EpistemicCircularity and write anything I want in it. Anyone else (yes, absolutely anyone else) can come along and make absolutely any changes to it that he wants to. (The editing interface is very simple; anyone intelligent enough to write or edit a Nupedia article will be able to figure it out without any trouble.) On the page I create, I can link to any other pages, and of course anyone can link to mine. The project is billed and pursued as a public resource. There are a few announced suggestions or rules. The concept actually seems to work well, as you can see here with the original wiki:

http://c2.com/cgi/wiki

Links are indicated by using CapitalizedWordsBunchedTogetherLikeThis.

If a wiki page exists, the word is underlined; if not, there is a question mark after the word, which is clickable, and which anyone can use to go and write something about the topic.

Setting up a wiki for Nupedia would be very easy; it can be done in literally ten minutes. (We've already found this out.)

As to Nupedia's use of a wiki, this is the ULTIMATE "open" and simple format for developing content. We have occasionally bandied about ideas for simpler, more open projects to either replace or supplement Nupedia.

It seems to me wikis can be implemented practically instantly, need very little maintenance, and in general are very low-risk. They're also a potentially great source for content. So there's little downside, as far as I can see. We can make wiki versions of all new Nupedia articles, too, and that can be a place where additional changes and commentary can be gleaned (authors could ignore what goes on on the wiki, of course—it's up to them). The content can be licensed under an open content license.

A Nupedia wiki would instruct users to try to make their entries resemble encyclopedia articles, but the usual wiki sort of banter would be permitted. This would make things more interesting to many users, who could *instantly* create, edit, and comment on articles. If a wiki article got to a high level it could be put into the regular Nupedia editorial process.

We would not integrate the Nupedia wiki into the rest of Nupedia (though wiki pages could link to regular Nupedia pages, there wouldn't be links back). It would be a completely separate part of the website. The search engine would not return wiki pages, and wiki pages wouldn't be listed among other regular Nupedia pages. We'd just have a link on the left or right hand column of the website, "Nupedia Wiki", and let people explore it if they're curious what it is. On the front page of the Nupedia wiki we'd make it ABSOLUTELY clear that this is experimental, that Nupedia editors don't have control of what goes on here, and that the quality of articles, discussion, etc., should not be taken as a reflection of the quality of articles, review, etc. on the main part of the Nupedia website.

Does anyone have an objection to our trying this out?

Larry

Eventually, Nupedia became Wikipedia, one of the most visited websites in the world. Not only would users be free to read the articles, but they would be free to write and edit the articles as well.

Wales and Sanger had to research how a traditional encyclopedia was put together, but they also had to research how a reader might make use of an online encyclopedia. Although some articles are loosely arranged by topic, Wales and Sanger recognized that a search feature within the site would allow audiences to quickly reach the articles they were looking for. Articles are then linked together with hyperlinks, allowing the user to jump from page to page much more quickly (hence, "wiki") than flipping pages in a printed encyclopedia.

Of course, the writers who contribute to Wikipedia have to research their topics. Usually, Wikipedia writers provide linked citations at the bottom of the page to let the reader know where they found the information that went into the article. If statements or claims are made without citing research, then editors usually mark the statement as "citation needed." Even though anyone can write and edit a Wikipedia entry, the research of others is required in order to make each article as correct and accurate as possible.

Because each edit is recorded, the reader, writer, or editor can view how the article has changed over time. Although you might have had previous writing instructors ask that you turn in prior drafts with a final essay, Wikipedia records every single change made, as well as the user who made the change. Editors also can include comments. This feature allows the writer or editor to research about the research and writing process, helping him or her to evaluate the quality of the research that was done, as well as the quality of the source material used to write the article.

Building

Link

Because Wikipedia is collaborative, Wales and Sanger needed to research and develop how such an open encyclopedia would work. Research more about the history of Wikipedia, particularly the changes that Wikipedia made to how the collaborative process should function. What research did they use to make these determinations? Who did they consider their audience to be? Write a short research report of your findings, and share it with the class.

Engine

Search

Open up a Wikipedia article (such as the featured article of the day) and click on the link that says "View history." Scroll through the history of the article and its edits, and discuss what changes were made. Do the changes include reasons for the edit? Do editors have conversations with each other about the process of editing? Does the editor provide any additional research to support the change she or he makes? What rhetorical appeals, such as *logos*, *pathos*, *ethos*, and *kairos*, are given when making or explaining edits? Write a short report based on your research.

Even if you simply use a Wikipedia article to research information, you need to perform similar research yourself and not use Wikipedia articles themselves as source material. Sometimes, editors miss information, and more than 4.5

million articles is a lot of information to research and edit. However, sometimes users will intentionally rewrite articles to make them inaccurate. For instance, in 2006, Stephen Colbert edited the Wikipedia article for "elephant" on his show *The Colbert Report*, prompting Wikipedia to ban him from future edits (Figure 6.3).

Known as Wikipedia vandalism, writers can change content that affects not only the quality of the article, but people who might be connected to the content of the article. This is another reason why you should never rely on Wikipedia as a research source for your own writing.

Figure 6.3
Stephen Colbert was banned from Wikipedia for this edit.

DIGITAL Connections

A False Wikipedia 'Biography'

By John Seigenthaler

This is a highly personal story about Internet character assassination. It could be your story.

I have no idea whose sick mind conceived the false, malicious "biography" that appeared under my name for 132 days on Wikipedia, the popular, online, free encyclopedia whose authors are unknown and virtually untraceable. There was more:

Consider the case of John Seigenthaler, Sr., a prominent and well-respected retired journalist, published in *USA Today*. In 2005, a user edited a Wikipedia article about him, including many untrue defamatory statements, mostly about his role in the assassinations of John F. Kennedy and his brother, Robert Kennedy.

"John Seigenthaler moved to the Soviet Union in 1971, and returned to the United States in 1984," Wikipedia said. "He started one of the country's largest public relations firms shortly thereafter."

At age 78, I thought I was beyond surprise or hurt at anything negative said about me. I was wrong. One sentence in the biography was true. I was Robert Kennedy's administrative assistant in the early 1960s. I also was his pallbearer. It was mind-boggling when my son, John Seigenthaler, journalist with *NBC News*, phoned later to say he found the same scurrilous text on Reference.com and Answers.com.

I had heard for weeks from teachers, journalists and historians about "the wonderful world of Wikipedia," where millions of people worldwide visit daily for quick reference "facts," composed and posted by people with no special expertise or knowledge—and sometimes by people with malice.

At my request, executives of the three websites now have removed the false content about me. But they don't know, and can't find out, who wrote the toxic sentences.

Anonymous author

I phoned Jimmy Wales, Wikipedia's founder and asked, "Do you . . . have any way to know who wrote that?"

"No, we don't," he said. Representatives of the other two websites said their computers are programmed to copy data verbatim from Wikipedia, never checking whether it is false or factual.

Naturally, I want to unmask my "biographer." And, I am interested in letting many people know that Wikipedia is a flawed and irresponsible research tool.

But searching cyberspace for the identity of people who post spurious information can be frustrating. I found on Wikipedia the registered IP (Internet Protocol) number of my "biographer"- 65-81-97-208. I traced it to a customer of BellSouth Internet. That company advertises a phone number to report "Abuse Issues." An electronic voice said all complaints must be e-mailed. My two e-mails were answered by identical form letters, advising me that the company would conduct an investigation but might not tell me the results. It was signed "Abuse Team."

Wales, Wikipedia's founder, told me that BellSouth would not be helpful. "We have trouble with people posting abusive things over and over and over," he said. "We block their IP numbers, and they sneak in another way. So we contact the service providers, and they are not very responsive."

After three weeks, hearing nothing further about the Abuse Team investigation, I phoned BellSouth's Atlanta corporate headquarters, which led to conversations between my lawyer and BellSouth's counsel. My only remote chance of getting the name, I learned, was to file a "John or Jane Doe" lawsuit against my "biographer." Major communications Internet companies are bound by federal privacy laws that protect the identity of their customers, even those who defame online. Only if a lawsuit resulted in a court subpoena would BellSouth give up the name.

Little legal recourse

Federal law also protects online corporations—BellSouth, AOL, MCI Wikipedia, etc.—from libel lawsuits. Section 230 of the Communications Decency Act, passed in 1996, specifically states that "no provider or user of an interactive computer service shall be treated as the publisher or speaker." That legalese means that, unlike print and broadcast companies, online service providers cannot be sued for disseminating defamatory attacks on citizens posted by others.

Recent low-profile court decisions document that Congress effectively has barred defamation in cyberspace. Wikipedia's website acknowledges that it is not responsible for inaccurate information, but Wales, in a recent C-Span interview with Brian Lamb, insisted that his website is accountable and that his community of thousands of volunteer editors (he said he has only one paid employee) corrects mistakes within minutes.

My experience refutes that. My "biography" was posted May 26. On May 29, one of Wales' volunteers "edited" it only by correcting the misspelling of the word "early." For four months, Wikipedia depicted me as a suspected assassin before Wales erased it from his website's history Oct. 5. The falsehoods remained on Answers.com and Reference.com for three more weeks.

In the C-Span interview, Wales said Wikipedia has "millions" of daily global visitors and is one of the world's busiest websites. His volunteer community runs the Wikipedia operation, he said. He funds his website through a non-profit foundation and estimated a 2006 budget of "about a million dollars."

And so we live in a universe of new media with phenomenal opportunities for worldwide communications and research—but populated by volunteer vandals with poison-pen intellects. Congress has enabled them and protects them.

When I was a child, my mother lectured me on the evils of "gossip." She held a feather pillow and said, "If I tear this open, the feathers will fly to the four winds, and I could never get them back in the pillow. That's how it is when you spread mean things about people."

For me, that pillow is a metaphor for Wikipedia.

Building

Link

Since the Seigenthaler incident, Wikipedia has made several changes to how a user may contribute to Wikipedia. Research some of these changes, and locate other acts of Wikipedia vandalism that prompted further changes. How did this vandalism affect the *ethos* of the person under attack? Write a report of your findings, and share it with the class.

Engine

Search

Assume that some of your online social media pages were vandalized, such as Facebook, Twitter, LinkedIn, or even Wikipedia (if you happen to have a page about you). What steps would you take to track down the vandal? How would you attempt to rebuild your *ethos*? Write a short paper that makes a claim for your approach, and support it with reasons and evidence.

Remixing Research

One of the most common practices of digital writing is remediating material from existing works into new ones. Often, this occurs in music, where an artist may sample an older music track and incorporate it into a new work. Figure 6.4 features a video of the song "Changes" by Tupac Shakur. This song borrows from the song "The Way It Is" by Bruce Hornsby and the Range.

Shakur uses Hornsby's work rhetorically, summoning for viewers an older song they may have heard that has similar themes of prejudice and hardships and then applying them to his own context. The combination helps orientate the viewer to the proper mood of the song.

Credit: Death Row Records

This kind of remixing is the most common characteristic of digital writing, appearing in nearly all the media that you consume. For instance, a typical news website such as CNN.com not only contains hypertext

Figure 6.4
Tupac Shakur's "Changes" remixes Bruce Hornsby and the Range's "The Way It Is."

www.youtube.com/ watch?v=eXvBjCO19QY

(HTML) but also photographs, video, podcasts, and other media. You might take this construction of hypermedia for granted now, but the current web experience only came about due to the interaction of all these media together.

While the web developed to most closely align with the logic of television, you can now see television adopting components of websites, such as on-screen information for email or Twitter accounts. CNN.com reuses video also shown on *CNN* the cable channel, and the cable channel will also display blog posts, email responses to questions, as well as videos posted on their website. Whenever you compose any digital text, you are probably also committing an act of remediation.

Rhetorical Continuities

Although you might typically think of remixing as a more recent method for composing works, especially digital works, remixing is actually a very old practice. When a new kind of media emerges, usually the first content presented in the new medium is a work from older media. After the invention of alphabetic writing, people didn't immediately invent new works specific to writing, such as the novel, but recorded oral works already circulating in their culture. When cinema was invented, some of the first films were book adaptations.

When considering elements to remix into your own projects that originally came from other sources, research each of the categories below to determine how the element fits and how it will affect the overall message you're attempting to convey. You should pay attention to the reasons why you make certain choices in your texts, and researching the elements you use is a major step in understanding why you might compose a text in a certain way.

Unfortunately, remixing can sometimes run into problems with copyright laws. Consider this *TEDx* Talk from Lawrence Lessig, who argues that current copyright laws "choke" creativity (Figure 6.5).

Credit: *TEDx*

Figure 6.5
Lawrence Lessig argues that current copyright laws limit our ability to be creative.

www.ted.com/talks/larry_lessig_says_the_law_is_strangling_creativity

The message's subject

If you're incorporating another text into your own design, you should know what it's about, its subject. Without this knowledge, you might include an image that has meanings contrary to your purpose, which may cause problems. While it's unlikely you would include a swastika in your design—since you're already familiar with some of its history and understand the negative reactions such an image would produce—other visuals have their own histories that can affect how an audience understands and interprets the work in which you include them.

Credit: Eddie Adams/Associated Press

Figure 6.6
Eddie Adams's photo alone
doesn't tell the whole story.

For example, Figure 6.6 depicts a photograph taken by Eddie Adams depicting General Nguyen Ngoc Loan, South Vietnam's national police chief, executing a Viet Cong captain, Nguyen Van Lem. This image would become one of the most iconic photos of the Vietnam War. However, many who see it often misinterpret the subject of the image.

The photograph depicts Loan just as he is about to pull the trigger of his gun, executing Lem. The image—and the video of the act, which was also shown on United States nightly news programs—helped to change U.S. sentiment against the war and spur the antiwar movement.

Opponents of the war claimed the image depicted the brutality of the U.S. allies in Vietnam. From their perspective, Loan played the villain, killing the victimized, unarmed Lem who was captive and helpless. However, this interpretation does not tell the whole story, and research into the larger subject and context needs to be examined.

Prior to the photograph's creation, the Viet Cong launched a military campaign—the Tet Offensive—which included death squads that targeted South Vietnamese National Police officers and their relatives. Lem, who led one of the death squads, was captured near the site of a mass grave containing thirty-four bodies and their relatives, six of whom were Loan's godchildren. South Vietnamese sources confirmed Lem's role in the killings, and Loan summarily executed him for his crimes, using his personal sidearm. While this knowledge perhaps doesn't excuse Loan's actions, it does put them in a greater perspective.

When originally running the story and photograph, *The New York Times* also included a photo of an infant killed by the Viet Cong juxtaposed next to Adams's photograph of Loan. However, Adams's image alone became remixed into other media forms and circulated without this balance, causing a more skewed perspective and damage to Loan's reputation.

Adams later lamented that his audience did not interpret Loan's actions as heroic, the way that he viewed them: "The general killed the Viet Cong; I killed the general with my camera. Still photographs are the most powerful weapon in the world. People believe them; but photographs do lie, even without manipulation. They are only half-truths. What the photograph didn't say was, 'What would you do if you were the general at that time and place on that hot day, and you caught the so-called bad guy after he blew away one, two or three American soldiers?'"

An ethical use of others' texts, or even an ethical interpretation of texts, asks you to research what's really going on before jumping to conclusions or before leading your audiences to particular assumptions. Of course, leading the audience toward a particular outcome is the purpose of rhetoric. However, conducting thorough research before selecting various elements for your own work can help you argue in a more ethical and honest way.

The writer's purpose

When using another's text in your own project, it's helpful to know the author's original purpose in creating it. As already discussed, Ramesses's main purposes for creating texts included propaganda. If you were to include photographs of his carvings in your own text, others might think you're trying to distribute propaganda yourself. Then again, they might just think you're using a dead pharaoh's wall carvings. However, such knowledge of Ramesses's work as propaganda might influence how others see your work as a whole.

What does including past propaganda say about the overall message you're creating? This inclusion might have negative repercussions, but they also may have positive effects if your work somehow reflects or criticizes the nature of propaganda. While another writer's purpose might not reflect your own, it can help you think about the message you're creating, provide insight, and help you think more critically about how you remix such images in your works.

The text's audience

Another image property to research is the original audience. Was the text meant for a pharaoh's slaves? Did a press photographer take an image to disseminate it to the general public? Or, did a famous celebrity take photos for personal reasons—intending no other audience than immediate family—that then became leaked or stolen? Or, did the celebrity hope that "private" images would become public as a way to get himself or herself into the news?

Like purpose, the original audience of a particular text may not align with your target audience, but knowing whom this image was intended for can help you understand the new image ecology you might be creating. Learning such details about audience also can help you place the text in its original historical context, and perhaps help you discover other details that inform how you might use the text in your design.

The message's influence

Many texts are influenced by previous images, and, in turn, influence subsequent images. The famous image of Barack Obama by artist Shepard Fairey (Figure 6.7) was influenced by a photograph taken by Mannie Garcia, an Associated Press photographer (Figure 6.8). Subsequent to Fairey's image, many others have incorporated his technique to produce their own portraits, including a website that allows you to create your own "Obama" version of an image. Fairey was taken to court for using this photo without permission, although Fairey claimed that his new, artistic interpretation constituted fair use. However, this argument doesn't help Fairey's *ethos* when he denies others the right to use his own artwork depicting Obama.

Credit: Shepard Fairey

Credit: AP/Mannie Garcia

Figure 6.7
Shepard Fairey was influenced by Mannie Garcia's photograph.

Figure 6.8
Mannie Garcia snapped the photo on which Fairey based his work.

Figure 6.9
Kirby Ferguson explains that "everything" is a remix.

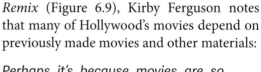

www.youtube.com/watch?v=Z-HuenDPZw0

In his short documentary, *Everything Is a Remix* (Figure 6.9), Kirby Ferguson notes that many of Hollywood's movies depend on previously made movies and other materials:

Perhaps it's because movies are so massively expensive to make; perhaps it's because graphic novels, TV shows, video games, books, and the like are such rich sources of material; or perhaps it's because audiences just prefer the familiar: whatever the reason, most box office hits rely heavily on existing material.

The movie *Pirates of the Caribbean* was based on Disney World's theme park, which further spawned three sequels. While you might generally think that toys based on television shows or movies come after their release, the movie *Transformers*, which now has multiple sequels, originally came from a cartoon created to help sell toys already on shelves at the time (Figure 6.10).

Credit: Hiroyuki Obara

Some of the biggest box office hits are influenced by other films. As Ferguson points out, George Lucas relied heavily on other films when creating *Star Wars*. Such influences included Joseph Campbell's analysis of myth and the classic hero story, *Flash Gordon*; Japanese director Akira Kurosawa; war films; westerns; and other science fiction films. As Ferguson concludes: George Lucas collected materials, he combined them, he transformed them. Without the films that preceded it, there could be no *Star Wars*. Creation requires influence. Everything we make is a remix of existing creations.

Figure 6.10
Transformers were toys before they were in cartoons or movies.

Lucas's originality comes not from the individual pieces of his film, but how he assembles them into a unique whole. While your own work will necessarily be influenced by other works, the overall design you create should have a uniqueness of its own.

Credit: The Everett Collection

Figure 6.11
If you were researching Zombie films, you should probably check out George Romero's *Night of the Living Dead*, one of the earliest zombie films.

From a research perspective, knowing how works were influenced and how they influenced other works can help you to understand more about how a particular visual was created and help you better create your own. For instance, the above knowledge about *Star Wars* helps you understand where different elements in the movie came from, as well as their history and lineage. This research can provide ideas for source materials for your own works. If you were making a movie and wanted to incorporate a sword-fighting scene, you might turn to Kurosawa or Lucas's works and use samurai or Jedi duels as templates. If you were telling a story about zombies, you would research other zombie-related materials (Figure 6.11). If you were creating a political poster, like Fairey, you might look at past political posters, research their influences, and research the subsequent posters they influenced as well.

Building

Link

Open a well-known website of a television channel, such as ESPN.com. Analyze how the site remediates its television content or other media. Then, discuss how its television coverage remediates its website. Write a short report that argues whether or not you think the site remediates its content effectively, or what it should do differently. Remember to include reasons and evidence to support your claim.

Engine

Search

Think of your favorite movie and research what other films, stories, or people may have influenced its creation. How significant was each of these influences? How do you think incorporating these prior works helps the film rhetorically according to appeals such as *logos, ethos, pathos*, or *kairos*? Write a short report that develops this claim, and include reasons and evidence to support it.

The text's details

While it's important to understand the main subject of a text—as the discussion of Adams's photograph illustrates—sometimes the details are just as important. When you analyze any type of text, you should pay close attention to the details included within the whole, and ask questions about why the writer included specific elements, where those elements come from, and what connotations they bring. Failing to research the particulars can create unforeseen problems if you incorporate such details without adequate investigation.

DIGITAL Connections

Gang Signs and a Sticker: Chicago Pulls Teen's Design

By David Schaper

"When you first look at the design, it's a beautiful design. It's recognizing Chicago's heroes," says former Chicago Police Superintendent Jody Weis.

But look a little more closely, and Weis sees something troubling.

In 2011, the city of Chicago held its annual contest in which high school students had the opportunity to design the city parking decal, a decal affixed to all automobile windshields of Chicago residents.

"You've got the hands . . . configured in such a way that are very similar to a particular gang's hand sign. So that's one part," Weis says. "If you look a little bit back—imagine yourself 10 feet away from this—you've got a couple of hands in a position that could be viewed as horns. That's another symbol of this particular gang."

The gang in question is the Maniac Latin Disciples, and Weis, now president of the Chicago Crime Commission, says even the large heart that forms the artwork's centerpiece is a main symbol of that gang.

"When you add the heart symbol, you add the hand signs, you add the hand placements—you can see where there might be a perception that this could be in some way reflecting on a particular gang."

Weis and others also point out that Pulgar's Facebook page—since taken down—had several gang-related photographs and comments.

But Pulgar, a freshman at a high school for children with emotional and learning disabilities, insists he is not in any gang and did not try to sneak gang symbols into his vehicle sticker design.

"Our design doesn't have nothing to do with no gangs. Nothing," Pulgar tearfully told Chicago's WGN-TV. "It don't have nothing to do with no gangs, no violence, no nothing."

The winning decal (Figure 6.12), designed by Chicago teen Herbie Pulgar, depicts a heart-enclosed skyline of Chicago along with various hands throwing up hats as symbols for "Chicago's Heroes": the police, firefighters, and emergency medical personnel that help keep the city safe. While the overall subject seems clear—celebrating local heroes—other elements may be interpreted in other ways. And they were, causing the city to reject using the decal even though Pulgar won the contest. David Schaper explains the controversy in this article from *NPR*.

Credit: City of Chicago's Clerk's Office

Figure 6.12
The details in Herbie Pulgar's design were upsetting to some.

Regardless of intent, perception of the final piece matters, and city officials had to choose the second-place design for the parking decals. While not necessarily derived from premade images, the hand signs are still visuals that signify certain meanings.

But in a city where gang violence terrorizes some neighborhoods, Chicago City Clerk Susana Mendoza says Pulgar's sticker design had to go, regardless of the boy's intent.

"I can't ask any Chicagoan to put on a city sticker that is mired in controversy related to gangs," Mendoza says. "So whether that was the intent or not, it doesn't matter. Because the perception is out there that there could be a correlation—and that's unacceptable."

Had Pulgar known this, he might have drawn the hands differently to avoid any connection to Chicago gangs. Although you might not expect students in a high school competition to undergo the kind of research covered in this chapter, the unfortunate outcome presented here shows the importance of researching the details of a particular image thoroughly before placing it into your project.

The text's genre

Beyond the content that makes up a text, the genre in which a text appears also has its own history. When considering writing a blog post, web page, tweet, status update, digital image, video, flyer, poster, or any other genre, you should research to determine why you might choose one genre over another.

Each kind of genre conveys information in different ways. A movie poster typically displays the title of the movie more prominently than other information, such as the production crew. However, the viewer can glance at the poster as a whole, and scan it as he or she likes.

A video, however, typically only allows the viewer to see it in a linear, controlled fashion. The viewer could fast-forward, pause, or rewind, but the video would typically make less sense.

Blogging allows for a more sustained discussion of a topic than microblogging, which usually only allows 140 characters to make a short, succinct point.

A proposal for a new car design, however, may be purposefully designed to be read differently by different audiences. A CEO or manager might only read the executive summary, while those in finance will read the budget, and engineers will read the technical aspects. Knowing how a genre is meant to be used is important when deciding which genre to use to distribute your message.

You might also consider subgenres. For example, the genre of film consists of many kinds of subgenres, such as drama, comedy, romantic comedy, horror, fantasy, and others. Each of these has further subgenres, with its own specific influences. Horror films can include such subtypes as slasher or zombie horror. You can probably think of others as well. Knowing the conventions and formulas for each of these subgenres can help you better understand how these films work, and help you better understand how to use them in your own works.

Typography

Like genres, typographies have their own histories as well. It's easy to forget that typefaces that come preloaded into word processor programs had to be designed and invented by a human being. Many of these typefaces were commissioned by an individual or group who wanted typography with a certain aesthetic—a particular look and feel.

Credit: Pbarnola

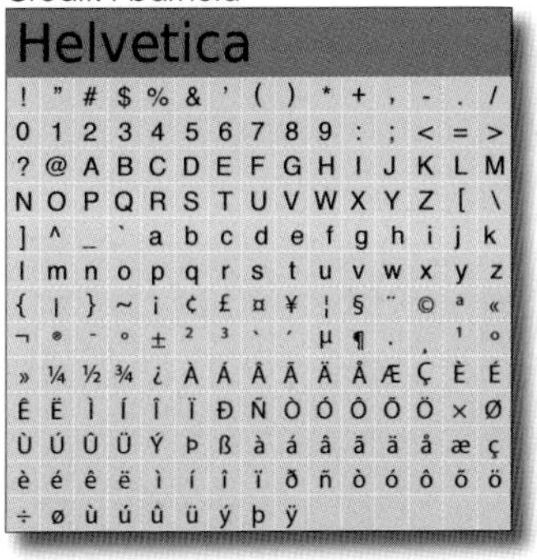

Figure 6.13
Helvetica remains a popular typeface.

The typefaces Helvetica (Figure 6.13), for instance, was designed by Swiss typeface designers Max Miedinger and Eduard Hoffmann in 1957. During this time period, designers were moving toward a cleaner, modernist look that was very simple and utilitarian. Because Helvetica displayed these characteristics that many designers were looking for, it became the designated font for hundreds of companies and organizations.

However, during the Vietnam War, younger designers felt that Helvetica came to symbolize the very companies they felt were perpetuating the war, and they started to create more unique typefaces that moved away from Helvetica's simple forms. Reaction to Helvetica today is mixed: Some designers feel it is so simple, easy, and timeless that it is an important typeface that should still be used. Other designers, however, feel that Helvetica is overused, constricting, and lazy.

When composing digital texts, you should determine if your final version will remain digital or be printed. Some typefaces read well on paper, but not on a computer monitor. Typefaces like Calibri were designed specifically to be read on screen. Researching your typefaces before you include them in a design can help you understand how audiences might react to different typefaces.

Color usage

Color choice requires extensive research, since colors can mean different things to different groups and individuals. While the United States and many western nations use the color red to symbolize danger, such as on a stop sign, some Asian countries consider red as a symbol of good luck or happiness. In Ireland, however, green is the color for good luck.

The chart in Figure 6.14 analyzes some of the moods associated with different colors in ten cultural contexts. Love, #53, is represented by red in Western/ American, Japanese, and Eastern European cultures, green in Hindu, yellow in Native American, and blue in African cultures. The color for a "truce" is white in most cultures—which you may recognize in the expression "waving the white flag"—except in Muslim and African cultures, in which the color silver represents this idea. Such differences don't preclude you from using any particular color, but you should be attuned to your audience's perceptions and associations about colors when making your selections. Research how your various audiences might respond to colors when considering your design choices.

Credit: David McCandless & AlwaysWithHonor.org

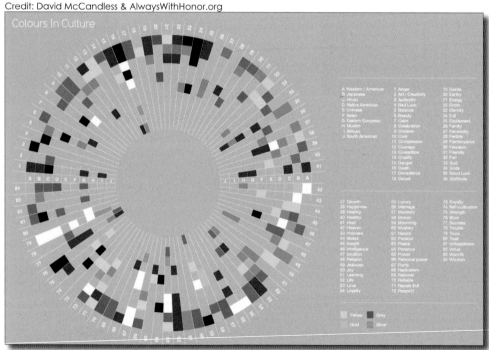

Figure 6.14
Colors mean different things to different cultures.

Composition techniques

When looking at a design, you might consider specific composition techniques that were used to create a particular effect. For example, low-key lighting (as seen in Figure 6.15), a method of lighting in which most of the frame is dark, was used in films in the early 1900s to depict "sinister" scenes. This technique is still used in many horror and suspense films, and it's easy to take for granted that scenes depicting dark subject matter should be lit darkly. However, the technique had to be invented, and part of this invention occurred when films began to shoot indoors or at night using artificial light.

Credit: Warner Brothers

Figure 6.15
Even modern movies still use low-key lighting to seem "sinister."

The technique of montage also has a rich history as well as specific theories related to its use. If you notice a particular technique in a visual, consider researching more about it, learning who invented it, the kinds of effects it is meant to have on an audience, or where it appears in other works. Such knowledge will help you think more professionally about how you use these techniques yourself.

Digital platforms

When considering a digital text, you also must research the digital tools needed to complete a project, as well as the platforms you might use to create and publish a text. For instance, if you create a video, should you distribute it on YouTube, which has a broad audience, or Vimeo, which is often considered more professional? If you're composing a blog, should you use WordPress, Blogger, LiveJournal, or some other option? How will your audience respond to each of these? What costs are involved? In terms of software, will you need access to professional-quality production software, such as the Adobe Creative Cloud, or will the photo editor that came with the computer suffice? Before putting too much effort into a project, determine which digital tools you'll need to create your digital text.

Search Engine

Online, search for a list of photographic or cinematic techniques, and choose one that interests you. Research this technique, including its invention, the first photos or films in which it appeared and the photographer or director who is most associated with it. Make a claim about how important you think this technique has been, and provide supporting reasons and evidence.

Link

With a partner, choose a movie you both enjoy. Identify the genre of the movie, as well as the director, time period, and other important elements. Next, identify previous movies that might have influenced it (based on your knowledge of the genre conventions and other films within the same genre), the kinds of movies that influenced the director, and any other information you feel is pertinent. Finally, what kinds of future films do you think this movie would influence? Write a short report on your results. In the report, make a claim about your data, and support that claim with reasons and evidence.

Ownership and Copyright

When looking for other texts to place in your own works, you have to be aware of copyright laws and how they affect you. Most works are copyrighted, a legal protection that designates the exclusive right the creator has to his or her intellectual property and can determine if it can be used by others, where, how often, and for how much compensation (Figure 6.16).

Figure 6.16
The copyright symbol designates that a work is copyrighted. However, a work can still be copyrighted without displaying this symbol.

Intellectual property is simply any original created work, such as music, a novel, a film, a poster, a photograph, computer program, or even one of your own college essays. If a work is protected by an existing copyright, you cannot use it without permission from the creator unless your project falls into a special category, such as fair use.

Generally, most of your class projects fall under fair use if they're noncommercial and for educational purposes. However, future projects beyond the classroom may not fall under this category. Below are some basic guidelines to follow when selecting works. However, what follows is not legal advice, and you'll have to conduct further research (or hire an intellectual property attorney) to make sure you can appropriate another person's intellectual works.

Fair use

Typically, work you complete for class will fall under "fair use," a section in copyright law that allows you to avoid seeking permission to use another's copyrighted work. Fair use, however, is a legal defense that can only be tested in court and must hold up to legal scrutiny if a particular copyright holder feels your use of his or her material isn't "fair." Here are four guidelines to research to determine if your overall project and use of copyrighted materials constitute the fair use doctrine. The better you meet all four criteria, the more likely you have used the work in good faith.

- The purpose and character of the use, including whether such use is commercial in nature or is for nonprofit educational purposes
- The nature of the copyrighted work
- The amount and substantiality of the portion used in relation to the copyrighted work
- The effect of the use upon the potential market for, or value of, the copyrighted work

The purpose and character of the work must be transformative in some way and not simply derivative. For instance, the law mentions the following specific uses: "criticism, comment, news reporting, teaching (including multiple copies for classroom use), scholarship, or research." While not every educational use falls under fair use, many do, including most of the projects you'll be working on.

The nature of the work often refers to what it expresses, fact or fiction. Generally, you can disseminate and incorporate facts into your works—such as journalistic reporting—much more readily than creative works.

The amount of the work you use is also important to consider. Generally, you should use as little of a copyrighted work as possible. If you were using a clip from a film, it should generally be 10 percent of the total film, or two to three minutes, whichever is less. If you were using a song, no more than 30 seconds should be used. The less of the original work you use, the more likely you'll be protected by fair use. However, even if the amount you use is very small, if it constitutes the "heart" of the work, fair use might not protect you.

Finally, courts will consider the effect your work has on the market value of the work for the copyright holder. The fewer people that will see your work, and the shorter the time period it will be available for viewing, the more likely that it will not unduly affect the potential financial interests of the owner.

Public domain

You can avoid dealing with fair use and copyright issues if you select works from the public domain. Usually, copyright only lasts for a limited period of time. If a work's copyright expires, then the work is in the public domain and can be used without restrictions. Currently, any work produced before 1923 is now in the public domain unless its author, or estate representing that author, has extended it (Figure 6.17).

Also, because they're paid for with public funds, most works produced by U.S. government agencies fall within the public domain. Some authors create work specifically for the public domain that may be reused and reproduced freely. Others utilize the copyright system of Creative Commons, which permits use in certain contexts and conditions, such as whether the work will be used for commercial or noncommercial purposes, if it will undergo modifications, if it is properly attributed, or as long as the new work may be shared as well (Figure 6.18).

Figure 6.17
This public domain symbol designates that a work is under the public domain and free to use without seeking permission.

Figure 6.18
Creative Commons brand symbol. Users who publish their works under Creative Commons can designate that they want all, some, or none of their rights protected.

Building

Link

The intent of copyright laws clearly states that "ideas" cannot be copyrighted, only their expression. Select an idea or concept that appears often in popular culture, such as zombies, vampires, aliens, etc. Then, find as many expressions of this idea as you can, either in movies, books, television, advertising, or other forms. Analyze how each of these media creates a new expression that can be copyrighted. Do any particular expressions seem to closely resemble others, perhaps creating a copyright infringement? Write a report in which you make a claim based on the questions above, and include reasons and evidence.

Engine

Search

Music presents one of the most difficult copyrights to obtain, often requiring several types of permissions. Research the general process for acquiring the right to reproduce copyrighted music. Who owns the copyright? Who owns distribution rights? What kinds of licenses are required? Compose a report of your findings, and share them with the class.

Filmic Research: A Digital Writing Analogy

As an example and analogy of the kinds of research you might have to conduct, consider how much research goes into a feature film. One has to screen the locations where a movie will be shot. One also has to screen the actors who will be cast in the film. However, before each of these selections can occur, the location scout, casting director, and other key personnel must have researched what they're looking for before performing each of these tasks. That is, the location scout must research the kinds of places in which the film takes place so the landscape best matches what the screenwriter and director have in mind. Likewise, the casting director should research the traits of the characters for which she'll cast so she knows what physical features to look for in the actors who audition for roles.

Once cast, the actors themselves have much research to do before they ever visit the set, have their makeup and hair done, or stand in front of a camera. For instance, if her role is based on a historical character, the actor will most likely want to research the biography of the person, learn about her traits, habits, patterns, friends, family, pets, and any other information that's available. If the character is a living person, the actor may want to talk to the person herself.

Johnny Depp, who has delivered some of the more bizarre and memorable performances in recent cinema, often thoroughly researches his roles and uses this research to create his own take on traditional, and not-so-traditional, characters.

Building

Link

Find examples of other actors who go to extreme lengths when researching their roles. What kinds of research do they perform? How do they research? How do they feel such research affects their performance? Thinking about it rhetorically, how do you think this research brings *logos, ethos, pathos,* or *kairos* to their roles? Do you think such research is necessary, or overkill? Why? Draft a short argument, complete with claim, reasons, and evidence that discusses your perspective.

Engine

Search

Imagine you were cast in the role of a space alien for an epic science fiction film. How would you start to research your role? What previous works would you look to? How would you try to develop your character's *ethos* through this research? Write a short report that argues for your approach, and support it with reasons and evidence.

DIGITAL Connections

Johnny Depp Explains How He Picked his Poison with the Mad Hatter

By Rachel Abramowitz

> Consider this article from Rachel Abramowitz from *The Los Angeles Times,* who describes Depp's preparation to play the Mad Hatter (Figure 6.19) in Tim Burton's *Alice in Wonderland*—part of which involves literally painting the character.

When he takes on a role, Johnny Depp often paints a watercolor portrait of the still-forming character to help find his face and personality. After putting the finishing touches on his painting for "Alice in Wonderland," Depp looked down at the Mad Hatter staring back at him from the canvas and giggled.

"I was thinking," the actor said, "'Oh my God, this one will get me fired!'"

Depp's extreme vision for the character…creates yet another vivid screen persona for the Hollywood chameleon who has played Sweeney Todd, Willy Wonka, Edward Scissorhands and a

Credit: Everett Collection

Figure 6.19
Johnny Depp as the Mad Hatter

certain scoundrel named Jack Sparrow. The 46-year-old actor said his Hatter's springy mass of tangerine hair became a particularly important detail because of one of the suspected origins of the term "Mad as a hatter."

In the 18th and 19th centuries, mercury was used in the manufacture of felt, and when used in hats it could be absorbed through the skin and affect the mind through maladies such as Korsakoff syndrome. Hatters and mill workers often fell victim to mercury poisoning which, in Lewis Carroll's time, had an orange tint—hence Depp's interest in adding brush strokes of that particular watercolor to his portrait.

"I think [the Mad Hatter] was poisoned—very, very poisoned," Depp said. "And I think it just took affect in all his nerves. It was coming out through his hair and through his fingernails, through his eyes."

Depp's research also took him down some unexpected literary rabbit holes with the writings of Carroll.

"There's a great line in the book where the Hatter says, 'I'm investigating things that begin with the letter 'M,''" Depp said. "So I started kind of doing a little researching, reading a bunch. And you start thinking about the letter 'M' and hatters and the term 'mad as a hatter' and 'mercury.'"

Depp was also intrigued by one of the Mad Hatter's nonsense questions during a dizzying tea party: "Why is a raven like a writing desk?" "I think he is referencing Edgar Allan Poe," Depp said, referring to the haunted author of "The Raven," which was published in 1845, two decades before Carroll's surreal tale reached the public. Depp let the two ideas germinate in his head and it informed his own Hatter concoction.

Director Tim Burton, whose background in art and animation is well known, also draws his characters, and when he and his star compared their handiwork they grinned like the Cheshire Cat. "They were," Depp says, "very close."

Depp's research is multifaceted, looking into the historical, literary, psychological, and physical aspects of his character-to-be (Figure 6.20). Depp looks into the historical instances of "mad hatter disease" brought about by mercury poisoning, a chemical used in the production of hats during the time Lewis Carroll wrote *Alice in Wonderland*, a chemical that still poisons us today (Figure 6.21). Such information influences how Depp paints his character's picture—such as the red hair and nails—and thus affects the choices of others involved in the production, such as hair and makeup artists.

Depp now has psychological (and physiological) motivation for why the Mad Hatter should be mad and can inhabit his character more convincingly. Finally, Depp researched the work on which the movie is based rather than just relying on the script. Carroll's text offers him insights into the Mad Hatter that the screenwriter might not have included, and these bits of information

Credit: Oskar Gustav Rejlander

Figure 6.20
Mad Hatter disease was a problem in Lewis Carroll's time.

Credit: Tom Friedel

Figure 6.21
Mercury poisoning is still an issue today, just not through the hatting industry.

helped Depp deliver a performance that is both faithful and unique.

This research is not only multilayered and multifaceted, but also collaborative. As already discussed, others besides the actors are researching on their own, such as the casting directors, who perform their own research on the Mad Hatter. And as Depp's final statement illustrates—that his and director Tim Burton's paintings of the Mad Hatter were "very close" (Figure 6.22)—this collaborative research eventually synthesizes into a shared vision of what the final project should look like.

Credit: The Art of Tim Burton

Figure 6.22
Tim Burton's painting of the Mad Hatter.

Rhetorical Continuities

This synthesis is not unlike writing a research paper, where all of the different sources used to make an argument should be arranged and integrated so they support the one voice of the author, rather than reading like disparate, unconnected statements. A large production requires all the actors and agents to research their own parts, distributing the work across the cast and crew, leaving it up to the director to make sure all the research distills into a coherent vision.

If the different elements in your own compositions become actors that you have to screen before casting, then you will need to research each of their roles sufficiently before including them in your text (and unfortunately, such elements can't research themselves). However, part of casting an actor involves looking at his prior work—what other roles he's performed—to help determine his suitability for a new role. Many images, techniques, genres, and other visual elements have their own history of roles that can help you determine how well they might fit. Luckily, since all these elements should be digital, they're easily changeable and rearrangeable. At least, more so than having to fire an actor and search for a new one.

Finally, *how much* research and *what kind* of research needs to be done depends on the type of film. Since *Alice in Wonderland* is based on a literary work, the cast and crew should read the work, research its creation, and perhaps research the author. They should also research the context in which the book was written, as Depp did, noting the historical moment and connections that influence the book and thus the film.

If the film is about the Civil War, then the producer, director, and actors have historical information to research, such as aspects of living and fighting in the Civil War, weapons of the time, meanings of colloquial vocabulary, or perhaps riding a horse.

If the movie takes place in outer space, then the production crew should research the environment of space, how features such as zero gravity or lack of atmosphere affect the way that physical actions might occur, as well as the psychological effects of living in space (Figure 6.23). This kind of environmental research must be done in addition to the other creative aspects that affect plotline and character development. Research becomes the most important part of making a successful film, and this occurs before the director ever shouts "action."

Credit: George Pantalos

Figure 6.23
To research and prepare to play NASA astronauts in *Apollo 13*, Tom Hanks and Kevin Bacon flew aboard a KC-135 "vomit comet." This aircraft can simulate zero gravity for up to 24 seconds.

Building

Link

Develop an idea for a movie. Once you have the basic concept, create a list of research goals necessary to understand the job that needs to be done (acting, designing sets, creating makeup effects, etc.). Choose one of these areas, and create a list of specific topics and sources you might use to find important information related to such research. What insights did you glean from researching for this kind of visual text? Write a report that explains your research findings and process.

Engine

Search

Think of your favorite film. Analyze the kinds of research you think the cast and crew needed to do in order to create the film. Did they have to perform historical research? Environmental research? Literary research? Scientific research? Did they have to research similar movies that came before and thus influenced the new production (as when a movie is remade)? Present your claims in a brief report, and include reasons and evidence.

KEY Terms

audience

color

composition technique

copyright

database

details

digital platform

fair use

genres

influence

primary source

public domain

purpose

remix

research

secondary source

subject

typography

website

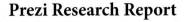

Prezi Research Report

For this assignment, research a historic image or video you might incorporate into a piece of digital writing. Research as many details as you can, such as the creator, subject, purpose, audience, influence, historical context, details, genre, and other aspects. Rather than a written report, however, compose your report as a Prezi presentation (Figure 6.24).

Credit: prezi.com

Figure 6.24
Prezi offers a more dynamic way to present than other software programs.

Prezi is a free online based presentation software that allows you to display information less linearly than Power-Point. Prezi allows you to pan and zoom across a single canvas, so you can look at multiple images simultaneously or zoom in on particular details. Prezi also allows the easy integration of images and video. Follow these basic instructions toward completing this project, although your instructor might have more details for you to consider.

1. **Select an image.** This image will hopefully be one you find motivating, appealing, or somehow interesting. You would do best to find an image that's fairly well known and has much information available for you to study. You might also think about the disciplines in which to look for an image: artistic, journalistic, scientific, nature-based, or biographical.

2. **Create a Prezi account.** Visit Prezi.com to start your account. Prezi accounts are free to set up, and if you use an ".edu" email address, you can get an "Edu Enjoy" plan for free, instead of paying a monthly fee.

3. **Start using Prezi.** It doesn't take long to learn how to use Prezi and the website offers a thorough tutorial—both written and in video—to get you started.

4. **Compose your Prezi.** Insert the information you've gathered about the image to start constructing your presentation. Prezi offers a few predesigned arrangements for organizing your material, but you also might sketch your layout on paper before integrating your materials online.

5. **Use images and video.** Presentations are usually better received when you include visuals for the audience to see rather than just lines of texts for them to read. From your research, what images can you include? What videos? Perhaps you've found experts discussing the image on YouTube you can include.

6. **Present your Prezi to the class.** When you present, do not read the text off the screen, but instead try to paraphrase with different words to explain the different elements of your image.

From DIGITAL Writers

As an example of a Prezi-based report, consider this annual report from the organization DonorsChoose.org.

DonorsChoose.org is an online charity that helps direct funds to educational projects in public school classrooms.

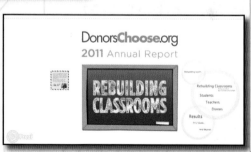

DonorsChoose.org Annual Report

prezi.com/6vkffcihisht/
donorschooseorg-fy11-annual-report/

You might also consider this Prezi by Jessica White, which is a report about writing reports.

Prezi by Jessica White

prezi.com/5jll5evtlfsv/report/

STUDENT Example

Nadine Vandergaast's presentation is available online.

Prezi by Nadine Vandergaast

prezi.com/um6_mzqw5dsu/heros-journey-research-report/

Consider this student example from Nadine Vandergaast, who compares and contrasts the heroic journey Harry Potter takes in the book and film versions of *Harry Potter and the Philosopher's Stone*.

Digital Genres and Modes

From the young age of 12, Malala Yousafzai began writing blogs for the BBC in which she described what it was like to live in Taliban-controlled Pakistan. Because of her blogging, Malala was often asked to be in various documentaries and interviews, and she became an activist for women's rights and access to education—for the region where she lived had banned girls from attending school. Her use of blogging and social media earned her a nomination from South African activist Desmond Tutu for the International Children's Peace Prize. However, her outspokenness also garnered fear and anger from those in control, and on October 9, 2012, a gunman, asking for her by name, shot her in the head.

Fortunately, Malala survived the attack and continues her work. From a few simple but brave blog posts, she now has written a book, has been awarded the National Youth Peace Prize of Pakistan, the Sakharov Prize, the Simone de Beauvoir Prize, and is the youngest child to be nominated for the Nobel Peace Prize. All because she wanted the right to go to school.

Unlike print, digital genres allow writers like Malala to connect much more quickly to their audience and more easily bypass those who might want to censor her. This chapter examines these digital genres, such as websites, blogs, and social media.

However, even though Malala uses a digital genre, she still uses traditional rhetorical modes, or the purposes for writing. Her blog incorporates description, helping the reader experience the sights, smells, sounds, and other elements of life in Pakistan; she uses exposition to inform the reader about her activities, daily routines, and the politics and challenges she faces; she uses narration to present this information in an interesting and captivating story; and finally,

she uses the mode of argumentation to argue that girls should be able to attend school and get an education.

Although Malala uses a blog to deliver her information, she uses modes that can apply to any genre. You can think of genre as a category of writing, and mode as the purpose. If Malala chose to write about her life in a diary, her modes would probably have remained very similar, even if the writing technology was very different. Malala could also use the modes of description, exposition, narration, and argumentation in a photo essay, video, a series of Facebook posts, or even a Twitter feed, all of which are categories of writing rather than the purpose for writing. Genre and mode are not mutually exclusive, but instead complementary: you can think of a genre as a container for a mode. Furthermore, more than one mode is usually used within a single text. As you read about each genre and mode, consider how the two can be integrated within each other.

Although any text could be converted into a digital text, some texts are more digitally native than others. For instance, an image created wholly in Photoshop might be considered a true digital image, while a painting that's merely scanned might be considered just a digital copy. While this book mostly avoids these distinctions, this chapter covers particular genres of digital texts that usually can't be created offline and scanned online. The discussions of the digital genres and modes below will include what each genre and mode entail, as well as why you might choose one over another. The genres of digital images and digital video, however, have been left out of this chapter and are covered in separate chapters, Chapters 8 and 9, respectively.

Given this chapter is called "Digital Genres and Modes," it may seem that it limits attention to a specific rhetorical element. However, while genre and modes might be the focus, you should think of genres and modes in relation to your audience, the text's message, and the medium and design that you incorporate into a particular genre. Since a rhetorical situation is always shifting and in flux, you should think about how your genre and modes for writing meet a particular environment and moment (kairos) and interact with the other parts of rhetoric and your audience's expectations.

Modes: Purposes and Shapes of Writing

While "genres" is a term for the different categories of documents that you might write (memos, emails, websites, videos), "modes" identifies the purpose for your writing—what the writing attempts to do. In this way, modes are incorporated into writing genres. For example, a website (genre = category)

may be created in order to explain (mode = purpose) an object or event. In addition, modes are often mixed together to complete a more robust, complex text that performs a variety of purposes. The following list (another genre) offers an overview and description (another mode) of the most common modes you may use in your own writing.

Argumentation

This is the predominant mode that you've read about so far in this book. An argument is simply a claim about your opinion that is supported with reasons and evidence for why an audience should accept the opinion as accurate. When you argue, the purpose is to convince your audience of this claim. Thus, as an argument, the mode of argumentation must adopt good practices of making an argument, discussed in Chapter 3. An argument should have an arguable topic, a claim, valid reasons, credible evidence, opposing arguments, an audience, and a conclusion.

Martin P. Hoerling's essay in Chapter 4 includes all of these elements. Hoerling argues that, although California is in the midst of a drought, this particular drought is not caused by global warming, as opposing arguments might suggest. Hoerling's reasons for his claim include historical trends and scientific evidence such as rainfall patterns and population growth. His audience includes those affected by the water shortage, and he concludes by noting that although global warming plays a part in droughts, the particular drought in California is primarily a result of many more factors.

For an example of argumentative writing that you may have already completed, the Execute assignment from Chapter 3 asks you to compose a response in the genre of a YouTube video. In the assignment, you are asked to present a counter argument to another YouTube video, providing your own claim, reasons for the claim, and evidence to support those reasons. This assignment has a clear mode (argumentation), and also a clear genre (video). The Execute assignment in Chapter 8 also asks you to write in the argumentative mode, but in yet another genre (photographs).

As a whole, this entire book teaches you how to write in the argumentative mode, but be aware that argumentation is a specific purpose for writing, and not all writing need be an explicit argument. The wall carving of Ramesses II, discussed at the beginning of Chapter 4, argues that Ramesses II was a great and powerful ruler, even if this claim isn't explicitly written with words. Instead, the wall carving describes the foundation which supports this point of view. As you'll see below, other modes can help you better convince, even if argumentation isn't their primary purpose.

Narration

This mode is used to tell a story about some event. For example, if you were going to discuss what you did on your summer vacation, the telling of this event would be a narration of what happened, in chronological order. Within longer, more complex texts, you might provide narration to provide details about an event before moving onto other modes that might explain why the event happened or what to do about it. Narration is the foundation of anecdotes, biography or autobiography, and storytelling.

Anecdote

This kind of narration provides the details of a short incident, often used to provide evidence toward some other purpose, such as argumentation or exposition. For example, in a cover letter for a job application, you might provide an anecdote in which you narrate about a successful work experience that you think will make you look favorable to the potential employer. If you were applying for a banking position, you might provide a short anecdote that shows your passion for the profession, such as something like: "I remember the thrill from executing my first loan. It was for the Davis family, who happened to be purchasing their first home. By helping the Davises navigate the financial landscape of buying a home, I got to see them fulfill their dream. It's these experiences that make me passionate about work in the financial sector." This short narrative helps to better show your audience some event and provide an appeal to pathos.

Biography or autobiography

While you're probably familiar with biography (and autobiography), these modes narrate the events of a person's life, either in whole or in part. Biography can often be used rhetorically to build ethos (or destroy it) by narrating life events as evidence for some claim. For example: if you were arguing that you should be elected president, you might include autobiographical narration to build evidence for your qualifications. As Julian Zelizer explains in his essay in Chapter 3, Jimmy Carter provided a short biography in a 1976 advertisement. As Zelizer writes, Carter "talked about his personal story in Georgia and used his own upbringing as the most important characteristic of the campaign." Carter used his autobiographical information not simply to inform viewers, but to persuade them that such a background as his will make him a better president. Carter mixes the narrative mode into the large mode of argumentation.

Storytelling

Narration can also be used to simply entertain the audience, framing an overall story for other purposes you might have, such as description or argumentation.

Many of Aesop's Fables attempt to make an important point, but do so through an entertaining story about animals rather than simply offer an abstract moral. For example, the story of the grasshopper and the ants, in which the grasshopper doesn't save enough food for the winter and perishes—unlike the prudent ants—makes the reader take interest in an emotionally engaging narrative with characters they grow to care about. Rather than just state "you should work hard and prepare for the future," the story shows the audience what happens to those who do not heed such advice. Used in this way, narration can make your writing more accessible and enjoyable than pure description or argumentation.

Description

The mode of description can be used to re-create sensory experience through written language, making the experience present to the audience through a written account. This sensory experience can include a written description for all the ways that you can sense the physical world, including sight, touch, smell, sound, and taste, and a writer might describe the experience of encountering an object or witnessing an event. For example, a zoologist who discovers a new species of animal might describe the animal through words, such as its shape, size, color, odor, texture, presence of features, and often in tandem with mathematical measurements. Even though a photograph or illustration might capture some of the animal's visual elements, a written description is needed to capture sensory experiences that an image cannot capture, such as how it feels, smells, tastes, or sounds. Description is utilized as a component of two sub-modes: classification and compare and contrast.

Classification

When you sort objects or ideas into groups based on similar characteristics, you classify them. You've probably been classifying from a very early age, sorting blocks by similar colors as a toddler, or letters into vowels and consonants. At various points, this book has classified some kinds of writing as "digital" writing, and other kinds as "alphabetic" writing. Using the example above, the zoologist might try to classify the animals within other groups based on the description. The zoologist might describe the animal as being warm-blooded and having mammary glands (thus, a mammal), but also being mostly hairless and shaped like a fish. Based on this description, the zoologist might classify the animal as a type of cetacean (whales and dolphins).

Compare and contrast

When you analyze how objects or ideas are similar to or different from one another, you are comparing and contrasting. The zoologist above compares the animal she found to those animals she already knows about in order to determine a similar group within which to classify it. However, she then contrasts it with these animals to determine how it's different and why it might be a new species. In this way, the mode of description is used to compare and contrast. If you were to sniff two different kinds of perfume, you might describe the smells that you notice in each one and describe how they are different. In one, you might smell pine, lemon, and jasmine, while in another you might detect leather, tobacco, and iris. Based on these descriptions, you might decide that they are similar in that they both use a floral extract (jasmine and iris), but very different based on the other ingredients.

Exposition

Writers use exposition when they need to teach the audience about some situation in order to further a claim. For example, you might explain how to complete some task, or inform the audience about a new policy that has been established. Let's say that you owned a saltwater fish store. At the end of the day, certain tasks related to feeding and cleaning the tanks need to be performed before closing the store so that the fish survive overnight. You might write a short manual to your employees that explains what tasks to complete, and how to complete these tasks so that all of your fish are alive when you open the next day. Such writing isn't arguing that the fish should be taken care; instead, this writing explains facts about how to do so. Exposition is an element of definition, exemplification, and cause and effect.

Definition

Often, writers must explain the definition of the term they present to their readers so that they understand the precise way that the writer is using the term within a given text. In such cases, the writer must provide a clear, precise definition for the term (or an object or an idea) through carefully crafted exposition. If you were comparing genetically modified apples with organic apples, you might need to define "apple" by identifying which variety of apples you were discussing to create an equal comparison. In your manual for the fish store, you might need to define different materials or objects for your employees. For example, if one of the steps instructed employees to test for pH levels for each tank using a pH probe, you might need to define what pH means (the acidity level of the water) as well as what a pH probe is (a sensor used to test the acidity level in some substance).

Exemplification

This form of exposition simply means to illustrate through an example. Sometimes, this example might only last a sentence or two. However, you might also need to provide a more extended example that lasts paragraphs or even pages. If you were going to discuss a topic, such as "The Dangers of Space Exploration," you might spend pages discussing all of the facts about the 1986 Challenger disaster in order to illustrate your point. In the fish store manual, you might provide an example of what a properly completed step looks like: "When you're done cleaning a tank, it should be free of algae on the sides of the glass, and the water should be crystal clear."

Cause and effect

While a narrative discusses some event in chronological order, the exposition of cause and effect is intended to explain why that event occurred, and what effects might have come about from it. In other words, writing to explain cause and effect specifically attempts to show the connections between one action and another. For example, after doing research into the Challenger explosion, you might conclude that the technical cause of the explosion was due to a faulty O-ring in one of the rocket boosters. However, you might further conclude that another cause was due to administrators who would not postpone the launch in order to check and repair the O-ring. In the fish store manual, you might provide an example of some of the steps, or provide an example of what could happen if the manual isn't followed: "The last time that these steps were not taken, 75 percent of the fish were dead the next day." This sentence displays the cause and effect related to using the manual and properly closing the store.

Along with other modes, exposition helps you to provide information within the context of larger purposes, which usually include convincing an audience of a particular point of view. Exposition can be used to present logical arguments (why something exists in such a way, or how something works) for why they should accept your overall claim. Although the fish store manual exists in order to inform the employee of how to close the shop, how it is written can also present an argument for why the manual should be followed, and why it is written in such a way. The use of definitions, exemplification, and cause and effect all contribute logical appeals in support of a larger argument. In fact, all of the modes discussed here can contribute to a larger argument, and so none of them need exist in isolation. The zoologist may use classification and compare and contrast forms of description in order to describe the species as a way to argue that the animal she found is indeed a new species of animal never discovered before. Just as genres and modes mix with each other, modes can mix with other modes to create complex arguments. Throughout the rest of the chapter, consider how these modes are incorporated into different kinds of genres.

Building

Link

Locate an advertisement, and analyze the modes that it uses. Does the advertisement write in order to tell a story? Does it attempt to demonstrate cause and effect? Does it describe its product? Does it try to make an argument to the audience? Or, does it use a combination of modes? After analyzing the advertisement, write a short paper in which you make a claim about which modes it uses, and support your claim with reasons and evidence.

Engine

Search

Although the modes in Malala's blog are briefly mentioned above, analyze at least five of her blog posts, and identify what modes she is using in each one. Does any blog post use just a single mode? Is there a blog post that uses more modes than others? If so, why? Based on your findings, develop a claim about how you see Malala using modes in her blog, and support your claim with reasons and evidence.

Genre Continuities

Before looking at genres that are specifically digital, this section considers the general category of "genre" and the specific features that all genres share when thinking about them rhetorically. Just as other rhetorical practices maintain continuities through time, the use of genres also share continuity in how they are used, even if these genres are as different as a clay tablet and a digital tablet.

Some traditional print genres include the following:

advertisement	instructions	obituary
application	invitation	personal essay
autobiographical essay	journal entries	personal letter
biographical sketch	letter to the editor	picture book
brochure	list	poem
business letter	magazine story	progress report
business report	map	receipt
chart	menu	recipe
comic strip	movie review	research report
definition	myth, tall tale, or fairy	schedule
diagram	tale	science article
encyclopedia article	newsletter	short story
ghost story	newspaper story	song lyrics
greeting card	novel	

As you can see, the list of genres, just in print, can become fairly long. Many of these items could be grouped into broader categories (for instance, personal letter and business letter are both letters), and some items might have subcategories of their own (brochure might include program brochure, travel brochure, museum brochure, school brochure, etc.).

Each of these genres is useful because they help define and predict audience use and expectations. For example, an audience uses a novel much differently than a set of instructions: one is for entertainment, the other for accomplishing a task. You could certainly write a set of instructions as a novel, but the audience would not be expecting this and would probably become irritated at having to follow a story when trying to complete the task at hand.

Tied to audience expectations, genres also have their own conventions and constraints. A business letter is always expected to have a date, greeting, author's address, recipient's address, introduction, body, conclusion, and closing. These are conventions that aren't found in song lyrics, even though lyrics too have many of these elements (a date when written, a recipient, an author, and perhaps even introduction, body, and closing). In addition, a business letter is often constrained from being too personal or too long, because the reader is most likely busy and does not have time to read more than a page or two.

Likewise, emails share many similarities with the expectations, conventions, and constraints of a letter, but they also have others that are uniquely digital. As discussed later in the chapter, emails share with letters the need to be brief, but rather than fit within the space of a 8.5" x 11" sheet of paper, the message must often fit within the space of a screen, which is becoming smaller as users shift from desktop to mobile devices. However, even though changes in the medium and design affect how genres change and develop, you can still ask how an audience will receive a genre, which affects how they will react to your message. In this way, a genre becomes an important rhetorical consideration when trying to argue to your audience, no matter if that genre is print or digital.

As you read through the rest of the chapter, remember that each digital genre shares these characteristics with other genres, even if the particulars of these characteristics change.

Websites

Of the digital genres you encounter on a daily basis, websites are probably the most frequent. You use them to search for information, look up sports news and scores, find out current events, check the weather, monitor your bank account, pay your bills online, as well as other digital writing tasks, such as blogging, tweeting, updating statuses, and other kinds of communication.

While much of this writing can be done through apps on a smartphone, these apps usually originate from and integrate a standard website. In these ways, websites provide a master genre for many other online genres, as you typically have to go to a website to engage with other media, such as videos, images, or audio.

Features of websites

Usually, a website will have at least one, if not all, of the following components that make this kind of digital genre particularly useful and powerful. When you write and view websites, consider how a site uses each of these parts, and how each part becomes a rhetorical consideration, not just a technical one.

Hypertext

Hypertext provides one of the characteristic features of the web, the ability to connect one document with another. Hypertext is any text, image, video, or other element that, when clicked, takes you to another page or element (even if that element is just a larger version, such as clicking a thumbnail image to get the full-size image). When this element is turned into hypertext, it becomes a hyperlink (or just "link"). Hypertext is usually identified some way in the document; you might make it a different color, place a border around it, or include a note to the reader that an element may be clicked.

Rhetorically, think about what strategy might be best when hyperlinking. Would blue text—which is familiar to most readers—be the best choice to identify a hyperlink, or might you use a different color to draw attention, such as red? Also, consider the text itself that you choose to hyperlink. Would certain words be more attractive to click on than others? For instance, some authors use provocative words or titles—referred to as "linkbait" or "clickbait"—to entice a reader to click on a link. However, doing so isn't always honest or ethical, so consider carefully how you present hyperlinks to a reader.

Navigation

Most sites use a clear navigation structure to help the user find the pages or information she is looking for on the website. Navigation menus usually appear in a conspicuous area of the page, such as along the top, left, or right sides, and they usually contain hyperlinks to the major pages of the website (Figure 7.1). To maintain consistency, these menus are usually duplicated on every page of the website.

Sometimes, the navigation menu may have a submenu for each major section that provides more detail about what's in each section. As a reader of websites, consider how you feel a website makes use of navigation menus to help the reader find information. Navigation menus should be clear, logically organized, and help the reader find information quickly. As a writer of websites, consider how you would create your own menu. Where would you place it? How detailed would it be? Depending on which blog platform you use for the assignment at the end of the chapter, you might have the ability to create a menu for your blog. Consider what users would most like to find on your page and how you can maximize their use of the menu.

Credit: NOAA

Figure 7.1
The National Oceanic and Atmospheric Administration uses three menus for navigating its site. How effective do you think this navigation scheme might be?

Building

You and your partner(s) are considering launching a website that sells surfboards, paddleboards, ocean kayaks, and related accessories. Research the range of products you intend to sell, and devise a navigation menu to help your audience find these products, as well as an overall site map for the website. How would you organize information to make it easy for your customers to find the products they want? Sketch a chart outlining your menu, as well as a list of your sitemap. In addition, write a brief explanation claiming why your approach would work. Remember to include reasons and evidence to support your claim.

Link

Engine

Locate three online articles from different websites that make use of hyperlinks. Analyze how these hyperlinks are constructed. Where do these hyperlinks go? What does the text say that is linked? How many hyperlinks appear in the article? Consider the rhetorical use of these hyperlinks. What does the author gain in linking certain text? Does he or she use too many hyperlinks, distracting the reader from reading the actual article? What color are the hyperlinks? Do any of the three articles use hyperlinks better than the others? Write a brief report of your analysis making a claim whether or not you think the author uses hyperlinks effectively.

Search

Web code

Many online applications allow you to create websites without knowing any code. For instance, Wix.com provides a variety of templates that you can customize to create your own website. As discussed below, many different blogging platforms allow you to post content and control layout, plugins, and many other elements of the website's design and function. While coding your own websites from scratch is beyond the scope of this introductory text, it's good to understand a few basics about how websites are typically coded.

Credit: W3Schools

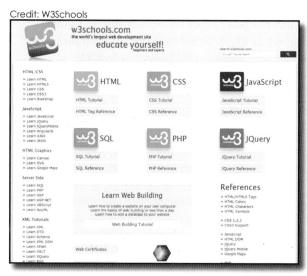

Figure 7.2
The website for W3Schools offers many free web-coding tutorials.

HTML

The most widespread and basic code used to create websites is HTML, which stands for hypertext markup language. HTML code provides the basic instructions necessary for a web browser to understand how to present a website for a reader (Figure 7.2). The code serves as instructions that let the browser know how to structure the content of the website and how this content should behave.

The basic structure of a website coded with HTML is made up of four basic tags:

<html> Instructs the browser that this is an HTML-coded page.

<head> Contains code at the "head" of the document that the browser reads pertaining to the site's style sheet, what the site is about, and other information not seen directly by the human viewer.

<title> Contains the title of the site, which is shown in the top bar of a web browser.

<body> Contains the content seen by the human viewer within the browser window.

Each of these sections are closed with an end tag </>. For instance, </body> closes the body, </title> closes the title, and so on.

CSS

Often, web authors will create the structure of a web page in HTML, but style it using CSS, or cascading style sheets. A CSS provides information on how the text, images, video, and other elements should look. A style sheet makes it easy to make broad changes across a whole website. This convenience helps you avoid having to make these changes page by page.

For instance, a first-level main header would probably be structured by the <h1> HTML tag. However, if you assign a style "class" to it, and give that class a style in the separate style sheet, then a change could be made quickly. The HTML code would read:

<h1 class="blueheader">Main Header</h1>

If this header was 14 pts, Arial, and blue, then the style sheet entry would look like this:

.blueheader {font-size: 14; font-face: arial; font-color: blue;}

Simply changing the font size from 14 to 16, or the color from blue to red, would change every instance of headers tagged with the class of "blueheader" on the site. Visit w3schools.com, which provides explanations, tutorials, and do-it-yourself instructions to help you learn to write CSS.

Metatags

Metatags are tags within the <head> section of a web page that provide information about the document, particularly a description about the web page, key words for the web page, the author, latest update, and other details.

This information is not shown in the browser to the viewer, nor does it provide information on how the site should be formatted. Instead, metatags help search engines locate, identify, and index a web page, so users can better find it during web searches. Thus, metatags are very important for search engine optimization (SEO). Chapter 5 provides more details on how to best compose metatags for SEO purposes.

Building

Link

Choose a single web page from a website (any will do). Right click on the site and select "View Source." The web browser should then show you the HTML code for the website. Based on what you've read about HTML, analyze how the page is constructed. What tags does it use? What are the purposes of these tags? Given what you know about how different audiences read a web page, how are these tags structured for human audiences? How are they structured for search engine robot audiences? How do the tags help bring rhetorical appeals, such as *logos*, *ethos*, *pathos*, or *kairos* to the document? Try repeating this with a web page from another website, and compare the two.

Engine

Search

Research the history of HTML code. Who developed it? How was it designed and why? Is the code used for anything other than websites? Write a short report of your findings and share them with the class.

Blogs

As a kind of website, weblogs, or just blogs, are perhaps the most frequently created kind of website by authors who are not professional web developers (Figure 7.3). It is estimated that a new blog is created every half-second, and 6.7 million people blog, and 46 million people view blogs each year on Blogger alone. As of February 2011, there were 156 million public blogs, and in 2012, Tumblr accounted for 77 million blogs and WordPress 56.6 million. This high number of blogs is mostly due to the wide (and free) availability of premade blogging web publishing platforms and templates available to the public, including blogging platforms such as WordPress, Blogger, Tumblr, or Typepad. You will most likely use one of these platforms for the project at the end of this chapter.

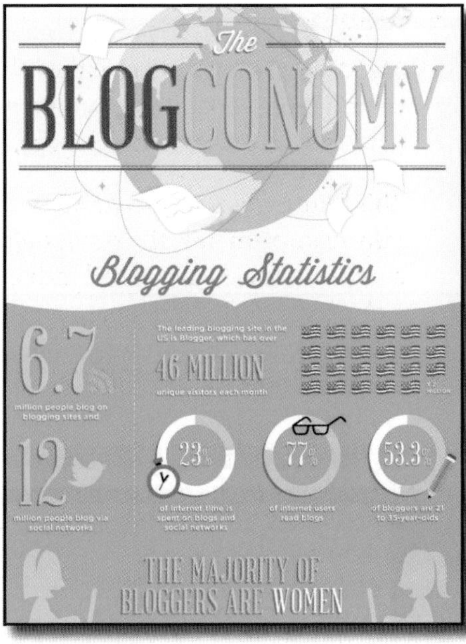

Blogs usually focus on a particular topic or discipline. For instance, political blogs usually don't cover celebrity gossip, and blogs about celebrities usually don't cover local environmental issues. Keeping a blog's topic focused helps to attract readers who are more engaged and interested in the content the author is writing about.

Figure 7.3
This infographic shows the popularity and use of blogs.

Blogs also can be composed in video form, referred to as vlogging (video logging). Often, vlogs are composed and uploaded via YouTube and kept on a YouTube channel or embedded into a blogging platform. Many vlogs serve entertainment purposes, such as Jenna Marbles (jennamarblesblog.com/) or Danisnotonfire (www.youtube.com/user/danisnotonfire), but others help create communities around shared hobbies and interests. Katie Pukrick Smells (www.youtube.com/user/Katie-PuckrikSmells) connects viewers interested in niche perfumes (Figure 7.4). Blogs and vlogs often go hand in hand, so consider how videos might be used to supplement, or even stand in for, a text-based blog.

Figure 7.4
In her video blog, Katie Puckrik discusses perfumes, and you can almost smell them through the video screen.

Most blogging platforms allow you to compose a post with what's called a WYSIWYG editing interface (What You See Is What You Get, pronounced "whiz-eee-wig"). A WYSIWYG editor shows you how your post will look in the browser,

Figure 7.5
Blogger allows you to use a WYSIWYG interface when composing posts.

Figure 7.6
In addition to a WYSIWYG interface, WordPress allows you to compose in HTML.

and allows you to edit text without having to code your own HTML tags (Figure 7.5).

For instance, to italicize text, you can simply highlight the text and click the "I" icon as in a word processor rather than place the text within the tags <i> </i> for italicize. Images, videos, and other elements can be inserted using drag-and-drop or menus as well. However, most blogging platforms also let you see the code so you can manipulate the design and layout more precisely if needed (Figure 7.6). Remember these elements and practices of blogging for when you execute your own blog at the end of the chapter.

Blogging platforms usually allow you to use a variety of predesigned templates. Most services provide several in-house templates, but you can usually search online for other templates made by professional and amateur designers. These templates are usually easy to install, and many are free to use.

Building

Link

Bring in a variety of blogs, including political, entertainment, technology, sports, and other domains. Examine how each blog attempts to stay current, create *ethos* for the author, and construct arguments within a limited space. How long are the posts for each kind of blog? Are some more image-heavy than others? Do they include categories and tags? If different, why do you think these differences exist among these different blog types? Develop a claim from these questions, and support it with reasons and evidence.

Engine

Besides the opening example of Malala, research other bloggers who have made major societal impacts through their blogs. Based on your findings, do you think anyone with access to a blog can change the world in such a way? Why or why not? Develop your perspective into a claim, and support it with reasons and evidence.

Microblogs are a subgenre of blogs, and you're probably most familiar with them through Twitter. Microblogs allow the user only a limited number of characters (usually 140), thus limiting the amount they can write in any one post. Tumblr also can be considered a microblog, as the content for each post is usually just an image or animated gif with a sentence or two explaining or commenting on the image. Vine, which allows you to create short, six-second videos, might be considered a form of microvlogging.

Like other websites, blogs usually have some sort of navigation menu. This can be as complex as different sections for different kinds of information, or simply a list of tags or the most recent posts. To facilitate navigation, most blogs incorporate a search box to make it easy to find a post on a particular topic.

However, blogs also use tags and categories to organize information and aid navigation (Figure 7.7). Just as hyperlinks can be used rhetorically, so can tags and categories that you apply to blog posts, tweets, images, and other digital texts. For instance, as mentioned above, tags and categories can help organize your material into logical relationships so that your reader can more easily navigate your text and argument. Tags and categories also can relate your argument to other conversations, giving the reader a sense of the larger discussion in which you're engaged.

Tags and categories are not the same genre, and should be used in different ways. Use categories to cluster information according to a group or topic.

Figure 7.7
The blog Videogum uses only a few categories as a navigation menu in order to organize its content (movies, TV, webjunk, photos).

For instance, if you had a blog about fishing, you might create the categories for fishing: "Spots," "Tackle," "Gear," and "Photos." These categories differentiate the

kind of material on your blog, but also are broad enough to include many kinds of posts. This way, if your audience wants to read about the tackle you use, but not look at your photos, the navigation is clear.

Generally, you should limit your categories to four to six so as not to confuse your reader with too many of them (Figure 7.8). Decide on your categories during your initial planning and design phase when constructing your blog. These categories will not only help your readers, but they'll also help you keep each post structured and focused toward a particular topic. As Bostjan Spetic writes, "readers who come to your blog for the first time are likely to use categories to navigate to posts that they're interested in. On the other hand, categories help bloggers make better writing decisions and keep them on track."

Tags operate differently. While categories are general and relatively broad, tags are more specific, honing in on particular figures, key words, and examples that all fit into broader categories (Figure 7.9). Again, as

Figure 7.8
Even though *Time* magazine voted The Everywhereist one of its top blogs in 2011, the site probably uses too many categories. Perhaps the author confused categories with tags.

Figure 7.9
The blog *The Truth About Cars* uses tags to organize information for its readers.

Spetic explains, "If you think of categories as sections in your favorite magazine or chapters in a book, think of tags as the index of key words you usually find at the end of a book or as key words used in articles in scientific journals." Going back to the fishing blog example, you might tag posts in the category "Spots" as "redfish" or "trout" to help further index the posts in that category. You also can apply these same tags across categories, helping your reader find all the posts on one of these tags. Thus, if a reader were to click on the tag "redfish," they could easily find all posts in all categories tagged as "redfish," including spots for redfish, tackle for redfish, gear for redfish, and photos of redfish. With a mouse click, tags help your reader quickly find specific information he or she is interested in.

When choosing tags, the following tips usually apply. First, limit your tags to only a few words, and only one when possible. Second, try to limit the number of tags you use. If you're considering using a new tag, check to see if there's another tag you already use that would work just as well (such as a synonym). If so, use existing tags rather than constantly creating new ones.

Third, once you establish repeatable tags, keep using them to help maintain consistency in organization for your reader. Although you will need to create new tags on occasion, try to fit your content within the tags you've already developed and with which your readers have become accustomed.

Building

Link

As in a previous assignment, you and your partner(s) are considering launching a website that sells surfboards, paddleboards, ocean kayaks, and related accessories. In addition to your stand-alone retail website, you decide to create a blog in which you write about the surfing lifestyle, review different products you sell, post images of customers using your products, and other kinds of information to help interest your readers in shopping from your site. Based on your site navigation, what categories and tags would you expect to use to help organize your posts into topics for your audience? Would you stick to the same navigation menu tabs on the website, or would you include others? Write a sample post of a few hundred words, and select a category and tags you would assign to it. Explain why you chose the tags you did, and include reasons and evidence for your choices.

Search Engine

In this chapter, the section on websites looked at metatags and writing for nonhuman audiences. Locate a few well-established blogs, and compare and contrast the use of metatags for these nonhuman audiences, and the use of categories and tags for human audiences. Are any of these tags the same? Are any different? Why do you think this is so? Draft a report with your analysis, and share it with the class.

Email

One of the oldest digital genres, and a genre that you've most likely encountered, is that of email. In fact, you might have sent your first email before sending "snail mail" through the postal service. Although familiar, email can have important conventions depending on situation, context, and audience, and should be rhetorically crafted to meet the needs of the reader.

All email has at least two components: a message header and a message body. The message header usually contains information about the sender, the recipient(s), the date/time, and a subject pertaining to the content of the message.

Rhetorical Continuities

Although the Internet has only been around since the 1990s, the first email was sent by Ray Tomlinson (to himself) in 1971, using early communication networks that would eventually be transformed into the Internet. Unlike Samuel Morse's first telegraph message ("What hath God wrought?"), or Alexander Graham Bell's famous first telephone message ("Mr. Watson—come here—I want to see you"), the first email was more modest and nonsensical, as Tomlinson writes that "The test messages were entirely forgettable. Most likely the first message was QWERTYIOP or something similar" (finance.yahoo.com/news/the-first-ever-email--the-first-tweet--and-12-other-famous-internet-firsts-181209886.html). In this way, email resembled the complaint that much instant online communication suffers from: lack of spelling, grammar, punctuation, and thought.

Sender

The sender is usually obvious: you. But how you configure your email settings can affect how the audience responds when seeing who the "sender" is. In many email programs, you can assign a name to your email address. You would most likely choose your real name. However, you can often use other names or nicknames that might be more appropriate. For the audience you plan to contact with this email address, choose something that best fits.

The email address you have also reflects upon your ethos. Sometimes, you have no choice as a company might assign you an email address. Often, these addresses are professional, include some element of your first and last name, and should cause no rhetorical problems. However, if you select your own email address and it's something less professional such as "honeybooboo1997," then your audience is less likely to take you seriously, if they ever open your email at all. They might simply assume that you're sending spam.

 **DIGITAL Connections**

Why Email Addresses Matter

by John August

Consider your inbox. You have seven new emails from strangers, with the following email addresses:

> This article, published on John August's website, offers a humorous yet practical look at how those receiving emails begin reading messages before they even open them.

1. smurf667@aol.com
2. bill@billwaldon.com
3. rem54mdds@sbcglobal.net
4. tommfs1982@hotmail.com
5. christina.alvarez@gmail.com
6. verdun.singh@stanford.edu
7. tammy@reallybigknockers.net

Which of these people do you expect has a website? Which do you suspect clicks a lot of animated banner ads? Which ones do you anticipate having the most succinct, well-written message?

Call it stereotyping. Call it filtering. But based on these seven email addresses, I know:

- Bill, Verdun, and Christina's names.
- tommfs1982 is probably 28 years old.

- rem54mdds is (in my opinion) a sucker for using SBC's email because it makes him less likely to switch to another provider.
- The AOL user either likes the Smurfs or has a name like Samantha Murphy.
- Verdun Singh goes to Stanford or works there in some capacity.
- tammy and I seem to have little in common. (And it might be spam.)

Based on just their email addresses, I start with mildly positive impressions for Bill, Christina, and Verdun. I start with mildly negative impressions for the other four. All that may change once I start reading — *but only if I start reading.*

Considering it takes five minutes to set up a free email address at a place like Gmail, why wouldn't you give yourself a better chance at a good read?

If you're preparing your first résumé or job application materials, create a new email address that has the best chance of establishing a positive ethos and persona with your audience.

Recipients

The recipient of the email also may seem obvious. However, multiple recipients may often be included in an email to which you're responding. You should ask yourself if you should "reply all" so that everyone sees your response, or if only the sender should see it. At a professional level, your colleagues' email boxes are most likely full of email they already have to read and attend to, and they might not appreciate another email, especially if the message doesn't really apply to them. Accidentally hitting "reply all" with personal or private information also can create unfortunate situations, sometimes just awkward or embarrassing ones, but sometimes potentially illegal situations if privileged information is accidentally distributed.

Also consider carefully when you forward someone else's email to other recipients. If you shared a comment or joke with only one close colleague, you probably wouldn't appreciate him forwarding the message to the whole organization, especially if they see that the original sender was you. In general, ask the original sender's permission first before forwarding. Remember that ethos unfolds through all your actions, so even forwarding someone else's emails can hurt your ethos when you write your own in the future.

Rhetorical Continuities

Researching online, locate nondigital examples of someone delivering a message to the wrong person, or delivering the wrong message to the right person. What were the results (did people get fired)? Write a report of your findings, and make a claim about how you see email in terms of this longer rhetorical history, and how writers in each situation might try to prevent this kind of accidental delivery.

Subject

The subject of the message also has rhetorical implications. The subject should be concise enough to be read quickly, yet specific enough to make it easy for your reader to identify the contents of the email. If the subject is too general, the reader may think it is not important enough to open, or simply delete it as spam.

You have several strategies when writing an email subject. First, consider placing the recipient's name in the subject line itself. The subject line becomes personal, and the reader most likely will want to know how the message affects her. Of course, you don't want to use this tactic (or any) too often or the audience will become accustomed to it and tune it out.

Second, vary the structure of the subject line to make it stand out from other messages. A brief subject of one or two words will often stand out among lengthier subjects, and vice versa. Remember, though, that your audience will appreciate a subject that is also descriptive of the message inside the email.

Third, don't format the subject lines the same way every time. This advice is usually easy to follow, for each email represents a different rhetorical situation. Varying the subject line in terms of both words and structure can break your reader's expectations and make them notice it.

Some techniques should be avoided, such as using "ALL CAPS" or including certain key words such as "FREE," which usually signals to the audience that the message contains spam.

Message body

Your goal when writing an email is often twofold. First, you want the recipient to open and read your email. If you've written a good subject line, then you should accomplish this goal. Once your audience performs the first act of opening the email, your next task is to persuade them to carry out the second goal, which is to take action upon your specific request in the email's message body. As former NFL head coach Herm Edwards has said, "you play to win the game . . . you don't play to just play it" (Figure 7.10). Similarly, you often don't write to just write, but you write to cause some action to occur.

Sometimes, the action required may be relatively passive. If you're simply acknowledging that you received an email, then there's nothing for your reader to "do" other than read your message. However, sometimes your email message attempts to solicit some action from your audience, such as a request for information, a demand for a refund, or a plea for volunteers. In such cases, you should make sure that what you want is explicitly stated in the body of the email message.

Figure 7.10
Herm Edwards makes it clear we don't just play for play's sake.

www.youtube.com/watch?v=b5-iJUuPWis

Depending on the length of the email, this request should appear in one or two places. First, the request should appear in the introduction so that the audience immediately knows what you want from them. If the email is particularly long (several paragraphs), you might also restate the request in the final line so that the last words the audience reads will remind them of what you'd like them to do.

Like your subject line, the body of an email should be brief. Since most of your readers most likely receive many emails each day, you want to make sure they can easily understand your message. Keeping the email's body concise is one way to do this.

Of course, how brief it is depends on the context and your audience. If you're writing back and forth to a friend, with whom you already have a prior conversation that you're continuing online, then you probably don't need to orient your friend to the reason that you're writing. For more professional uses, however, you should clearly indicate why you're contacting the audience.

In the first line or two, explain your reason for writing. Are you applying for a position through email? Are you asking for a refund? Are you contacting your congressman about a particular issue? Place this information first.

For each subsequent paragraph, include topic sentences or headers to help your reader quickly navigate the email and decide which information is most useful to him or her. These paragraphs should, again, be brief, and sometimes as short as a single sentence if it provides particularly important information. Because most emails are read on a computer monitor, each paragraph should not extend past the bottom of the monitor frame so that the viewer doesn't have to scroll through an individual paragraph. Given that many people read emails on smartphones and tablets, you might pay extra attention to how much space you think each paragraph will take up on a smaller screen.

If your message is particularly long, or requires intricate formatting, you can upload the document as an attachment that can be read or printed elsewhere by your audience. In this case, you would provide a brief email explaining the purpose of the email, and call attention to the attachment that provides more detail (and remember to actually attach the document) (Figure 7.11).

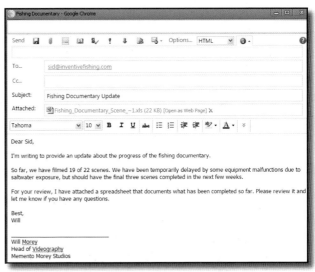

Figure 7.11
The email provides short, clear sentences, tells the reader exactly what the writer wants, takes up little screen height, and includes an attachment of a longer report.

Signature

While your name may appear in the subject line next to your email address, you may also want to consider including a signature at the end of the message.

In addition to your full name, email signatures usually also include your contact information, including your job title, company, phone number, and other pertinent information. You may include your postal address, but this might make the signature unnecessarily long, and not every reader needs this information.

You should also include your email address, as this does not always readily appear in the "From" line (sometimes it shows your name instead). If you have a website, you can also include its URL. You also can place social media

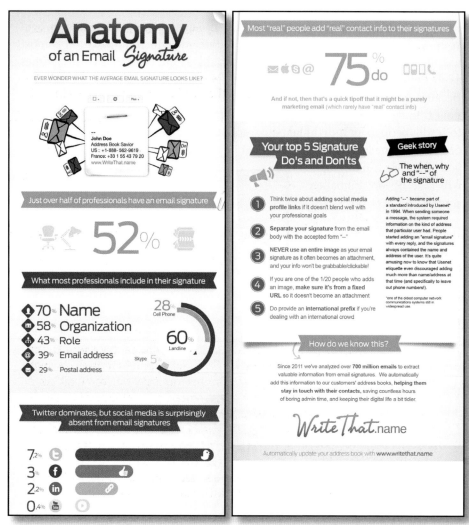

Figure 7.12
Like any part of an email, the signature can also be rhetorical, as what you include can affect how your audience responds to your writing.

information in the signature, but as Figure 7.12 shows, most signatures do not include this information. However, doing so could help your reader learn more about you (assuming your social media pages have information you want them to read).

Unless your company requires it, don't place your logo in the signature, as it often slows the speed of the email's download, and might be included as an attachment instead, confusing the reader about what's important and what isn't.

You may have also noticed that some authors include a quote or message that provides insight into their beliefs or philosophy. While often harmless, such messages could offend your audience, hurting your ethos and their willingness to act on your request.

Most email programs will allow you to create a standard signature that will be included in every email you send, avoiding the need for you to rewrite it in each email (Figure 7.13). In addition, these programs will also let you set secondary signatures for replies and forwarded messages so that the signature doesn't constantly repeat in between messages, making the email difficult to scan.

Figure 7.13
Gmail allows the user to create a custom email signature.

Building

Find three examples of private emails that were accidentally sent to the wrong recipient (or were forwarded without the original sender knowing). For instance, a government official who accidentally hit "reply all," or a celebrity whose friend (or ex-friend) forwarded an embarrassing email. In each case, what was the result of the accidental distribution? Did the author lose his job? Did another party sue him? Could any of the authors have taken steps to prevent this situation? How do these accidents affect the *ethos* of the author? Write a report in which you make a claim about whether or not you feel these accidents were harmful to the author or not. Make sure to support your claim with reasons and evidence.

Engine

Record all the subject lines from emails you receive over the course of a week (if you regularly delete emails, start recording them over the upcoming week before you delete them). What rhetorical strategies do you think the authors considered when writing the subject line? Do any use a high volume of words? Are some only one or two words? Do any grossly misrepresent the content of the email? Did you think some were spam that turned out not to be (and vice versa)? How do the subject lines use the rhetorical appeals of *logos, ethos, pathos,* and *kairos*? Develop a claim based on your analysis, and support it with reasons and evidence.

Social Media

Andreas Kaplan and Michael Haenlein have defined social media as "a group of Internet-based applications that build on the ideological and technological foundations of web 2.0, and that allow the creation and exchange of user-generated content." Basically, any Internet-based platform that you can write with, in words or images, either by creating new content or interacting with existing content, qualifies as social media. Given that many sites offer ways to create your own account, or reply with comments, many pages can be considered social media. For instance, the genre of blogs discussed above is usually considered a form of social media, mainly because most blogs allow readers to leave comments.

Platforms and text forms

This section discusses social media in two ways. Since so many websites can qualify as social media, this section limits discussion to only some of the major social media platforms such as Twitter, Facebook, YouTube, and LinkedIn. Then, it looks at different categories of texts that can be created and shared on social media, such as text messages, comments, and memes. These genres circulate among most of the social media platforms.

You are probably very familiar with many social media platforms. In fact, you probably already use many of them regularly and already know how to create profiles, set up accounts, add photos, and use other features available on each platform. So rather than offering a detailed tutorial on how to set up each account—tutorials that may quickly be found online—this section focuses on a few rhetorical tips that can help you use each platform more effectively to communicate with your audience. Because your audience for each of these platforms can be very large and often unintended, you should be careful what you post. If a message should stay private, consider using another genre to send the message.

Twitter

Because individual Twitter posts are limited to 140 characters, this platform obviously isn't very good for distributing large amounts of textual information. And although you can add images, video, and other media, such sharing is usually done in the form of hyperlinks, sending the reader off to another page. In addition, it can sometimes be difficult to make your tweet stand out among all the other tweets on your reader's page.

Instead, Twitter's strength is in its brevity and speed. You can usually type or read 140 characters rather quickly, and readers may appreciate the conciseness.

Similar to an email subject line, your tweets need to be specific, but you have a bit more room for an important detail or two.

You can also "mention" other users in your tweets by including the @ character followed by their Twitter username. This can alert the user that you wish to include them in a particular conversation as a means to "tag" your audience. Use this feature when you're trying to target a few specific people rather than all of the Twitterverse.

Remember that your tweets are generally public, so everything you tweet can affect your ethos as a writer. If you plan to use Twitter to communicate and persuade your audience to take some action, then your tweets should generally have some value for the reader. Post tweets that show your expertise, your connection to the community you're trying to reach, or information useful to your followers. Your audience will better trust your credibility as a writer.

Hashtags

The hashtag (#) allows you to connect your message with other conversations in a variety of social media platforms, helping users to find your tweet when searching for specific topics. Hashtags largely originated with the advent of Twitter, but now, most social media platforms support hashtagging and searching. Twitter has even capitalized on the phenomenon by offering paid trending tags to as a form of advertising. These tags can and most often do occur spontaneously, and you can create your own tag if another doesn't suit your purposes. However, you should generally use a short tag that others will recognize in the context of your message.

DIGITAL Connections

How to Create a Great Hashtag to Advertise Your Business

by Deborah Sweeney

It goes without saying that if a business has a Twitter account, they'll probably be including a hashtag in their tweets. Or several hashtags, many of which may be generic key words to better attract new fans to follow them with (#business #branding #tips), but some will be

In this article published on socialmediatoday.com, Deborah Sweeney discusses the gravity of a good hashtag. What trending hashtags have you seen in sponsorship of a brand or company?

created specifically for the business, by the business. For some companies, especially those with less hashtag crafting expertise, this fun activity can easily turn stressful if all you have on your mind is the need for trending speed and to go viral in the span of a few hours. What's a brand fresh to this #PoundSignScene to do? As my own company works on building a hashtag for a contest we have coming up later this month, I picked up a few tips along the way to help your custom made hashtag stand out from the crowd.

1. **Conduct research.**
   While you'll never be able to trademark a hashtag for your personal use, it's important to keep an eye out on whether or not the hashtag you have in mind is unique to what the

> How do you think Sweeney would respond to Twitter's "Promoted Trends" offers to businesses to pay for a trending hashtag?

business does and how they do it. The simple way to do this is to type in the hashtag into the search toolbar and see what else shows up and in what capacity. #RulesoftheDunk might sound just right for a basketball team's account, but it's a hashtag that makes a regular appearance on Oreo's feed to talk cookies with. You can use that hashtag if you like, but remember that in doing so you might confuse other Twitter users when your "rules of the dunk" don't include a glass of milk on the side.

2. **Integrate your brand's name (or product) into the mix.**
   Don't take this tip too literally, especially if you have a business name that's pretty long. You don't have to put your entire brand name into a hashtag, and it doesn't mean you don't have to concentrate on skimping out on being creative either. Just keep a few small elements in the hashtag that will keep it from being confused with another brand's. A great example of a company that does this well is Victoria's Secret with their #AskAnAngel hashtags. Q&As catch the eye when the subject of the chat is identified and in the case of VS, long noted for referring to their models as "angels," it's a safe bet that you'll be sending your tweet questions to a Victoria's Secret Angel to answer.

3. **Keep it on the short side—and easy to read.**
   Hashtags are at their best when they're to the point, and you have no trouble reading or typing them out. Avoid placing two of the same letters together, unless one is capitalized—a hashtag like #letsstoppoverty is slightly better when spelled, #LetsStopPoverty, or even shorter at #StopPoverty. Caps go a long way in making the

hashtag stand out legibly. Additionally, keep in mind that you can't include punctuation or Emojis in a hashtag, just in case you were looking to include that thumbs up symbol everywhere you tweet. And while we're on the topic of everywhere, use your hashtag when it's most appropriate. You don't need it in every tweet you send out, and it won't fit into the context of every message either. That only means one thing . . . time for you and your business to get cracking on making more unique hashtags!

Facebook

You may use Facebook every day (or every minute), and you may only use it for social interaction with friends. However, Facebook can be a powerful tool for quickly spreading information to broader audiences.

What you post on Facebook can significantly affect your ethos as a writer, whether or not you actually use Facebook to communicate argumentatively. Even if you set your profile to private, some information still leaks through, allowing anonymous browsers to see images, comments, or other details you'd rather not have others see. First and foremost, only post information to Facebook you feel comfortable sharing with most of the general public.

As a platform, Facebook quickly allows you to share text, images, video, links, and other kinds of media. However, since Facebook adopted the new "timeline" layout, which organizes information like a scrapbook, individual posts may be hard to locate by a viewer. In addition, unless another Facebook user is friends with just you, your messages will be competing for space on the reader's timeline along with all of their other friends' updates. This relationship also becomes two-way, as you will now see their posts on your timeline as well.

Facebook can be more useful if you create a Facebook Page or Group. A page becomes more of a one-way interaction where users can like your page and receive your updates, without theirs appearing on your wall. Pages are usually used for business and organizations rather than single individuals.

A Facebook Group allows a collection of individuals to gather on Facebook to share information about a common interest or topic. Such spaces can be useful for gathering a specific audience you can direct your message to. Of course, you first have to build that audience if you're starting a new group. However, you also can join existing groups, and use these groups to reach new readers who may be open to your message. For instance, if you were attempting to gather donations for a local animal shelter, you might join local groups that are known pet lovers and solicit donations there.

Building

Share stories of times you have accidentally sent a social media or text message to the wrong person or a message that didn't convey what you intended. How might you have avoided sending the wrong message? Develop a list of best practices you would recommend to a friend so she or he doesn't make the same mistakes. Although this is just a list, provide reasons and evidence to support your list items.

Engine

Search

Locate a website that helps you make memes, such as www.quickmeme. com. Using some local issue as your exigency, create your own meme that uses a well-known image or concept to reframe the issue. What new insight do you feel is gained by looking at the issue through your meme? What rhetorical appeals do you think are used in your meme (*ethos, pathos, logos, kairos*)? Write a brief explanation for your choice, and share your meme with the class.

YouTube

When it comes to reaching an audience, YouTube videos are 50 times more likely to be found on the first page of a Google search than videos from other sites. Thus, if you're posting videos online, YouTube gives you the best search engine optimization results. However, you still need to create good content for users to stay and view your videos. Creating digital videos will be discussed more in Chapter 9, but when you post on YouTube, make sure your content has value for the audience, either by providing informative content about an issue, product, or current event, or by holding entertainment value (or both). For example, look at the local advertisement created for a taxidermy shop in Ojai, California, in Figure 7.14. Finally, make good use of categories, tags, and comments to help facilitate interaction among your viewers.

Figure 7.14
Is that Chuck Norris? Nope, Chuck Testa.

LinkedIn

Unlike the other platforms, LinkedIn is more "social" and less "media." The site functions primarily as a database of professional contacts and colleagues so that individuals can find each other for networking. Think of LinkedIn more as an online, networked résumé than a place to update general audiences about daily events, and carefully consider your audience, who will most likely expect formal, clear, and correct language and relevant information pertaining to your professional credentials.

Consider these tips when writing your own LinkedIn profile:

Research your goals for using LinkedIn.

Like any writing situation, consider why you're on LinkedIn. Do you want to find a new job? Find colleagues? Hire employees?

Use a face pic.

Unlike profile pictures on other social media outlets, which may be more artistic or whimsical, the profile pic on your LinkedIn page should be professional and show your face. A headshot often works best. You can change the privacy setting so that only your connections can see your face if you don't want anonymous users knowing what you look like.

Use LinkedIn offline.

As you build connections and meet people in person, you can use the profile pictures of others to help you remember these contacts in case you run into them again.

Write an engaging headline.

Your headline can be you job title, such as "Staff Writer," but it can also be a bit more descriptive or creative. For instance, if you're seeking an internship or your first job, you might write, "Talented Writer Seeking Internship," rather than simply listing your name and university. However, keep this headline clear and concise.

Update your page.

Although you won't post on LinkedIn as regularly as on other social media platforms, you can still update your status to show recent projects or other work completed. You also might post interesting or relevant news to your field. These posts will usually appear in the feed of your connections, making you more visible.

Write about yourself.

Since LinkedIn works more like a résumé, your profile should be focused on you, not where you work or the school you attend.

Use sections in your profile.

LinkedIn provides various sections and categories to help you organize your information, such as volunteer experience, projects, foreign languages, and other facts you may want to highlight. Select those sections you want audiences to focus on, and make them stand out.

Join groups.

Find groups that formed based on the same interests and expertise as you. For instance, if you study or work in bioengineering, find (or create) bioengineering groups, and join in the groups' conversation. Doing so will help you learn more from others, increase your visibility, and help build goodwill among this audience.

Building

Locate a business, organization, or celebrity that uses at least five of the social media platforms listed in this chapter. How does the group or person make use of each platform? Does the person integrate the platforms (putting the same information on Twitter and Facebook, for instance)? Does the person employ any of the tips mentioned above? Do you notice any poor choices the person makes? Write an essay that argues whether or not you feel this person's use of social media is effective, and support your claim with reasons and evidence.

Engine

Examine social media platforms that aren't listed in this chapter. How do these platforms compare? How are they similar? How are they different? What do they offer that the social media platforms listed above don't? Do they have specific audiences or topics? Do some offer better opportunities to make use of rhetorical appeals such as *ethos, pathos, kairos,* or *logos*? Develop a claim based on your responses, and support it with reasons and evidence.

Text messages and comments

You're probably very familiar with text messages (also called short message services, or SMS). Besides texting your friends, you might text your boss, coworkers, and perhaps even your professors. You might have received texts from an airline, emergency workers, or your university. Some believe that texting has become so widespread that it will eventually replace email as the preferred means of sending text-based messages (if it hasn't already).

However, you might consider a few good practices when sending texts, especially if you find yourself sending texts in more professional writing situations. Like emails, the tone of a text message can be difficult to determine, and also like emails, you can accidentally send them to the wrong recipient. Also, because many texting applications offer autocorrect, you might accidentally send the wrong message to the right person if the autocorrect replaces your right word with the wrong one (Figure 7.15).

Figure 7.15
Sometimes an autocorrect fail can cause even bigger fails.

If you're writing for a more formal audience, avoid acronyms, such as "B4" for "before," unless you're familiar with the audience and know they won't have a problem with the informality. Also consider that some readers might receive the text message in their email program, which may appear strange in this other genre. Many people who frequently compose texts for business include a phrase such as "Sent from my smartphone, please excuse any typos" so that the audience knows that any mistakes were probably caused by trying to type while walking or on a small thumb-based keyboard.

 **DIGITAL Connections**

Texting in Business: Not a Good Idea

by James Kendrick

Texting. We all do it. It's so easy to fire off a quick text message to communicate with family or friends. It's become so commonplace that many of us are now doing it for work. But that's not a good idea.

Text messaging has come a long way since the early days. In the beginning carriers charged us per message and

Remember, not all audiences may be comfortable with texting, and those that are might not appreciate substituting "CU@8" for "see you at 8." James Kendrick, in fact, recommends that you not use texting at all for business in this article from zdnet.com.

stories were commonplace detailing how texters were getting massive phone bills. Over time the carriers had to bend to customers' wishes, leading to near free service today.

Free messaging led most of us to start texting all the time. It's an easy way to get in touch with personal acquaintances without worrying if they'll get the message right away. This ease of use has led texting to make its way to the workplace.

Communicating with coworkers is important, even if a given message seems innocuous. If it has to do with work then every message should be treated the same as any other, and that means it is important. Email is much better for this than texting.

There are several reasons why work communications should almost always be done with email and not via text message:

- Text messages can give the impression that what's being conveyed to a coworker is not important.
- Work communications done with both texting and email don't send a cohesive image for work teams.
- Email leaves a digital paper trail for both sender and recipient that resides with all email about work.

Note that texting is fine for personal messages such as telling Bob where you'll meet him for lunch. It's not necessary to never text at work, but only for messages that aren't work-related. If it's about a project or status, for example, then it should go into an email.

Although established social media platforms only allow a certain amount of customization, one option you can typically control on such sites is the comment feature. The decision to allow comments is a personal and rhetorical one (Figure 7.16). Do you want others to be able to interact and respond to what you write online, or do you wish to more carefully control the message? You may want, for instance, to create the perception that your YouTube channel or blog is friendly, inviting, and open to the opinions

Figure 7.16
YouTube and other social media sites usually let you control the comments section.

of others. This creates goodwill between you and a reader and affects how your ethos as a writer is perceived.

Facebook's major comment area, called a "wall," allows those with access to one's account (a user's "friends") to post messages, photos, and various comments. For most users, these interactive, communicative features make social media worth using. However, for companies using Facebook to advertise their brand, the environment of the wall can pose particular problems.

Memes

Richard Dawkins, an evolutionary biologist, first used the term "meme" in his 1976 book, *The Selfish Gene*. Analogous to "gene" a meme transmits cultural information rather than genetic information. The important aspect of a meme, like a gene, is that its information spreads. Figure 7.17 provides a *TEDx* talk by Susan Blackmore that describes memes in more detail.

Unlike text messages and comments, memes usually use images, with a bit of text, to make their point, although any idea that spreads can be considered a meme. For instance, the idea that Barack Obama wasn't a United States citizen, even though untrue, was an idea that caught on and was shared among various populations. The phrase, "going postal," was used for any mass shooting, not just those by postal employees. A meme doesn't have to be correct; it only has to spread.

Figure 7.17
Susan Blackmore explains the origin and workings of a meme.

www.youtube.com/watch?feature=player_embedded&v=fQ_9-Qx5Hz4

Memes can be effective at appealing to emotion (pathos) by making your audience laugh and view you more favorably as a speaker (ethos). So although memes can be fun and entertaining, they also can be used to help convince an audience. Memes are most rhetorically powerful when they juxtapose one well-known idea with another in order to produce new meanings. For instance, on November 18, 2011, students at the University of California-Davis formed a human chain as part of the Occupy protests going on at the time. The students refused to obey police who asked them to leave. When they refused, UC Davis

Figure 7.18
This video shows UC Davis Police officer Lieutenant John Pike pepper spraying students on campus. Don't spray me, bro!

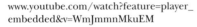

www.youtube.com/watch?feature=player_embedded&v=WmJmmnMkuEM

Figure 7.19
Would you like some pepper with your liberty?

Police Officer Lieutenant John Pike and another officer sprayed the group with pepper spray (Figure 7.18)

As one form of response, many students and other outraged citizens created memes juxtaposing Pike with historical events and places in order to make a statement that this kind of behavior cannot stand in a democracy. Figure 7.19 is a meme that places Pike as the figure of the Statue of Liberty, only this time with a can of pepper spray. This meme makes a comment on the state of liberty in the United States: Citizens can no longer protest without fear of physical harm.

Since they're usually small image files overlaid with little text, memes can circulate quickly among many social media platforms, such as Facebook, Twitter, Tumblr, and others. In addition to the example above, memes can be used to make a political statement, spread awareness of current events, or to spread information about some cause or issue.

Building

Link

Consider the reasons why a company (besides a pharmaceutical company) may or may not want a social media page that allows comments. What are the reasons for including comments? Why wouldn't a particular company want comments? How can comments help or hurt the company's image and its message? Providing examples of both, develop a claim based on your reasons, and support it with evidence.

Engine

Recall a website that uses a variety of media genres, such as print, images, video, podcasts, or even video games. Do you find this integration of various media in a single electronic environment to be effective or distracting? Why or why not? Is any media genre missing that should be included? How would you redesign the environment to better fit its purpose and target audience? Develop your answers into a claim, and support it with reasons and evidence.

Avatars

If you have a Facebook, Twitter, or LinkedIn account, or you play World of Warcraft or are on Second Life, then you probably have some sort of profile pic or image that you use to associate with your accounts. In general terms, this image can be referred to as an avatar, which makes up the totality of your online persona. How you choose to construct your avatar can have important implications for your ethos as a writer, affecting how your readers respond to you.

Avatars can range from a simple photographic headshot to more stylized renderings like cartoons or abstract figures. The kind and style of avatar you decide to create depends on the audience you hope to reach. If you're looking to develop a fun and whimsical persona, then a more informal, characterized avatar would work well. However, if you are attempting to create an avatar for more professional use, then you might consider a more formal picture (Figure 7.20).

Figure 7.20
These avatar icons make use of a face and logo.

DIGITAL Connections

How to Create the Right Avatar for You and Your Brand

By Mihaela Lica

I always advise against using logos as avatars. They are cold and somehow insinuate that the ones using them are not there to communicate, but to sell.

If you have a business, you could use your logo as your avatar. This might be best if you have a very large company and need an avatar that represents many people who might be using the company's digital writing platforms.

People in social networks respond better to human faces than to iconic avatars. It's in human nature to trust more the face behind a business than the business logo. Even more: statistics show that people tend to click more on banners depicting human faces than anything else. If this is true for banner advertising, then it is logically true for social networks, right?

So, what should you use as your avatar if your focus is not entirely personal? A company logo is a good branding tool, but on a social network, like Twitter for example, it's simply inappropriate. When it comes to brands, the "consumers" simply prefer to know who they are talking to.

Lica goes on to say that the avatar might use a combination of human face and company logo, as long as the face is personal, someone the audience would want to have a conversation with (Figure 7.20).

However, a logo also can come across as impersonal and not connect as well with the audience. Consider Mihaela Lica's advice.

However, your avatar is more than simply the image that accompanies your social media platforms. Your avatar is your entire digital, online persona that includes not just a small profile pic but the totality of what you do online. For instance, photos of your recent vacation, wedding, or Saturday night's party can become part of how people see "you" on the Internet (and thus off the Internet) and become enfolded into your total avatar. Thus, what you show and say online constantly composes and revises your avatar and has ramifications for how people treat you offline, as Justine Sacco found out. Sacco, the director of communications for InterActive Corp—a company that owns several online sites including Match.com and Vimeo—sent a tweet as she was leaving on a trip to South Africa (Figure 7.21).

Figure 7.21
This tweet was not only offensive, it also cost Sacco her job.

Sacco's tweet received a huge backlash from the audiences that saw it and quickly prompted InterActive Corp to fire her. This tweet also significantly hurt her ethos as a speaker, will probably make it hard for her to land another job, and ruined her online identity and reputation. As the director of communications, she should have known that such a tweet was not only hurtful and inappropriate, but also rhetorically damaging to her and her company. She most likely took much time and effort to craft a particular avatar for herself, one that she ruined quite quickly through Twitter.

Building

Choose five well-known companies or individuals that have multiple online social media accounts such as Facebook, Twitter, YouTube, LinkedIn, Tumblr, or more. Study how the avatar changes from one site to another. Are the avatars and images the same from site to site, or does the author change the avatar and images for each site? If the author keeps the same avatar, what are the rhetorical advantages for doing so? If the author changes the avatar, how does this change reflect the context of the site and make for a better rhetorical appeal? How do the avatars use the rhetorical appeals of *logos*, *pathos*, *ethos*, and *kairos*? Develop a claim based on these questions, and support it with reasons and evidence.

Engine

The word *avatar* originally comes from the Sanskrit word *avatara*. Research the meaning and history of this word—how was it used in Indian languages and how was it subsequently adopted and used in English? How did this word come to be used for online personas? Does this word seem to fit and adequately describe the overall experience of what happens when you put yourself online? Can you think of any other words that might be a better substitute for avatar? Write a report based on your research, and suggest alternatives for "avatar," and share them with the class. In addition, develop a claim based on your substitutes for avatar, and support them with reasons and evidence.

KEY Terms

anecdote	definition
argumentation	description
autobiography	exemplification
bibliography	exposition
cause and effect	mode
classification	narration
compare and contrast	storytelling

Blog

While you might keep a blog for this class or write a blog on your own already, this Execute will focus on creating a focused, sustained blog and some suggestions for developing an audience and keeping them engaged. According to Technorati, a website that studies and tracks blogs, a new blog is created every half-second (that's 120 per minute). However, many of these blogs are quickly abandoned by their creators and are considered "dead."

When you create your blog, use the rhetorical tetrahedron to consider its audience, message, and design. You already know your medium (the Internet, text, visuals) and your genre (a blog), but consider how the other elements of the rhetorical tetrahedron interact with these predetermined elements. In addition, the following suggestions will help you sustain a blog over a longer period of time and reach your target audience.

Write Good Content

You may have heard the phrase "content is king." No matter how slick or fancy your blog may look, users won't return to it if you don't include good content. Try to post information that will help your readers, or at least content that is interesting or entertaining. This, more than anything, will help you build and retain a long-lasting readership.

Read Other Blogs

Reading other blogs can be a great way to see what other bloggers are posting, how they compose posts, and how they interact with their readers. While you don't have to do everything other bloggers do, studying other bloggers can help you write better content for your own site, even if the other blogs are on different topics. Just as you read other essays to help you write better essays, reading other blogs can help you write your own blog better.

Blog Regularly

Readers won't frequent your blog if you don't keep it fresh with new material. Try to blog regularly, preferably several times a week. If a reader returns to your page and doesn't find new content, she or he may move on to other sites that offer something current.

Create a Bank

In order to help you blog regularly, consider making a bank of prewritten blog posts. This bank allows you to quickly add a new post if you don't have time or can't think of anything to write for that day. However, make sure these posts are not tied to any current event; if you submit the post a year after the event happened, then the post obviously won't be timely. Add posts on current events when those events are still current, seizing the kairotic moment.

Chunk Your Text

When reading online, readers generally prefer short chunks of text rather than long, dense paragraphs. If you're composing a longer blog post, make sure to break it up into smaller, digestible paragraphs of only a few sentences.

Proofread

Part of building up and sustaining a readership involves *ethos*. As a writer, spelling and grammatical errors can quickly erode your *ethos*, so make sure you proofread your text before you publish your posts. Errors in spelling also can affect SEO (for instance, if you misspell a key word), so proofreading affects how both human and nonhuman audiences interact with your site.

Post Images and Multimedia

In addition to small, chunked text, images and videos help to break up writing as well as provide illustrations, examples, and more interactive ways to engage with your content. You can add images, videos, podcasts, or other media that help support your written text.

Disseminate New Posts

When you add a new post to your blog, disseminate the news via social media platforms such as Facebook or Twitter. If you visit the technology blog Mashable. com and visit its social media pages, you'll notice that its representatives post and tweet about their articles, thereby allowing their readership to know when new material is on the site.

Write for Nonhuman Audiences

In order for web robots to better find and index your blog, use the SEO practices noted in Chapter 5, especially those related to selecting titles for your blog posts and including key words within the written content.

Interact with Other Bloggers

In addition to sending out blog updates through social media, you also can engage with other bloggers who might direct traffic to your site. Interacting with other bloggers is a great way to engage with the larger blogging community and establish yourself as an expert in your particular niche.

Choose a Niche

Speaking of niches, choose one that is not too broad but not too narrow. For instance, if you blog about sports, you might select a particular sport to blog about, or even a particular team. This would narrow down your focus and give you plenty to blog about (but not so much it would be overwhelming). However, blogging about an individual player on a team might be too narrow a focus, since your readership would be much smaller and you would have less to blog about on a weekly basis.

Blog Comments

Most blogs allow you to activate a "comments" section, where your readers can respond to your posts. You can usually turn this section "off" in the blog template, so you wouldn't have to worry about keeping up with comments or worry about negative comments that could hurt your argument or offend other readers. However, allowing comments from readers can help to create a larger sense of belonging and participation among the users, and it might create a larger sense of community, helping to keep readers coming back for more. If you do allow comments, you need to be aware that some readers will post negative comments no matter what you write. This practice is referred to as "trolling," and arguing with such posters (called "trolls") can sometimes make things worse. If possible, you might set your comment section so you have to moderate comments before they're posted. This allows you to see the comments before all your readers do, so only those comments you approve will appear publically.

Respond to User Comments

If you do allow users to comment on your blog, try to respond to each one. This helps you establish a good rapport with your audience, gives your readership a sense of belonging, and helps your *ethos* as a writer. However, try to make the responses meaningful. Don't simply include "thanks!" when responding to a compliment, but direct the reader to other resources related to that compliment, showing the reader you have more to offer as an expert on your topic.

Tag Your Posts

For organizational purposes and to help readers find related posts on particular topics, tag your posts with descriptive key words.

List Your Blog in Directories

Blog directories will help generate more exposure to your blog. You can visit the site below to find out more about directories, including a list of 23 blog directories where you can submit your blog information. There are many more blog directories, but this should get you started: http://www.searchenginejournal.com/20-essential-blog-directories-to-submit-your-blog-to/5998/.

From DIGITAL Writers

Djenne Djenno by Sophie Sarin
djennedjenno.blogspot.com/

There are many blogs that you might research when designing your own, but consider the blog *Djenne Djenno* by Sophie Sarin, who uses the blog to record her attempts at opening (and keeping open) a small hotel in the ancient trading town of Djenne in Mali.

Sarin is a Swedish-born English citizen who started a mud hotel in the ancient West African town of Djenne in Mali.

STUDENT Example

Avogadro Salad, student blog

avogadrosalad.wordpress.com

In the second example, Sarah Almeda created this blog, *Avogadro Salad*, for her honors chemistry class when only a sophomore in high school. Consider how she uses good blogging and digital writing practices to inform her reader about concepts in chemistry.

CHAPTER **8**

Digital Images

As you've seen in Chapter 2, digital photographs can be a powerful form of digital rhetoric. Cruz uses his images to argue a point that's important to him. However, behind the push-button act of taking a digital image lie other factors you might consider. For instance, while the first digital camera was invented in 1975, the first digital photograph was not taken with this camera, but created from a traditional photograph even further back in 1957 when Russell Kirsch scanned a photo of his three-month-old son (Figure 8.1). While digital photography and digital imaging have come a long way, this example offers some important points that still pertain today that you should consider when thinking about writing with digital images: not all digital images are photographs; digital images can be created in many different ways, and even older media can become digital.

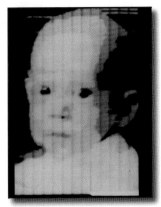

Figure 8.1
This photograph was taken 18 years before the first digital camera was invented, yet it is the first digital photograph.

Still, all digital images are created with some sort of digital technology. Diagrams, charts, and signs are created with an image design or editing software. Three-dimensional models are often designed in special software used by architects and builders. Most digital photographs are taken by a smartphone, a fact that touches on two of the most important aspects of digital images: they can be shared and edited quickly.

As this example shows, then, simply taking a digital photograph or making a diagram with digital software is not the last step in the process of making digital images; they must also be converted to different file types, edited for

Figure 8.2
Image categories and their descriptions

Screen captures can be useful images for documenting online activity.

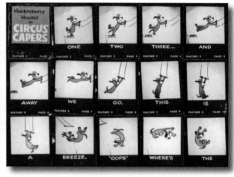

Animations provide a dynamic image that can be used to show a reader how to complete a process of several steps.

Icons are usually simple abstractions of some object that usually convey more information than what their simple images present.

Photographs are useful for documenting an event or providing a high level of detail.

Diagrams are usually simple renderings, often in the form of line drawings that help to make some object more abstract, focusing in on particular elements.

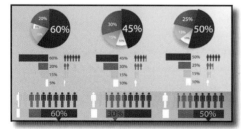

Charts help to show numerical information or processes in a more visual way. Common charts include pie charts, organizational charts, and flow charts.

Maps display geographic positions and relationships. In addition to simply showing a geographical location, maps can also include weather patterns, animal migrations, or a map to buried treasure.

emphasis or correction, or combined with other images in order to make more complex, robust arguments. Thus, beyond the technology of making digital images also exists rhetorical techniques for making and using digital images and crafting them into arguments.

This chapter introduces you to three facets of digital images: the categories of digital images, the rhetorics of digital images, and the ethics of using digital images. As discussed earlier in this text, this chapter assumes that most images created today become digital at some point in their lives. Although much of the information here applies to all images, it mainly focuses on the digital aspects of images.

As you read about the various ways digital images are created in terms of technological, categorical, and rhetorical approaches, consider how these elements align with some of the rhetorical concepts you've learned already. For instance, how does a particular rhetorical technique affect audience? What kind of and how many writers are required? How does a specific medium encourage particular design and image category choices, and vice versa; how do particular techniques encourage one medium over another? Keep these questions in mind as you read through the chapter.

Image Categories and Rhetorics

While the terms "graphic" or "visual" are often used as a broader category for static visuals created on a computer, this chapter has used the term "image" instead. Many subcategories of images exist that you might have to create. When you decide to include an image in your texts, consider which category of image is most appropriate for your purpose in writing, your audience's needs, and the medium and design of your document. The images in Figure 8.2 provide examples of the most common categories of images.

Building

Link

Choose one of the image categories on the previous page and research its history. For instance, when was the first pie chart created? How is it often used? Are there any ethical concerns with this kind of image? How does this image make use of the rhetorical appeals of *logos*, *ethos*, *pathos*, or *kairos*? Write a short essay in which you develop a claim based on your findings, and support it with reasons and evidence.

In addition to knowing the technology of making images, you also need to know the rhetoric of making images. This section discusses different ways to understand and compose images, whether digital or analog, and can help you make better rhetorical choices to create a certain kind of image in a certain way. Although the topics covered below are in a chapter focused on images, they also can apply to digital videos and text.

Analogy

Analogies are one of the most basic structures of communication and are present in how humans understand the world through both alphabetic writing and writing with images. For example, when you use a map, you're using an analogy to make sense of the world (or a part of it). The map is not the territory itself but an analogous representation.

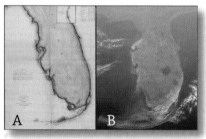

Figure 8.3
A map creates an analogical relationship with the land it represents.

That is, the outline of Florida on a map (A) is analogous to the actual coastline of Florida (B), setting up the formula A is to B (Figure 8.3).

Credit: Spitfire19

Figure 8.4
Map depicting the electoral votes from states during the 2008 presidential election. In this example, the color red is associated with the Republican Party and blue is for the Democratic Party.

On a larger scale, a model of the solar system provides another analogy for how the planets are arranged spatially at a given point in time. Because you are used to such analogies, you are not confused when someone points to a map and says, "you're here"; you know she means the place the map represents, not the actual spot on the map.

Analogies may appear in a variety of subtypes, such as associations, comparisons, correspondences, metaphors, proverbs, idioms, and icons. A complex analogy like a map may be comprehensive and include several of these analogical types. The scale on a map may be used for comparisons in distances, while color coding may be used to create associations, such as using the colors red and blue when discussing Republican or Democratic representations of certain US states (Figure 8.4). On topographical maps, the proximity of lines around a mountain indicates an association of elevation and gradient (the closer the lines, the steeper the slope). On a weather map, however, lines represent isobars and indicate wind speed (the closer the lines, the higher the wind speed).

Rhetorical Continuities

Another kind of analogy used in oral, print, and visual narratives is the proportional analogy. As a formula, proportional analogies might be written, A is to B as C is to D. In other words, the character (A) in her situation (B) is analogous to me (C) in my situation (D). Also called a structural portrait, this kind of analogy helps the audience identify with a character in a book or movie.

For instance, in a crime drama, you might identify with the victim because you have undergone a similar event. In science fiction or fantasy, you might identify with a character like Luke Skywalker, feeling stuck at home and wanting to escape and find adventure. The proportional analogy would be Luke (A) feels trapped and restless in Tatooine (B) just as you (C) feel trapped in your hometown (D).

Building

Link

Perform an Internet search for "visual analogy." What kinds of examples does the search return? Analyze what analogy the image is attempting to communicate and whether or not you feel it is effective. Does the analogy make use of the rhetorical appeals of *logos, ethos, pathos,* or *kairos*? Write a short essay in which you develop a claim based on your findings, and support it with reasons and evidence.

Engine

Search

Research the mascot of your college or university or the mascot of your favorite sports team. What kind of analogy is being made between the mascot (cardinal, lion, gator, tiger, etc.) and the university or town of the team? Does this analogy fit, or does it seem forced? How does this analogy image make use of the rhetorical appeals of *logos, ethos, pathos,* or *kairos*? Write a short essay in which you develop a claim based on your findings, and support it with reasons and evidence.

Metaphor

Metaphor is a type of analogy that you use every day in many situations. If you've ever claimed that a test was a "slam dunk," you've used a metaphor to

express how easy it was or how well you did (Figure 8.5). Metaphors help express ideas by using something familiar from one domain (such as a slam dunk in basketball) and applying it to another (test taking). Metaphors (which in Greek means "to carry over") help carry across meanings that might otherwise be difficult to grasp. Obviously, doing well on a test is not too difficult to communicate. You might simply note that it was easy, or use a number of other metaphors: you aced the test; you passed it with flying colors; it was no sweat; it was easy as pie.

Figure 8.5
This is a picture of a literal slam dunk, although the term can be used metaphorically as well.

Metaphors also appear in images that are seen every day. Rather than using words to represent concepts between domains, images are used. Consider the image in Figure 8.6. Here, a gas hose is depicted in the shape of a noose, juxtaposing the domains of gasoline consumption with that of capital punishment or suicide. The noose helps to carry across the idea that gasoline consumption (either through high gas prices or the reliance on foreign and domestic oil) provides a means of hanging oneself.

Figure 8.6
This image suggests that society is hanging itself through its use of gasoline.

Visual metaphors such as this one are used heavily in advertising, although they may be harder to pick out. During the 2010 Super Bowl, Snickers ran a commercial featuring Betty White and Abe Vigoda playing football (Figure 8.7). View the commercial, and consider the following questions:

- What is the metaphor being used in this advertisement? That is, what is the "vehicle" that attempts to convey meaning to the audience?

- Although reinforced with the tagline, "You're not you when you're hungry," how well do you think the metaphor conveys this meaning without that additional text? Are there other meanings you interpreted before viewing the tagline?

■ If the audience doesn't know who Betty White or Abe Vigoda is, do you think the advertisement is still effective? Why or why not?

How you select a metaphor depends on audience and context. If you suspect your audience has never played or seen a basketball game, then you might not want to use the "slam dunk" metaphor. Just as word choice is important when writing text, image choice is important when converging media into multimodal compositions.

Credit: Mars/BBDO North America

Figure 8.7
If you're not you when you're hungry, are you like Betty White?

www.youtube.com
watch?v=UbMN7wvIw_s&feature=youtu.be

Certainly, composing metaphors will be one of the primary techniques you will use to write through images. Having a good understanding of how others make metaphors through images will improve your ability to select and compose metaphors that suit your purpose.

Building

Find an advertisement that uses metaphor to make an argument. How does the metaphor make a claim and provide evidence about the product or service of the ad? In other words, how does the metaphor make an argument? Write an analysis of this relationship between the product and the metaphor used, and share your findings with the class.

Link

Engine

Although you may not have chosen a major yet, select a specialized term in your field (or something that interests you), and develop a metaphor to help explain the term to someone who is unfamiliar with it. Exchange your metaphor with a classmate's and test whether your metaphor was effective. In addition, research the specialized term, and consider how it might already provide a metaphor (for instance, why do police call the location of a crime a "scene"?). How does this metaphor make use of the rhetorical appeals of *logos, ethos, pathos,* or *kairos*? Write a short essay in which you develop a claim based on your findings, and support it with reasons and evidence.

Search

Metonymy

Metonymy is a kind of metaphor that uses part-to-whole relationships to stand in for another idea, and it can offer you ways to succinctly represent an idea through image. You may have encountered these terms from their literary context. Metonymy occurs when a speaker represents a larger idea or process by mentioning a smaller piece of that larger whole. For instance, the phrase "Washington passed the budget today" uses the location "Washington" to represent the larger organization of the federal government. "Washington" itself isn't the government, but provides a metaphor that stands in for the idea of government, and you usually understand what someone means when she uses the term this way.

Consider the request "Lend me your ears." You probably don't interpret this literally to mean "Remove your ears from your body, and lend them to me." Instead, the speaker most likely means this metaphorically, as in "Give me your attention," and this task may even be specific to the ears: "Listen to me." The ears, however, stand in for the larger idea of giving one's attention rather than actually lending the ears themselves (Figure 8.8).

Credit: Andreas Praefcke

Figure 8.8
The phrase "lend me your ears" usually means to "listen."

In a visual example, a cross sometimes serves as a metonymic function for Christ and Christianity. Similarly, the Star of David or the crescent moon and five-pointed star does the same for Jewish and Islamic faiths respectively. A country's flag may perform this function as well. When you see the United States flag, you typically think "America." In this way, any brand mark can become an image that serves a metonymic function. Over time, this metonymic function can lose its transparency so the brand mark seems to *be* the thing it stands for.

Building

Link

Think of as many sayings as you can, such as "Lend me your ears," that have a metonymic function. If it's not obvious, research how the saying came about. Report your findings to the class.

Search Engine

Read through news reports, or watch news reports on television, about large organizations such as governments or corporations. Pay attention to the language used in these reports, and note how many uses of metonymy occur. Do the reports use the organization as a whole to refer to the actions of unnamed individuals? Visually, do they present a brand mark to stand in for the organization? How do you think this use of metonymy makes use of the rhetorical appeals of *logos, ethos, pathos,* or *kairos*? Write a short essay in which you develop a claim based on your findings, and support it with reasons and evidence.

Synecdoche

Synecdoche is another kind of metaphor that is very similar to metonymy, and the two are easily confused. While metonymy stands in for some larger process or idea, synecdoche occurs when a part of a person or object stands in for the whole of an actual physical object or group of people.

Synecdoche can provide a powerful narrative element if used properly and can simplify an image by playing to the audience's imagination by only showing a part of a larger picture. If you've ever seen the movie *Jaws*, you most likely remember the shark's dorsal fin cutting through the water (along with hearing the famous theme music).

Spielberg, because the animatronic shark kept breaking down, resorted to showing either none of the shark, or just the dorsal fin (Figure 8.9). Most critics agree and argue that the absence of the shark makes it more terrifying because the audience has to use their imagination.

Music, to the extent that it provides a theme for a particular character, can also serve as a metaphor via synecdoche. Whenever the *Jaws* theme plays, the audience knows the shark is present.

Credit: Mary Evans/Universal Pictures/ Courtesy Everett Collection

Figure 8.9
This dorsal fin from the shark in *Jaws* performs a synecdochal function.

Besides just a part for a whole, however, synecdoche has a few other modes. It also can:

- Represent a part via a whole: such instances include using "car" to refer to any and all automobiles, including trucks, or using "meat" to refer to any animal flesh.

■ Refer to a larger class: Although "Kleenex" is a brand name, many use it to refer to any kind of tissue.

■ Refer to an object made of a certain material by mentioning that material: you've done this if you've ever referred to your credit card as "plastic."

■ Refer to the contents by citing its container: rather than saying beer, you might refer to it by its container, such as a bottle or a keg.

Building

Link

Choose an animal and create a brand mark for it based on a part of the whole. For instance, if you choose a tiger, you could use the paw (as in Clemson University's athletic brand mark), or you might choose its stripes (as the Cincinnati Bengals football team does). Think about how that particular part creates meaning for the brand mark. Next, repeat this exercise with a different part of the animal. How does the meaning change from one brand mark to another? How does the changing of the part change the rhetorical appeals of *logos*, *ethos*, *pathos*, or *kairos*? Write a short essay in which you develop a claim based on your findings, and support it with reasons and evidence.

Engine

Search

As mentioned above, sound also can serve to create synecdoche. Think of, or rewatch, a favorite movie or television show, preferably one that is suspenseful or dramatic. How does the film use music or sound effects to associate particular sounds with certain characters or moods? How does this use of sound affect the rhetorical appeals of *logos*, *ethos*, *pathos*, or *kairos*? Write a short essay in which you develop a claim based on your findings, and support it with reasons and evidence.

Deductive arguments

Deductive arguments derive from deductive reasoning, which usually has three parts: 1) a major premise, 2) a minor premise, and 3) a conclusion. One of the most common examples of deductive reasoning comes from the statement that Socrates is mortal because he is a man.

Major Premise: All men are mortal.

This major premise sets up the situation or conditions under which a test case is applied, which appears in the minor premise.

Minor Premise: Socrates is a man.

If Socrates is a man, and all men are mortal, then the conclusion is easily reached.

Conclusion: Socrates is mortal.

While you might consider mortality to be somewhat scientific, deductive reasoning might be expressed argumentatively. For example,

Major Premise: Smoking marijuana is unhealthy.

Minor Premise: Alexia smokes marijuana.

Conclusion: Alexia is unhealthy.

As you have probably already concluded, the outcome of a deductive reasoning depends upon the ingredients put into the the statement being made. Rather than expressing a clear-cut fact, the above example makes an argument about what constitutes an unhealthy state of being. This argument relies upon a major premise that is also argumentative (i.e., whether or not smoking marijuana is unhealthy). One might argue that such reasoning is invalid because little evidence exists to support the major premise. Alternatively, even if sufficient evidence or common opinion supports the claim of the major premise, Alexia might be unhealthy because of other factors, or she might be completely healthy despite the accuracy of the major premise.

Deductive argument relies upon this structure of deductive reasoning but omits one of the elements, either the major or minor premise, or the conclusion. This omission creates a kind of puzzle or riddle that requires the audience to fill in the missing part themselves. Deductive argument provides a kind of pleasure to the audience once they figure it out, the way you experience pleasure when you get the punch line of a joke. In addition, because the audience fills in the missing part themselves, they're more likely to remember it. This is one reason advertisements rely heavily on deductive argument. Many of the Geico commercials, such as the one in Figure 8.10, rely upon deductive arguments to convey their message.

Credit: Geico/The Martin Agency

Figure 8.10
Do woodchucks chuck wood?
If so, then Geico can save you money on your car insurance, according to the argument they construct.
www.youtube.com/
watch?v=4faBo4PdFpU&feature=youtu.be

In this commercial, the announcer states the major premise in the form of a question, asking "Can Geico really save you 15 percent or more on car insurance?" He then asks a rhetorical question, "Do woodchucks chuck wood?" The overall major premise would be, "Geico can save you 15 percent or more on car insurance if woodchucks chuck wood." The commercial then fills in the minor premise through a visual demonstration, showing that woodchucks do indeed chuck wood. The conclusion, "Since woodchucks chuck wood, Geico can save one up to 15 percent on car insurance," is left for the viewer to figure out. This structure has worked well for Geico, and the company has adapted it for many other commercials.

Building

Link

Create your own example of deductive reasoning based on something familiar. For example, deductive reasoning based on my dog might be as follows:

> Major Premise: Border collies are smart dogs.
> Minor Premise: My dog is a Border collie.
> Conclusion: My dog is smart.

Once you have your example, create a deductive argument from it. For the example above, you might simply state, "My dog, a Border collie, is smart," omitting the major premise.

Engine

Search

Using the example created in the exercise above, try to express the deductive argument as an image. How did you adapt words into an image? What elements were included or excluded? How do you think the rhetorical appeals of *logos*, *ethos*, *pathos*, or *kairos* change? Write a short essay in which you develop a claim based on your findings, and support it with reasons and evidence.

Text and Image Relationships

Texts and images usually coexist in a document in some way, either as a figure with a caption, a title with a painting, or simply a company's brand name on an advertisement. Two primary kinds of relationships between text and image include anchorage and relay. If one of the main ways a reader tries to interpret an image is through language, then anchorage and relay are two modes of interpretation. However, they also are modes of production. That is, they may become rhetorical techniques to relate image and text.

If you heed the cliché "a picture is worth a thousand words," anchorage and relay aid to fix those thousand words to only a few specific ones you might want the reader to focus on. When juxtaposed with an image, a title or caption helps to situate what the picture is about, and this is a rhetorical strategy, whittling down all the possibilities of what the image means to only the one intended by the author. Results are not guaranteed, of course, but anchorage and relay can help maximize the intended message.

Anchorage

As its term suggests, anchorage helps to fix the meaning of an image so the audience can better interpret it. Consider the picture and caption in Figure 8.11. You probably already know this picture as the image of President Barack Obama and some of his cabinet watching the raid on Osama Bin Laden's compound in May 2011. In fact, the caption that accompanies the image on one of CNN's pages tells as much: "U.S. President Barack Obama was able to monitor the raid that led to the death of Osama bin Laden 'in real time' from the White House, it has been disclosed." However, if you didn't have that caption to "anchor" the message of the photograph, what other meanings might you come up with?

Credit: Pete Souza

Figure 8.11
Depending on the caption, this image can be anchored in many ways.

You could list the people in the picture; describe the colors of their clothes; analyze their demeanor. Also, without the caption to explain what they're watching, you might conclude they're focused on the final minutes of a close basketball game. Such a caption also would have larger consequences for how you might subsequently view the president himself (for instance, why would they be using the situation room for this superfluous purpose?).

The caption, however, typically restrains the audience from reading "too much" from a photograph; it aids in narrowing the focus from a thousand words to only a few, and thus affects how the audience understands photographs.

The caption of the photo in Figure 8.11 directs the reader toward Obama, toward his intense gaze at the monitor out of the picture frame (one that you know is there from the focus of all of the spectators in the room, but also from the caption letting the reader know the action of the photograph). The very action ascribed to Obama, that of "monitoring," provides an ideological reading positioning the president as someone engaged in the operation, supervising as commander in chief.

Credit: Pete Souza

Figure 8.12
The caption on Fox News gives a different interpretation.

The same picture on the Fox News website has a different caption, which provides a different understanding of the picture: "Top-level officials get updated on the status of the mission to kill Osama bin Laden" (Figure 8.12). The caption no longer puts the focus on Obama but on all the officials in the room, so Obama is no longer as important. Moreover, the caption doesn't indicate these officials are watching the operation in "real time," only that they are receiving updates.

Relay

While anchorage most commonly occurs with fixed images, relay operates alongside moving images, such as film, or images in a sequence, such as a comic strip. While anchorage fixes the meaning of an image, relay develops meaning through the back and forth interplay between image and text to create a larger narrative than either provide individually.

Figure 8.13
The text in the speech balloon helps the reader understand what's going on in the image as a whole.

For example, imagine a comic strip with just images. The text balloons help provide context for the images and move the story along (Figure 8.13). Without text, comics would be difficult to interpret. Alternatively, imagine a comic strip with no pictures, and only text balloons. Such a comic would be equally unfulfilling in its narrative structure.

Such would be the same for a film without sound. Dialogue and music often provide information and clues that move the images of the story along through a plot or some other narrative. When serving as a relay rather than an anchor, text helps the image by moving its meaning along from one image to the next, filling out the parts of the world the audience needs to know when encountering the next image that doesn't show the whole picture.

Engine

Search

Find a comic strip from the comic section in your local newspaper or online. Without looking at the comics themselves, cover the speech balloons with a strip of paper. Next, try to deduce the plot of the comic from just the images, writing down your interpretations as you proceed. After a few tries, remove the paper and see how your narrative compares to the actual balloons. Share your comic with the class, both in its original form and how you interpreted it.

Building

Link

Locate the same picture or photograph on at least three different websites and note how the caption changes. How do these different captions affect the meaning that you take away from the photograph? What different ideological meanings do you think these captions create? What key words in the captions do you think have the most effect toward these different meanings? How does the caption make use of the rhetorical appeals of *logos, ethos, pathos,* or *kairos*? Write a short essay in which you develop a claim based on your findings, and support it with reasons and evidence. Then, write your own caption for this image, and share it with the class.

Rhetorical Continuities

Puns have long been used to create multiple associations and for rhetorical effect, whether in oral discourse, written documents, or through images. For instance, look at the image in Figure 8.14 of a "semiconductor."

Typically, you might think of a semiconductor as an element in computer circuitry. In this visual pun, however, a man is conducting semi trucks, making him a "semi conductor." Like the effect produced by many puns, your first response might be to groan. However, the associations created by overlapping the two meanings can provide new insights to each of these ideas. As a practice, Gregory L. Ulmer has

Figure 8.14
This image creates a visual pun on "semi conductor."

developed the term "puncept" to describe a kind of concept-making based on the pun. By using a pun like an analogy—relating two things that may seem dissimilar—an argument or new understanding can be made that can make your audience think. The puncept can be used in any application of rhetoric, from oral to digital.

Juxtaposition

Images (and text) are usually always present with other images. Look at a typical website, from CNN and ESPN to eBay or Facebook, and images always exist near other images. These images are juxtaposed, placed together in a single space. Often, the presence of any particular image next to another may be accidental. Different images on a news site may have little to do with one another, other than both being related to the day's current events. The images juxtaposed on your Facebook page go together because they come from your friends (or ad banners based on your interests), but, otherwise, there isn't much thought in placing images together in such ways. Juxtaposition, however, can be used in a purposeful, rhetorical way to create meaning and communicate ideas to an audience. While you inhabit a visual world full of juxtaposed images, here you'll look at juxtaposing as a rhetorical move to make an argument.

Credit: Chris Gee

Figure 8.15
What does the juxtaposition of this toy tricycle and tank say to you?

Juxtaposition offers a powerful technique for creating your own visual arguments. Figure 8.15 depicts two very different kinds of transportation: a play toy tricycle and a tank. The first of these you've probably used as a very young child, while most of the audience have probably never driven a tank. What meaning is created by combining these two items? From a stylistic perspective, you could argue that the large tank imposes itself upon the smaller tricycle and threatens to crush it (or fire upon it).

You also might consider how the two vehicles serve as analogies for those who use them. A young child most likely uses the tricycle, while a young adult probably operates the tank. Each object, the tricycle and the tank, might represent aspects of a single individual at different stages of his life, prompting questions, such as, "how can someone who innocently used a tricycle now wage war in an armor-plated vehicle?" Other aspects, such as color, lend to this analysis. The tricycle is bright, multicolored, which might signal the curiosity and optimism of childhood, while the "olive drab" color of the tank is just that—drab—

suggesting a loss of optimistic spirit. When placed together, these objects offer a trajectory of their user's life. A single image juxtaposing two simple objects can offer many new modes of thought than each object presented alone.

Rhetorical Continuities

Advertisements exist in many forms, from analog to digital. These advertisements may employ different techniques (for example, web ads are clickable, while print ads are not), but they also make use of similar rhetorical techniques and appeals. Locate a print magazine or newspaper that also has an online presence. Collect various advertisements from these sources that appear both in the print and online versions of the magazine. Analyze the difference between print ads and the online ads. How do they employ similar rhetorical techniques and appeals, such as *logos, ethos, pathos,* or *kairos*? How do they use different techniques? Why would you expect one medium to be better than the other for certain rhetorical appeals? Develop a claim based on your analysis, and write a brief report. Make sure to support your claim with reasons and evidence.

Building

Link

Select two images, and juxtapose them by using a photo editor. Analyze the image, and consider what new meanings emerge between the two objects. What relationships can you think of between them that you might not have noticed before? How does the juxtaposition make use of the rhetorical appeals of *logos, ethos, pathos,* or *kairos*? Write a short essay in which you develop a claim based on your results, and support it with reasons and evidence.

Engine

Search

Find and analyze an icon or brand mark that juxtaposes two images, such as the brand mark used by United Way. Without any research into the brand mark, what associations does juxtaposing the elements in the brand mark create? What message do you think the company or organization was attempting to communicate? How does this brand mark make use of the rhetorical appeals of *logos, ethos, pathos,* or *kairos*? When you've finished, research the company's intent when designing the brand mark, and compare what you've found with your original ideas about the brand mark's design. Write a short essay in which you develop a claim based on your findings, and support it with reasons and evidence.

Denotation

Look at the image in Figure 8.16. If you had to describe the picture with words, how would you do it? Take a minute to write down as many words as you can think of.

Figure 8.16
How would you describe this image?

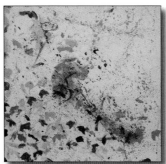

Figure 8.17
What words would you use to describe this painting?

Which words did you use? How did you describe the image? Did you write a definition? Did you describe features such as colors and shapes? Did you define it by naming a category it fits into?

How about the image in Figure 8.17? Is it a bit trickier to do? What words would you use to describe this image?

This image is more difficult to describe and requires different terms in order to say "what it is." For instance, it doesn't seem to have recognizable relationships between parts that follow linguistic grammar. There is no clear subject (noun) doing something (verb) to an object. So besides naming its colors, what else could you say about it?

Naming an image in this way defines its "essence," its literate definition, or in semiotic terms, its denotative message. The denotative meaning usually refers to the abstract meaning of a signifier, that is, what something "is" apart from what it "means."

Denotation is the "literal" meaning of a sign (or image). The denotation of a linguistic sign is the literal meaning, or dictionary definition. Similarly, the denotation of an image is what you and anyone else would literally see when you view the image. If you wanted to make a denotative description of an image, you would describe the image in the most objective and unbiased way you could.

Figure 8.18
What are the denotative meanings of the United States flag?

Usually when you see a symbolic object as familiar as the American flag (Figure 8.18), you don't think of "red, white, and blue" as simply colors; when you "read" a symbolic object like the American flag, you not only see the colors and the shapes of the stars and stripes, but you also see the symbolic meanings those colors and shapes represent.

The denotative meaning does not include any of the flag's symbolic meanings. Denotation is a literal description of the visual elements in the image:

> *A photo of the American flag on a flagpole. The flag has dark stars on a blue background in the upper-left corner, and white and red horizontal stripes. The flag appears to fold like it is waving in the wind. It appears against a blue sky and is backlit by the sun . . .*

Engine

Search

Find an original version of a music video, and attempt to write your own literal version of the lyrics. What visual elements do you find yourself including? Which do you seem to exclude? Why? Share your literal version with the class, and write a short essay in which you develop a claim based on your video's goals, and support it with reasons and evidence.

Building

Link

Visit YouTube, and find a "literal version" of a music video. These videos attempt to provide the denotative message of the video as the lyrics of the song to explain what occurs visually. These literal versions change the lyrics and the actual song itself to give a denotative description of the video. Analyze the literal version of the video you find, or the one in Figure 8.19. What does the denotation mainly focus on? What kind of meta-analysis occurs through the lyrics? What do the lyrics miss? Write a short essay in which you develop a claim based on your results, and support it with reasons and evidence.

Credit: "Rainbow Connection" and Rob O'Hara

Figure 8.19
Literal version of "Rainbow Connection."

www.youtube.com/watch?v=Ywvwp0aQz-o&feature=youtu.be

Connotation

Look again at the rose image (Figure 8.16). The section on denotation discussed that the denotative message is the literal message apart from symbolic meanings or association. Connotation, however, pertains to those messages of an image that include the symbolic levels.

What connotative, symbolic messages might an image of a rose invoke? Romance? Love? Valentine's Day? You can probably come up with many. Connotation provides the image with a set of cultural conventions that help the reader navigate and make sense of an image and, in some ways, provide the audience with an image's meaning. You didn't always associate a rose with romance but learned that this flower and behavior have been connected in the past, so the rose becomes symbolic. The rose comes to signify ideas beyond its denotative meaning.

The stylistic techniques and elements used when taking a photograph are all elements of connotation. Typically, an audience is unaware of these techniques (and probably can't tell which settings a photographer used), but these are still design choices selected to create specific effects. Such effects also may be "recorded" into the denotative meaning but are meant to evoke connotative meanings.

For example, using a black-and-white setting might convey a feeling of nostalgia or timelessness, while framing a subject at a long distance against an expansive backdrop might create a feeling of smallness compared to the vast space. Because any photograph or video relies on such choices (even if made without much thought), there is no clean separation between denotation and connotation. Even if a photographer attempted to capture an image of an apple, that apple is not simply a thing by itself but related to the larger context in which the photo was taken.

DIGITAL Connections

"Miles Away From Ordinary" Ad Description

By Jonathan C. Hall

In these days of wane for traditional media advertising, Corona's "Miles Away From Ordinary" ad campaign seems almost quaint. While most

> As an example of connotation, consider Jonathan C. Hall's description of a Corona beer advertisement.

marketers are looking to guerrilla and viral techniques to spend less and circumvent the kind of instinctive consumer ad resistance I expressed above, Corona simply blanketed the mass media—from 30-second spots on primetime TV to graphic wraps on the trucks of their distributors to those banner-flying planes that buzz up and down the Jersey Shore in summer—with the visual and aural sensations of a subdued tropical beach, a picture always completed by that iconic Corona bottle and obligatory lime wedge.

Whether in web, TV, print and outdoor media, Corona ads consistently offer a flight of the senses to an idyllic, tropical place "miles away" from our ordinary worries and woes. Beach scenes and ocean sounds are powerful triggers of the so-called "relaxation response"—some psychotherapists use these exact tools to help patients cope with anxiety. The Corona drinkers in these scenes silence their cell phones and engage in other stress-neutralizing activities. A trope in the ads is the use of the Corona bottle in fanciful optical experiments: a bikini-clad woman appears to swing on a hammock between two Corona bottles (pictured in Figure 8.20); a beer-drinking beach-goer re-positions his Corona bottle to block his view of less attractive neighbors; a crescent moon over tropical waters appears in the mouth of a Corona bottle as if it were a lime wedge. These images emerge from the kind of

Credit: Corona/Cramer-Krasselt

Figure 8.20
Corona attempts to show a mood that's "miles away."

idle mental play that only occurs to a vacationing mind. All of these media ladle onto us, day after day, the promises and meanings of the Corona brand: namely, that drinking Corona is tantamount to a temporary escape, a vacation, from the punishing, daily fray of our *ordinary* modern lives. But how could Corona beer itself, that sad drink, ever deliver on such a promise? How could *I* have enjoyed the stuff?

Alcohol content is certainly part of it. But I suspect the phenomenon also has something to do with what Baylor College of Medicine researchers found with Coke drinkers: that brand knowledge can have "a dramatic influence on expressed behavioral preferences and on the measured brain responses" to beverages. In other words, all those ad dollars spent by Coca-Cola over the years haven't been just to persuade us to buy Coke; they've also been part of the content of the product experience.

Of course, that mood, that experience, might be different for each person. Such ads, however, assume their audience has a certain shared set of ideas so that connotation might be achieved. Corona hopes that most Americans associate the beach with vacation (as well as some of its international audience), and thus drinking their beverage will induce that atmosphere. Someone who hates the beach or is afraid of the ocean, however, might have a negative reaction to such images, although she or he might still understand what the advertisement is trying to evoke.

Building

Link

Locate a brand mark from a familiar company, such as the "Golden Arches" of McDonald's or Target's "target." Research what the brand mark means, why it was designed or selected, and other details that affect its connoted message. What message do you think the company was trying to convey by using a particular brand mark? Do you think the brand mark is successful at this message, or could it be improved? How does the brand mark make use of the rhetorical appeals of *logos, ethos, pathos,* or *kairos*? Write a short essay in which you develop a claim based on your results, and support it with reasons and evidence.

Engine

Search

Locate a print ad for your favorite food. What kind of "experience" do you think the ad is trying to convey? What elements in the advertisement add to that message? How does the ad make use of the rhetorical appeals of *logos, ethos, pathos,* or *kairos*? Write a short essay in which you develop a claim based on your findings, and support it with reasons and evidence.

Visual narrative

Typically, a narrative is simply a method for telling a story. While you're probably familiar with narrative as it appears in books, narrative also can use images to tell a story, and sometimes much more efficiently and emotionally.

For example, Charles Minard's map of Napoleon's Russian campaign of 1812 (Figure 8.21) uses a visual design to tell the story of how badly this campaign ended for Napoleon. Minard overlays geographic details with the directional line of Napoleon's march (tan indicates marching to Russia, black represents coming back), with the thickness of this line indicating the size of Napoleon's army. By following the tan/black line along the map, you can see just how few of Napoleon's army remained by the end of the campaign without reading about a single battle. In this one visual, you quickly get the narrative of what happened.

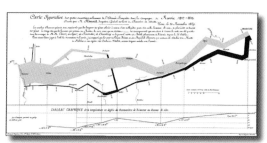

Figure 8.21
In a single glance, you can see how badly Napoleon was beaten by the Russians.

Credit: Chipotle/CAA Marketing and Nexus Productions

As a video example of a visual narrative, Figure 8.22 depicts a Chipotle commercial that tells the story of a farmer who turned to factory methods of farming. He realizes he made a mistake and

Figure 8.22
This music video attempts to tell a story to make an argument.
https://www.youtube.com/watch?v=aMfSGt6rHos

returns to his former practices. Although Willie Nelson's cover of Coldplay's "The Scientist" relays this message thematically, the visuals provide the main narration of the story and attempt to persuade the audience that Chipotle only buys agricultural products that sustain the environment and animal well-being.

Building Link

Create a visual narrative that tells the story of one of your school's recent athletic seasons. You may complete this assignment in a variety of ways, via an image collage that contains multiple images from each important moment, or as a video narrated with audio dialogue. Even though this is a story, include a claim about the season, and support it with reasons and evidence.

Engine

Choose a commercial that is online, and analyze its narrative structure. Does the commercial tell a story? If so, does it mainly use visuals, written text, narration, or a combination of these? Which of the three, if any, dominate? How does the narrative in the commercial tie into the larger narrative of the company or organization as a whole? How does the commercial make use of the rhetorical appeals of *logos, ethos, pathos,* or *kairos*? Write a short essay in which you develop a claim based on your findings, and support it with reasons and evidence.

Adaptation

If you've ever seen a Disney movie, you've mostly likely seen a visual adaptation of a written work. The narrative in the movie *Aladdin* comes from the Middle Eastern folktale, "Aladdin's Wonderful Lamp," while the movie *The Little Mermaid* is adapted from a tale by Hans Christian Andersen (Figure 8.23). Many visual works you see—from historical epics, like *Troy,* to modern bestsellers, like *Harry Potter*—originate in print and are adapted into other media from television and film to video games.

Credit: Hans Christian Andersen

Figure 8.23
Disney wasn't the first to draw a little mermaid.

Of course, an adaptation isn't an exact copy of the original but rather an adapted version of one medium into another. In a broader sense, adaptation is a process in which an individual or group changes to better live in their environment. Similarly, a novel "as is" wouldn't work well as a movie and would need major changes for the new medium.

Rhetorical Continuities

This principle of adaptation can be applied to written texts as well. For instance, you would typically adapt your writing style when sending a professor an email versus sending your friend an email. You also would write a text message or Twitter update differently than you would an answer on a test. While the content for each might be the same, you would adapt the style for each audience and medium.

Credit: Sesame Workshop and Columbia Pictures

Figure 8.24
These two Draculas were adapted for very different audiences.

When you consider adaptation, think more broadly than the kind of filmic adaptation you're used to, and, instead, think of how a particular message might be adapted for a particular genre and for a particular audience. An adaptation of Bram Stoker's *Dracula* would be much different for a children's cartoon compared with an adult-rated movie (Figure 8.24).

Building

Link

Choose a short poem. Using video clips from the Internet, create a visual adaptation of the poem by integrating images with the poem's words. How does the meaning of the poem change once you create it as a visual? How does the visual poem make use of the rhetorical appeals of *logos*, *ethos*, *pathos*, or *kairos*? Write a short essay in which you develop a claim based on your findings, and support it with reasons and evidence.

Engine

Search

Research a film you've seen lately or one you remember seeing as a child. Was this film adapted from other sources? If so, what other adaptations have been made from the original? Create a diagram mapping the various relationships between the original and all of the adaptations produced from it. If the film you researched wasn't adapted, choose another, or look up *The Little Mermaid* and complete this exercise using this film as a starting point. Share your diagram and results with the class.

Photomontage

A photomontage is made of several images stitched together into a single visual. Rather than compressing time in the mode of a film montage, an image montage juxtaposes images that might not fit within the same space of a single camera shot. Photomontages might be used for scientific purposes, such as

Credit: NASA

Figure 8.25
Photomontage of the surface of Mars

Credit: Peter Kennard

Figure 8.26
What argument is
Peter Kennard trying
to make with his
photomontage?

Credit: Unknown/Charles Maxwell/Lance Cheung

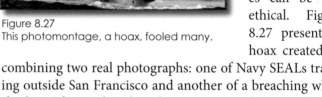
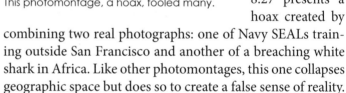

Figure 8.27
This photomontage, a hoax, fooled many.

the photomontage of the surface of planet Mars in Figure 8.25, or to create visual metaphors. Such montages can be used for rhetorical purposes and create visual arguments, as in Figure 8.26, a photomontage by Peter Kennard, which combines photos of the Earth, a screaming mouth, and what appear to be warheads to suggest a response that the Earth might have due to the arms race and current eco-crisis, according to the work's creator.

However, some photomontages can be unethical. Figure 8.27 presents a hoax created by combining two real photographs: one of Navy SEALs training outside San Francisco and another of a breaching white shark in Africa. Like other photomontages, this one collapses geographic space but does so to create a false sense of reality.

While you might create images such as these for fun, to practice photo editing skills, or to make an argument, the creator of this montage (who still remains unknown) tried to pass off the photo as real and even claimed that it was the 2001 National Geographic Photo of the Year. Depending on how you intend to use a photo, you must be careful about the ethical (or even legal) consequences of photo composition and manipulation.

Building

Link

Find one montage each from a television show and a movie. Compare the two montage sequences. What features do they have in common? How do they differ? What are the formal features? How many seconds does the director dedicate to each part of the montage? How many parts are there? What else do you notice? How do the montages make use of the rhetorical appeals of *logos*, *ethos*, *pathos*, or *kairos*? Write a short essay in which you develop a claim based on your results, and support it with reasons and evidence.

Search Engine

Using a video camera—either a camcorder or a video camera on your phone—take photos of each part of your day, and try to create a photomontage depicting the whole day in a single view. What narrative emerges from your photomontage? Share your photomontage with the class, and revise your montage based on their feedback.

Image Ethics

Digital images and image editors make it very easy to make and manipulate images. While some manipulations might be fine for your own personal use, there are many ethical reasons why you might want to avoid creating certain kinds of images or applying a certain editing function to existing images, especially for images you intend to use for public or professional reasons (as seen in the Helicopter Shark photomontage). Follow the guidelines below if you're unsure about a particular ethical approach.

Copyright and permissions

As discussed in Chapter 6, most of the images you create for education purposes will probably fall under fair use. However, for other uses you will most likely need to gain permission from the original creator of the image. Using others' images not only constitutes a form of plagiarism, but it also might result in legal repercussions, even if you alter the image. For instance, Figure 8.28 shows an original photo by Art Rogers on the left that was used to develop the sculpture by Jeff Koons on the right. A judge determined that the sculpture was too much like the photograph and ordered Koons to pay monetary damages to Rogers. If you are using an image for academic work, make sure you cite it correctly.

Figure 8.28
A judge ruled that Jeff Koons's sculpture (right) was too much like Art Rogers's photograph (left).

Manipulation

You can manipulate an image in many ways. For instance, cropping out important parts of an image can conceal parts that might be important to the overall context of the image. You could make an image confusing, unclear, or inaccurate by skewing its proportions, applying filters, or pixelating the image. These all affect how the audience reads the image, or whether they can read it at all.

DIGITAL Connections

The Associated Press is Not *Vogue*, Fired Photoshopping Photographer Learns

By Sara Morrison

Digitally altering photographs might be accepted—expected, really—when it comes to magazines like *Vogue*, but it's a big no-no when it comes to news organizations. Yet that's what one Pulitzer-winning AP photographer chose to do to a photo he took in Syria in September.

The manipulation of an image is often considered unethical, especially by journalistic outlets. Consider Narciso Contreras, an Associated Press photographer and Pulitzer Prize winner, who was fired for manipulating one of his photos (Figure 8.29) from this article published in *The Wire*.

Figure 8.29
In this altered photograph (bottom), Contreras removed another photographer's equipment from the original (top).

Narciso Contreras was part of a team of five AP photographers who won a Pulitzer for breaking news photography last year for their work in Syria. The AP also posted a video of Contreras discussing his work to YouTube last June, and he spoke to the *Guardian* and *Time* about working in a country in the middle of a bloody and brutal civil war in December 2012.

"He's showing us the reality of the situation in Aleppo, which is surely a difficult place to work," AP vice president and director of photography Santiago Lyon told *Time*.

Contreras was not just a random freelancer who took a few photos for the AP; he was one of the organization's best photographers on the ground in Syria, and since October 2012, he's filed almost 500 photos for the wire organization.

And in one of them, taken last September, he chose to edit another journalist's camera out of a shot of a Syrian rebel taking cover. Contreras thought the camera would "distract viewers," according to the AP's story about itself, which did not mention how Contreras' ethical lapse was discovered.

"I took the wrong decision when I removed the camera . . . I feel ashamed about that," Contreras told the AP. "You can go through my archives and you can find that this is a single case that happened probably at one very stressed moment, at one very difficult situation, but yeah, it happened to me, so I have to assume the consequences."

Those consequences will be harsh: Contreras "will not work for the AP again in any capacity," said vice president and director of photography Santiago Lyon. And, though the AP found no evidence that any of his other photos were altered, all of them—including the six that were part of the Pulitzer-winning package—are no longer available for commercial licensing. They've already been removed from the AP's image search.

It's a sad end to Contreras' once very promising career with the AP, especially over what was, essentially, a cosmetic change that didn't alter the news value of the photo. But it's not like he didn't know this could have happened to him. Three years ago, Miguel Tovar, also a freelancer, edited a photo to remove his shadow. Rival wire service Reuters has also had photoshop scandals. In 2006, freelancer Adnan Hajj was fired for (badly) photoshopping extra plumes of smoke in a photo of the aftermath of an Israeli airstrike in Beirut. He also photoshopped a photo of an Israeli jet fighter to show it firing three missiles instead of one. Like Contreras, their photos were removed from their employers' photo libraries.

The AP has come down just about as hard on its staff reporters as it did its freelance photographer. Last year, three journalists were fired after an article about Virginia's then-gubernatorial candidate, Terry McAuliffe, had to be retracted.

Accuracy

If you're creating an image to illustrate or present information, make sure the image is accurate at showing that information. You also should consider the way that text anchors the reading of an image. Words that inaccurately describe the image will lead the viewer to inaccurately understand the image, unethically leading them to wrong conclusions.

Building

Link

Locate a recent photograph of a well-known event across at least 10 different online news sources. How does the caption influence how you understand the image? Do you find some captions more ethical than others in their accuracy? How do the captions affect the use of the rhetorical appeals of *logos, ethos, pathos,* or *kairos*? Write a short essay in which you develop a claim based on your examination of all 10 outlets, and support it with reasons and evidence.

Engine

Search

Research the steps in gaining permission to use a photo from a major image resource, such as the Associated Press, Reuters, or Getty Images. Write a short set of instructions informing someone else how to get permission from one of these resources. Then, adapt those instructions into a diagram such as a flowchart.

KEY Terms

adaptation	manipulation
analogy	map
anchorage	metaphor
chart	metonymy
connotation	photograph
crop	photomontage
denotation	puncept
diagram	relay
ethics	screen capture
icon	synecdoche
juxtaposition	visual narrative

Photo Essay

For this assignment, produce a photo essay that makes an argument or relates some story, either fictional or based on real events. A photo essay is an arrangement of images used to tell a story to an audience or express a real-life event. Often, the images provide an emotionally charged narrative that captures details the written word cannot. These photographs are arranged in a specific order to tell this story, usually chronologically.

The guidelines below offer some considerations and a place to start. However, use your imagination, and go beyond these suggestions. Of course, follow other instructions from your instructor, who will provide details about length, topics, or specific requirements. Classes that don't have access to cameras can also complete this assignment with found images on the web.

As you script your photo essay and then finalize it in visual form, remember to reference the rhetorical tetrahedron, and ask yourself questions about the essay's audience, message, and design (the medium and genre are, of course, photos and essay). Also think about how you can use *logos, ethos, pathos,* and *kairos* in composing your essay.

Choose a Topic: A photo essay, like a written essay, first requires that you choose your topic—that you determine what you'd like to write about. As with other writing, find a topic that interests you, one that calls you to write. If you plan on creating this photo essay by taking your own photographs, make sure you're able to get the shots you want.

Research: As with any writing assignment, much of the work comes before you start writing. Research where you'll take most of your photographs, so you can ensure you can bring the right equipment. Will you need a tripod? Extra lighting? Study how the environment will play a role, and plan accordingly.

Finally, consider how you will get to your locations. Unless your class has a large travel budget, you probably won't be able to take your own photographs in remote locations. In addition, make sure you are safe when taking your own photographs, and ask for permission when shooting on private property or other locations that require it.

Find your angle: Try to find an angle or specific story within the story. In other words, what makes your particular essay interesting or unique? Good research will help reveal the angle (or several angles) you might take.

Plan: Before you enter the field with your camera, or find your images online, try to plan the story you'd like to tell. What's the argument you plan to make with the story? Make a script, treatment, and storyboard of the essay, or make a list of the photos you need to shoot. Determine which best suits your purposes, and plan out your essay before you get too deep in production. Sometimes, however, you might compose your story after you have taken your photographs, using them to help find the story or narrative arc. If so, you can still organize and plan your essay using the above techniques, which can help you figure out how to arrange them into an argument.

Pinpoint the emotional tone: Determine what emotional tone you want to establish with your photographs. Are you trying to express joy, hate, fear, sadness, regret, or a range of emotions? Discover whatever emotional angle you feel tells the best narrative, and use photographs that convey those emotions to connect with your audience.

Take multiple photos: While you should have a shot list of specific photographs you'll need, take multiple shots of each of those items on the list. Sometimes the first shot will be out of focus or include some undesirable element, so taking several shots of the same list item can ensure you have usable photographs when you begin to edit and arrange your essay.

Consider captions: Many photo essays include captions that help guide the reader through the essay. However, don't let captions take over and undercut the power your photographs can provide on their own. Use the captions according to the advice in this chapter, such as pointing out important details the audience might miss, explaining the general events occurring in the photograph, or expressing your particular focus. When including specific details, make sure you check that any factual information is correct.

Arrange: Once you have selected your photographs, determine the best arrangement that will express your argument (remember, arguments can be implicit). Does one photograph offer a "claim" or "conclusion" more than another? Does your essay have a narrative arc with a beginning, middle, and end? Order and reorder your photographs to try different arrangements before deciding on any particular order.

Review and revise: As with any essay, you should have a peer review your essay and give you feedback. If possible, compose a specific list of questions you would like your reviewer to answer about your essay; this will make the review session more productive. After you have feedback, revise your photo essay.

Distribute: Once you have selected and arranged your photographs and have written any captions you want to include, determine how you might best distribute the essay in its final form. You can certainly create a photo essay through a word processor, but you might consider integrating the photos into a website, blog, Prezi, PowerPoint, or even design your own booklet. Of course, the final delivery form should satisfy whatever audience you're trying to reach, as well as the requirements made by your instructor.

From DIGITAL Writers

The New York Times photo blog
lens.blogs.nytimes.com/?_r=0

There are many photo essays you might research when designing your own, but consider the photo essays posted by *The New York Times's Lens* blog, which hosts a variety of photographic narratives that tell stories from diverse parts of the world.

STUDENT Example

Student photo essay
stephaniajune.blogspot.com/2005/11/out-and-about-in-ferndale.html

The student who composed this photo essay documents how the community of Ferndale, Michigan shows support for the gay and lesbian community across its many businesses.

CHAPTER 9

Digital Video

In 2005, Jawed Karim posted a video of himself at the San Diego Zoo, creatively titled, "Me at the zoo" (Figure 9.1). Although the video only lasts 18 seconds, this was the beginning of YouTube, started by Karim, Chad Hurley, and Steve Chen. Their purpose was to create a video-sharing site that allowed anyone to post videos of everyday events and to make the site searchable, so videos could be found easily. Today, YouTube stores not just the mundane videos, but also the extraordinary moments, as well as corporate videos from companies, organizations, and celebrities. Digital video has become a major online medium.

Although digital video existed before YouTube, this was the first site that made it easy to share videos with other people. Previously, video files were comparatively large in size and, therefore, difficult to quickly send through the Internet. Now, due in part to YouTube and new video compression technologies, a researcher in Antarctica can share daily video with her university lab in Minnesota in a matter of minutes.

Figure 9.1
"Me at the zoo" was the first video posted to YouTube. Yes, Jawed. Elephant trunks are cool.
www.youtube.com/
watch?v=jNQXAC9IVRw

Digital video technologies have also become more affordable, portable, and easy to use. In fact, almost everyone can take video through their smart phone. Because of the ease of use and distribution, the world is sharing events that would have taken days to spread by other means, and without the filter of government agencies or corporate interests who could have stopped viewers from seeing what they didn't want seen.

For instance, since 2006, you might have viewed light-hearted videos, such as "Charlie bit my finger," fundraising campaigns, such as the Ice Bucket Challenge, or have been introduced to Justin Bieber, whose career was launched partially due to digital video. But you might have also seen more important events, such as video direct from US soldiers fighting in Iraq and Afghanistan, video from the 2011 Japan earthquake and tsunami, or the death of Nedā Āghā-Soltān, an aspiring Iranian musician whose violent death by gunshot was captured by an amateur digital videographer and uploaded that night. *Time* magazine has called her shooting, "The most widely witnessed death in human history." In comparison, consider that the famous homemade film reel of President John F. Kennedy's assassination didn't broadcast on network television until 1975, twelve years after the event took place.

Digital Video

Since digital video is another writing technology you might use to communicate, it's important you understand how to shoot and post videos, so you can tap into this powerful writing technology for your own purposes. However, this task is not just technical, but also rhetorical and aesthetic. Whether you have a smartphone that can record video or a more expensive digital video camcorder, the basics of camera angles and shot selection are relatively similar to shooting analog film.

This chapter won't cover all the technical basics of your individual video recording device (see your device's user manual for this information). However, it will discuss some basics for how to shoot video more conscientiously.

As you read about the various ways to script, compose, and shoot digital video, consider how these elements can be used rhetorically. For instance, how does a particular camera angle affect the audience? What kind and how many writers are required to create a script? How does the medium of video encourage particular design and genre choices, and vice versa? Keep these questions in mind as you read through the chapter.

Types of digital video

There are many types of digital videos you can produce and a variety of ways you can distribute them—from YouTube and Vimeo, sites that permit longer videos up to full-length feature films, to Vine, a video-sharing service that allows you to create short, six-second videos. Although the following list is not exhaustive, it covers some of the more popular kinds of digital videos that can serve a variety of purposes.

- **Vlog:** As discussed in Chapter 7, "vlog" stands for "video blog," a blog that is distributed via digital video. Vlogs are usually short videos of two to five minutes that focus on the topic of the site or channel in which they're located. Vlogs may be scripted or spontaneous, although recording will most likely be smoother if you at least have a rough outline of what you plan to talk about.

- **Interview:** An interview is simply a discussion between a host and a single respondent or larger group. Interview questions should be planned in advance, although you might come up with others as the interview progresses. Specific camera angles for interview videos are discussed later in the chapter.

- **Tutorial:** A video-based tutorial instructs the viewer how to accomplish some task. These videos should be well scripted, and shots should include you actually completing the tasks as you describe them to the viewer.

- **Review:** A review provides an evaluation of some product or service for the viewer. When possible, include shots of you using the product or service, as well as its best and worst features.

- **Essay or presentation:** A video essay provides a way to make an argument, just as you would in a traditional essay. However, a video essay allows you to incoporate images and sound to help make your point.

  Video presentations can simply be Powerpoint or Prezi presentations that are recorded, either with you giving the presentation live, or screencapturing the presentation and then adding voice-over narration. Video presentations allow you to deliver your presentation to a larger audience.

- **Résumé:** A video résumé transforms a print résumé into a dynamic showcase of your skills and abilities. A video résumé is not simply a reading of your print résumé, but uses the power of digital video to tell a story about what you can do for an employer.

- **Documentary:** A documentary is a video that investigates some question or problem. The video might make an argument, but its primary goal is to show the audience some slice or perspective of the world they might not have seen before. Although traditionally composed of celluloid film, digital video has allowed anyone with a camera to make his or her own documentary.

- **Feature film:** Although also traditionally composed of celluloid film, most feature films you see in the theater are composed either with digital video cameras, or are heavily edited with digital video tools in postproduction. Although you probably don't have access to actors, producers, special effects editors, and the entire crew that helps make a large-scale feature film, you can still make use of digital video to create your own narratives.

Digital Video Rhetorics

Although video shares many of the same rhetorical elements you've looked at in this book, you should also understand rhetorical techniques specific to the medium of video. How you position and capture video is as important as what you capture, and the methods below will help your audience better interpret your intended message. In addition, many of these techniques can apply to shooting digital still images.

Zooming and framing

When composing a video, you often use the viewfinder to make sure your desired subject is in the shot. The two techniques to ensure the subject appears correctly include zooming in or out to appropriately place the subject, and framing the subject within the viewfinder.

When shooting a particular subject, usually a person, there are generally four shot types that are created by the camera's zoom (or by physically moving the camera nearer or farther from the subject): wide shot, medium shot, close-up, and extreme close-up.

- **Wide shot:** This shot zooms the camera lens as wide as possible, showing the subject surrounded by the context of his environment. Use this shot to show the relationship between a subject and his surroundings (Figure 9.2).

- **Medium Shot:** This shot zooms in a bit, but still shows some context around the subject of the shot (Figure 9.3).

- **Close-up:** For this shot, the camera lens is zoomed in farther, usually showing a subject's head and shoulders (Figure 9.4).

- **Extreme close-up:** This shot is the opposite of the wide shot. In general, little background is shown, and the camera is zoomed in on the subject's face, or even only part of the face (Figure 9.5).

Figure 9.2
This example shows a wide shot of the subject.

Figure 9.3
This medium shot zooms in on the subject, but still provides background context.

Figure 9.4
Close-up shots usually focus on the subject's face.

Figure 9.5
An extreme close-up provides even more focus and detail on a subject.

Of course, the subject doesn't have to be a person, and the interesting part of the person may not be her face; it may be a tattoo, item of clothing, or some other feature. What you choose to focus on tells the audience what you want them to think is important, just as you might boldface or italicize a word you want to be stressed in a written document.

When placing a person or object in a shot, you also should be aware of how that person or object fits within the frame of the camera lens. For instance, you don't want an important part to be out of frame, nor do you want irrelevant scenery, props, or equipment to appear in the frame. Generally, consider headroom, chin room, and nose room when filming a person.

- **Headroom:** This term refers to the amount of space between the top of the subject's head and the top of the frame (Figure 9.6). Usually, unless it's an extreme close-up, you don't want to "cut off" part of your subject's head.

- **Chin room:** Just as you don't want to cut off the top of your subject's head, you also shouldn't cut off her or his chin (Figure 9.7).

Figure 9.6
These images show bad use of headroom (left) and good use of headroom (right).

Figure 9.7
The left image provides plenty of chin room for the subject, while the right image nearly cuts off the chin.

Figure 9.8
The left image provides adequate space into which the subject can look, speak, and act, while the right image provides no space.

■ **Nose room:** This term refers to the amount of space between the subject and the area to which he or she is looking or speaking (Figure 9.8). If you were to place the frame opposite the subject's face too close to his mouth, then it would appear as if he was talking into a wall.

Building

With a still or video camera, practice composing each of the shot types and framing techniques discussed above. How can different ways of composing enact the rhetorical appeals of *logos*, *ethos*, *pathos*, and *kairos*? Develop a claim based on your research, support it with reasons and evidence, and then share your images with the class.

Engine

Find examples in which a head, chin, or nose is "cut" from the subject. Do you think this cutting was intentional or accidental? Does the cutting detract from watching the subject? Do such cuts detract from the videographer's *ethos*? Develop a claim based on your research, and support it with reasons and evidence.

Camera angles

Most of the shots discussed above consider subjects that are mostly level with the camera. However, you can also vary the camera angle to create different relationships between the subject and the audience, thus creating rhetorical effects mostly through power relationships.

Figure 9.9
A low angle shot places the subject in a superior position to the audience.

- **Low angle:** If you place the camera below the subject's height, you confer a status of superiority to the subject because it now looks down upon the viewer (Figure 9.9). This angle also might be chosen to show an aerial background behind the subject.

- **High angle:** As an alternative to the low angle shot, the high angle confers the audience's superiority over the subject (Figure 9.10). If the audience

Figure 9.10
The high angle connotes a sense of superiority over the subject.

is seeing through the point of view of another character, then it would associate a position of power through this character's eyes, as he or she is looking down upon the other character. High angle shots also can be used to provide unique perspectives and show more background information, such as an aerial flyover.

Figure 9.11
The Dutch angle tilts the camera to provide a canted view.

- **Dutch angle:** This angle tilts the camera, so the scene is shot at a sideways angle, providing a dynamic and disorientating view to the audience (Figure 9.11).

Figure 9.12
This swimming shark provides a vector of direction.

These angles also help you create lines and vectors within your shots (Figure 9.12). If you've had a basic design class, you've learned that vertical lines create a sense of strength, horizontal lines a sense of stability, and angled lines a sense of movement or uneasiness. Lines perform the same functions when they appear in video as well. For instance, an image of a tall building shot from a low angle can symbolize strength and power. The panning of a calm ocean can suggest serenity. Diagonal lines, perhaps produced by a Dutch angle, can create dynamic shots.

Building Link

In addition to the three angles mentioned above, research other camera angles that have been invented. What was the original use for these camera perspectives? What problems did they solve? How are they used today? Develop a claim based on your research, and support it with reasons and evidence.

Search Engine

With a camera, photograph or video an object from multiple camera angles. How does the viewer's relation to the object change with each change in angle? Which do you find the most pleasing? Which do you find the strangest? Do different angles reveal some details that others don't? Develop a claim based on your research, and support it with reasons and evidence.

Rule of thirds

Typically, you might think if you want to emphasize a subject, you should place it in the middle of your viewing frame when shooting video. However, asymmetrical designs are often more engaging and dynamic to viewers. When working with space in your frame, one technique you might consider is the "rule of thirds." This rule divides the image in your viewfinder into nine segments by virtually dividing the image with two horizontal rules and two vertical rules (see Figure 9.13). Any major compositional elements should lie somewhere near one of the four intersections of these lines. For instance, rather than aligning your main object in the center of the frame, you would align it on one of the four vertices, which gives your shot a more dynamic feeling or greater sense of depth and context.

Credit: Chaky

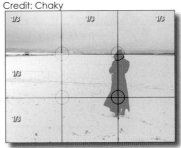

Figure 9.13
The focal point of this image is emphasized through the rule of thirds.

The rule of thirds in some ways is a shortcut to creating designs with an aesthetic use of spatial arrangements. A more precise layout follows the "Golden Mean," displayed by the Fibonacci spiral (Figure 9.14). When overlaid on several photographs, notice how the major area of focus aligns with the spiral. Another shortcut to this Golden Mean, then, is to divide the composition into fifths rather than thirds and align your major point of interest along the two-fifths or three-fifths lines in any direction (portrait or landscape). However, the rule of thirds will generally produce good results, and many video cameras have a feature that simulates gridlines in your viewfinder, allowing you to align your subject with one of the four intersection points.

Credit: Raiana Tomazini

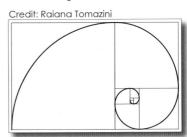

Figure 9.14
Fibonacci spiral

You can usually notice the rule of thirds while watching television, specifically during interview scenes. For example, this still from *The Office* in Figure 9.15 uses the rule of thirds to position the interviewee's head in the upper right intersection point. If filming your own interviews, you should make use of these upper two points, positioning your subject's face in either of these two spots.

Credit: NBCUniversal

Figure 9.15
Many interviews use the rule of thirds to arrange their shots.

Building

Link

As discussed above, television shows, such as *The Office*, use the rule of thirds during their "interview" sequences. Locate other instances of television or films that use this technique, either fictional shows or news programs. Do you find these uses of the rule of thirds effective? Develop a claim based on your research, and support it with reasons and evidence.

Engine

Search

Using a camera—either provided by your class or just a cell phone camera—practice taking photos of a variety of objects using the rule of thirds. However, also take a series of photos placing objects in other orientations. In a photo editor, overlay a rule-of-thirds grid onto the images, seeing how well your images align with this principle. Share your images with the class, and discuss which photos are more engaging and whether the rule of thirds improves the composition of your images. How does the rule of thirds enact any of the rhetorical appeals of *logos, ethos, kairos,* or *pathos*?

Using multiple cameras

Multiple cameras, or multiple camera positions, can make your video more dynamic, offer varying perspectives, and provide more information for the viewer. Two techniques to ensure the best result include the 180-degree rule and creating sequences out of multiple shots.

If you were shooting a scene between two people, such as an interview scene, you might place cameras in two positions, one aimed at the interviewer, and one at the interviewee. When setting up a shot such as this, always keep the cameras on the same side of the subjects. In other words, imagine a line separates the cameras from the subjects, a line that can never be crossed (Figure 9.16). This is called the 180-degree rule. If you were shooting the interviewer from one side so she appeared on the left of the frame, but moved the camera across this line and shot the interviewee from the same position, the audience would become confused since it would appear that neither was talking to the other (Figure 9.17). In terms of *logos*, breaking this rule would seem illogical to the audience.

Figure 9.16
When filming two people interacting with each other, keep the cameras on the same side of an imaginary line.

Figure 9.17
While the top sequence makes sense to us as two people talking to each other, the bottom sequence does not.

Besides alternating camera positions between two subjects, you also can alter camera positions on a single subject. For instance, if you were filming an instructional sequence on how to tie a fishing knot, you could shoot the entire action from one fixed position called a static shot. However, audiences often prefer dynamic shots, shots that move or cut to close-ups for more interesting perspectives. Instead of just one perspective, consider the shot from several perspectives, providing more interest to the viewers and giving them more information through different angles (Figure 9.18).

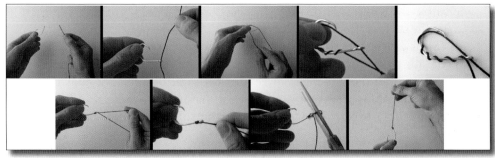

Figure 9.18
The action of tying a knot becomes much more interesting once a dynamic sequence is created.

When composing a sequence, have the subject perform the complete action for each angle so you have plenty of options when editing. For the example above, the subject should tie the knot four different times with the entire action being captured from each angle.

Building

Link

Think of a mundane task you perform regularly, such as making a sandwich, turning on your computer, or getting on a bike. Create a sequence that would break the action into at least six different shots, and create rough sketches for each shot. Why did you choose to focus on some elements over others? What do you hope the audience's reaction would be? How would the scene change if you replaced some shots with others? Which rhetorical appeals do you think are most important in this sequence? Share your sequence with the class, and discuss these choices.

Engine

Search

Watch your favorite television show, and pay attention to how the director composes a sequence out of a single event, such as getting into a car and driving, to more complicated action sequences. Describe each shot and what information it provides that wouldn't be available from just a single, static camera position. Develop a claim based on your research, and support it with reasons and evidence.

Montage

If you've ever seen *Team America: World Police* by *South Park* creators, Matt Stone and Trey Parker, you might remember these lyrics. They offer commentary about the filmmaking process of montage, a technique used to reduce a longer period of narrative time down to a few minutes, so a movie doesn't have to last many months to tell a whole story. As an example, watch the *Team America* montage clip in Figure 9.19.

Credit: Paramount/Courtesy Everett Collection

Figure 9.19
Team America shows how to make a montage.
www.youtube.com/
watch?v=oJc0PxeikfA&feature=youtu.be

This montage occurs at a point in the film when the movie's main character, Gary Johnston, needs to gain physical fitness and skill after becoming depressed and despondent from an earlier failure. As the lyrics explain, a montage shows "a passage of time" with "a lot of things happening at once" in only a few minutes (or even seconds), for "to show it all would take too long." Using this logic, the montage depicts Johnston target shooting, running on a treadmill, practicing martial arts, shaving, flying in a simulator, strength training, reading, as well as a few clips of other characters to maintain the context of why he's preparing. Obviously, even though Johnston's training only takes "one day," all of these actions would be too long to show in a full-length film.

While a montage is actually composed when editing, you need to consider all the shots you need to take that will go into the montage. Therefore, create a plan to include and record the scenes for a montage before you get to the editing phase.

Search Engine

Using a video camera—either a camcorder or a video camera on your phone—take brief video clips from each part of your day and try to create a montage depicting the whole day in two minutes or less. Share your montage with the class, and revise your montage based on their feedback.

Building

Link

Watch the montage scene from *Rocky IV* (Figure 9.20), in which Rocky prepares in the Russian countryside to fight his main opponent, Drago. As you watch, write down the answers to the following questions: What are all the activities you notice in the montage? How long do you think it would take all of these activities in real time? How does the montage order and link the scenes together to create a narrative arc? How does this particular montage use comparison and contrast to create a narrative? Develop a claim based on your research, and support it with reasons and evidence.

Credit: MGM/United Artists

Figure 9.20
The *Rocky* movies make frequent use of montage scenes.
www.youtube.com/watch?v=rV7rjT_
dGbY&feature=youtu.be

Digital Video Writing

This section covers the kinds of writing that are necessary to produce digital video, writing that may range from a traditional research report to help you produce other documents, a script for a video, a list of shooting locations, or something as simple as a timeline to keep you on track so you can successfully produce the final

Figure 9.21
Although this is one kind of "script," you'll write many other kinds when creating visual texts.

visual output (Figure 9.21). Writing in words has always been an important tool for writing in images, and this chapter will cover the ways traditional writing can transfer to digital outputs that may not even contain words.

Screenplays

When you think of writing for film or video, the script or screenplay probably first comes to mind. The screenplay provides the plan for the movie, the detailed outline for how to produce the visual and audio elements of the film. When a writer composes a screenplay, she is obviously writing words, but words meant to be transformed into images. These words need to be clear and easily adaptable to a visual camera shot or an action by an actor. When writing a script, one writes the visual elements, what the audience will see. Although you probably won't produce a screenplay for a full-length movie in your class, understanding the function and terminology of screenplays and how to write them can help you produce better digital texts, whether they're for a photo essay or a short YouTube clip.

The screenwriter also composes what the audience hears, such as the dialogue or sound effects (the film's musical soundtrack is usually composed by a professional musician). However, as discussed in Figure 9.22, a film's dialogue—which many will probably assume is the most important writing in the screenplay—can be the least important part.

As Lawrence Kasdan notes in the video, "The biggest misconception about screenwriting is that the screenwriter writes the dialogue and someone comes up with the other stuff" (Figure 9.22). So what is this "other stuff?" Dick Clement states that a screenplay includes the "architecture" or structure of the story. This structure typically follows some sort of narrative arc, with a beginning, middle, and end. Figure 9.23 shows Freytag's Pyramid, a diagram that helps explain the basic structure of narratives.

Credit: Academy of Motion Picture Arts and Sciences

Figure 9.22
There are some misconceptions about being a screenwriter.
www.oscars.org/video/watch/screenwriters_misconception.html

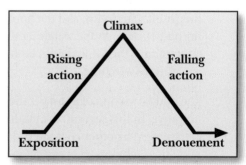

Figure 9.23
Freytag's Pyramid diagrams the structure of a film's story.

Rhetorical Continuities

Aristotle, in describing ancient Greek drama, identified three main parts to a well-written play: a beginning, middle, and end. Gustav Freytag, a German playwright and novelist, designed a five-part pyramid with which he explains typical dramatic structure. Freytag's pyramid derives from a five-act play, in which the following parts appear: exposition, rising action, climax, falling action, and dénouement. While Freytag based his pyramid on plays, this analytical device also can be used to understand other kinds of narratives, including fiction, film, and television.

The beginning of a story offers critical information, introductions to the main characters, and familiarity with the setting. In addition, the beginning presents the audience with a "hook"—some situation that captures their attention and interest. You can think of a hook as the exigency of the film. What is the problem facing the characters? What question is the director trying to explore? In other words, why is this story being told, and why is the audience compelled to watch it?

When considering that a typical screenplay is about 120 pages (with one page equivalent to one minute of screen time), this hook should occur in the first 10 pages of the script (or the first 10 minutes of a movie). Of course, many of the videos produced on a daily basis aren't two hours long, so you should consider getting to the hook sooner. If the video is informative rather than narrative (for example, an instructional video rather than a story), then this beginning should introduce the reader to those providing the information, what organizations they're affiliated with, and the hook, which can be thought of as the reason why the audience might be watching the video. If the video is a review of the latest smartphone, then this should be stated early to let the audience know what and why they're watching.

The middle section of a story is the longest and provides the rising action of the narrative. In this section, the main character attempts to solve a problem, but is complicated by other characters or situations. These characters have their own problems (subplots) that can get in the way of the main character's motivation or sometimes correspond with it. Often, alliances are formed between characters with similar interests.

You can see this typical structure played out in the movie, *The Hangover*. The hook, the problem the characters confront, comes when Phil (Bradley Cooper), Stu (Ed Helms), and Alan (Zach Galifianakis) can't remember where they left their friend, Doug (Justin Bartha), who is soon to be married. Besides their hangover-induced amnesia, other problems complicate the search for their friend, such as awakening to find their hotel room in shambles as well as finding a baby and a live tiger (Figure 9.24).

They further discover that they've stolen a police car (for which they're arrested), Stu has married a stripper, they have stolen $80,000 from a flamboyant gangster, and the tiger belongs to former boxer Mike Tyson. The main plot of the movie develops as the characters figure out how all of these complications occurred and trace them through the previous night to find Doug. Although the movie is a bit exaggerated in terms of its probability, it provides a useful example of how to include obstacles and subplots in the story that still drive the main plot.

Credit: ©Warner Brothers/Courtesy Everett Collection

Figure 9.24
The Hangover introduces many complications for the protagonists to overcome.

Following the rising action, the story ends with a climax, the highest point of the rising action. The climax marks a point of transition for the protagonist. This final act provides the key moment at which the plot will turn toward its fulfillment.

However, the climax itself is not the end of the story. After this final buildup, a falling action occurs in which the actual conclusion is revealed. Often, the ending is still contingent, still in doubt, and could go in either direction. The hero could win, or lose. Phil, Stu, and Alan might find Doug in time for his wedding, or they might not.

The actual conclusion, also called the dénouement, presents the outcome of the climax, and allows all of the unresolved situations in the film to become solved or untied (Figure 9.25). The dénouement may come quickly before the final scene of the film (such as Brody's killing of the shark right before he and Hooper swim back to shore in *Jaws*), or a more lengthy conclusion, as in *The Hangover*, in which the final wedding scene depicts Stu breaking up with his controlling girlfriend, and the friends finding

Credit: Martino Altomonte

Figure 9.25
Dénouement literally means to "unknot," and describes the resolution to the story. In this painting, Alexander the Great cuts the Gordian knot, creating a dénouement or final solution to his problem of untying it.

a camera with images of their forgotten exploits. Although the plot resolves when they find Doug and get him to the wedding, the falling action continues for several minutes before the final scene occurs.

In addition to dialogue and the basic structure, Brian Helgeland explains that screenwriters have to write all of the smaller details as well, including the exterior shots, such as bridge explosions, car chases, fight sequences, and other action. In John August's words:

> Dialogue is a hugely important part of movies, but it's really one of the smaller parts of movies. The screenwriter's the person who figures out what's gonna happen, and when it's gonna happen, and how it's gonna happen ... the screenwriter creates a plan for making the whole movie.

While a screenwriter won't create all the writing that goes into a film on his own, he does create the blueprint from which much of the other writing develops. As discussed in Chapter 6, most of the research that goes into movies derives from what the cast and crew read in the script.

DIGITAL Connections

```
EXT. BEL AIR BAY CLUB --
PACIFIC PALISADES, CA --
MORNING

It's a beautiful spring
morning in the Palisades.
High atop the cliffs, looking
out over the Pacific Ocean, sits the exclusive BEL AIR BAY
CLUB. Workers bustle about the lawn, setting up a high-end
wedding.

A STRING QUARTET warms up. A team of FLORISTS arrange
centerpieces. CATERERS set the white linen tables...

INT. BRIDAL SUITE -- DAY

A simple, classic wedding dress hangs on a closet door in
this sun-drenched bridal suite. Sitting at the makeup table,
surrounded by her bridesmaids, is the beautiful bride, TRACY
TURNER, 20's. She's busy doing her makeup.

Just then, Tracy's rich, stern FATHER, 50's, blows in.

MR. TURNER

        Any word from Doug?
```

As an example of a screenplay, consider this early script segment from *The Hangover*.

The way he spits out "Doug"
tells us all we need to know
about how Mr. Turner feels
about his future son-in-law.

TRACY

                No, but I'm sure
he's--

Just then, Tracy's CELLPHONE
rings. She quickly answers it.

TRACY (CONT'D)

                Hello?

INTERCUT WITH:

EXT. MOJAVE DESERT -- MORNING

Heat-waves rise off the Mojave.
Standing at a lone, dust
covered pay phone in the
middle of the desert is

VICK LENNON

He's in his late 20's, tall,
rugged—and currently a mess.
His shirt is ripped open, his
aviator sunglasses are bent,
his lip is bloodied, and he
clearly hasn't slept in days.

VICK

            Tracy, it's Vick.

Parked on the dirt road behind Vick is his near-totalled
1967 Cadillac Deville convertible; it's scratched, dented,
filthy -- and missing its passenger side door.

Slouched inside are TWO OTHER GUYS, also looking like hell.

TRACY

            Hey Vick!

VICK

            Listen, honey...The bachelor party got a
            little out of control and, well...we lost
        Doug.

TRACY

            (her jaw dropping)
            What?! But we're getting married in like four
            hours!

These first few pages of the script provide brief descriptions of the characters for the actors who play them, the costume designers who dress them, and the make-up artists who need to add effects, such as a bloody lip, not to mention set designers and whoever must procure the 1967 Cadillac Deville convertible.

However, these first pages of the script clearly provide something even more important: the hook. Very quickly, the audience understands the problem: there is a wedding planned to take place in four hours and Doug, the groom, is missing. The rest of the film shows the previous 40 hours and how the situation unfolded, and makes the audience wonder if Doug will actually get to his wedding.

```
Vick squints at the rising sun.
VICK
                 Yeah, that's not gonna happen.
CUT TO:
TITLE OVER BLACK: 40 HOURS EARLIER
CUT TO:
EXT. THE 10 FREEWAY -- DAY
The top down, The Who's "Baba O'Riley" blasting from the
stereo, Vick's pristine Cadillac convertible rockets down
Highway 10 towards Nevada.
At the wheel is Vick, looking as sharp as his Caddy in a
half open shirt and mint condition aviators.
Sitting shotgun is the groom, DOUG BILLINGS, late 20's,
handsome, barefoot, crunchy—an all around great guy.
Behind Vick sits ALAN MERVISH, late 20's, an anal tax
attorney from Connecticut, his Izod shirt tucked into his
khakis. He's currently applying sun screen to his forehead.
Next to Alan is STU PRYCE, late 20's, former high school
linebacker and lovably dimwitted father of two. He drums the
back of the front seat to the music, totally pumped, like
this is his first time out of the house in years. Because it
is.
```

When writing your own scripts, you don't need to include all of the elements of a Hollywood screenplay, but they provide important information to different audiences about different facets of a project's production. Most importantly, your script should provide the narrative of your visual text. However, other instructions help to inform those working with you (or even remind yourself) how certain scenes should be composed. Together, the narrative outline and technical instructions provide a blueprint for completing your project.

Building

Link

Choose a short story, comic, or other story not already in movie or film form. Write a screenplay of this story as a film. How would you provide details about interior or exterior shots? How would you provide character descriptions? What would you want others to know who might be working on its production? What parts would you remove from the original story, and what parts would you add? Develop a claim based on your responses, and support it with reasons and evidence.

Engine

Write down your favorite five or ten movies. If you can, revisit the first 10 to 20 minutes of each movie, and note when the hook occurs. What aspects of the hook make it compelling to keep watching the film? Why is it interesting? Do you feel it occurs too late, too early, or at an appropriate time? Answer these questions about each movie, and develop a claim based on your responses. Support the claim with reasons and evidence.

Dialogue

According to the screenwriters in Figure 9.22, dialogue isn't the most important part of writing for a film. However, it represents what the audience hears and still plays a major role. When writing dialogue for your own project, there are several guidelines you can follow to make it sound more authentic and believable.

Read

Find a variety of scripts that contain different kinds of dialogue, and read them. Note how the dialogue is written to mimic spoken language and what cues the screenwriter provides to the actors for guidance. The more scripts you read, the more familiar you'll become with how to write good dialogue. You can also use plays in addition to scripts.

Speak

In addition to reading the dialogue in the screenplays you find, try speaking the dialogue out loud. This will give you a sense of how the written word translates into a spoken performance. You might also watch clips of film as you follow along in the screenplay to hear how the lines of dialogue are delivered by actors.

Cause and effect

Typically, dialogue should follow a natural flow from one line to another, in which the response spoken by a character makes sense based on the line that came before. In other words, dialogue should feed off itself. If a character's line states, "Why did you burn the house down?" the following line might be something like, "It's the only way I could stop the infestation of the alien virus," not "I need to get some bread." The lines should be logically connected.

Motivate the dialogue

When characters speak, it's typically because they want something from another character. Dialogue should be motivated by these desires of the character. What is the character trying to accomplish in the scene, and how does speaking help her or him to do this? When writing narration for video that is expository, what is your motivation for the narration? What are you trying to point out with words that isn't evident in the images? How does narration help you make your point to the audience?

Don't infodump

Often in science fiction books and films, at some point the author has to explain the new world she is introducing or explain how some piece of technology works. This technique is called an "infodump" because the author is dumping a lot of information through dialogue that is often forced, clunky, and unnatural. Of course, this can also occur with places or situations you are familiar with, where the director might find it necessary to bring the reader up to speed on some aspect of the story. However, instead of including this information through dialogue, try to use actions, props, or other visual elements to convey the information rather than dialogue that doesn't ring true. Let the audience pick up on the visual cues and subtext of the film. Show them, don't tell them.

Perform

Once you've written your own dialogue, speak it, and have others speak it as well. As with any writing that provides instructions, you should user-test your material to make sure it does what you want. You should perform your writing even if that writing is voice-over narration.

Revise

Consider bringing in a third party to listen to your dialogue, asking him or her to make notes about your performance for you to review. After you've performed your dialogue, revise those areas that sound forced or unnatural. Perform the new lines, and revise again as needed.

These are just a few tips to help you craft dialogue in your projects. They apply to both fictional narratives as well as nonfiction, expository works. Study carefully how other writers craft scripts, not just those for the traditional Hollywood film, but also for television, documentaries, nature shows, or other kinds of programs. Finally, consider looking at genre-specific scripts, such as horror, suspense, mystery, romance, or science fiction, if you have narrowed your interests to a precise genre.

Building

Link

Craft a short scene between two characters that primarily features dialogue. Follow the guidelines above, making sure the dialogue helps the characters to achieve some goal and that dialogue from one character feeds into the following line of the other character. When you've completed the script, perform it before the class, and get their feedback on the quality of your dialogue.

Engine

Search

Because of each panel's limited space, comic books require sparse use of dialogue, relying on dialogue that is tightly crafted and highly motivated. Bring in a comic book or graphic novel and study the dialogue. Compare this dialogue to what you might find in a film, play, or novel. Do you notice any differences? Similarities? Does the dialogue serve other functions that it doesn't in other genres? Develop a claim based on your findings, and support it with reasons and evidence.

Narration

Unlike dialogue, voice-over narration isn't meant to sound like "natural" speech, so your goals for producing this kind of writing are very different. Rather than just telling a fictional story, narration might be used to try to sell something (advertising), inform (public service announcement), explain (nature documentary), or persuade (social or political documentary). Just like any piece of writing, you should understand your purpose for the narration as well as your audience.

- Are you writing to a general audience in which you should choose basic diction, so people from a wide range of educational backgrounds can understand it?

- Are you writing for children, so that you must discuss complex concepts in simple ways?

- Are you writing narration for other specialists, who might expect disciplinary language?

Each of these audiences come with its own constraints and expectations and will determine how you should script your narration. However, narration should sound more like natural speech than the essays you compose in other writing classes.

While timing is important when delivering dialogue, it's extremely important when crafting narration. Not only do you have a limited amount of time into which you must fit all you'd like to say, but you also must decide when to include narration. You must decide when visuals might need some sort of narration to enhance the viewer's understanding and when it might be better to include silence, letting the power of the image speak for itself, allowing the audience's imagination to work without other input. Remember that images can evoke powerful emotional responses in your audience. You will most likely find that using images to elicit emotional reactions will be more effective than using narration to tell the audience what to feel in a particular scene.

Narration shouldn't be used to tell the story but rather to comment on the visual aspects of the story. Action should be shown, not told about. However, some narration can be used to comment on the action of the scene that might be unclear to viewers. This technique is common in nature documentaries, in which the camera may show some activity performed by an animal, with the narrator explaining exactly what the animal is doing (building a nest, courting a mate, or ambushing prey) (Figure 9.26).

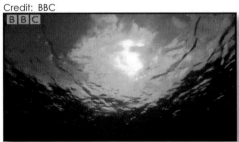

Credit: BBC

Figure 9.26
The BBC series, *Planet Earth,* uses narration to describe the various creatures and landscapes. To what extent do you also think the narration contributes toward storytelling?
www.youtube.com/watch?v=3-uA8t7-msY

In cases in which this activity is obvious, the narrator might indicate how the activity is happening or some other biological fact about the creature. For instance, in a scene showing two cuttlefish courting each other, the narration might explain the purpose of their complex color changes or how these changes occur biologically.

For fiction, voice-over narration should not be a device that suddenly appears in a film but a particular style that permeates the film as a whole (Figure 9.27). Narration shouldn't happen once, but occur regularly throughout the movie, as in *Fight Club*, in which the main, nameless character, played by Edward Norton, continually narrates events and his thoughts to the audience.

Bad examples of narration occur when directors use it to fill in plot holes due to a poorly written script. While this is true of fictional narratives, it also can be

Credit: Everett Collection

Figure 9.27
The opening scene from *The Assassination of Jesse James by the Coward Robert Ford* uses voice-over narration to provide information about the main character.
www.youtube.com/watch?v=r2gY_e1ZKD8

true of nonfiction, expository scripts as well. Make sure your original script for any kind of video is complete and provides a thorough blueprint that expresses your point, even if narration is removed.

Just as you should read other scripts to better write your own scripts, and read other dialogue to better write your own dialogue, you should read and listen to other examples of voice-over narration to help you better write narration. Listen to many different kinds of narration and to specific instances that align with your particular goals. If you're creating an advertisement, seek out these examples. If you're producing your own nature documentary, turn on the Discovery Channel and pay attention to how the narration on its programs is crafted. Learn from the examples of others.

Also, just as with dialogue, user-test your narration. Let others read your narration, as well as listen to you speak it aloud. You also can ask others to read it aloud, so you can hear it yourself. If you're casting someone else to narrate, let the person read over it a few times, and, if possible, adjust the language or sentence structure to better suit the person's speaking style. You might also include cues for how you want certain lines or words to be delivered, such as cues for emphasis, volume, or tone.

Edit the script to make sure the narration is consistent for speech style, including tone of voice, use of first, second, or third person, and the use of contractions. Make sure the narration at the beginning of the script has the same style as the narration at the end of the script.

Finally, pay attention to your transitions, so each sentence logically flows into the next and the narration makes sense with what occurs onscreen. You don't want the narration to detract from the visual elements, only to reinforce or add to them. When you feel the written narration is polished, record it and listen to it through your sound editor, so you can hear how it will sound when outputted through speakers, experiencing it the way your audience will.

Building

Find documentary footage that is re-narrated and placed on YouTube, such as the "Honey Badger" clip in Figure 9.28. Discuss the role tone has when adding narration to an image. How is this similar to anchorage (Chapter 8)? How would the same words, delivered differently, produce another interpretation of the clip? How would the voice of a particular actor influence how you receive the video? How does the narration add rhetorical appeals to the video, such as *logos*, *pathos*, *ethos*, or *kairos*? Take the raw footage from one of these clips, and write and record your own narration. Share your remixed video with the class, as well as the original, and discuss how narration plays a role in audience reception.

Figure 9.28
That honey badger is nasty!
www.youtube.com/watch?v=4r7wHMg5Yjg

Engine

Many commercials use voice-over narration delivered by famous celebrities, yet often these celebrities aren't given name credit. For example, Gene Hackman provides the narration for Lowe's commercials (the hardware store), while Jeff Bridges narrates many commercials for the car company, Hyundai. Although many viewers might recognize the voice, most probably cannot identify the name the voice belongs to. Why do you think companies would hire such celebrities for their voice alone, rather than use less expensive voice talent? What do they gain? What rhetorical appeals are used by doing so? Develop a claim based on your research, and support it with reasons and evidence.

Storyboards

Often, before shooting a film directly from the script, directors will create storyboards to provide a visual representation of the shots they hope to produce. Storyboards help make shooting go more smoothly, as they provide an intermediary translation of what a particular shot should look like before spending time and money on set with equipment and actors. A storyboard also can give the entire production staff a clearer idea about the overall process and final vision. Storyboarding can be a time-consuming process, but it is extremely important toward getting the final look you're after. Consider the clip in Figure 9.29 of Steven Spielberg discussing his storyboard process.

Credit: AFI

If you're creating a storyboard for a visual production, such as video, start with your script. Although it provides general instructions for how to create the movie, it leaves a lot of room for the director and actors to insert their own creative ideas. The storyboard will help fill in these details and provide visual life to the words in the screenplay. Read through it, and try to break down each scene into individual shots (a shot consists of a segment of footage with no cuts), with each storyboard panel representing one shot. After reading through the script, you should have developed a shot list from which you can create the storyboard (as well as shoot the actual footage).

Figure 9.29
Steven Spielberg on storyboarding
www.youtube.com/
watch?v=nBH89Y0Xj7c

As you read the script and evaluate each shot, consider including information about each of the following aspects of your video when creating your final list and the corresponding storyboard panels:

- location for each shot
- number of actors in the shot
- important props or set pieces
- important camera directions for the shot (aerial, close up, zoom in)
- movement of characters or objects
- movement of camera (is it fixed or does it move with the action?)
- lighting needs
- special effects

Although you'll have a more complete idea of your film if you storyboard every shot, this isn't always necessary. Sometimes you only need to consider the most important sequences or the general unfolding of a scene. Often, a basic sketch will give you enough clarity that you can set up the equipment, help the actors perform their roles, and start shooting. You also can improvise and go off-storyboard if you or other collaborative members have ideas on location. While you typically don't want to improvise the entire project, be flexible with your script and storyboard, and revise when inspiration strikes. This can be especially important if uncontrollable elements interfere with your previous plans, such as changing weather conditions, other natural phenomena, or the general unforeseen occurrence.

Rhetorical Continuities

Storyboards aren't restricted to video. They can be useful when designing websites in order to lay out the site's design and flow from the home page to other pages. You also can use them for podcasts, helping you lay out when to include your own narration, when to include preexisting clips, or as a way to add voice-over directions or other notes. If you were writing a printed output, such as a novel, you also could use a storyboard to help you organize the plotline or figure out where to add subplots, character introductions, or other important elements to the story. Storyboards allow you to further rearrange all the pieces to easily experiment and see if other sequences might produce better results.

Several techniques can be used to create your own storyboard, and, like all writing activities, you'll discover the strategies that work best for you. When you think of storyboarding, you might think of hundreds of hand-drawn images posted onto a wall to lay out an entire sequence (Figure 9.30). While this is certainly one method, several software applications can help make the task easier and more transportable.

Graphic design programs, such as Adobe Photoshop, Adobe Illustrator, or Gimp, can be used to digitally sketch the scenes and save them in a variety of image formats. If you decide to hand-draw your scenes, you might scan the sketches to send them to collaborators and insert them into programs such as Microsoft PowerPoint or Prezi to more easily arrange their order (Figure 9.31). In either case, consider using the slug lines from

Credit: wiredfly.blogspot.com

Figure 9.30
Storyboards can easily take up a whole wall.

wiredfly.blogspot.com/2010_04_01_
archive.html

the script as the titles for each card so you clearly understand where and when each scene occurs.

Credit: Prezi by Jasmine Creed

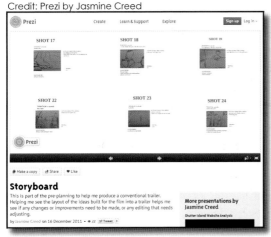

Figure 9.31
A Prezi can be a useful tool for creating storyboards.

prezi.com/iihdlkhrsg8l/storyboard/

Once you have your rough sequence completed, you can use the storyboard as a checklist, making sure you capture each shot. A storyboard also makes it easier to shoot out of sequence and still ensure you capture all of the shots you need, as well as make sure you put them in the correct, final order. Finally, consider including any dialogue in the scene next to the appropriate images. This technique can help you better understand how the images flow together and might help you catch any images that are logically out of order.

If, like Spielberg, you're not good at drawing, you could find preexisting images that represent what you're trying to convey in the final shot, or take photographs that mimic the description in the screenplay. As a worst-case scenario, you also could write textual descriptions of each scene that are more complete than the details in the script. Regardless, a storyboard is important and should be drafted before shooting begins. Together with the instructions of the script, the storyboard can offer the best blueprint that assures you create a well-designed, quality production.

Building

Link

Revisit the earlier prompt that asked you to create a short screenplay based on a short story, comic, or other story not already in movie form. Create a shot list and storyboard for your screenplay. In addition to images, consider including other direction and dialogue to help orient the viewer. Finally, place your storyboard in a digital format, such as Prezi, and share it with the class.

Search Engine

Create a storyboard for a traditional essay you wrote for another class. How would you convey the information from this essay in images? How would you break up the essay into individual shots? How would you incorporate the rhetorical appeals of *logo*, *ethos*, *pathos*, and *kairos*? Once you've finished, share both the storyboard and original essay with a peer or the class and get their feedback.

Supporting documents

In addition to screenplays, dialogue, narration, storyboards, and captions, a variety of other kinds of writing can help you plan, draft, and organize your project, so it comes together as you envision it. Not all of these written documents will be necessary for every project, so use them at your discretion, according to what helps you stay on track and complete the assignment.

Logline

A logline is a brief synopsis of a work, typically a film, that is usually twenty-five to fifty words or less. While the logline can tell an audience what a movie is about, it's also very useful for an author at the beginning of the writing process to keep her focused on the final goal of the film. In this way, the logline can be thought of as the main thesis statement of the film, helping the writer keep track of the story she wants to tell. For example, a logline for a movie about King Tut might state:

> *As a boy ruler of Ancient Egypt, King Tutankhamen had to contend with conspiring advisors and jealous generals, one of which would take his life.*

This logline focuses the story on the mystery of how King Tut died, making it a historical mystery film. One could redirect the intention of the film, and its thesis, toward a romance by restating the logline as:

> *Despite falling deeply in love with a local slave girl, King Tut is advised to marry his half-sister, Ankhesenamun, for political reasons. He must decide between love and duty.*

Treatments

Before writing a full script, screenwriters or film producers will often write a film treatment that provides a comprehensive outline for the movie. A treatment is usually between thirty and sixty pages, and includes full descriptions for each scene. If a film script is not solicited by a studio, screenwriters often will write and distribute a presentation treatment to pique interest from potential collaborators rather than taking the time to draft a full screenplay. If you have an idea for a video production, a treatment can help you organize and provide detail for each scene before fleshing out camera directions and full dialogue.

Descriptions

One of the more common kinds of writing you'll probably compose includes descriptions. In order to work collaboratively, or even to provide reminders to yourself, you should write descriptions of characters, places, events, plotlines, scenery, props, special effects, music, or any other element that might be incorporated into your production (Figure 9.32). Since it's typically cheaper to write these descriptions before trying to film them, they can save you time and money, and give others a sense of the visual aesthetic you're trying to achieve.

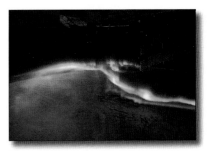

Figure 9.32
How would you describe your idea for a special effect to someone else?

When writing descriptions, try to use active verbs and precise language when possible. You want the reader to have a very clear understanding of your vision, so include concrete language with sensory details such as colors, textures, sounds, as well as comparisons with things the reader might already be familiar with. Finally, besides physical details, also describe the mood that a character, setting, or scene evokes.

Lists

Although you've probably created many lists, it's important to remember this valuable writing genre. Lists can help organize complex information into either step-by-step guides, or simply provide a reminder of things to do. When composing digital writing projects, you should maintain many lists, including lists of:

- characters
- settings
- shots
- images
- sounds

- props
- permissions

As you can see, sometimes you need to create a list of lists to write. Determining these lists before you start composing—as well as keeping track of fine points such as permissions during the process—will help you be more efficient and ensure you attend to all of the details.

Summaries

When working collaboratively, often you'll need to write information or task lists to other members of your team, describing what they need to know or what to accomplish. When describing parts of the product, you might need to compose summaries for these collaborators who may not need all the information you have, making the information more digestible and more quickly accessible.

In addition, not all audiences need access to the same level of detail. While the actors might only need a general summary of the shooting locations, the set designer will need to know much more, including not only the details of the physical environment but also its history or other important information to make sure all of the elements such as trees, furniture, vehicles, animals, props, costumes, or other elements belong in the location and aren't out of place.

Rhetorical Continuities

When conducting research for your project—whether video-based or not—you'll need to condense that research into basic, usable material for yourself as well. Summarizing will enable you to quickly recall information to mind and help you work more efficiently. Writing summaries of your research also will help you better master the material of your project.

When you compose summaries, you have to decide what to leave in, and what to leave out. When beginning your research, first make sure you understand the content of what you're reading. Then, edit the original piece by highlighting the key points and crossing out what you feel is superfluous information. You can always go back to the master document if you need to find these details. Rather than copying sentences from the original piece word-for-word, try to rewrite the information in your own words. You can further edit your own subsequent writings in the same way before distributing them to others.

Digital Video Technologies

Once you've understood the rhetorical aspects of writing with video, and writing for video, you should also understand a few technologies and technical details about digital video to help you produce digital video. Although it's beyond the scope of this book to provide instructions on every video camcorder or every video editing program, there are some basic technical choices you should consider when creating a new digital video.

Screen settings

There are a few initial settings you might want to decide upon before you begin shooting video, and some other considerations once you've finished. While you might not always be able to select some of these settings because of the particular limitations of your device, keep them in mind if they're available in your camera's settings or editing program. When creating a video, you have three important choices to make regarding screen settings: the screen dimensions, the aspect ratio, and the frame rate.

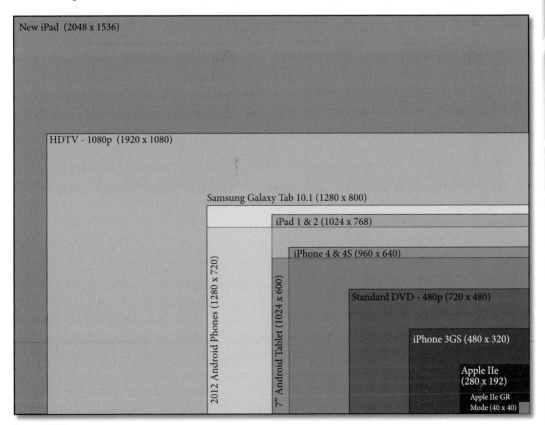

Figure 9.33
These are some of the screen resolutions used by many popular digital devices.

Screen dimensions

Since your digital videos will probably be viewed on a digital device such as a computer monitor, smartphone, or tablet, you should consider the most common screen dimensions for each of these displays (Figure 9.33). Ideally, your video will be easily viewable on any size screen. However, research which size screen you expect your audience to use most of the time and optimize your audience's viewing by using this screen dimension.

Aspect ratio

Many camera settings also provide you with the option of setting the aspect ratio. You typically have two choices, 4:3 and 16:9. This ratio refers to the ratio of horizontal units (width) to vertical units (height) (Figure 9.34). The 4:3 ratio provides a narrower field of view and is common on older monitors and televisions before the ratio of 16:9—often referred to as "widescreen"—became popular. Given that most digital video appears on widescreen monitors with a 16:9 ratio, consider using this aspect ratio. In addition, 16:9 delivers more visual information to the viewer since it provides a wider field of view.

Figure 9.34
As you can see, the 16:9 aspect ratio (left) is wider than 4:3 (right) and provides more visual information.

Frame rate

You also may be able to set the frame rate of your camera. While theatrical films have traditionally shot footage at 24 fps (frames per second), digital video usually records at 30 fps, but it is not uncommon to have the option of shooting at 60 fps. Generally, 60 fps provides smoother motion because there are more images per second, so this frame rate is ideal when filming motion, such as sports or moving subjects. However, this frame rate also requires more light and should be used mostly outdoors or in very bright environments. In low light situations, or situations in which the subjects are not moving quickly, 30 fps is your best bet. In addition, since most online video is 30 fps, if you plan on integrating your own digital video footage with clips taken from online sources such as YouTube, you should probably choose 30 fps so the frame rates will all be the same.

Building

Link

Browse various websites that use video, and determine whether the sites post videos in 4:3 or 16:9 aspect ratios. How many do you find of each? Is one more predominant than the other? Why do you think this is so? What advantages do you think the website authors considered when choosing an aspect ratio for their particular sites? Develop a claim based on your research, and support it with reasons and evidence.

Engine

Search

Research the different frame rates used when shooting film and video. What was the original frame rate that was widely adopted? Why was this frame rate chosen? Why did other frame rates develop? What are the best uses for each frame rate? Develop a claim based on your research, and support it with reasons and evidence.

Storing video

When considering where to store videos, you have three main domains to consider: storage on the device itself, saving and formatting the video for other devices, and uploading video to online sites. Generally, you select storage media based on two characteristics: capacity and data transfer speed. You need storage media with enough capacity to record the video.

Device storage

In general, one hour of full HD video takes up 11–12 gigabytes (GB); thus, a 4GB SD card will only store about 20 minutes of video. The data transfer rate of the storage media affects the quality of the video. For SD cards, consider using a Class 10 card, if possible. Once recorded, transfer your video to another storage device on the platform you'll use for editing. Your editing will usually go smoother if these files are stored locally on your computer, and you can then delete the files from your camera's storage so you can shoot more content.

Saving and formatting

After editing, the best quality file format for saving your video is the format you recorded the video in. For instance, if your video camera records video as an MP4, then you should save your final video as an MP4. However, the best quality video also produces the biggest file size, which might make it difficult to upload and view on the Internet. Instead, you might choose to save the file in a smaller, compressed format. The video will lose some quality, but it will play better when streamed online. Also consider that saving can sometimes take a long time and usually cannot be stopped once started. Make sure you have enough time in a computer lab or at home before beginning the process.

Uploading video

Once you have captured and edited video, you can now upload the video for distribution online or through other storage devices such as a Flash USB drive or a portable hard drive. If you're uploading the video to the Internet, consider which website provides the best audience and distribution. For instance, YouTube has a much wider audience and better search engine results, but Vimeo is sometimes considered more professional. See Chapters 6 and 11 for more information about how to choose the best video sharing websites.

Building

Link

Make a list of all video file formats that have been developed. Choose three of these file types, and research who created the file type, when it was created, and for what purpose. What problem did these file formats solve? Develop a claim based on your research, and support it with reasons and evidence.

Engine

Search

Research the different video sharing sites that are available (YouTube and Vimeo are just two of the possibilities). Create a list, and include the features of each site, and evaluate their pros and cons. What are the best uses for each site? How might each site affect the *ethos, pathos, logos,* or *kairos* of the video? Develop a claim based on your research, and support it with reasons and evidence.

KEY Terms

180-degree rule
aspect ratio
audio
caption
chin room
close-up
description
dialogue
Dutch angle
extreme close-up
frame rate
framing
headroom
high angle
instructions
list

logline
low angle
medium shot
montage
narration
nose room
rule of thirds
screen dimension
screenplay
script
sequence
storyboard
summary
treatment
wide shot

Video Essay

For this activity, create a video essay that makes a claim and supports it with reasons and evidence. An argument can be explicit or implicit, and much of your supporting evidence may offer examples that make your point implicitly based on metaphor or analogy, appealing to pathos rather than logos. Of course, you can construct an explicit argument through video as well (Figure 9.35).

Although your instructor will provide you with more specific guidelines for your video essay, the overall project should:

■ last 3–5 minutes in length

■ provide a thesis or claim with reasons and evidence

■ include a short research report

■ include a script

■ include a rough cut prior to revising, editing, and proofing

■ include a one-page memo detailing what changes were made during the revision process

As you've already learned from the previous chapters, much alphabetic writing will go into this project before the video is even shot. Rather than just cobbling together a video, take serious care during the prewriting phase of this project to make sure it comes together in a clear, coherent, and professional manner. While the quality of the video and audio will depend on the available resources you have in your class or on campus, the quality of the video's content depends on the amount of time and effort you put into its research and preparation. As a general process, consider the following steps toward completing your video essay.

Figure 9.35
This essay about the pencil was produced by students trying to make an explicit argument (through the persona of Nicolas Cage).

www.youtube.com/watch?v=3BEc5CDju_k

Choose a topic: A video essay, like a written essay or photo essay, first requires that you choose your topic—that you determine what you'd like to produce your video about. As with other kinds of writing, find a topic that interests you, one that calls you to write.

Research your topic: As with any writing assignment, much of the work comes before you start writing. You also should plan, as you think about your script, what kinds of footage you're capable of shooting and what video already exists for you to incorporate. As with the photo essay, unless your class has a large travel budget, you probably won't be able to take your own video of remote locations. In addition, make sure you are safe when taking your own video, and ask for permission when shooting on private property or other locations that require it.

Plan and draft: Before picking up the camera, plan your initial components and the structure of your argument. This plan can include writing an essay first—making sure you have a claim, reasons, and evidence—or it can offer a more basic outline of the argument and the major scenes and visuals you hope to include. Once you clarify the main points for yourself, you can start to think more visually, developing a script that will depict the scenes you hope to show as well as any audio you might use, including any voice-over narration. This step can be the most important and may determine if your project fails or succeeds.

Create a storyboard: Once you've completed a script, create a storyboard that depicts each shot. The storyboard will be invaluable as both a conceptual tool—helping you to see your video before you actually assemble and edit it—as well as an organizational tool, providing a framework for visually arranging your script and making sure you account for all the shots you might need.

Create a shot list and gather footage: Once you have a script, you can create a shot list. This list will provide an important resource to ensure that you gather all of the video footage you'll need. On the list, note which footage you plan to shoot yourself and which footage you plan to use from archival sources. Dividing your list this way can help you manage your time since the footage you shoot yourself will probably take longer to gather than archival footage. When producing video, try to gather this footage as early as possible, as editing will be more time consuming than you may realize and is often the longest part of the process.

Add narration: Although your project may not require it, you may want to add voice-over narration to your video to comment on the footage or to maintain the argumentative arc. Include this narration in your script and record all narration before starting the revision process.

Create a rough cut: After you have gathered your footage and recorded any narration you'll need, use your storyboards as a guide to assemble your clips into a single rough cut of your video essay. Try to complete as much of the video as possible so you will have a better idea of how you might revise the piece.

Revise, edit, proof: Revise the rough-cut by starting with the large-scale changes first. Notice where the gaps in argument occur, which shots and scenes look bad, and which look bad when sequenced together. Once you've accomplished revision, you can begin to edit transitions and other elements before performing a final proof. Remember, ask peers to review your work as well, since they can offer input on problems you might not notice.

Save and distribute: as you work, save your video file often. Once you've finished, consider what file format you'll need to distribute it in, such as DVD or the web, and in which formats, such as MPEG, AVI, MOV, or other formats. Whatever distribution method you plan, research what file formats are acceptable and research the specifics of those file formats. While your video might look good in the video editor, it can look lousy if you save it in the wrong format.

From DIGITAL Writers

Eula Biss & John Bresland
ODE TO EVERY THING

05:19

There are many video essays you might research when designing your own, but consider the video essay below from Eula Biss, an American nonfiction writer, and John Bresland, an essayist who works in film, radio, and print.

Video essay from Eula Biss and John Bresland

requitedjournal.com/index.php?/form/eula-biss-and-john-bresland/

STUDENT Example

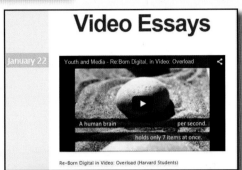

Re-Born Digital, in Video: Identities (Harvard Students)

Visit the Tumblr URL to watch several student examples of video essays. They range in topic from research and reporting to commentaries on digital identities. What elements do you note in the student examples that are similar to those in the professional example above?

Student video essays

videoessays.tumblr.com/

CHAPTER 10

Digital Editing

If you've ever sat through the credits for a large-scale blockbuster movie, you may have noticed how many people are involved in a film's production. Directors, best boys, key grips, stunt crew, catering, and costume designers make up just a few of the important roles. However, some of the most important crew members are the editors. Looking at the film *Avengers: Age of Ultron*, the editorial department was composed of 45 people, but 69 crew members had the term, "editor," in their title. Editing for this film consisted of more than just making cuts, but also editing sounds, music, special effects, and animation, to name just a few. Although the head editors of each of these areas might make the final decisions in consulation with the film editor, director, and producer, editing a film is basically a huge process of peer review, with the head editors getting input and feedback from all the assistant editors and other crew members who contribute to the film. Although the technology and scale differ, the process of editing a film is not wholly different from editing a paper.

Thus, one of the most important stages in any writing process is the step of editing. This step is important not only for alphabetic text, but also for documents composed through digital writing. Of course, editing for digital media is much different than editing for spelling, grammar, and other issues you might typically think of when writing traditional papers. For example, when writing HTML, you must also edit at the code level, which has its own rules of syntax and usage. Or in video, once a

Credit: Starz Entertainment

Figure 10.1
Most directors will tell you that a good movie requires good editing.
www.youtube.com/
watch?v=xJcQgQHR78Q

director has captured the raw footage via a camera, an editor (with the help of many other editors) takes that footage and assembles it into a final format (Figure 10.1).

The video editor is not concerned with comma splices or dangling participles, but with the cuts, film splices, and transitions needed to create a coherent whole out of many hours of footage, often taken at different times and in different locations. During this process, the editor looks through the footage for consistency between the shots, props, scenery, and other elements, and revises the work to make the film match the final vision shared by the director and producer.

Similarly, a writer using HTML to build a web page is probably more concerned with <body> tags and <meta> tags than with comma splices as she tries to make sure all the code works properly.

However, a web editor who must attend to both the code that the computer sees, as well as the text and images that a human sees, must be concerned with comma splices, image edits, and proper coding. In this case, you can see how editing for digital texts requires juggling between different mediums, and is often collaborative between different content experts.

Credit: Andrew Toos

"No, go ahead and critique my mss. I'm always ok ... after the initial reaction."

Figure 10.2
If you're editing your peer's work, be tactful when offering criticism.

This chapter will cover techniques that will help during the editing and revising process for digital text, image, video, and traditional writing because all of these digital media are intertwined during the production process. While digital writing requires its own set of specific practices when editing, some basic underlying principles govern all types of revision, and here you'll learn both. While editing may not be pleasant, as Figure 10.2 indicates, it's an important and necessary process.

General Editing Guidelines

When editing, consider how a particular change affects the message, how your various audiences will view the change, how that change affects the overall design, or how an edit will enhance or detract from *logos*, *ethos*, *pathos*, and *kairos*. Whether you are editing text, images, or video, the following three guidelines should be followed to make your editing more efficient and timely.

Save early and often

Whether you're editing in a word processor, an image editor, a video editor, a blog interface, or any other digital writing platform, save your work early and often to avoid losing any of it. You also should back up the file in multiple locations and on different devices. For instance, save a copy on your hard drive, on the Internet, and on a USB flash drive. As you save, consider creating different file names (such as including the date) as well so you can keep track of the most recent version.

Pay attention to space

With traditional print-based media, you can only fit so much information on a page before you run out of space. Thus, it may seem that digital writing genres allow you to have infinite space, providing as much room as you need. However, remember that online readers typically prefer a paragraph to be no larger than the size of their computer screen, and with many readers switching to their smartphones or tablets to check email or browse the web, these screens are becoming smaller. Web audiences also prefer not to scroll too much. When you edit a document, account for the size of the screen your audience may be using and try to design documents that will best fit within those spaces. This guideline applies to text and visual media, for no one wants to scroll down in order to see the rest of an image.

Be timely

When publishing in print, the time between the initial draft and final copy can take years. This length of time allows the input of many editors in order to make the text as correct, accurate, and clear as possible. However, digital writing designed for online delivery is often instantaneous. How often do you let a text message sit before sending it? For such digital genres, the editing process needs to be just as instantaneous, requiring you to check for format, errors, and other issues very quickly. But digital editing is timely in another sense. It's nearly impossible to return to a printed document and revise it should new information make the text incorrect or irrelevant. Online documents, however, can be revised based on new information, so they often require regular editing. If you continue to maintain the blog you created from Chapter 7, consider returning to and revising any posts that need to be edited as new information becomes available.

Building

Choose a variety of blogs, websites, or other digital texts, and view them on a variety of devices, such as computers, smartphones, or tablets. How does the page design fit on each screen? Does the website change depending on the device you view it on? As an editor, what suggestions would you make to the website authors toward accommodating a variety of screen types? Develop a claim based on your responses, and support it with reasons and evidence.

Engine

Return to the blog you created in Chapter 7, and revise each post for timeliness. Is there new information that would make your posts more complete or accurate? Would you let the audience know about these revisions, or make revisions without directly referencing the changes (for instance, some journalistic outlets will let readers know of changes, corrections, or retractions)? How does updating your blog affect your *ethos* as a writer? How are *logos*, *kairos*, or *pathos* affected? Create a list of all the changes, as well as why you decided to make (or not make) the changes. Develop a claim based on your responses, and support it with reasons and evidence.

Levels of Editing

Figure 10.3
Revising entails working with the text as a whole.

Although you might lump terms, such as proofreading, editing, and revising, into one group, the three activities are quite different and will be addressed separately throughout the rest of this chapter. As you work on editing and revising, keep in mind the different roles each plays, as well as the strategies and goals for this step in the writing process. Use the inverted triangle in Figure 10.3 as you follow the editing process, starting with the broader changes (revising), continuing with more detailed changes in smaller sections (editing), and finishing with corrections (proofreading).

The revision process

When looking over your initial draft of a project—whether text, image, or video—you should first make changes on a large scale. Revising focuses on the whole document, making larger structural, design, and argumentative changes rather than picking apart the smaller details. While you'll eventually get to these smaller matters in editing and proofreading, you should start with the bigger picture. This is the work of revising (Figure 10.3).

Text revision

When you revise, you're literally "looking again" at your initial draft. The best way to start the revision process, then, is by rereading what you have already written. As mentioned above, don't focus on the smaller details at this point, but instead look for the bigger issues that might prevent your audience from understanding your argument.

When revising your text—whether an essay, report, script, or proposal— start with the largest scale and work inward. For instance, if you're working on a traditional essay, you should revise your larger argument, check that all of the paragraphs in the document support that argument, and ensure that these paragraphs are grouped into sections that make sense. Once you have the general order figured out, you can then move down to individual sections, then to individual paragraphs, reordering them if necessary and deleting what you don't need. If you were to edit and proofread prior to this step, you might be proofreading paragraphs you would later delete anyway, wasting much of your time. Always work from large to small, from the big picture to the details.

You might find that you need to add an entire section to strengthen your argument, building on what you already have, or you may decide to remove a whole section that doesn't make sense. Make these large-scale changes to the paper now before you worry about individual words and sentences. However, during the revision process you should make the decision about the tone and voice you want to use, as this affects how every paragraph and sentence will be read and interpreted by the reader. Consider the following steps for revising a document.

Steps for revision

- **Focus on purpose:** Take a general overview of your document and revisit the main reasons you're writing, the purpose of the text, the audience, and any information that should be included. In other words, do you think the writing will accomplish your goal?

- **Reorganize:** When you reorganize, group similar evidence together, or change the order of your points starting with the least important and moving toward most important, or vice versa.

- **Refine the main ideas:** As you can see, most of the revision process focuses on the ideas in the text rather than the text's mechanics. Decide if your thesis statement needs refocusing and revision, and check that each section and individual paragraph has a clear topic.

- **Improve the argument:** Although you probably have many reasons and much evidence to support your claim by the time you finish your first draft, you can always revise the argument by adding additional points. Particularly, add counterarguments that seem to disprove your claim, and then argue why these counterarguments are wrong by offering counter evidence as a rebuttal. By acknowledging these other voices in the final draft, you'll improve your goodwill with the audience and strengthen your argument.

- **Delete the unnecessary:** Although it's often hard to delete large sections of text once you've composed them, sometimes a paragraph or an entire page doesn't add to your argument. Be honest about text that should stay in and text that needs to be deleted. If you save multiple copies during your revision process, you can always reclaim them if you change your mind (Figure 10.4).

Figure 10.4
Editing often requires the writer to cut much of what you've already written.
https://www.youtube.com/watch?v=7vRhOdf-6co

- **Determine the best tone:** Although your tone may seem like a small element of your writing, it affects the work on a large scale, and inconsistencies across the document can confuse or annoy the reader. Read through your document, and make sure your tone and voice seem consistent throughout the piece. This revision step is especially important if you collaborate on a document, and each partner writes separate sections. During revision, you should make the tone of voice consistent throughout, so the document seems as if just one person had written it.

Not all of your work needs revision, and sometimes you might accidentally revise for the worse as you cut and paste, moving sections or paragraphs around trying to find the best fit. Even if you think you'll cut a paragraph, save it in another file in case you end up reusing some of its content. To help ensure you don't lose this work forever by over-editing, save your work as you revise, but save it under a new file name from time to time. Sometimes you might want to revert back to a prior version you think sounded better, and if you simply save over your existing file you'll lose that version forever. As mentioned earlier, this advice also applies to writing with images or video: Save multiple versions as you progress through the revision process.

Peer review

In addition to rereading your own work, a document can be reread by giving it to others for review. Having peers read your work will give you other perspectives. Most of the time, you are so familiar with your own work you might skip over and leave out important information your reader might not know, or organize information in a way that is unclear to other readers. Peer reviewers can "test" your document to help ensure your audience can understand your argument. Your audience might still disagree with you, but at least a well-revised argument is less likely to be misinterpreted.

Think about asking your reviewer to consider the following principles (or follow them yourself if you're reviewing someone else's writing).

Strategies for effective peer review as the reviewer

- **Research:** Ask the author a few questions before you start, such as who the audience is, what he wants the audience to do after reading, as well as his purpose and the exigence. This will help orient your review toward the author's goals and focus your review.

- **Scan, then read:** After you've asked the author about her audience, purpose, and desired action, scan the document to determine the overall argument, organization, and ideas. Once you have a feel for these general aspects, read the document more carefully to determine where the document succeeds, and where it needs work.

- **Focus on the writing:** As you read through the document and begin to offer suggestions (either orally or in writing), remember that you are giving feedback about a written document, and not the author himself. Keep your comments document-specific. For example, instead of saying "You do a poor job in creating transitions," instead say, "The paper's transitions could be a bit stronger." This perspective helps ensure that the author doesn't get defensive and listens to your advice.

- **Praise:** As you review, you should focus on the strengths of the writing for a few reasons. First, the author might not be aware of these strengths in her writing, so pointing them out can help her maintain these strengths in the future. Second, positive comments can help temper less positive news about what needs to be fixed. Thus, you might state: "Overall, this paragraph has a strong topic sentence and great evidence. You might strengthen the closing to really bring these points home for the reader." In this case, even the suggested revision is framed in how it will positively impact the paragraph rather than as something "bad" that needs to be corrected.

- **Be honest:** Although you should praise what the author does well, you don't want to offer praise when the author hasn't actually earned it. In other words, don't praise something just to be nice; be honest about what does, and doesn't work.

- **Specify:** When you offer a suggestion to a writer, try to describe precisely what should be revised, and when possible, why. Rather than making a general statement, such as "The paper needs better evidence for its argument," or "The order isn't very logical," think of the author's overall goals and be more specific. You might suggest instead that "Given that the audience will be more receptive to examples that impact them personally, you might research them further, and include evidence that shows how your argument affects them directly."

One way to be specific is to make sure important elements are present in the writing. For instance, you might check to make sure the following elements are present and clear.

- **Introduction:** Does the writer clearly introduce his topic to the audience?

- **Claim:** Does the writer offer his claim clearly and early in the document?

- **Reasons:** Does the writer present reasons for his claim?

- **Evidence:** Does the writer offer evidence for his reasons?

- **Topic sentences:** Does the writer clarify the subject of a paragraph by introducing it with a topic sentence?

- **Transitions:** Does the writer transition logically from one idea to the next?

- **Conclusion:** Does the writer reemphasize his claim and make it clear why it should be important to the reader?

- **Prescribe:** As the last example shows, you should try to offer prescriptive advice rather than just point to the problem areas. Offer possible solutions the author can use to revise her document, such as "You might reorder your evidence from least important to most important, so the reader is left with the most powerful example at the end." Such prescriptive statements will help the writer take the next step toward revision.

These peer revision strategies apply to any medium. For instance, if you're having someone review a video, you should still listen, record, avoid becoming defensive, and thank the reviewer. Once you've covered these large, global issues in your text, you can then proceed to editing and proofreading. Working in this order will save you time and help you revise with more efficiency and focus.

A good peer reviewer reads the document according to the steps above, and must include comments that are instructive and clear for you, the author. To help facilitate this process, you might include your own list of areas you want the reviewer to focus on, such as clarity of thesis statements, the effectiveness of the evidence you use, or how you incorporate counterarguments. The important point here is that you must communicate with the peer reviewer during this process, not just hand him the document, and let him review the document in isolation. Revision is collaborative.

During peer review sessions that occur in class, you're often able to be present with the reviewer as she reads and remarks upon your writing. Receiving such comments can be difficult, but remember that all writers need to revise before delivering a document to an audience. It's much better to receive feedback at this point in the writing process than after you've disseminated the document to a larger audience. Try to keep a positive, open mind as you receive comments from your readers and realize they are helping you make a better argument.

During such sessions, consider the following actions you can take to get the most from your reviewer.

Strategies for effective peer review as the author

- **Come prepared:** When you ask a reviewer to look over a draft, it should be as complete and polished as possible. In other words, your draft should not be rough and written the night before. You'll get much better feedback if the reviewer is not distracted by lots of small errors you can quickly fix on your own. In addition, come to the meeting with your own concerns about your writing. For instance, if you feel a particular piece of evidence might be weak, or you have particular struggles with certain grammatical features, you might ask the reviewer to pay attention to these before she begins. You might also prepare an "author's note" for the reviewer that lists some of this information, as well as your intended audience, purpose, and outcome that you want from your document. This way the reviewer can try to match your expectations with how the document actually meets them.

- **Listen and record:** As your reviewer discusses the changes that he thinks you should make, stay silent and record each suggestion. Since time spent with the reviewer is precious, you need to take advantage and make sure you leave the meeting with all the information. You don't want to forget what the reviewer stated, which you are likely to do once you leave the review. In addition, your reviewer is likely to forget as well, so you won't simply be able to inquire about a suggestion later through email.

- **Save comments and questions for the end:** Part of listening well includes remaining silent and letting the reviewer talk you through her suggestions. Try to save any questions you have for the end of the session, and you might jot these down along with your other notes. Try only to speak if the reviewer asks you a specific question about your intent, audience, or some other strategy she might need to understand before making her own suggestion.

- **Don't defend yourself:** This step is easy if you abide by the first two rules, but you might sometimes feel the need to defend yourself if you think the reviewer misunderstood your writing or is otherwise unfairly critical. Remember, however, if you think the reviewer misunderstood your writing, then your intended audiences probably will, too. Instead of becoming defensive, keep taking notes and take the advice positively. The reviewer just saved your writing from going out into the world less clear and complete than it could be.

- **Thank the reviewer, clarify notes:** When the reviewer has offered all his advice, thank him for helping you out, and then ask any questions you might have written down during the process. Do not use the questions to attack his understanding of your document, but instead to clarify his feedback or to discuss other rhetorical and organizational strategies to get further feedback.

If you're reviewing outside of class, you can still adopt these principles. Remember this as well: ultimately, you're the author. You have final editorial control and can accept or reject the feedback given to you by the reviewer. Thus, if you find that the peer reviewer misunderstood something you think your intended audience will understand, ignore the related comments. However, most likely your reviewer will help you clarify much of your writing and help make it better. Encourage a dialogue with your reviewer. Sometimes

- **Resizing/Scaling:** Your image may be too large or too small for the final document in which you plan to use it. Decreasing an image size is easy without losing too much detail. However, increasing an image's size often results in pixilation or fuzziness. Most online images have 72 dots per inch (dpi), and you can't increase them without significant pixilation. However, you can often scan hard copy images at a high resolution and enlarge them for other purposes.

- **Artistic manipulations:** Most photo editors have a wide array of filters or other ways to manipulate and customize an image. For instance, you might remove color information, turning an image to black and white. You might make a photograph appear to be a watercolor (Figure 10.5). Research what options your photo editor has—or research how to perform the effect you want—and revise your image so it best fits the goals of your project.

Figure 10.5
The "watercolor" filter in Adobe Photoshop was used to edit this photo.

Like text, it's best to perform these revisions before you start with other details, such as removing red eye or adjusting colors, as these steps may be completely unnecessary, depending on the large-scale changes you make.

Video revision

Before you worry about editing individual cuts, you should revise your video as a whole. Ideally, you wrote an excellent script that was relatively free of plot holes or gaps in argument and provided a clear blueprint for producing your project. From this footage, you should assemble the rough cut of the video, stitching the shots together into a complete draft. However, once you capture the script on film, you might be surprised that a certain scene or shot doesn't look as expected. Some scenes might even need to be re-shot. Here are a few steps you might take when revising video.

- **Assemble:** In a video editor (Figure 10.6), assemble a complete version of your video.

- **View:** Once you have a complete rough cut, watch the draft and take notes, paying attention to the large-scale issues you see. Do some scenes seem out of place? Does the order of the shots seem logical? Do you notice any gaps in argument or narrative that would confuse the audience? Does the hook appear close enough to the beginning? You also may want to have a peer view the rough cut with you.

■ **Reassemble:**
Revise your video based on your notes, and reassemble the shots into a new version.

■ **Review:**
Watch this new version, repeating the process.

Figure 10.6
A video editor allows you to combine individual clips to create larger sequences.

Most of your video revision strategy should focus on arranging individual parts into a whole. Once you assemble the pieces according to your script and storyboard, you can better judge if a particular order doesn't make sense or would be more effective if altered. Much like a written text, you may decide you want to reorder the scenes to present a more persuasive story or narrative. If you're not happy with what you see, don't be afraid to completely alter the video from your original script or idea. You may find that playing with the footage in the video editor, such as dragging and dropping scenes into new arrangements, can help you think visually about your project and help you come up with new ideas for revision.

Building

Link

Select several video clips, and assemble at least three different rough cuts by changing the sequence of the clips. How does each arrangement differ from the others? Do they all make sense in their own way, or does one particular order seem most effective? How do the rhetorical appeals of *logos*, *ethos*, *pathos*, and *kairos* change with these revisions? Share your three versions with the class, and get their opinion as well. Then, develop a claim based on your responses, and support it with reasons and evidence.

Engine

Search

Locate an essay you have written for another class. If you were going to make a video based on this essay, how would you revise the essay to make it better fit a visual medium? Would you change the order of its major points? Would you change when you present your major thesis? Write a short report that lists the changes and explains your rationale behind them, and share them with the class.

Editing

While revision deals with the global structure of the document, editing usually addresses the next step down, the details and technical aspects (Figure 10.7). Since editing is usually performed once a draft is already finished, this step is usually given the least amount of attention due to time constraints or general neglect. However, thoroughly editing your text can make it much more professional and acceptable to audiences. Many readers or viewers love to find a misspelled word, a misplaced comma, or a poorly edited image and chide the author for his or her carelessness. As an author, such mistakes harm your *ethos*, so don't give audiences a chance to find these errors.

Figure 10.7
Editing looks for more detailed changes.

Text editing

When editing text—rather than revising or proofreading—your goal is to improve the readability of the document for your audience. You may rewrite sentences for clarity, cohesiveness, grammatical correctness, or change entire paragraphs to meet these goals. When editing, you should also check for consistency. Do you use the same formatting throughout? Do you write out all numbers, or use numerals? Are abbreviations consistent throughout? Does the document use a single style format, such as MLA or APA?

For the most part, editing and proofreading occur at the surface level of writing. But while simple proofreading only checks if a word is spelled correctly, editing requires that you make decisions about the appropriateness and placement of words. When editing, you're making decisions about what to leave in and what to leave out. Does one word best fit the argument you're trying to make, or would another work better? Would a word receive more emphasis if it were placed at the end of the sentence rather than the beginning? These are important questions to tackle before moving on to proofreading. In general, editing requires that you consider:

- the placement of individual words,
- deleting unnecessary words,
- revising awkward or grammatically incorrect phrasing,
- moving sentences or paragraphs,
- editing transitional words between sentences,
- punctuation choices,
- formatting choices, such as paragraph form versus a bulleted list,
- adjusting the tone to make sure it's consistent, and
- checking that any references or citations are correct.

As discussed in Chapter 7, many digital genres such as email, microblogging, and text messages need to be specific yet concise. In addition, it's often difficult for an audience to understand your tone from such brief writing. Follow these guidelines to help you edit length, tone, and style.

Trim unnecessary excess

Look for parts of the writing that seem repetitive or information that doesn't support your main goal. Consider cutting these words, phrases, sentences, or paragraphs so your reader has less to read while still taking away your main points.

Clarify things

Make sure your language is clear. For instance, is it clear which noun a pronoun belongs to, or what word an adjective or adverb modifies? Are any sentences ambiguous in meaning? Does an unnecessary comma make a sentence confusing? Does the word order of a phrase or sentence make sense? You might understand what you're trying to communicate, but will your audience?

Be concise

When editing for concision, cut down on wordiness and excessive information. Wordiness occurs when a few words could be substituted for several in the sentence. Try to cut unnecessary phrases, modifiers, or clauses. To cut excessive information, ask yourself if facts, descriptions, dates, names, or other information is really necessary for them to understand your meaning. If you don't think some information helps your argument—or worse, detracts from it—cut it out.

Attend to style

Consider your style in terms of delivery and audience. As already discussed, online writing tends to be shorter than print-based writing, so you might adopt shorter sentences and paragraphs. You also might use visual cues to signal style, such as boldface, use of color, and spatial arrangement between elements on screen. You also might consider if your audience will expect a style that can be read by anyone, or if you're writing for professionals and can use jargon or discipline-specific terminology.

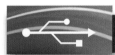

DIGITAL Connections

The Importance of Thoughtful Editing (Or: Why I Tear Apart Manuscripts Like a Rabid Dog)

By Maura Lammers

July 13, 2012

> Consider this article about editing from Maura Lammers in a piece for *The Missouri Review*.

Throughout June, I edited the first draft of a novel for a friend of a friend. He was a first-time writer and I was the first person to read his 600+ page novel. Though I'd never edited a novel before, my creative writing classes and current position here at *The Missouri Review* convinced him I was up for the task. When we first met, the author asked me if I was a tough editor, and I told him yes.

"That's good," he said. "I don't want you to go easy on me. I want you to be honest."

"Okay," I told him. "I'll tear it apart."

"Tearing apart" is the nickname I have for my editing style. To define tearing apart: when the constructive criticism for a piece of writing purposefully outweighs the praise. If I'm tearing apart a manuscript, I won't return the document to the writer until I've filled all the margins with notes. Although I always make sure to highlight great moments in whatever I'm reading, I relentlessly search for weak moments. I nit-pick over word choice, circle unimpressive images, cross out irrelevant sentences, and engage the writer in my notes by asking questions about the story as I go. In general, I won't stop editing until the manuscript is covered in colored ink.

Often, when I return a document and the writer sees my edits, they look like a truck just backed over their foot. Their gut instinct, always, is that my edits are solely negative and that I hated their writing. Once the writer reads my actual comments and realizes that I didn't write "YOU SUCK" in the margins, they don't seem quite so pained. In the case of the author whose novel I edited, when I met with him a week ago I gave him a three page outline addressing the main issues he needs to fix in his final draft, then discussed these issues at length for two hours. By the end, he said, "Honestly, I thought you were going to be meaner." The fact that he felt this way, even after I suggested he cut entire chapters from the novel, illustrates the benefits of tearing apart a manuscript. Even though I recommended major cuts, I offered so many suggestions for revision that the author didn't feel stunted. Most importantly, the amount of detail and attention I gave to each page proved that I cared about his writing. He trusted my opinion because he knew I cared.

Undoubtedly, there are professional editors, professors, and even fellow students, who edit the same way I do. This "tear it apart" idea is not unique to me, and probably carries many other snazzy names. However, during the three undergraduate writing workshops I've had, no one has ever torn one of my short stories apart. Yes, I received plenty of positive and negative feedback for each story. But no one ever handed me back a story covered in elaborate edits and said, "This is all right, but it's not great yet. Let's work on making it great." This isn't because I'm a talented writer. Rather, it's because no one will look me in the eye and bluntly tell me what's holding my story back from reaching its full potential.

While I've encountered many helpful fellow students in my past workshops, every workshop inevitably contains at least one person from the following two groups: the Cheerleaders and the Naysayers. The Cheerleaders focus on the positive aspects of a story either because a) they aren't experienced enough to recognize the weak points in a story, or b) they don't want to hurt the writer's feelings with negative comments. The Naysayers, however, are writers who either a) can't intelligently articulate their negative thoughts apart from saying, "I don't know, this just fell flat," or b) won't offer thoughtful criticism because they think the story is simply a hopeless case. Whether it's through overly positive or overly negative feedback, Cheerleaders and Naysayers produce the same result: vague, useless editing.

With my own work, historically, the Cheerleaders compliment the details or the overall tone of the piece. The Naysayers sometimes argue that the description is overwhelming. I'm quick to tune out the fluff and the snide remarks, and once the workshop ends I gather everyone's notes in a pile and put them away with the draft. It's not until months later, when I pull out the same story for a final edit and read with a more detached gaze, that I always notice the mistakes no one brought up during workshop: shaky plot points, wandering thematic elements, and too-neat dialogue. These are the kinds of mistakes that become more apparent during a second read-through or, arguably, a slow tear-it-apart first read. In these moments, I wonder if the Cheerleaders and Naysayers (as well as my uncategorized peers) actually felt my writing was great—or if they all suspected my story was a hopeless case, and were just too polite or lazy to tell me so.

This kind of bad attitude, this need to privately dismiss our peers' imperfect first drafts, is what leads to poor editing in workshops, which eventually manifests itself into unexceptional writing. It's true that only a handful of the writers in my past workshops will ever see their work published in a prestigious journal. It's true that many of us will never finish writing a novel, much less see it in print. It's true that most of us received an A for effort, regardless of whether our writing was flawed or flawless. But to dismiss any individual work as a hopeless case is nothing short of unfair. No piece of writing is a hopeless case. If an editor reads closely and analyzes the details, tears it apart page by page, he or she can always help lead the writer to a more fulfilling final draft. It's not just about finding mistakes. It's about investing the time and energy to show the writer that you believe in their work. Even if it means using a lot of ink.

Text editing tools

Unlike editing on paper, digital editing on a word processor provides a variety of tools to make editing easier and more efficient. Consider using the following features, which are found on most word processors, when you edit text.

Cut and paste

As its name suggests, the cut and paste feature used to be literal—one had to literally cut a printed page, rearrange text, and paste the pieces together with glue. The term has now become a metaphor for copying digital text to the computer's memory and placing it somewhere else. This feature allows you to not only cut and paste in a single document, but also between documents.

Copy

This feature saves text to the computer's memory so you can insert it elsewhere. You can copy to reproduce others' works as well as copy your own editing comments and place them elsewhere in a work.

Search and replace

Perhaps one of the most useful tools when it comes to editing, search and replace allows you to search for a particular word, phrase, punctuation, or other piece of text and replace it with another. For instance, if you need to replace "iphone" with "iPhone," search and replace will help you replace every instance of one with the other in a single step.

Spell-check

This feature can be very useful; however, it will not correct words that are spelled correctly but used incorrectly. For example, spell-check will miss the error in the sentence "The whether outside is frightful" because "whether" is spelled correctly (the sentence really refers to "weather").

Grammar check

The grammar check feature can help catch grammatical and stylistic errors, especially when words may be used incorrectly according to standard grammatical rules. The feature also can provide readability statistics, such as the percentage of passive sentences and the writing's reading grade level.

Thesaurus

Most word processors include a thesaurus for help in identifying synonyms or antonyms. This feature can be useful when attempting to replace a repeated or overused word, so the writing style is more pleasant.

Track changes

As you edit a document, you may turn on the track changes feature so all of your changes and suggestions are recorded. This feature allows you (or the author whose writing you're editing) to see both your revisions and her original text.

Comments

In addition to track changes, you also can insert marginalia comments in case you have a question or advice for the author, or if you're the author, a reminder or comment for yourself to insert text at a later time.

Highlight

This feature allows you to highlight text in order to call attention to it, and is usually available in a variety of colors, allowing you to color code different kinds of edits.

Image editing

When editing an image or composition that uses visuals, you should consider many of the elements you would for a written text. If you're creating an informational graphic about the price of gasoline, you should check that you use only one term—gasoline or gas—in the visual, otherwise you may confuse your readers. If you're using various colors in this information graphic to represent different suppliers of gasoline, editing ensures those colors are consistent.

You also might consider technical aspects of editing in a photo editor. For example, you could find it beneficial for an audience if you were to adjust the contrast, brightness, hues, or sharpness of an image so it's easier to read and understand. You might blur out individuals' faces to protect their identity (Figure 10.8). You might remove dust or other blemishes from an image so it's clearer.

Figure 10.8
The blur tool can be used to protect a subject's identity.

However, if you're using a photograph for journalistic purposes, there is only so much photo editing you should perform while still maintaining factual, journalistic integrity. For example, check out the recommended photo editor adjustments suggested by the news agency, Reuters, using the QR code to the right.

reuters.com

When shooting photographs for Reuters, the organization only permits a certain amount of postproduction done to the photos so the original content is not substantially changed. However, if you intend to use your photograph for rhetorical purposes, to persuade rather than to present facts, then you should feel freer to manipulate images to express your argument (without, of course, outright lying to your readers through an image; they should understand and recognize your attempt at purposeful editing).

You also should edit across text and image. Make sure the figure number for each image corresponds to what you've indicated in the body of the text. Check that any textual descriptions in the text match the image to which it refers, and make sure the captions reflect the context for why you included the image.

Finally, save the image in the correct format. If you're using the image for the web, you can save it as a JPG, PNG, or GIF at 72 dots per inch (dpi) and in RGB color. If you're using the image for print, then save it as an EPS, TIFF, or even PDF at 300 dpi or higher and in CMYK color. Although file formats might not seem like image editing, selecting the right format is an important part of ensuring your image will appear the way you intend it to.

Video editing

After revising and before proofreading, the step of editing video becomes one of the most important parts of the postproduction process. While revising leads to a rough cut and concerns the larger story or argument you're trying to make, and while proofing removes the smaller blemishes, editing removes the traces that it was ever edited at all. This may sound paradoxical, but good editing appears seamless. In other words, the best editors make their work disappear so the audience focuses on the story rather than transitions.

When editing, you should focus on the transitions between shots and scenes. These transitions—such as cuts, wipes, or dissolves—should appear at points where the audience would expect some sort of change (Figure 10.9). Use the following guidelines when editing your own video at the level of transitions.

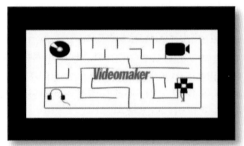

Figure 10.9
Brandon Pinard, from *Videomaker* magazine, discusses some common transitions.

www.youtube.com/watch?v=iCEdSGeFCCA

Motivate your transitions

When you make a cut, you should have some reason for doing so and that reason should be apparent to the audience. If one character reaches out his hand to offer money to someone, you might then transition to a shot of the outstretched hand holding the money. However, the cut should only happen after the character has outstretched his hand so the audience sees this important movement.

Cut during action

If the camera focuses on a car moving down the street, you should cut in the middle of that movement; the audience doesn't need to see the car traveling the whole distance.

Use close-ups

Video does best as a medium when it uses close-ups of characters, objects, or other points of interest. Use establishing shots to give the audience a sense of location or context, but transition to close-ups to show better detail.

Transition after your visual statement

Because each shot should be motivated, it shows some statement that you intend to make. Once that goal has been accomplished, any remaining action in the shot serves little purpose and you can then cut away.

Old and new

Just like writing a traditional essay, in video old information should be presented before new information. For objects, places, or characters that may already be familiar, you only need to dedicate a few seconds before transitioning to another shot.

Base tempo on context

The timing of your transitions should match the tone or mood of your scene. A quiet picnic by a lake should probably have longer shots than a fast-paced action scene, which will probably make use of short, quick cuts to heighten its intensity and suspense.

Include B-roll

When watching an interview between two people, you might notice that the scene includes shots in addition to the interviewer and interviewee. This footage is known as B-roll, and may include images relevant to the topic being discussed. Adding B-roll can make the scene more interesting or provide valuable information that enhances the verbal conversation.

Cut it out

Although most of the guidelines above instruct you to add materials into your video project, you should also be equally willing to remove shots from the final cut. If you think any added footage or B-roll detracts from the message you're trying to communicate, use your instinct and remove it.

These guidelines only apply to continuity editing, when you are attempting to tell a linear story and make the audience forget about the medium they are viewing. Sometimes, you may want the audience to be aware they're watching a video, so you may use more jarring cuts to get their attention or make a statement about video itself. When editing video and selecting appropriate transitions, you're making rhetorical choices that affect how an audience receives your argument. Even though all of your footage has been shot, some of the most important parts of the video writing process occur when the camera is turned off.

Building

Link

Choose a short video clip from YouTube or another video source. Using a video editor, change the transitions in the clip to any kind other than what is currently used. Show both the original version and new version to your peers, and discuss how the same footage with new transitions changes it (or doesn't).

Engine

Search

Locate a famous example of a journalistic photograph that was manipulated prior to its printing. For instance, Figure 10.10 shows a photo from the 1970 Kent State University shootings in which a sign post was removed. Write a report that examines the context of the photo's manipulation, including why and how it was manipulated, the reaction by the public when the manipulation was discovered, and how the journalistic community reacted to the ethics of the manipulation. Develop a claim based on your research, and support it with reasons and evidence.

© 1970 Valley News-Dispatch and John Filo

Figure 10.10
This famous photograph from the 1970 Kent State shootings was altered by removing the post above the woman's head.

Proofreading

While the steps of editing and revising usually attend to the larger work as a whole, proofreading looks for the smaller mistakes (Figure 10.11). With traditional alphabetic writing, such mistakes usually occur at the level of spelling, punctuation, misuse of words, alignment, format, or other errors of consistency.

Text proofreading

You've most likely proofread a text document, either your own or a peer's. Some general strategies can help ensure you proofread more efficiently and accurately. These tips apply equally to a traditional term paper or the captions you might write for an image.

Forget your writing

The best way to catch errors in your own writing is to forget what you wrote, making it less familiar. Often, when you read your own work, you know it so well you gloss

Figure 10.11
Proofread your text as the last step.

over the sentences because you've already read them so many times. When you've finished drafting a piece, put it away for as long as you can. A week or more would be ideal, but even a day or a few hours will help. The more you can forget what you wrote, the better.

Find a proofreader

Because of your familiarity with your own work, you can easily miss errors when proofreading your own document. As an alternative, try finding a proofreader unfamiliar with your work who can help identify errors or other issues with your writing.

Proofread backward

Another method to defamiliarize your writing is to read it backward. This helps break the flow of normal reading, forcing you to slow down and pay attention to details. You can read backward at three different levels: 1) word by word, which helps you pay attention to spelling errors; 2) sentence by sentence, which helps you identify problems with sentence structure; and 3) paragraph by paragraph, which helps you ensure that each paragraph coheres as a whole and that you use correct punctuation.

Read aloud

You can also try reading your work aloud. This technique not only slows down your reading so you don't skip over errors, but it also helps you catch mistakes by hearing them, making yourself more conscious of sentence structure and wordiness. Asking peers to read aloud can also be a very effective technique. Since they are unfamiliar with the work, they will be especially sensitive to confusing sentences or questionable word choice.

DIGITAL Connections

A Cautionary Poem

By Anonymous

I have a spelling chequer.
It came with my pea sea.
It plane lee marques four my revue
Miss steaks eye kin knot sea.

Eye strike a quay and type a word
And weight four it two say
Weather eye am wrong oar write.
It shows me strait a weigh.

A checker is a bless sing,
It freeze yew lodes of thyme.
It helps me right awl stiles two reed,
And aides me when aye rime.

Each frays come posed up on my screen
Eye trussed too bee a joule.
The chequer pours o'er every word
To cheque sum spelling rule.

Bee fore wee had hour checkers
Hour spelling mite decline,
And if we're lacks oar have a laps,
We wood bee maid too wine.

Butt now bee cause my spelling
Is chequed with such grate flare,
Their are know faults with in my cite,
Of nun eye am a wear.

Now spelling does knot phase me,
It does knot bring a tier.
My pay purrs awl due glad den
With rapped words fare as hear.

To rite with care is quite a feet
Of witch won should bee proud,
And wee mussed dew the best wee can,
Sew floors are knot aloud.

You might have a habit of letting the computer's spellchecker catch any proofreading errors for you. But, as this poem published on the website *The Proof Angel* demonstrates, a computer can only check if a word is spelled correctly, not if the right word is being used. Sarah Perkins, the website's editor, notes that this anonymous poem offers a comical look at proofing.

Sow ewe can sea why aye do prays
Such soft where four pea seas,
And why eye brake in two averse
Buy righting won too pleas.

Eye ran this poem threw it,
I'm shore your glad two no.
Its letter perfect all the weigh.
My checker tolled me sew.

Image proofreading

Before printing a final diagram, illustration, photograph, or other visual design, you should proof the final draft to ensure it will look as you intended. When you proof a visual, you are checking to see how it will appear on the final medium you have chosen, whether that medium is a book, poster, flyer, television, or computer screen. If you were designing a brochure, you should have a proof printed to ensure that colors, fonts, arrangement, alignment, and other elements appear correctly. If they don't, you can go back and correct these errors before ordering a large quantity of them from a printing vendor. The following checklist offers some suggestions of elements to look for, and it can apply to print documents as well.

- Does the image need to be touched up for errors or blemishes, such as red eye, skin tones, or color correction? For example, Figure 10.12 shows a photograph of a politician on a political mailer. In the image on the left you can see that the camera lighting is reflected in the candidate's eyes. The image on the right has been edited to remove most of the lights.

Figure 10.12
This photo was edited to remove the camera lights from the subject's eyes (photo on the right).

- Does the image need to be cropped in order to remove unwanted elements or to focus in on a particular feature?

- Does the image appear in the correct place within a larger document? If it is a figure, does it appear near the text that refers to it?

- Does the image need a caption? If so, is the caption's text free of errors?

- If a text is made up of many images, are all the images present? Are these images labeled correctly and appear in the right order?

- For more complex visual documents such as brochures, manuals, or visual essays, are all the sections or pages present? Do they appear in the proper order? Do they have (or require) page numbers?

- Are all the elements of the design aligned correctly? Are the margins consistent on each page or section?

- Are all the fonts of the document correct and consistent, including both typefaces and font sizes?

While this isn't an exhaustive list of all the aspects you might proof, it will help you check the major details of the image and any document in which the image occurs. As always, ask a peer to review these details for anything you might overlook. In addition, consider printing out your documents and proofing them in hardcopy. When a reader views text on a screen, he or she tends to skip over words more often and, therefore, miss more errors. Reading a draft on paper will help you or your reviewer catch more mistakes.

If the final version isn't digital, the last production step is printing, which usually requires a significant financial investment. You should proof the final version two or three times, with as many eyes as possible, to notice any mistakes before the printing press starts.

Video proofreading

Once the main sequence of the video is assembled and you've cleaned up the rough cut, you can then carefully analyze and proof the footage to notice any details that might have been missed.

Sometimes, editing errors occur. As you know from *The Empire Strikes Back*, Darth Vader cuts off Luke's right hand during their lightsaber battle. Luke later gains a mechanical hand, covered by a black glove (Figure 10.13).

However, during the speeder scene on Endor in the sequel *Return of the Jedi*, Luke's glove switches from his right hand, to his left hand, and then back to his right hand (Figure 10.14). This error is most likely due to a shot that was horizontally reversed by the editor to make it look like the camera angle was changed.

Credit: Lucasfilm

Credit: Lucasfilm

Figure 10.13
Most of you know that Luke Skywalker lost his right hand in a lightsaber duel with Darth Vader.

Figure 10.14
This shot of Luke reverses the image and disrupts continuity, making it appear that Luke's glove has disappeared.

Sometimes continuity errors can be the fault of the actors or the crew. In the film *Prometheus*, the character Shaw isn't wearing gloves in a scene on the planet's surface. The scene cuts away to another shot, but when it returns to Shaw, she is suddenly wearing gloves. In other cases, the error occurs because of factually incorrect information in a script. Again, in *Prometheus*, the ship travels 35 light years to reach the alien planet (205.8 trillion miles). However, in one scene, Charlize Theron's character states they are half a billion miles from Earth. Since the distance from Earth to Saturn is a little more than 755 million miles (more than half a billion), the ship hasn't even made it out of the solar system, much less to an alien planet, according to her estimate (Figure 10.15).

Neil deGrasse Tyson
@neiltyson
Follow

Prometheus goes 35 light yrs into space, but Charlize Theron gaffes "We're a half billion miles from Earth" – just past Jupiter

← Reply ⟲ Retweet ★ Favorite
1:32 AM - 8 Jun 12 via TweetDeck - Embed this Tweet

Figure 10.15
Astrophysicist Neil deGrasse Tyson called out *Prometheus's* factual error on Twitter.

When proofing your own video, check for the following errors. While some errors might be difficult to change—such as errors in the original footage—you can usually use transitions to cut away from any major problems or expand the size of the screen outside of the viewable margins so errors on the periphery disappear.

Continuity

These errors occur when some aspect of the scene—such as the character's clothing, props, or position are inconsistent from one shot to the next. The glove examples above are errors of continuity. If you were filming an instructional video about how to change a light bulb but took several days to film this action, you might make sure the talent wears the same shirt each day to make it look like all the action occurred in a single day, thereby maintaining continuity. Sometimes you can change these errors in postproduction, either through digital effects or by simply cropping undesirable elements from the shot.

Factual

These errors occur when some image, prop, line of dialogue, or scene presents information that is factually incorrect or historically inaccurate. For example, a factual error would occur if characters in a Revolutionary War movie were wearing boots worn during the Civil War.

Plot hole

This error occurs when some part of the film doesn't make sense given what the audience already knows to be true, thus creating a logical error in the plot. Sometimes editing scenes out of order causes plot holes and a simple reordering of scenes is necessary. Other times, however, plot holes result from a poorly written script and should have been caught before shooting commenced. Of course, if you're not creating a fictional-based video, you can look for gaps in a logical argument rather than plot.

Revealing

This type of error appears when some part of the wardrobe, props, or set is meant to be hidden but is accidentally revealed to the audience, usually at the edge of the shot. In the movie *Snow White and the Huntsman*, Snow White rides a horse bareback through the forest, without the aid of saddle or reigns. However, in a few of the shots where the horse is trapped in the mud, the audience can see a thin set of reigns used by the actor to help control the horse (Figure 10.16).

Credit: Universal Studios

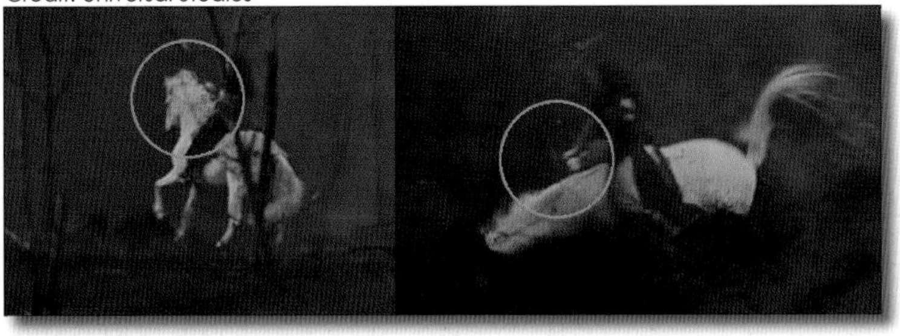

Figure 10.16
While most shots show Snow White riding a horse without reigns, this shot accidentally reveals them.

Visible crew/equipment

Sometimes, a piece of equipment, such as an overhead microphone, drops into the picture frame. This can destroy the suspension of disbelief and call attention to itself as a movie. Sometimes, such mistakes can be cropped out of the frame. These errors also occur if something reflective in the scene reveals the camera and crew or if crew members happen to be on the set (Figure 10.17).

Another technique used for proofreading written text is to look for only one kind of error at a time. In this technique, you would make one pass looking for punctuation mistakes, and another pass looking for spelling mistakes. Similarly, when proofing an image, you might look for only one kind of error, such as visible equipment, before moving on to continuity errors.

Credit: Walt Disney Pictures

Figure 10.17
A crew member accidentally appears in this shot from *Pirates of the Caribbean: Curse of the Black Pearl.*

Rhetorical Continuities

Like proofreading a written document, you can also proof video by watching each shot or scene in reverse sequence. This will prevent you from getting distracted by the unfolding story and help you focus on catching mistakes, just as reading your own work backward helps to make it less familiar.

Building

Link

Look at Figure 10.18. On the right side, you'll notice a tree in the frame. Research how you might remove the tree in a photo editor. What options do you have? Which technique do you think is best? Try removing the tree using all of the options, and show the class your final, edited image.

Figure 10.18
How can you edit this image to remove the tree?

Engine

Search

Find a digital image of yourself or a friend. Through an online search engine, research how to remove blemishes or red eye from a photograph. With a photo editor, edit your image using these techniques. Then create your own set of instructions informing someone else how to perform these edits. Allow a peer to user-test these instructions on his or her own image.

KEY Terms

CMYK

continuity error

editing

factual error

photo editor

plot hole

proofreading

revealing error

revising

video editor

visible crew/equipment error

Remix Essay

For this activity, create a remix essay that makes a claim about digital writing.

In other words, you will select text from other sources and remix these sources to create your own argument about digital writing. You might write about digital writing practices, or you might write about digital writing technologies.

Although the requirements for this assignment might vary depending on your instructor, follow the guidelines below unless told otherwise.

- You should use at least 10 sources in your remix essay.

- Your excerpts should be at least three words, but no more than 20.

- You may only add your own words that are single-word conjunctions such as "and," "but," "or," "however," "although," etc.

- Your essay should be at least 1,200 words.

- You should consistently cite all sources in MLA, APA, or another appropriate style.

This assignment will be challenging, but it will give you a better idea of how to create a remixed text, as well as how to edit various sources so these different authors and texts come together and ultimately speak with one message (yours).

From ▯I▯I▯AL Writers

Keeli Fricks
Professor Sean Morey
ENGL 475 – Remix Essay
11/10/12

Augmented Reality Glasses and Blue Light
Exposure

"[T]he 'message' of any medium or technology is the change of scale or pace or pattern that it introduces into human affairs."[1] I argue that "a . . . massive new *gestalt* or pattern has been"[2] "introduced into an ancient way of life by the intensification of a single factor,"[3] "the electric light."[4] "[T]he new patterns"[5] "introduced into our affairs"[6] "a new level of"[7] "blue light exposure"[8], "which can not only impact our sleep, but also increase our risk of cancer."[9] "[I]n today's world of modern technology and late-night work and entertainment habits"[10], "we use white LED lights (blue light) and stare into laptop (blue light) and high-def TV (blue light) screens. We use our iPhones (blue light) or Androids (blue light) in bed, even waking up in the middle of the night just to check our email (blue light)".[11] "[T]he effects of blue light exposure"[12] "affects our sleep cycle"[13] "which, in turn,"[14] "may have a range of other health effects."[15] "In a word, the message of the electric light is total change."[16] "The message of"[17] "some... new technology"[18] like "Augmented reality (AR)"[19], however, "does not need"[20] "to be an amplification of"[21] "already existing patterns".[22]

"Different types of artificial light sources"[23] "ended the regime of night and day, of indoors and out-of-doors."[24] "Bright, blue light which makes sense being outside,"[25] "that's going to, again, be a direct stimulator of cortical activity."[26] "Blue light from a 10:00 AM sky, blue light from your computer screen at midnight—it makes no difference to our circadian rhythms"[27], "our internal, approximately 24-hour cycle of biochemical, physiological, and behavioral processes."[28] "It's all the same to our bodies, because for millions of years blue light *meant* daylight, not a late night blog comment section or reruns of *The Daily Show*. And it's the blue light specifically that appears to monitor our sleep patterns the most."[29] "So let's talk a little bit more . . . about exactly how light does influence sleep rhythms and hormones that regulate sleep like melatonin and cortisol."[30]

"Every living thing, from fungus to bacteria to plant to animal, has a circadian rhythm. External cues called zeitgebers . . . help synchronize or alter our rhythms; they include temperature, nutrition, meal timing, social interactions pharmacological intervention . . . and, most prominently, the light/dark cycle of the earth."[31] "Light will enter into the eye, and it affects the specialized cells that are called intrinsically photosensitive retinal ganglion cells. . . . And those will transmit their signal back into the hypothalamus. . . . And near that hypothalamus is this suprachiasmatic nucleus . . . and that is the master clock in the brain—and the body."[32] "The clock in the brain synchronizes with the environment, and then all of the clocks—because there's a clock in all cells in the body—will then synchronize with the master clock." [33] "And what you see is that we know that at certain times of day, of course at night, melatonin levels go up, body temperature starts to drop, cortisol levels are low, and what happens is at different parts of the day there are different phase relationships."[34]

"When one is in good health, all these clocks are in sync, so that the body's activities will be properly coordinated."[35] Unfortunately, "it's not just sleep that's affected."[36] "When circadian rhythms are disrupted, disease often results."[37] "Infertility may often be due to disrupted circadian rhythms."[38] "Obesity, too, may be a circadian rhythm disorder."[39] "Immune function follows a circadian rhythm"[40] and therefore "time of infection matters"[41]. "Disturbing our circadian rhythms with improper light exposure may have a range of other health effects, including, but not limited to: increased risk of breast cancer"[42], "increased susceptibility to skin cancer"[43], and "increased risk of metabolic syndrome and obesity-related diseases"[44]. "Just a single 'pulse' of artificial light at night disrupts the circadian mode of cell division."[45] "Another study showed that the blue light emitted from alarm clocks and other digital devices suppresses melatonin production in a dose-dependent manner."[46] "This means that"[47] "the things that do matter are the intensity of the light, the wavelength or the spectrum, and then the duration or how long light is acting on the eye."[48]

"Disrupted circadian rhythms"[49] "is a natural adjunct of electric technology."[50] "It is the" "consequence of ever" "changing... forms of"[51] "the electric light".[52] "[A]ny new technology"[53] "that causes us to conform to the pattern of experience presented"[54] "in such a way" "that blue light"[55] "exposure. . . . may have a significant effect on . . . melatonin secretion when using these devices at night" "has almost invariably"[56] "drastic health consequences as shown by current science."[57] "If we trouble to scrutinize" "a new technology"[58] like "augmented reality technology"[59], "it does not follow that we are prepared to accept the consequences."[60]

"As augmented reality becomes more pervasive,"[61] "the potential for"[62] "the consequences of"[63] "blue light exposure" "to... [move] to the mainstream"[64], "to cause these"[65] "widespread health problems"[66], "will be greater"[67]. "We will see AR become a part of everyday life, impacting our sense of the world, our education, our medical analysis and treatment, our entertainment"[68] "and overall health"[69]. "Newer glasses-oriented displays are more likely to be worn on a daily basis and thus make a mobile AR system that provides the capabilities of a head-mounted display a possibility. With contact lens displays or lightweight glasses displays, the mobile AR experience can become totally seamless with your everyday life."[70] "The very nature of"[71] "displays that are worn like helmets, glasses, . . . with the trend being toward lightweight glasses"[72], encourages "daily use of these sets"[73] "and maybe even"[74] "all day, every day"[75] "use of these"[76].

I am "concerned precisely with accelerated media changes as a kind of massacre of"[77] "our circadian rhythms"[78]. "Head-based [displays] such as glasses"[79] "and other devices with self-luminous electronic displays are"[80] "light emitting devices"[81], "beaming directly into the eyes of those present and affecting the secretion of their melatonin"[82]. "Because blue light is most effective at disrupting circadian rhythms, wearing goggles that filter out blue light can help preserve normal melatonin rhythms."[83] "With... glasses displays"[84], it "is not necessary"[85] "to continue to"[86] "amplify or accelerate existing patterns".[87] "Instead they have"[88] "the ability to"[89] "act as the"[90] "blue-blocking lenses"[91] themselves "with the use of"[92] "a. . . . filter. . . . placed in front"[93]. This "would permit the"[94] "use of the"[95] "amber-lensed goggles once the sun has gone down"[96] "to seep into the mainstream"[97] "and . . . to improve"[98] "levels of general fitness and health".[99]

Endnotes

1   Marshall McLuhan, *Understanding Media: The Extensions of Man*, (Cambridge, Massachusetts: The MIT Press, 1964), 8.

2   Ibid., 54.

3   Ibid., 124.

4   Ibid., 9.

5   Ibid., 7.

6   Ibid.

7   Ibid., 160

8   Paul Jaminet and Shou-Ching Jaminet, *Perfect Health Diet*, (New York, New York: Scribner, 2012). Kindle Location 6378 of 12572. Kindle Edition.

9   Chris Kresser, "9 Steps to Perfect Health - #8: Get More Sleep." *ChrisKresser* (blog), February 22, 2013, chriskresser.com/9-steps-to-perfect-health-8-sleep-more-deeply

10 Chris Kresser, "How artificial light is wrecking your sleep, and what to do about it," *ChrisKresser* (blog), February 22, 2013, chriskresser.com/how-artificial-light-is-wrecking-your-sleep-and-what-to-do-about-it.

11 Ibid.

12 Chris Kresser, "How artificial light is wrecking your sleep."

13 Mark Sisson, "How Light Affects Our Sleep," *Mark's Daily Apple* (blog), March 04, 2010, www.marksdailyapple.com/how-light-affects-our-sleep/

14 McLuhan, *Understanding Media*, 142.

15 Mark Sisson, "How to Conduct a Personal Experiment."

16 McLuhan, *Understanding Media*, 52.

17 Ibid., 9.

18 Ibid., 239.

19 Alan Craig, *Understanding Augmented Reality: Concepts and Applications*, (Waltham, Massachusetts: Morgan Kaufmann, 2013), 255.

20 McLuhan, *Understanding Media*, 80.

21 Ibid., 172.

22 Ibid., 52.

23 Vic Costello, *Multimedia Foundations: core concepts for digital design*, (Waltham, Massachusetts: Focal Press, 2012), 296.

24 Ibid., 52.

25 Chris Kresser and Dan Pardi, *Why Most People Are Sleep-deprived and What to do About it*, podcast audio, Real Health Radio, 56:45, accessed November 16, 2013, chriskresser.com/why-most-people-are-sleep-deprived-and-what-to-do-about-it.

26 Ibid.

27 Mark Sisson, "How Light Affects Our Sleep."

28 Ibid.

29 Ibid.

30 Chris Kresser and Dan Pardi, *Why Most People Are Sleep-deprived and What to do About it*.

31 Mark Sisson, "How Light Affects Our Sleep."

32 Chris Kresser and Dan Pardi, *Why Most People Are Sleep-deprived and What to do About it*.

33 Ibid.

34 Ibid.

35 Paul and Shou-Ching Jaminet, *Perfect Health Diet*, Kindle Location 6303

36 Mark Sisson, "How to Conduct a Personal Experiment."

37 Paul and Shou-Ching Jaminet, *Perfect Health Diet*, Kindle Location 6303

38 Ibid.

39 Ibid.

40 Ibid., Kindle Location 6312

41 Ibid.

42 Mark Sisson, "How to Conduct a Personal Experiment."

43 Ibid.

44 Ibid.

45 Chris Kresser, "9 Steps to Perfect Health - #8: Get More Sleep."

46 Ibid.

47 McLuhan, *Understanding Media*, 58.

48 Chris Kresser and Dan Pardi, *Why Most People Are Sleep-deprived and What to do About it*.

49 Mark Sisson, "How to Conduct a Personal Experiment."

50 McLuhan, *Understanding Media*, 5.

51 Ibid., 186.

52 Ibid., 348.

53 Ibid., 7.

54 Ibid., 329.

55 Mark Sisson, "How Light Affects Our Sleep."

56 Mark Sisson, "Are Your Canned Foods Safe To Eat?: A BPA-Free Buying Guide," *Mark's Daily Apple* (blog), January 12, 2012, www.marksdailyapple.com/are-your-canned-foods-safe-to-eat-a-bpa-free-buying-guide/#axzz2lCtb8kpn

57 Mark Sisson, "Is It All Just A "Paleofantasy"?," *Mark's Daily Apple* (blog), April 03, 2013, www.marksdailyapple.com/is-it-all-just-a-paleofantasy/#axzz2lCt9kmRz

58 Ibid., 177.

59 Alan B. Craig, *Understanding Augmented Reality*, 256.

60 McLuhan, *Understanding Media*, 161.

61 Alan B. Craig, *Understanding Augmented Reality*, 264.

62 Costello, *Multimedia Foundations*, 274.

63 McLuhan, *Understanding Media*, 183.

64 Alan B. Craig, *Understanding Augmented Reality*, 255.

65 McLuhan, *Understanding Media*, 192.

66 Mark Sisson, "Is It All Just A "Paleofantasy"?," *Mark's Daily Apple* (blog), April 03, 2013, www.marksdailyapple.com/is-it-all-just-a-paleofantasy/#axzz2lCt9kmRz

67 Paul and Shou-Ching Jaminet, *Perfect Health Diet*, Kindle Location 1530.

68 Alan B. Craig, *Understanding Augmented Reality*, 255.

69 Mark Sisson, "How Noise Impacts Your Health," *Mark's Daily Apple* (blog), April 14, 2011, www.

marksdailyapple.com/how-noise-impacts-your-health/#axzz2lDAoIaJ4

70   Alan B. Craig, *Understanding Augmented Reality*, 210-11.

71   McLuhan, *Understanding Media,* 255.

72   Alan B. Craig, *Understanding Augmented Reality*, 97.

73   McLuhan, *Understanding Media,* 329.

74   Mark Sisson, "Dear Mark: Bodyweight or Barbells, Restaurant Traps, Primal Egg Coffee Stability, and Post-Exercise Insomnia," *Mark's Daily Apple* (blog), October 14, 2013, www.marksdailyapple.com/bodyweight-or-barbells-restaurant-traps-primal-egg-coffee-stability-post-exercise-insomnia/#axzz2lDIEqqNh

75   Mark Sisson, "7 Things You May Be Doing That Impair Workout Recovery," *Mark's Daily Apple* (blog), August 14, 2013, www.marksdailyapple.com/7-things-impair-workout-recovery/#axzz2lDLgEvU4

76   McLuhan, *Understanding Media,* 329.

77   Ibid., 16.

78   Paul and Shou-Ching Jaminet, *Perfect Health Diet*, Kindle Location 6322.

79   Alan B. Craig, *Understanding Augmented Reality*, 215.

80   Chris Kresser, "How artificial light is wrecking your sleep, and what to do about it."

81   Ibid.

82   Mark Sisson, "How to Conduct a Personal Experiment."

83   Paul and Shou-Ching Jaminet, *Perfect Health Diet*, Kindle Location 6359.

84   Alan B. Craig, *Understanding Augmented Reality*, 211.

85   McLuhan, *Understanding Media*, 159.

86   Mark Sisson, "Are You Living an Active or Passive Life," *Mark's Daily Apple* (blog), September 27, 2011, www.marksdailyapple.com/are-you-living-an-active-or-passive-life/#axzz2lDa4hJxM

87   McLuhan, *Understanding Media*, 8.

88   Ibid., 110.

89   Ibid., 244.

90   Ibid., 273.

91   Chris Kresser, "How artificial light is wrecking your sleep, and what to do about it."

92   McLuhan, *Understanding Media*, 352.

93   Costello, *Multimedia Foundations*, 327.

94   McLuhan, *Understanding Media*, 319.

95   Ibid., 341.

96   Chris Kresser, "How artificial light is wrecking your sleep, and what to do about it."

97   Mark Sisson, "Is Conventional Wisdom Set in Stone," *Mark's Daily Apple* (blog), September 9, 2009, www.marksdailyapple.com/is-conventional-wisdom-set-in-stone/#axzz2lDfPdgZy.

98   Mark Sisson, "How to Improve Thoracic Spine Mobility," *Mark's Daily Apple* (blog), May 7, 2010, www.marksdailyapple.com/how-to-improve-thoracic-spine-mobility/#axzz2lDgLmnp3.

99   Mark Sisson, "A Case Against Cardio (from a former mileage king)," *Mark's Daily Apple* (blog), June 20, 2007, www.marksdailyapple.com/case-against-cardio/#axzz2lDftknD5.

CHAPTER 11

Digital Delivery

The ancient Greek orator, Demosthenes (Figure 11.1), once claimed that delivery was the most important aspect of rhetoric. You might laboriously struggle through researching a project, crafting a script, drawing storyboards, shooting video, creating images, revising, editing, proofreading, and all the other steps in the process. However, if you don't effectively deliver your final project, then you won't reach your intended audience and your message will go unheard.

Figure 11.1
Demosthenes was considered by many ancient rhetoricians as the greatest of orators.

You might stay up all night writing that final paper, but if your alarm fails you in the morning, or your email attachment doesn't go through, your instructor will never receive your work and you won't receive credit.

Rhetorical Continuities

Without effective delivery, your audience may be unaware that you have attempted to get their attention at all. However, delivery not only affects the physical reception of communication but also whether an audience accepts the premise of your message. How you say something can be as important as what you say, and this chapter explains different considerations for how to deliver your digital texts, whether those considerations are as simple as where to post a printed document in the community, different websites to upload videos for particular audiences, or even something as complex as search engine optimization for blogs so audiences can find them more easily.

For Demosthenes and classical Greeks, delivery had several components, most of which involved the orator's physical presence in front of the Greek assembly. The most important aspect was probably vocal projection and verbal articulation. Orators had to be able to project their voice and fill the space but also know how to alternate between loud and soft volumes to draw in their audience.

Two famous anecdotes tell how Demosthenes would practice his speeches at the seashore, shouting above the volume of the surf (Figure 11.2). He also would put pebbles in his mouth, trying to articulate his words despite the stony impediments.

These stories show that delivery happens well before one is actually ready to deliver a work. Although you don't need to practice speaking with pebbles in your mouth in order to deliver a video online, you might think of what a digital situation requires. For instance, your message might be better received if you already have a positive *ethos* as an author. Or, if you were disseminating digital projects through your website, then your website should look the part as well, showing your audience what kind of aesthetic design or quality to expect.

Credit: Jean-Jules-Antoine Lecomte du Nouÿ

Figure 11.2
The ancient Greek orator, Demosthenes, used to deliver to the roaring ocean.

Credit: Gilbert Austin

Figure 11.3
These are a few gestures that used to be taught to students of delivery.

Besides the voice, classical delivery also included attention to the rest of the body. Orators would have to be aware of their posture, their facial expressions, when and how they walked, and their arm and hand gestures (Figure 11.3). Roman teachers of rhetoric also emphasized that students should pay attention to clothing, jewelry, and grooming as well, and when it was acceptable to remove one's outer garments (Figure 11.4).

You might associate many of these guidelines with acting in a scene, either in a play or on a movie set. An actor must not only remember her lines and how to stress each word but also her physical acting beyond the voice. An actor can say much without

Credit: John Robert Charlton

Figure 11.4
Lady Gaga makes careful use of clothing in all her public appearances.

saying a word, and so she must be fully aware of how she moves her body at all times. In these ways, an orator and an actor do not differ much in the techniques they use to either persuade or entertain. In fact, the Greek word for delivery, *hypokrisis*, became synonymous with acting. The Latin word for delivery, *actio*, speaks for itself.

The following chapter discusses contemporary modes of delivery that occur through three primary media: text, images, and video. As you read about delivery techniques in each of these media, consider how each medium changes the possibilities for delivery and how you might invent new ways to deliver that aren't covered in this chapter. Also, consider how the larger environment plays a role in what kinds of delivery are possible and how to creatively use that environment to deliver your message.

Delivery Through Text

While delivery, either through acting on camera or acting on stage, has clear connections with digital writing that include images and video, you should first consider delivery's role in more traditional texts. When communication occurs face to face, in your audience's presence, then the body is important for communication. However, once you write down your message on some medium and send it across the city, state, country, world, or solar system, your body stays with you, not with your message, and the

Figure 11.5
The act of signing can often determine how others will act.

two become separated. In print culture, a piece of paper serves as your "body," which is still divided according to a human physiology with the "header" at the top of the page, the "footer" at the bottom of the page, and the "body" in the middle. Of course, a piece of paper can't make facial expressions, pace across the stage, or gesture to a crowd. For the most part, it remains passive and does not "act." However, print documents, especially legal documents such as laws, determine how one should act (Figure 11.5).

How, then, might a static piece of paper "act"? Your favorite book obviously moves you in some way, creating an emotional response and connection. This appeal to emotion is one of the principle functions of delivery. Aristotle bemoaned the ability of orators to use delivery in place of logic when persuading an audience. Aristotle felt the best argument was the most reasoned, logical one, not the one best delivered.

Rhetorical Continuities

Documents we might have once printed we now send electronically. Emails, text messages, or blog posts can all "act" on our behalf much like a letter. For the moment, however, leave aside the fact that digital texts can be sent with other media (such as images), or the instantaneous feedback (i.e., through comments). Consider, for the sake of this section, how a printed document must deliver information, and fold this thinking into what you know about digital documents composed primarily of text.

Humans don't only think with the logical parts of their left brain hemisphere and must address the whole brain when making an appeal, especially with visual media. Such visual media include physical bodies (just watch any physical comic), but also the media you use when you can't be present, including paper.

Credit: Nathan Beach

Figure 11.6
High-quality paper can increase your writing's delivery.

For instance, if you submitted your résumé to an employer and one copy was printed on clean, high-quality résumé paper and another printed on thin, standard copy paper, which do you think would most impress the employer? All other factors being equal (i.e., the same résumé, the same type of job), the résumé printed on high-quality paper will probably look (and feel) more professional and persuade this potential employer that you care about getting this job and that you will hopefully bring this same attention to detail to the workplace (Figure 11.6).

Medium, typography, and layout

Your choice of medium—even if simply choosing one kind of paper over another, or one social media platform over another—affects how the audience responds to the message and becomes an important factor in delivering that message. As Marshall McLuhan (Figure 11.7) wrote, "the medium is the message" and reaches the audience at a level beyond the actual content. What kind of message do you want to send with your medium?

Typography, layout, and other textual features also can change how the audience receives a message.

Figure 11.7
Marshall McLuhan famously wrote "the medium is the message."

While you might think of these features as elements of style, you also can think of them as choices of delivery. Just as an orator has a variety of hand gestures, writers have a variety of typefaces, and changing a typeface can affect how an audience interprets one's writing.

For example, look at the text in Figure 11.8. This text is the same as in the previous paragraph, except that it appears in the typeface Comic Sans MS. While the rest of this book is written in Times New Roman, a very standard typeface used for professional applications, Comic Sans MS doesn't exude the same mood or expectations, and so you would not expect to read a business report that uses this typeface.

Typography, layout, and other textual features can also change how the audience receives a message. While you might think of these features as elements of style, you can also think of them as choices of delivery. Just as an orator has a variety of hand gestures, writers have a variety of typefaces, and changing a typeface can affect how an audience interprets one's writing.

Figure 11.8
Comic Sans can make any text more "comical."

DIGITAL Connections

Cavaliers Owner Dan Gilbert Addresses Cleveland in Comic Sans: Why We Facepalm

By Robert Quigley

In case you haven't heard, the only news in the world today is that LeBron James decided that he is going to play basketball for the Miami Heat instead of the New York Knicks or the Cleveland Cavaliers. This has made some people in Cleveland very sad, including the team's owner, Dan Gilbert.

Dan Gilbert was so upset, in fact, that he wrote a very angry open letter to Cleveland fans, laden with surprising capitalizations and lines like "The self-declared former 'King' will be

In 2010, LeBron James (Figure 11.9), a professional basketball player for the Cleveland Cavaliers, announced that he was signing with the Miami Heat. The Cavaliers' majority owner, Dan Gilbert (Figure 11.10), wrote a letter to Cavaliers fans about the decision and placed it on his team's website. Many reactions to Gilbert's letter focused not on the content of his message (although, certainly, some critics focused on this), but that he delivered his message in Comic Sans. Consider Robert Quigley's take on Gilbert's typeface "decision" published on themarysue.com.

taking the 'curse' with him down south. And until he does 'right' by Cleveland and Ohio, James (and the town where he plays) will unfortunately own this dreaded spell and bad karma," and "I PERSONALLY GUARANTEE THAT THE CLEVELAND CAVALIERS WILL WIN AN NBA CHAMPIONSHIP BEFORE THE SELF-TITLED FORMER 'KING' WINS ONE. You can take it to the bank."

We will leave it to our sporting brethren at *SportsGrid* to parse the meaning and sporty implications of all of this to the world of people who care about sports. For our part, the most important thing to note about Dan Gilbert's letter is that it was written in Comic Sans. Comic Sans.

As you may be aware, Comic Sans is a Vincent Connare-designed font with promising enough origins—Connare was partly inspired by John Costanza's lettering for *The Dark Knight Returns* and Dave Gibbons' lettering for *Watchmen*—but it has since blossomed into a long history of infamy, thanks in large measure to its inclusion in Windows 95. While Connare says the font was never intended for wide-

According to Quigley, you can assume that any use of Comic Sans will instantly destroy your *ethos* as a designer and thus your delivery. You might find a use for the typeface from time to time (for instance, comic book speech bubbles), but you would need to use it with extreme caution. Just as certain gestures or facial expressions might be used at appropriate moments to deliver a speech, typefaces and other typographical elements can provide tools for expressing aesthetic and emotional content, such as Gilbert's attempt to "shout" by writing some of his sentences in ALL CAPS. Each typeface has specific uses—whether for body text, headers, footnotes, indexes, title pages, advertisements, web pages, or other situations and contexts.

Credit: Keith Allison

Figure 11.9
Lebron James as a member of the Cleveland Cavaliers

I don't always write letters

but when i do, i use comic sans

Figure 11.10
Perhaps Comic Sans isn't the best typeface choice for a CEO?

spread use, the lighthearted, readable font has since been inappropriately used the world over, for things like, say, composing office memos, or announcing one's feelings to millions about the star basketball player on their franchise departing in a cold attempt to woo the Chinese market.

Comic Sans is widely hated by designers primarily for the inappropriate uses to which people turn it, Gilbert's letter being a prime example. But there are deeper, more design-specific reasons: Gibbons, *The Watchmen* letterer whose work partly inspired the font, blasted it in an interview with *The Guardian*:

> As figure 11.11 demonstrates, individual typefaces each have their own message to deliver, and choosing the wrong typeface can be counterproductive to your rhetorical goals.

"It's just a shame they couldn't have used just the original font, because it's a real mess. I think it's a particularly ugly letter form," he says. "The other thing that really bugs me is that they've used an upper case 'I' with bars on it: it looks completely wrong to the comic eye. And when you see store fronts done in it, it's horrible."

Another major Comic Sans complaint concerns the font's kerning, or spacing between letters: By default, there's some odd and uneven spacing which breaks the flow of reading. There's even a designer-led movement to ban Comic Sans. From afar, all of the Comic Sans hate might sound a little heavy in response to a font which was originally "only intended for Microsoft's cartoon dog, Rover." But when a billionaire sports team owner makes a heavy, angry, somewhat crazy announcement to be read by millions in a zany, unbalanced font, it all sort of makes sense.

Figure 11.11
Although "toy" and Comic Sans might go together, Comic Sans and the subject of weapons probably don't.

Color in text

Color, of course, also becomes an important tool when trying to deliver a message through text and visual design. Audiences often associate certain colors with particular meanings and emotions. For instance, white and black are often used to signify themes of good and evil. The colors green and brown depict earthy, naturalistic feelings, while blue can be melancholic. When writing in professional settings, however, you should be very conscious of the color choices you make, especially when writing for international and transnational audiences, and audiences with different cultural backgrounds. As you remember from Chapter 6, Figure 6.14 (p. 212) shows how different cultures respond to colors differently, and you should choose colors that are rhetorically appropriate for each audience and situation.

Building

Link

Find several official memos or other documents from the White House, your college or university, or other institution. Create different versions of the documents by altering their typography. Use a variety of typefaces and colors to provide a range of changes. How do the new versions compare to the originals? Show the new documents to your class. Ask them how they respond to the documents. Do they take them less seriously, even though the documents are from serious, government and professional institutions and the content remains the same? As an alternative, find a funny, humorous piece of writing, and put it in a very serious typeface. Do you notice the opposite effect? How does the change in typeface affect the rhetorical appeals of *logos*, *ethos*, *pathos*, and *kairos*? Develop a claim based on your responses above, and support it with reasons and evidence.

Engine

Search

In order for paper to "deliver," it has to travel from person to person. Research the history of letter transport, from human runners, the pony express, to modern day transit. Write a report on your findings, and share them with the class, discussing what you and your peers discovered. Then, develop a claim about delivery based on your research, and support it with reasons and evidence.

Delivery Through Visuals

Despite the typographical and layout changes you can make with print, the technology is still fairly limited in terms of delivery. Even when print becomes highly circulated through the Internet, no longer limited to the "delivery" of postal mail, the actual document doesn't do much once you start reading it. Other media, especially electronic media, offer other possibilities for delivery not available with print. In general, learning to write with these media is the goal of this book so that you're not limited to expression through alphabetic text alone.

Although they're also static, still images can offer the emotional component of delivery in a way much different from print. You have already learned how visuals attempt to evoke emotional responses from an audience by tapping into evocative images, using connotation to create associations, creating visual metaphors to suggest connections, or developing concepts to suggest new ways of thinking. Still images also can show poses, gestures, facial expressions, and other features of a human body that print can only abstractly mimic. An image can make the human body visible again, offering a seemingly more direct connection with the author even though he or she may be thousands of miles away (or even deceased).

Strategic choice and placement

An image also can deliver content much more quickly than print. The placement of a billboard in different environments can affect how the audience views it, and a typical billboard needs to deliver information quickly and efficiently to the motorist driving by. If the billboard presented its information in print alone, it would be much more difficult to read while driving down the road than a billboard with an image and some text for anchorage.

For example, Figure 11.12 shows a billboard promoting vegetarianism. The billboard juxtaposes a piglet and a puppy, suggesting equality between the species. The text offers a rhetorical question: "Why love one but eat the other?" with the main claim presented as "Choose Vegetarian." The image of the piglet and puppy provide a visual representation of the implicit argument of the animals' equality, and no other words are needed. The image also creates an emotional connection, portraying the two animals with "puppy dog eyes" that make a plea to the viewer.

Credit: Mercy for Animals

Figure 11.12
This billboard argues that the audience should treat pigs and dogs equally.

However, an alternative, text-based billboard would need more commentary in addition to the existing text, such as: "You should consider a pig and a dog to have equal worth. Both are cute animals—too cute to slaughter." Obviously, an image makes more impact emotionally and also delivers that information much more quickly, allowing a passing motorist to absorb the image and text and make the connection the billboard is arguing for. As the cliché goes, an image is worth a thousand words; only a few words are provided above, and you could probably come up with many more to describe the picture and its message. But even if the billboard was filled with a thousand words, such text would be rhetorically ineffective compared to a well-designed image, and delivery would fail.

DIGITAL Connections

The Kennedy-Nixon Presidential Debates, 1960

by Erica Tyner Allen

On 26 September 1960, 70 million U.S. viewers tuned in to watch Senator John Kennedy of Massachusetts and Vice President Richard Nixon in the first-ever televised presidential debate.

> Erica Tyner Allen writes about the visual impact of the first American presidential debate to ever be televised in 1960.

It was the first of four televised "Great Debates" between Kennedy and Nixon. The first debate centered on domestic issues. The high point of the second debate, on 7 October, was disagreement over U.S. involvement in two small islands off the coast of China, and on 13 October, Nixon and Kennedy continued this dispute. On 21 October, the final debate, the candidates focused on American relations with Cuba.

The Great Debates marked television's grand entrance into presidential politics. They afforded the first real opportunity for voters to see their candidates in competition, and the visual contrast was dramatic. In August, Nixon had seriously injured his knee and spent two weeks in the hospital. By the time of the first debate he was still twenty pounds underweight, his pallor still poor. He arrived at the debate in an ill-fitting shirt, and refused make-up to improve his color and lighten his perpetual "5:00 o'clock shadow." Kennedy, by contrast, had spent early September campaigning in California. He was tan and confident and well-rested. "I had never seen him looking so fit," Nixon later wrote.

In substance, the candidates were much more evenly matched. Indeed, those who heard the first debate on the radio pronounced Nixon the winner. But the 70 million who watched television saw a candidate still sickly and obviously discomforted by Kennedy's smooth delivery and charisma. Those television viewers focused on what they saw, not what they heard. Studies of the audience indicated that, among television viewers, Kennedy was perceived the winner of the first debate by a very large margin.

The televised Great Debates had a significant impact on voters in 1960, on national elections since, and, indeed, on our concerns for democracy itself. The impact on the election of 1960 was significant, albeit subtle. Commentators broadly agree that the first debate accelerated Democratic support for Kennedy. In hindsight, however, it seems the debates were not, as once thought, the turning-point in the election. Rather than encouraging viewers to change their vote, the debates appear to have simply solidified prior allegiances. In short, many would argue that Kennedy would have won the election with or without the Great Debates.

When using video, sound, or both, many more aspects of the body become prevalent again. This fact became apparent in 1960 when Richard Nixon and John F. Kennedy appeared in the first presidential debate broadcasted on television (Figure 11.13).

Figure 11.13
John F. Kennedy and Richard Nixon appeared in the first televised presidential debate.

www.youtube.com/watch?v=C6Xn4ipHiwE

Yet voters in 1960 did vote with the Great Debates in mind. At election time, more than half of all voters reported that the Great Debates had influenced their opinion; 6% reported that their vote was the result of the debates alone. Regardless of whether the debates changed the election result, voters pointed to the debates as a significant reason for electing Kennedy.

The Great Debates had a significant impact beyond the election of 1960 as well. They served as precedent around the world: Soon after the debates, Germany, Sweden, Finland, Italy, and Japan established debates between contenders to national office. Moreover, the Great Debates created a precedent in American presidential politics. Federal laws requiring that all candidates receive equal air-time stymied debates for the next three elections, as did Nixon's refusal to debate in 1968 and 1972. Yet by 1976, the law and the candidates had both changed, and ever since, presidential debates, in one form or another, have been a fixture of U.S. presidential politics.

Perhaps most important, the Great Debates forced citizens to rethink how democracy would work in a television era. To what extent does television change debate, indeed, change campaigning altogether? What is the difference between a debate that "just happens" to be broadcast and one specifically crafted for television? What is lost in the latter? Do televised debates really help us to evaluate the relative competencies of the candidates, to evaluate policy options, to increase voter participation and intellectual engagement, to strengthen national unity? Fundamentally, such events lead to worries that television emphasizes the visual, when visual attributes seem not the best, nor most reliable, indicators of a great leader. Yet other views express confidence that televised presidential debates remain one of the most effective means to operate a direct democracy. The issue then becomes one of improved form rather than changed forum.

> From Kennedy's tan and fitness level to Nixon's pale complexion and rehabilitating physique, the body suddenly becomes much more important to anyone on television.

The Nixon-Kennedy debates of 1960 brought these questions to the floor. Perhaps as no other single event, the Great Debates forced us to ponder the role of television in democratic life.

Rhetorical Continuities

Like print, video often uses the same elements of color, typography, transitions, and other visual features that help the audience make sense of the document. However, video sometimes uses these elements in slightly different ways. Look at the section "Digital Techniques for Video" in Appendix B for more information.

Building

Think of the more memorable theme songs from television shows. Often, these songs create a connection between the viewer and the show, whetting their emotional appetite and preparing them for the rest of the program. Recall theme songs without lyrics, and—with a video editor—swap songs between show openings, many of which can be found online. How does changing the theme song alter how you respond to the introduction? How do you think these theme songs function in delivering the show to the audience? Where else might the theme song be used besides the beginning of the show? How does this increase the show's delivery to an audience? How does the song affect the rhetorical appeals of *logos, ethos, pathos,* and *kairos*? Develop a claim based on your responses above, and support it with reasons and evidence.

Engine

Research a particular photographic or filmic technique, such as a wipe transition, montage, use of a fish-eye lens, etc. Why was this technique invented? What is its primary purpose? How can this technique be thought of as rhetorical, and how can it help delivery? Develop a claim based on your responses above, and support it with reasons and evidence.

Distribution

You also can think of delivery in terms of distribution. Once a movie is finished, the film distributor must consider the best outlets for disseminating the film. The kind of distribution you're probably most familiar with is a theatrical release. This kind of distribution usually receives the most media attention and promotion.

However, if a film isn't likely to do well in the theater, the distributor might consider delivering the film through video, simply called "straight-to-video" release (or now, straight-to-DVD). In some cases, the distributor may use both options at once, called a simultaneous release. The film may be distributed through television, either through network or cable channels, or video-on-demand. Some filmmakers don't have the backing of a large-scale distributor and may deliver their films online.

Because you probably don't have a large-scale distributor, you will have to distribute your work in other ways. Text documents, images, and smaller files can easily be emailed directly or posted to the web. From there, you can link the document to Facebook or Twitter. You might even place the documents on a website and optimize the site's content and descriptions for intermediary audiences such as search engine robots. As you can probably see, delivering to audiences you know is not a problem; delivering to those you don't can be more challenging. Use nonhuman audiences such as web robots to help disseminate your documents to those audiences you don't know but might benefit somehow from seeing your texts. For advice on how to reach web robots and better deliver your texts on the web, return to the Nonhuman digital audiences section and review the information on search engine optimization in Chapter 5.

For delivering video, you most likely know about YouTube and Vimeo. Each of these sites can affect delivery differently. YouTube has much more traffic than Vimeo, so, in theory, you have a better chance of someone finding your video. However, more videos also mean more competition during a search, so your audience might not find your video. Vimeo has fewer visitors but offers more customization, including the ability to place your own brand mark on your video and cleaner, higher-quality uploaded videos. However, Vimeo charges a small fee for some of its services, while YouTube is completely free. You should research the pros and cons of any site you're considering as a delivery platform, and determine how your audience will respond when viewing the video on a particular site.

Another web video delivery alternative is Vine, a video-sharing and social media service that allows the user to post looping, six-second videos. Although this short form doesn't provide enough time for a detailed message or argument, it can be quickly viewed, shared, and therefore circulated among many people. The short length requires you to think carefully about your message's concision, but it can help increase its distribution.

Of course, not all of the documents you deliver will be online. As discussed earlier in this text, a flyer for a lost dog will probably be distributed in hard copy around the neighborhood. In addition to aspects such as typography, layout, or color, how and where you place your document matters.

Building

Link

Select three online sites that allow you to upload, store, and share photos. What are the differences between these sites? What are the pros and cons of each? What are the different audiences for each site (e.g., personal versus business use)? How do you think each site would affect a photo's delivery differently? How does each site affect the rhetorical appeals of *logos, ethos, pathos,* and *kairos*? Develop a claim based on your responses above, and support it with reasons and evidence.

Engine

Create a list of the different file formats in which an image can be saved. Research each format, noting the intended purpose and use of the format type. How might these formats influence a file's delivery? How does each format affect the image's viewing and dissemination differently? How does this information influence how you think about saving your own images in the future? Develop a claim based on your responses above, and support it with reasons and evidence.

Environment

The environment and location also play a part in delivery. Auditoriums are designed to maximize an orator's volume and carry his or her voice to the back row (Figure 11.14). They're also designed so that every seated audience member can see the speaker on stage. Recording studios are soundproofed so noises from the outside environment don't disturb the vocal talent or dilute the recording process. Likewise, the environment in which you place your text will play a huge part in how that message is delivered and received.

Figure 11.14
Auditoriums are specially designed to maximize sound acoustics.

DIGITAL Connections

Atheist Group Targets Muslims, Jews with 'Myth' Billboards in Arabic and Hebrew

By Dan Merica

The billboard wars between atheists and believers have raged for years now, especially around New York City, and a national atheist group is poised to take the battle a step further with billboards in Muslim and Jewish enclaves bearing messages in Arabic and Hebrew.

Knowing your target audience and deciding on a location often go hand in hand in maximizing delivery. Consider this story from Dan Merica (CNN) that demonstrates how the organization American Atheists places billboards (Figure 11.15) in strategic environments to best deliver its message to its target audience.

American Atheists, a national organization, will unveil the billboards Monday on Broadway in heavily Muslim Paterson, New Jersey and in a heavily Jewish Brooklyn neighborhood, immediately after the Williamsburg Bridge.

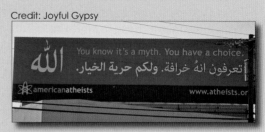

Credit: Joyful Gypsy

Figure 11.15
The group American Atheists has a difficult time placing their billboards without controversy.

"You know it's a myth . . . and you have a choice," the billboards say. The Paterson version is in English and Arabic, and the Brooklyn one in English and Hebrew. To the right of the text on the Arabic sign is the word for God, Allah. To the right of the text on the Hebrew sign is the word for God, Yahweh.

Dave Silverman, the president of American Atheists, said the signs are intended to reach atheists in the Muslim and Jewish enclaves who may feel isolated because they are surrounded by believers.

"Those communities are designed to keep atheists in the ranks," he says. "If there are atheists in those communities, we are reaching out to them. We are letting them know that we see them, we acknowledge them and they don't have to live that way if they don't want to."

Silverman says the signs advertise the American Atheists' upcoming convention and an atheist rally, called the Reason Rally, in Washington next month.

Atheists have long pointed to surveys that suggest atheists and agnostics make up between 3% and 4% of the U.S. population. That number increases when Americans unaffiliated with any religion are included. The Pew Center's U.S. Religious Landscape Survey found that 16% are unaffiliated, though only a fraction of those are avowed atheists and agnostics.

Silverman acknowledges that the pair of new billboards will likely cause a stir.

"People are going to be upset," he says. "That is not our concern."

"We are not trying to inflame anything," he continued. "We are trying to advertise our existence to atheists in those communities. The objective is not to inflame but rather to advertise the atheist movement in the Muslim and Jewish community."

The billboards will be up for one month and cost American Atheists, based in New Jersey, less than $15,000 each, according to Silverman.

Mohamed Elfilali, executive director of the Islamic Center of Passaic County, laughed when he learned the Arabic billboard would go up in the same town as his office. He says he's surprised that someone is spending money on such a sign.

"It is not the first and won't be the last time people have said things about God or religion," Elfilali says. "I respect people's opinion about God; obviously they are entitled to it. I don't think God is a myth, but that doesn't exclude people to have a different opinion."

But Elfilali bemoaned the billboards as another example of a hyper-polarized world.

"Sadly, there is a need to polarize society as opposed to build bridges," he says. "That is the century that we live in. It is very polarized, very politicized."

Rabbi Serge Lippe of the Brooklyn Heights Synagogue had a similar response.

"The great thing about America is we are marketplace for ideas," he says. "People put up awful, inappropriate billboards expressing their ideas and that is embraced."

But Lippe acknowledged that there are a lot of agnostic and atheist Jews. A recent Gallup survey found 53% of Jews identified as nonreligious. Among American Jews, 17% identified as very religious and 30% identified as moderately religious.

"When you have two Jews in the room, you have three opinions," joked Lippe.

American Atheists have used the word "myth" to describe religion and God on billboards before. Last November, the organization went up with a billboard immediately before the New Jersey entrance to the Lincoln tunnel that showed the three wise men heading to Bethlehem and stated "You KNOW it's a Myth. This Season, Celebrate Reason."

At the time, the American Atheists said the billboard was to encourage Atheists to come out of the closet with their beliefs and to dispel the myth that Christianity owns the solstice season.

The Christmas billboard led to a "counter punch" by the Catholic League, a New York-based Catholic advocacy group. The Catholic League put up a competing billboard that said, "You Know It's Real: This Season Celebrate Jesus."

Silverman says his group's billboard campaigns will continue long into the future.

"There will be more billboards," Silverman says. "We are not going to be limiting to Muslims and Jews, we are going to be putting up multiple billboards in multiple communities in order to get atheists to come out of the closet."

The billboard in Figure 11.16 depicts a fishing lure from the fishing goods company, Rapala. One of these billboards is placed at the Florida Turnpike exit ramp for the Florida Keys. A few environmental factors make the placement of this billboard rhetorically effective: 1) many people coming to the Keys do so to fish; 2) the exit bends past the sign, making it hard to miss; 3) traffic slows down to 35 mph, so the driver should have plenty of time to see it. While their lure gets "more hits than Google," the ad probably gets more hits than a Google ad over the course of a year.

Credit: Steve Baird

Figure 11.16
Rapala is hoping that fish aren't the only species that take their bait.

When considering delivery and environment, you might use the ecological concept of niche as a way to think about your audience. In the field of ecology, a niche is a specific role or category that a species occupies within an environment. That role is defined, in part, by its relation to the niches of other plants or animals.

In general, each species specializes in a particular way of surviving, and living within this niche helps to ensure that it has resources other animals can't use. When thinking about delivery, you might ask several questions about niche and delivery. For example: Do you have a product or argument that no one else has? If so, you might choose language that explains how it's unique. On the other hand, you might have a product that many people can use, but you want to target a specific group of people who best fit your intended audience. In advertising, each of these groups would be an example of a "niche market."

Depending on the kind of college or university you're attending, apartments close to campus are often the most desirable to students since they can walk to campus. This kind of property is the equivalent of beachfront property on the coasts. Companies that own such apartments have a desirable niche product, and should focus their marketing on this fact (Figure 11.17). Of course, these companies also have a specific, niche audience: university students, staff, and faculty.

To most effectively deliver its message, the company, most likely, will target its marketing to these three populations. Although anyone who lives in the same town could be a potential tenant, the most likely viewer to respond to such advertisements would be someone connected to the school. For this example, then, the location of the product—as well as the specific niche it inhabits among the kinds of apartments available—affects how the marketing director would attempt to reach her audience, ultimately affecting how the message becomes delivered.

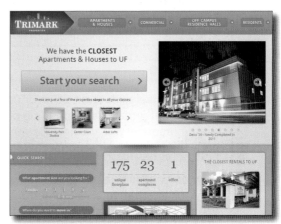

Figure 11.17
This web page for a property management company tries to deliver a niche product (apartments close to campus) to niche consumers (students).

As the examples above indicate, failure to thoughtfully consider the environment in which you deliver a text can cause viewers to miss it, or even cause that text's destruction. Consider the following guidelines toward better delivery in a particular environment.

- Where is the best location to reach your intended audience?
- What will your audience be doing in this location?
- How can you best integrate your text into the environment?
- How might an electronic environment affect your text?
- How might a natural environment affect your text?

These guidelines will help ensure that—once placed in a particular environment—your text has the best chance of reaching your audience and optimizing delivery.

Building

Link

Walk through your campus, paying attention to where visuals appear. Create a list of niches into which these visuals might fall. Once you have noticed all the niches in use, see if you can identify niches that aren't being occupied by a particular visual. How might these unused spaces be rhetorically effective or enacted? How might it aid a text's delivery? How does each space affect the rhetorical appeals of *logos*, *ethos*, *pathos*, and *kairos*? Develop a claim based on your responses above, and support it with reasons and evidence.

Engine

Search

Often, a university's auditorium or coliseum can be rearranged into a variety of configurations, depending on the event being held. For example, event personnel will arrange the venue for a graduation ceremony differently than for a musical concert. Research the different options available for your local venue and the different purposes for each arrangement. How do you think each formation affects delivery differently? Can you think of alternative arrangements that would be more effective? How does the change in arrangement affect the rhetorical appeals of *logos*, *ethos*, *pathos*, and *kairos*? Develop a claim based on your responses above, and support it with reasons and evidence.

KEY Terms

color	gesture
Comic Sans	layout
delivery	Marshall McLuhan
Demosthenes	niche
distribution	typography
environment	Vimeo
facial expression	Vine
format	YouTube

Video Résumé

For this activity, you'll create a video résumé, a visual version of your résumé that allows you to make different kinds of persuasive appeals that you can't in a printed résumé.

If you've watched the television show *How I Met Your Mother*, or if you are familiar with the show's character, Barney Stinson (played by Neil Patrick Harris), then you might have seen his "Awesome Video Résumé" (Figure 11.18).

Although a humorous example, Stinson's video is able to convey many qualities that one cannot communicate in a typical print-based résumé, such as making an emotional connection with the viewer. Moreover, he can demonstrate some of the qualities he proclaims, such as attention to detail through the details of the shots.

This example shows how attention-grabbing a video résumé can be, which is especially needed when trying to stand out in a stack of other

Credit: 20th Century Fox Television

Figure 11.18
Barney Stinson has a very imaginative video résumé.

www.barneysvideoresume.com/

applicants. While video résumés don't completely replace traditional résumés, they do offer a valuable supplement and can be vital when applying to jobs that require demonstration of new media skills. A video résumé can demonstrate your portfolio of work in a condensed, visual, and efficient way.

Because you can compose a video résumé in many ways, the following guidelines offer some basic strategies and techniques rather than a strict how-to guide. Also, a simple YouTube search for "video résumé" will produce many examples on which you might model your own.

Like the actors mentioned above, a résumé "acts" on your behalf, letting the potential employer see certain aspects of you. Carefully consider what kind of "character" you want a potential employer to see as you craft the video.

Also, remember to read the rhetorical situation through the rhetorical tetrahedron. What kind of audience does a video résumé address? What is its message? How should you design it? How can you effectively use *logos, ethos, pathos,* and *kairos*? Keep these questions in mind as you read through the following guidelines.

Start with a traditional résumé: Although you're creating a video résumé, just like any video production, a written script will greatly help. This is where your traditional résumé comes in. If you don't have one already, create a list of the following:

- education history
- work experience
- activities you performed for each job
- skills (such as computer skills, foreign language fluency)
- awards
- other qualifications (such as certificates or licenses)

This list will help you develop your overall narrative for the video even though you might not use every item on the list.

Determine your audience: Like any document, determine your audience. Are you targeting a specific company? A specific industry? Once you know who you're asking to work for, research the company and determine how your experience and skills match up with what it's looking for. You can also study the company's own website materials to determine smaller details, such as how to dress on camera (is the company formal or casual?). After sketching the audience and determining what details from your résumé the company is most likely to find appealing, you can start developing a more complete script.

Tell the story of your résumé: You should incorporate some of the résumé items into your video résumé based on this audience, but unlike your résumé, which is essentially just a list of accomplishments, your video résumé should be an argument. In the video, you should have a pitch, a claim for why the company should hire you, with your accomplishments and skills as reasons and evidence for that claim. Do not simply recite your traditional résumé, but tell a story about the items on your résumé. However, just like your traditional résumé (and like Barney's), start with your name—ideally both spoken by you, and superimposed in text—this way potential employers both hear it and see it.

Incorporate aesthetic elements: Because you're not simply reading your résumé but performing it, incorporate graphics, music, and other elements to create an overall atmosphere. While you don't need fighter jets soaring through the sky to create a metaphor for how awesome you are, you can use other images that might convey positive associations. Just make sure they're tasteful, and not tacky. If you're unsure, ask a friend.

Make your résumé relevant: As mentioned above, a video résumé should not be used for just any kind of job. For example, you probably wouldn't submit a video résumé for a technical editing job. Instead, save the video résumé for jobs where showing off your personality would be beneficial (such as sales jobs), or for jobs where you need to show off visual production skills, such as a graphic designer or video editor.

Be bold and creative: While you don't need to be as creative as Barney—who uses Hollywood effects, stunts, and other unrealistic techniques—you can still think of creative ways to tell your story. For example, consider the video résumé by Matthew Epstein (Figure 11.19).

Although Epstein didn't land the job with Google, he did get hired by another company to do his dream job. And although Epstein is bold in his approach, he nicely integrates his skillset and knowledge of the company into his dialogue, showing how he would perfectly fit with the Google team. While you don't necessarily need to create this level of performance, you can still create an interesting narrative that tells a company about what you do, and what you can do for it. In addition, by marketing himself, Epstein is showing his marketing skills and not just talking about them.

Credit: Matthew Epstein

Figure 11.19
Matthew Epstein eventually landed his dream job with this video résumé.

www.youtube.com/
watch?v=HRHFEDyHIsc

Stay professional: Although you want to develop a creative idea, make sure you still demonstrate professionalism and that you would be an invaluable employee who would work hard and infuse talent into the company. For example, unlike Epstein, you probably shouldn't appear in your video résumé without pants. And unless you're making a specific point by wearing a Batman costume, you should probably stick to more traditional clothing. Of course, the research you do about the company can tell you if it has a culture of three-piece suits or deck shoes and khakis. So unless it conflicts with a particular effect or rhetorical move, keep your speech, clothing, and general appearance as professional as is appropriate.

Keep it brief: Keep your video short (unless it's particularly engaging, such as Epstein's), usually around a minute but no more than two. Most viewers of online videos don't like to watch more than one to three minutes at a time, and as you've probably noticed, most résumés are only a page long.

Rehearse: Don't assume you'll be able to complete your video résumé in one take. Performing in front of a camera can be a strange experience, even when there is no one else in the room watching. Practice your story and script in front of the camera, and watch these early attempts to improve your enunciation, posture, gestures, and other body movements. Also, practice adding stress to important words and delivering the script naturally, not as if you're reading from a page.

Prepare the recording environment: Make sure the environment where you're shooting the video résumé is ideal. Check the lighting in the room, listen for ambient sound or outside noises the microphone might pick up, and try to alter the surroundings until you eliminate these unwanted elements.

Deliver well: After you've watched your rehearsal videos, refine your delivery. Try to act casual, and remember not to look or sound like you're simply reading the script. However, you can place your script below the camera to use as a guide, but not to read from. If you're recording from a webcam, you can potentially leave your script on-screen. When you close the video, repeat your name, thank the audience for watching, and leave them with a smile.

Review: Like the other video assignments in this book, you should have other eyes look at the video and give you feedback. Consider their suggestions, and add them to your revision list. Technically, check the video's sound and image quality and listen for unwanted noises. Finally, note the segments you might cut out and what parts you need to reshoot because of poor delivery or other accidents.

Edit and revise: Once you've reviewed the video and reshot any necessary video, use the techniques in Chapters 9 and 10 to edit the video into a final cut, incorporating any images, title sequences, or other effects you want to include.

Distribute: Although you can distribute your video résumé widely, you might want to be more selective in where you post a professional résumé. For instance, should you place it on YouTube, it may remain there forever, and old video résumés will show only past experience when you may have had several other jobs since. Instead, some job-finding websites such as CareerBuilder have options to upload a video résumé, or you could host it on a separate server and send employers the direct URL. YouTube can always be a backup option, but it might not be the best one. Also, like Epstein's résumé, include a link to your traditional résumé either embedded in the video, or in hypertext directly below it. This way, potential employers can find out more about you should they be interested.

From DIGITAL Writers

Credit: Michael Chow

Michael Chow video résumé

www.youtube.com/
watch?v=I1SVvcdCF1Q

In addition to the video résumés above, consider this video résumé from Michael Chow, an undergraduate who majored in chemistry at Hong Kong Baptist University.

Digital Documentation

Documentation of Digital Sources

When you incorporate someone else's material into your own work—whether that material is writing, image, video, sound, or other kinds of texts—it's important you provide a citation for the original source. Citing sources is important because you need to give proper credit to the individual or group who created the original material. If you fail to do so, you have plagiarized that material, for the lack of a citation suggests you are presenting someone else's work as your own.

However, in addition to the ethical reasons why you should cite source material is another: to provide the reader with links back to your train of thought and line of argument. In other words, you typically cite another work in order to help bolster your particular argument. Sometimes, in order to study and better understand your argument, the readers need to be able to return to the original source material and read it for themselves. If you fail to include a citation, they will find it difficult to locate the original material and fully understand your own argument.

Citations also help the reader understand how you build upon other conversations and other authors' works. When you cite, you are essentially remixing other sources into your own work, and this is not much different from a musician remixing prior material into new songs. Although the new song often has a different message, the original lends its history and original context to the new song, helping the audience understand part of the new song's message through its connection to this history. Your own writing, when it makes use of sources, connects with these sources' histories as well, but only if you provide citations so the audience can make these connections as they read.

Since the development of the World Wide Web in 1993, citing sources has become a bit more complicated. While it might be easy to cite a print edition of *Moby Dick*, citing this same classic novel becomes more complicated if you're referencing the book as an electronic file on the website of an online database that is, in turn, sponsored by a government institution. In addition, digitally native sources such as YouTube videos, tweets from Twitter accounts, Facebook posts, blogs, and other online materials require their own specific citation formats that account for elements such as time, date posted, date of access, usernames, and URLs.

To account for these changes, the major citation styles such as MLA, APA, and Chicago Manual of Style have created citation formats specific to this digital evolution. The citation styles for commonly cited sources below provide these updated citation formats.

The two most common formatting styles you're likely to encounter are developed by the Modern Language Association (MLA) and American Psychological Association (APA). These two styles differ in slight ways, and the examples below illustrate the differences of each. For more information on these styles, you can visit the MLA website, style.mla.org, and the APA style website, www.apastyle.org.

Formatting for the Printed Page

When writing and publishing in print, MLA and APA have different formatting requirements for the document as a whole. See below for a summary of these differences.

MLA

Spacing:	Double
Margins:	1 inch all around
Typeface:	Standard (i.e., Times New Roman)
Font size:	12 pt.
Cover page:	No (unless requested by instructor)
Page numbers:	Upper-right hand side, starting with Page 1
Indent each paragraph:	Yes

Sources:	Sources are included at the end in a section titled "Works Cited"
Identifying information:	On the first page in the upper left, provide your name, you instructor's name, the course, and the date
Other requirements:	Center and double-space the title; add another space after the title and before the first paragraph

APA

Spacing:	Double
Margins:	1 inch all around
Typeface:	Standard (i.e., Times New Roman)
Font size:	12 pt.
Cover page:	Yes; the cover (or title) page should include the title of the paper, your name on the second line, and the name of your college on the third line; all information should be centered; the cover page should also include a header, flush left, with the words "Running Head: Title of Your Paper"; remember to include your actual title rather than the text above
Page numbers:	Upper-right hand side, starting with Page 1
Indent each paragraph:	Yes
Sources:	Sources are included at the end in a section titled "References"
Identifying information:	On the first page in the upper left, provide your name, you instructor's name, the course, and the date
Other requirements:	*Running heads*: in addition to the cover page, your paper should have running heads, positioned flush left, that include the title of

your paper and the page number, such as: "Title of Your Paper 23"; note that after the cover page, you should remove the words "Running Head"

Abstract: The second page of your paper should include an abstract of 150-200 words that provides a summary of the major argument and points of your paper; your essay would then begin on the third page

Commonly Cited Print Sources

Although you will cite many digital sources in your work, you will still rely on print sources, from books to journals to magazines, as well. The following citation formats apply to these print sources. The MLA formats are listed first for each print source, followed by the APA formatting.

MLA

As mentioned above, MLA and APA differ in slight ways. One of the key differences between the two styles is the manner in which each accounts for variances in source publication medium. The most recent edition of the MLA style guide, MLA 8, no longer distinguishes between citation formats for digital or print sources, though this appendix, for ease of use, still offers examples of how to format the most commonly used sources. Instead, in an effort to streamline the citation process, MLA 8 relies on a set of 9 elements common to most source types. If a given element is not relevant to the type of source you're citing (e.g. page numbers on a web page) it should be omitted from your Works Cited entry. Each element is followed by the punctuation mark shown below, and the last elements should be followed by a period.

(1)Author. (2)Title of Source. (3)Title of Container, (4)Other

Contributors, (5)Version, (6)Number, (7)Publisher, (8)

Publication Date, (9)Location.

In the examples listed below, only the elements available for the sample citation are listed in the example format. Prior to MLA 8, we were required to include "n. pag." if no page numbers were available for our source and "n.d." if we didn't have a publication date. That is no longer the case. If you have a source type that contains page numbers and the example of that source type here does not include them, you should include them in your Works Cited. MLA 8 recognizes that not all sources have all of the core elements, and even two of the same type sources may not have all of the same core elements. As noted above, if a source is missing any of the core elements, simply omit them from your Works Cited entry. MLA 8 has omitted the requirement for including "n. pag." If a source has no page numbers, and it has also omitted the need for "n.d." if no publication date is provided. In this supplement, in-text citation formats are provided only for unusual circumstances.

Books

Works with one author are listed Lastname, Firstname. Two authors are listed in the order they appear, separated by a comma, the first Lastname, Firstname, and the second Firstname Lastname. If you have a book with three or more authors, list only the first author that appears, followed by a comma and "et al.".

Author. *Title of Source*. Publisher, Publication Date.

Works cited entry

Diffenbaugh, Vanessa. *The Language of Flowers*. Ballantine, 2011.

In-text citation for one author

(Diffenbaugh 101), (Bardes and Gossett 11), (Wysocki, et al. 7).

Book with an author and editor

Author. *Title of Source*. Other Contributors, Publisher, Publication

Date.

Works cited entry

Foster, Hannah Webster. *The Coquette*. Edited by Cathy N. Davidson,

Oxford UP, 1986.

Book with an editor instead of an author

In MLA 8, the term "author" spans a range of possibilities. The individual who fits the author role for your Works Cited may actually be an editor, translator, performer, creator, adapter, director, illustrator, or narrator. The key question to consider when determining whom to list as your author is: "Who or what aspect in this work am I focusing on in my discussion?" For example, if you're discussing the choices an editor made regarding what to include in an anthology, collection, or reader, you would list the editor in the author position: Lastname, Firstname, editor. If you're discussion the quality of a translation, you would list the translator(s) as the author: Lastname, Firstname, translator.

In-text citation

Any direct references to the content of an edited work would have their own individual citations, and in-text citations would reference those specific entries rather than the work as a whole. Otherwise, you should follow normal author-date format for in-text citations.

Chapter in a Book

> Author. "Title of Source." *Title of Container*, Other Contributors,
>
> Publisher, Publication Date, Location.

Works cited entry

One of the main differences between MLA 8 and previous editions of the style guide is the inclusion in MLA 8 of "p." to indicate the location of a document on a single page and "pp." to indicate a page range.

> Samuels, Shirley. "Introduction." *The Culture of Sentiment: Race,*
>
> *Gender, and Sentimentality in Nineteenth-Century America,*
>
> edited by Shirley Samuels, Oxford UP, 1992, pp. 1–8.

Scholarly article in a print journal

> Author, "Title of Source." *Title of Container*, Number,
>
> Publication Date, Location.

Works Cited Entry

> Ziser, Michael. "Emersonian Terrorism: John Brown, Islam, and
>
> Postsecular Violence." *American Literature*, vol. 82, no. 2,
>
> 2010, pp. 333–60.

Book Reviews and Editorials

MLA 8 does not differentiate between an editorial or books review and other types of sources. The main difference will be that editorials don't often list an author, so the Works Cited entry will begin with the editorial's title. If your book review is titled, simply list it in the Title of Source element. If your review is untitled, however, you will list your title as "Review of *Title of Book*, by Author of Book."

In-text citation

Follow normal author-page number format for in-text citations, unless you have no author, in which case you will use the source's title, or a shortened version of it, in the in-text citation. Use the same formatting for the title as appears in the Works Cited entry (i.e., italics for longer works and quotation marks for shorter works).

Magazine article

Author. "Title of Source." *Title of Container*, Publication Date,

Location.

Works cited entry

Hilmantel, Robin, and Lambeth Hochwald. "America's 51 Best Mail-

Order Foods." *Everyday with Rachael Ray*, July/Aug. 2015, pp.

92–97.

Government document

When citing a document published by a government agency, if no author is provided, list the author as the name of the government, followed by a comma and the name of the agency. Name any organization units of which the agency is part (as e.g. the Senate is part of Congress) between the name of the government and the agency. In other words, all the names are organized from largest to smallest. It is also advisable, but not necessary to include the number and session of Congress from which the document emerged, and/or specify the document's type and number (e.g. House Report 615).

Author. *Title of Source*. Publisher, Publication Date, Optional

Elements.

Works cited entry

> United States, Congress, Senate, Committee on Energy and Natural
>
> Resources. *Hearing on the Geopolitics of Oil.* Government
>
> Printing Office, 2007. 110th Congress, 1st session.

In-text citation

Though this citation technically has an author, you should use a shortened version of the work's title in place of the author's name in the in-text citation. Often, if a work cites one government document, it will likely cite others as well, and using the title rather than the "author" will help readers distinguish between your sources. If you are, however, citing only one government document, you may choose to cite the author in-text as the first government entity listed.

> (United States 43).

or

> (*Geopolitics of Oil* 43).

Online edition of a book or novel

Sources often have more than one container, each smaller container "nested" within a larger one. This is often the case, especially with online sources. Journal articles located through JSTOR, books read on Google Books, or television shows watched on Netflix all provide instances of sources held in multiple containers. In your Works Cited, you should attempt to account for all the containers enclosing your source. To do this, you will simply add the core elements 3-9 (Title of Container through Location), omitting irrelevant or unavailable elements, to the end of the entry until all additional containers are accounted for. Note that a period should follow the last element in each container.

> Author. *Title of Source.* Publisher, Publication Date. *Title of Container,*
>
> Location.

Works cited entry

In this Works Cited entry, since a novel is a "self contained" source, it serves as the first Container while Google Books serves as the second. Also, since the publication date is the last element of the first container, you'll notice it is followed by a period.

Diffenbaugh, Vanessa. *The Language of Flowers*. Ballantine, 2011.

Google Books, books.google.com/books?id=dD9_uTXl7roC.

In-text citation

In the case of digital sources, try to indicate the location of the material you cite by referencing page number(s), paragraph numbers "par.", sections "sec.", or chapters "ch.", etc. If no such indicators are available, simply list the author's last name in the parenthetical citation followed by a comma and a shortened version of the source title.

(Diffenbaugh, ch. 3).

Scholarly article in an online database

Author. "Title of Source." *Title of Container*, Number, Publication

Date, Location. *Title of Container*, Location.

Works cited entry

Ziser, Michael. "Emersonian Terrorism: John Brown, Islam, and

Postsecular Violence." *American Literature*, vol. 82, no. 2,

2010, pp. 333-60. *EBSCO*, search.ebscohost.com/login.

aspx?direct=true&db=aph&AN=50986884&site=ehost-

live&scope=site.

Article in a journal published online

If the article you're citing appears in both print and online versions, but the online version does not employ page numbers, simply omit the page numbers from the Location element. If the journal is strictly an online publication, no indication of pagination is required.

Author. "Title of Source." *Title of Container*, Number, Publication

Date, Location.

Works cited entry

> Dolby, Nadine. "Research in Youth Culture and Policy: Current
>
> Conditions and Future Directions." *Social Work and Society:*
>
> *The International Online-Only Journal*, vol. 6, no. 2, 2008,
>
> www.socwork.net/ses/article/view/60/362.

Book reviews and editorials published online

The same circumstances apply to online book reviews and editorials as to print ones. You may, however, also have a second container to include in your citation.

> "Of Mines and Men." *Wall Street Journal*, 24 Oct. 2003, www.wsj.com/
>
> public/page/editorials.html.

In-text citation

Follow normal author-page number format for in-text citations. If no author is listed, use a shortened version of the title.

> ("Mines").

Magazine article from an online database

Magazine and newspaper articles found in online databases are cited in the same fashion.

> Author. "Title of Source." *Title of Container*, Publication Date. *Title of*
>
> *Container*, Location.

Works cited entry

> Tyre, Peg. "Standardized Tests in College?: Why U.S. Universities are
>
> Implementing a No Child Left Behind-style Accountability
>
> Program." *Newsweek Web Exclusive*, 16 Nov. 2007. *Newsweek*,
>
> www.newsweek.com/standardized-tests-college-96211.

Online magazine article

> Author. "Title of Source." *Title of Container*, Date of Publication. *Title of Container*, Location.

Works cited entry

> Hilmantel, Robin, and Lambeth Hochwald. "America's 51 Best Mail-Order Foods." *Everyday with Rachael Ray*, July/Aug. 2015. *Everyday with Rachael Ray*, www.rachaelraymag.com/mailorder.

Website

Websites often do not list authors. The example included here does provide an author; however, if the source you're citing does not list one, simply omit that element and begin your Work Cited entry with the website's title. Furthermore, in MLA 8, if your website is made available through an organization, such as a museum, library, or university or any of its departments, that organization is considered the publisher.

> Author. *Title of Source*. Publisher, Publication Date, Location.

Works cited entry

> Felluga, Dino. *Guide to Literary and Critical Theory*. Purdue U, 31 Jan. 2011. www.cla.purdue.edu/english/theory.

Page on a website

> Author. "Title of Source." *Title of Container*, Publisher, Publication Date, Location.

Works cited entry

> Felluga, Dino. "Introduction to Narratology." *Guide to Literary and Critical Theory*, Purdue U, 31 Jan. 2011, www.cla.purdue.edu/english/theory/narratology/index.html.

Image from a website (including painting, sculpture, or photograph)

For electronic reproductions of images housed in a museum or collection, the museum or collection name fills the Publisher element, and the website name is the Title of Container. Additionally, and especially for older works including artworks or publications, you have the option of including the date of original creation or publication. Note that this date will appear immediately following the Title of Source element, and is itself followed by a period.

> Author. *Title of Source*. Optional Element. *Title of Container*,
>
> Publisher, Publication Date, Location.

Works cited entry

> Goya, Francisco. *The Family of Charles IV*. 1800. Museo Nacional
>
> del Prado, Madrid. *Museo Nacional del Prado*, 2016, www.
>
> museodelprado.es/en/the-collection/art-work/the-family-of-
>
> carlos-iv/f47898fc-aa1c-48f6-a779-71759e417e74.

In-text citation

If an image or work of art is to be cited in text, it should be accompanied by a figure or screen shot of the image in the text itself. The full citation information should be included in the caption for the image. There are no parenthetical citation requirements for this type of source.

For web-only or digital images

> Author. "Title of Work." *Title of Container*, Publisher, Publication
>
> Date, Location.

Works cited entry

> Brandy, Chloe. "Great Horned Owl Family." *Webshots*, American
>
> Greetings, 22 May 2006, community.webshots.com/user/
>
> brandychloe.

If the title of the work is unavailable or the work has no title, provide a brief description of the image, neither italicized, nor in quotation marks, using sentence rather than title capitalization.

> Stack of books. *Google Images*, Pyxl, 12 Jan. 2015, thinkpyxl.com/
>
> blog/wp-content/uploads/2015/01/Books.jpg.

Listserve, discussion group, or blog/podcast/vlog post

In any of these instances, the listserve, discussion group, or blog/podcast/vlog post title or subject line will act as the Title of Source. Furthermore, though the poster's username/handle can fill the Author element, if the user's actual name is also listed, include it in brackets after the username/handle.

> Author. "Title of Source." *Title of Container*, Publisher, Publication
>
> Date, Location.

Works cited entry

> Salmar1515 [Sal Hernandez]. "Re: Best Strategy: Fenced
>
> Pastures vs. Max Number of Rooms?" *BoardGameGeek*,
>
> BoardGameGeek, 29 Sept. 2008, boardgamegeek.com/
>
> thread/343929/best-strategyfenced-pastures-vs-max-
>
> number-rooms.

In-text citation

If the user's full name is not listed, use the username/handle in the in-text citation; otherwise, use the individual's actual last name.

> (Hernandez, "Best Strategy").

Government document online

In the example provided, the government document does have an author listed. In this case, as the government agency(ies) is the entity providing the document for public view, it/they become the Publisher. In this case, the document has two agencies of one government responsible for publication, so they are all listed from largest to smallest and separated by a forward slash (/).

> Author. "Title of Source." *Title of Container*, Publisher, Publication
>
> Date, Location. *Title of Container*, Location.

Works cited entry

> Snyder, Howard N. "Law Enforcement and Juvenile Crime." *Office of*
>
> *Juvenile Justice and Delinquency*, United States / Department
>
> of Justice / Office of Justice Programs, Dec. 2001, pp. 1-32.
>
> *National Criminal Justice Reference Service*, www.ncjrs.gov/
>
> pdffiles1/ojjdp/191031.pdf.

Government document in online database

Please see the example above, as it comes from an online database, the National Criminal Justice Reference Service.

Web videos (YouTube/Vimeo/Vine, etc.)

When citing online videos, the poster's username serves as the Author.

> Author. "Title of Source." *Title of Container*, Publication Date,
>
> Location.

Works cited entry

> Late Night with Seth Myers. "Amy Poehler and Seth Reunite for a
>
> New Really!?!" *YouTube*, 24 June 2015, www.youtube.com/
>
> watch?v=KmEoKXgBvSl.

Twitter

Short, untitled messages, such as Tweets, are cited by typing the full text of the message, without any changes and enclosed in quotation marks, in the Title element.

> Author. "Title of Source." *Title of Container*, Publication Date,
>
> Location.

Works cited entry

> @tombrokaw. "SC demonstrated why all the debates are the engines of this campaign." *Twitter*, 22 Jan. 2012, 3:06 a.m., twitter.com/tombrokaw/status/160996868971704320.

Email

When citing an email, use the subject line as the Title of Source.

> Author. "Title of Source." Other Contributors, Date of Publication.

Works cited entry

> Doe, Jane. "Re: Victorian Flower Meaning." received by Vanessa Diffenbaugh, 25 June 2015.

Book on a digital text archive or database

> Author. *Title of Source*. Optional Element. *Title of Container*, Publisher, Publication Date, Location. *Title of Container*, Location.

Works cited entry

> Alcott, Louisa May. *Work: A Story of Experience*. 1873. *Early American Fiction Full-Text Database*, U of Virginia, 2002, etext.lib.virginia.edu/eaf/. *Literature Online [ProQuest]*. gateway.proquest.com/openurl?ctx_ver=Z39.88-2003&xri:pqil:res_ver=0.2&res_id=xri:lion&rft_id=xri:lion:ft:pr:Z000719846:0.

Online film (Netflix, Hulu, Amazon, etc.)

As mentioned above, media productions require creative consideration of who to include in the Author element or whether to include an Author element at all. If you're focusing on the contributions of one actor, you would list that actor in the Author element, followed by a comma and the word, "performer." If you're focusing on the director's cinematic choices, you would list the director as the Author, followed by a comma and the word, "director." However, if you're focusing specifically on an episode of a television show or a movie as a whole work (as in the example provided below), you would skip the Author element altogether, and begin with the Title of Source. Regardless of who fits the Author element or if you include one, you should try to include either the director/creator or the main actors either as Author or Other Contributors.

Title of Source. Other Contributors, Publisher, Publication Date. *Title of Container*, Location.

Works cited entry

V for Vendetta. Created by Lilly and Lana Wachowski, as "The Wachowskis," Warner Bros., 2006. *Netflix*, www.netflix.com/watch/70039175?trackId=14170034&tctx=15%2C2%2Cfc83ee96-8cc3-4a21-834f-9cd6731acf5a_ROOT.

Online television episode or program (Netflix, Hulu, Amazon, etc.)

"Title of Source." *Title of Container*, Other Contributors, Publisher, Publication Date. *Title of Container*, Location.

Works cited entry

"Amelia Porter." *Criminal Minds*, created by Jeff Davis season 10, episode 10, CBS, 10 Dec. 2014. *Netflix*, www.netflix.com/watch/80066873?trackId=14170289&tctx=0%2C9%2C89948cf9-17ac-4ec7-b8f4-6f3c2bc40f32-18545977.

eBook (Kindle, Nook, etc.)

Kindle, Nook, and other eBook file types are treated as containers.

Works cited entry

> Diffenbaugh, Vanessa. *The Language of Flowers*. Ballantine, 2011.
>
> *Kindle*, Random House, 23 Aug. 2011.

eAudiobook (Librivox, Audible, etc.)

Audible and other audio-book file types are handled as container.

> Author. *Title of Source*. Publisher, Publication Date. *Title of Container*,
>
> Other Contributors, Publisher, Publication Date.

Works cited entry

> Diffenbaugh, Vanessa. *The Language of Flowers*. Ballantine, 2011.
>
> *Audible*, narrated by Tara Sands, Random House Audio, 23
>
> Aug. 2011.

Social media (Facebook, Google+, etc.)

If the post you are documenting is titled, use that title. However, since most social media posts are not titled, you have a few options for how to fill the Title element for MLA 8. First, if the post is one, short, simple sentence, then use that sentence as your title. If the post is longer, use just the first sentence as your title. If neither of these is the case, use the first 12-15 words of the post as your title. Your author will be the poster's name or username/handle.

> Author. "Title of Source." *Title of Container*, Publication Date,
>
> Location.

Works cited entry

> Criminal Minds. "Big News: Morgan's office officially has a new
>
> occupant." *Facebook*, 21 Apr. 2016, 2:04 p.m., www.facebook.
>
> com/CriminalMinds/?fref=ts.

Sound recording

Author. "Title of Source." *Title of Container*, Version, Publisher, Publication Date.

Works cited entry

Florence and the Machine. "Dog Days are Over." *Lungs*, deluxe edition, Universal Island Records, 27 Feb. 2011.

Audiobook

Author. *Title of Source*. Other Contributors, Publisher, Publication Date.

Works cited entry

Diffenbaugh, Vanessa. *The Language of Flowers*. narrated by Tara Sands, Random House Audio, 23 Aug. 2011.

Personal interview

Author. Other Contributors, Publication Date.

Works cited entry

Doe, Jane. Interviewed by John Smith, 25 June 2015.

Speech/lecture/address

When citing an unusual type of work, you have the option of identifying the type with a descriptive term. If the source you're citing is published, then use that publication information; however, if you attended a live address or speech, then the event or circumstances take the place of the publisher and publication date as in the example provided below. Of course, if the source does not have a title (such as a class lecture), simply skip that element.

Author. "Title of Source." Publisher, Publication Date, Location.

Optional Elements.

Works cited entry

> Matuozzi, Robert. "Archive Trauma." Archive Trouble, MLA Annual
>
> Convention, Hyatt Regency, Chicago, 29 Dec. 2007. Address.

Film on DVD or BluRay

> *Title of Source*. Other Contributors, Publisher, Publication Date.

Works cited entry

> *The Help*. Directed by Tate Taylor, performances by Emma Stone and
>
> Octavia Spencer, Dreamworks, 2011.

Television program or episode

> "Title of Source." *Title of Container*, Publisher, Publication Date.

Works cited entry

> "Amelia Porter." *Criminal Minds*, CBS, 14 Jan. 2015.

APA

Book with one author

> Lastname, First Initial. (Year of Publication). *Title of book*. City and
>
> State of Publication: Publisher.

References entry

> Diffenbaugh, V. (2011). *The language of flowers*. New York, NY:
>
> Ballantine.

In-text citation

> (Diffenbaugh, 2011).

Book with more than one author

> Lastname, First Initial, & Lastname, First Initial. (Year of
>
> Publication). *Title of book*. City and State of Publication:
>
> Publisher.

References entry

> Bardes, B., & Gossett, S. (1990). *Declarations of independence: Women*
>
> *and political power in nineteenth-century American fiction*.
>
> New Brunswick, NJ: Rutgers University Press.

In-text citation

> (Bardes & Gossett 1990).

Book with more than three authors

If a book has three to seven authors, list all authors in the References list. If a book has more than seven authors, list the first six authors as usual, but after the sixth author's name use an ellipses in place of the author names, then provide the final author name.

In-text citation

For a work with three to five authors, list all authors the first time you cite the work in-text, then list only the first author's name followed by "et al." in each subsequent citation. For works with six or more authors, use only the first author's name in all citations followed by et al.

Book with an author and editor

> Lastname, First Initial. (Year of Publication). *Title of book* (Editor's First
>
> Initial Lastname, Ed.). City and State of Publication: Publisher.

References entry

> Foster, H. W. (1986). *The coquette* (C. N. Davidson, Ed.). Oxford:
>
> Oxford University Press.

In-text citation

> (Foster, 1986).

Book with an editor instead of an author

Lastname, First Initial. (Ed.). *Title of book*. City and State of Publication: Publisher.

References entry

Samuels, S. (Ed.). (1992). *The culture of sentiment: Race, gender, and sentimentality in nineteenth-century America*. New York, NY: Oxford University Press.

Scholarly article in a print journal

Lastname, First Initial. (Year of Publication) Title of article. *Title of Journal, Volume*(Issue), Pages.

References entry

Ziser, M. (2010). Emersonian terrorism: John Brown, Islam, and postsecular violence. *American Literature, 82*(2), 333-360.

In-text citation

(Ziser, 2010).

Book review

Review Author Lastname, First Initial. (Year of Publication). Title of review (if applicable). [Review of the book *Title of book*, by Author First Initial Lastname]. *Title of Periodical*, Page(s).

References entry

Stephenson, M. S. (2015). [Review of the book *Apocalyptic sentimentalism: Love and fear in U.S. antebellum literature* by K. Pelletier]. *Choice*, 1500.

In-text citation

(Stephenson, 2015).

Editorial

Editorial title. [Editorial]. (Year, Month Day of Publication).

Publication Name. Page Number(s).

References entry

Of mines and men. [Editorial]. (2003, October 24). *Wall Street*

Journal, p. A14.

In-text citation

For editorial with named authors, use standard author-year format. However, as editorials often do not list an author, if none is given then use a shortened version of the editorial's title followed by the publication year for in-text citation.

(Of mines and men, 2003).

Magazine article

Lastname, First Initial. (Year, Month of Publication). Title of article.

Title of Periodical, Pages.

References entry

Hilmantel, R., & Hochwald, L. (2015, July). America's 51 best mail-

order foods. *Everyday with Rachael Ray*, 92-99.

In-text citation

(Hilmantel & Hochwald, 2015, pp. 92–99).

Government document

If identified, cite the publication's author; otherwise, start with the name of the national government, followed by the agency (including any subdivisions or agencies) that serves as the organizational author. For congressional documents, include the Congress number and the session of the hearing or when the resolution was passed.

National Government. Agency. Subdivision. Sub-agency. (Year)

Document Title. City and State of Publication: Publisher.

References entry

United States. Senate. Committee on energy and natural resources.

(2007). *Hearing on the geopolitics of oil*. Washington, DC:

Government Printing Office.

In-text citation

When a source's author is unknown, use a shortened version of the work's title in place of the author's name in the in-text citation.

(*Geopolitics of oil*, 2007).

Electronic books (On websites, in databases, or via audio)

Lastname, First Initial. (Year of Publication). *Title of book*. Retrieved

from URL.

References entry

Diffenbaugh, V. (2011) *The language of flowers*. Retrieved from

https://books.google.com/books.

In-text citation

(Diffenbaugh, 2011).

If your text does not list page numbers, use "n. pag." in place of the page number for the in-text citation.

Scholarly article in an online database or article in an online journal

APA does not require database information in citations because databases change over time. If your article is available in print, format your references entry as you would for a print article. If your article is difficult to locate or is only available online, include a web page or database URL.

Book review published online

Review Author Lastname, First Initial. Title of review (if applicable). [Review of the book *Title of book*]. *Title of Periodical.* Retrieved from URL.

References entry

Stephenson, M.S. (2015) [Review of the book *Apocalyptic sentimentalism: Love and fear in U.S. antebellum literature*]. *Choice.* Retrieved from http://www.cro3.org.ezproxy.mtsu. edu/content/52/9/1500.

In-text citation

(Stephenson, 2015).

Editorial published online

Editorial title. [Editorial]. (Year, Month Day of Publication). Retrieved from URL.

References entry

Of mines and men. [Editorial]. (2003, October 24). Retrieved from http://www.wsj.com/public/page/editorials.html.

In-text citation

(Of mines and men, 2003).

Online magazine article

Lastname, First Initial. (Year, Month of Publication). Title of article. *Title of Periodical.* Retrieved from URL.

References entry

> Hilmantel, R., & Hochwald, L. (2015, July). America's 51 best mail-
>
> order foods. *Everyday with Rachael Ray*. Retrieved from
>
> http://www.rachaelraymag.com/mailorder.

In-text citation

> (Hilmantel & Hochwald, 2015).

Website

> Lastname, First Initial (if known). (Date of Publication). *Website Title*.
>
> Retrieved from URL.

References entry

> Felluga, D. (2011, January 31). *Guide to Literary and Critical Theory*.
>
> Retrieved from https://www.cla.purdue.edu/english/theory/.

In-text citation

> (Felluga).

If your website does not list an author or creator, use a shortened version of the website title for your in-text citation instead.
> (*Literary and Critical Theory*).

Page on a website

When a web source consists of more than a single page, provide a URL that links to the home page or entry page for the document, but using the same format as that for a website as noted above.

Image from a website (including a painting, sculpture, or photograph)

> Lastname, First Initial of artist. (Year Created). *Title of work*.
>
> [Format]. Retrieved from URL.

References entry

Goya, F. (1800). *The Family of Charles IV*. 1800. [Painting]. Retrieved from https://www.museodelprado.es/en/the-collection/online-gallery/on-line-gallery/obra/the-family-of-carlos-iv/.

In-text citation

(Goya, 1800).

Blog or vlog post

First Initial Lastname of Editor, Screen Name, Author, or Compiler (if available). (Date of Posting). Posting title. [Web log comment]. Retrieved from URL.

References entry for blog

S. Hernandez. (2008, September 29) Best strategy: Fenced pastures vs. max number of rooms? [Web log comment] Retrieved from https://boardgamegeek.com/thread/343929/best-strategy-fenced-pastures-vs-max-number-rooms.

In-text citation

(Hernandez 2008).

References entry for vlog

Psychology video blog #3 [Video file]. Retrieved from http://www.youtube.com/watch?v=lqM90eQi5-M.

In-text citation

(Psychology video).

Government document online

> National Government. Agency. Subdivision. Sub-agency. (Year).
>
> *Document title.* Retrieved from URL.

References entry

> United States. Senate. Committee on energy and natural resources.
>
> (2007). *Hearing on the geopolitics of oil.* Retrieved from
>
> http://www.energy.senate.gov/public/index.cfm/hearings-
>
> and-business-meetings?ID=c1dc2207-58ee-44b2-b7f2-
>
> dcf834684a54.

In-text citation

When a source's author is unknown, use a shortened version of the work's title in place of the author's name in the in-text citation.

> *(Geopolitics of oil*, 2007).

Web videos (YouTube/Vimeo/Vine, etc.)

APA recommends writers use the same format to reference an online video, television episode, or film as for referencing a website.

Twitter

> Lastname, Firstname (username). "Full Text of Tweet." Date and Time
>
> of Posting. Tweet.

References entry

> Brokaw, Tom (tombrokaw). "SC demonstrated why all the debates
>
> are the engines of this campaign." 22 January 2012, 3:06 a.m.
>
> Tweet.

In-text citation

> (Brokaw).

Social media (Facebook, Google+, Twitter, etc.)

> Lastname, First Initial or Username. (Year, Month Day Posted). Title or first sentence of message or full text of Tweet. Message posted to (or archived at) URL.

References entry

> Criminal Minds. (2015, June 25). Fall can't come soon enough. Message posted to https://www.facebook.com/CriminalMinds.

Email

Emails are not included in the References list; however, they are cited in-text as follows:

> (First Initial. Lastname of author, personal communication, June 25 2015).

eBook (Kindle, Nook, etc.)

> Lastname, First Initial. (Date of Publication). *Title of book.* [ebook Version]. DOI or Retrieved from URL.

References entry

> Diffenbaugh, V. (2011) *The language of flowers.* [Kindle DX version]. Retrieved from http://www.amazon.com.

In-text citation

> (Diffenbaugh, 2011).

Audio and video podcasts

> Lastname, First Initial. (Date of Publication). *Title of podcast* [Audio podcast]. Retrieved from URL.

References entry

> Fleming, J. (2012, November 25). *Rex Jung on Neuroscience of Creativity* [Audio podcast]. Retrieved from http://www.ttbook.org/book/rex-jung-neuroscience-creativity.

In-text citation

> (Fleming, 2012).

Film on DVD

> Producer Lastname, First Initial (Producer), & Director Lastname, First Initial (Director). (Date of Release). *Film title* (Motion picture). Country of origin: Studio or distributor.

References entry

> Silver, J. (Producer) & Wachowski, A. & Wachowski, L. (Directors). (1999). *The matrix* (Motion picture). USA: Warner Brothers.

In-text citation

> (*The matrix*).

Television series episode

> Writer Lastname, First Initial (Writer), & Director Lastname, First Initial (Director). (Date of broadcast or copyright). Title of episode. [Television series episode]. In First Initial Lastname (Producer), *Series Title*. City, state of origin: Studio or Distributor.

References entry

> Davis, J. & Watson, S. L. (Writers), & Riley, A. (Director). (2015, January 14). Amelia Porter. [Television series episode]. In R. Dunkle (Producer), *Criminal Minds*. New York, NY: CBS.

In-text citation

> (Davis and Watson, 2015).

Sound recording

> Artist, Band, or Songwriter. (Date of copyright). Song title. [Recorded by artist if different from song writer]. On *Title of album.* [Medium of recording]. Location: Label. (Recording date if different from copyright date).

References entry

> Taupin, B. (1975). Someone saved my life tonight [Recorded by Elton John]. On *Captain fantastic and the brown dirt cowboy.* [CD]. London, England: Big Pig Music Limited.

In-text citation

> (Taupin, 1975).

Audiobook
Follow the same citation guidelines for an audiobook as you would for a sound recording.

Personal interview
No personal communications, including interviews, are included in an APA References list. Instead, cite the interview in-text as follows:

> (E. Robbins, personal communication, January 4, 2001).

Speech/lecture/address
To cite a speech, lecture, or other address, you should have a documented source for it whether in text, video, or recorded audio. Use the relevant citation guidelines for your particular medium from the list above.

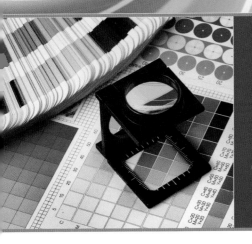

Digital Tools and Techniques

Although this book has covered a wide range of rhetorical appeals, media choices, and genres you can use when engaged in digital writing, there are a few more digital tools and techniques you might consider, especially if you are new to using some of the digital platforms necessary to complete this book's various assignments.

Digital Tools

When creating the projects in this book, there are a variety of free tools and tutorials available. For instance, if you don't have access to Adobe products (such as Photoshop), open source image editors such as the GIMP offer nearly as many features. If you do have access to commercial products, many tutorials exist that can walk you through any tool or technique you might need to learn. Below is a list of such tools and techniques.

Free Photoeditors
- GIMP: http://getgimp.com

Free Layout Editors
- Scribus: http://www.scribus.net/canvas/Scribus

Free Video Editors
- Lightworks: http://www.lwks.com/ (tutorial:http://www.youtube.com/watch?v=YRYNAvZJawQ)
- VideoLAN: http://www.videolan.org/ (tutorial:http://www.youtube.com/watch?v=_XTeCwhMNnM)

GIMP Tutorials
- http://www.youtube.com/watch?v=8LmW5ndnEqw
- http://www.youtube.com/watch?v=kOSmn-NeqBA

- http://www.youtube.com/watch?v=xG1eApVSnkY

Adobe Photoshop Tutorials
- http://www.youtube.com/watch?v=Dy2d4H3VHew
- http://www.youtube.com/watch?v=xS5uh5TCXcU
- http://www.youtube.com/watch?v=o-u-OYz2qaU

Adobe InDesign Tutorials
- http://www.youtube.com/watch?v=bYUTNfqEx-Q
- http://www.youtube.com/watch?v=F4I809YXmZ4
- http://www.youtube.com/watch?v=MHfDZvbychc

Adobe Premiere Tutorials
- http://www.youtube.com/playlist?list=PLOToExFaWoNKcTa-ARw5-VmGTBalH9Zoly

Windows Live Movie Maker Tutorials
- http://www.youtube.com/watch?v=Sdte6mxMZzg

Apple iMovie Tutorials
- http://www.youtube.com/watch?v=fFuLi8D-qGk

In addition to these technical tools and techniques, there are also some rhetorical techniques you might consider when developing texts with these applications.

Digital Techniques for Print

In addition to the tools for writing digitally, there are also many techniques for using these tools and rhetorical choices specific to digital writing. For example, aspects such as the genre and format of the document greatly affect how a reader responds. Consider how the following rhetorical choices can affect how a document becomes distributed and received by the audience.

Genre

The term "genre" can cover a range of meanings. For instance, in a written essay, itself a genre, you might choose subgenres such as satire, parody, or opinion. You could select a range of technical writing genres such as letters, memos, reports, manuals, or other kinds of documents. For example, often letters are used in more formal situations with audiences outside of your organization, while memos are used for more informal, internal situations. Film, as this text has already discussed, has a wide array of genres and subgenres as well, including documentary, comedy, drama, romance, suspense, fantasy, or science fiction. Your photographs might fall under the genres of fashion, advertising, still life, fine art, nature, travel, architectural, portrait, or photojournalism. As you plan your project, consider how the audience will react to the genre you chose. This reaction affects the document's overall delivery.

Format

When you think of format, you might think of the formal aspects of a document, such as the page size, margins, layout, or spacing. While this type of format certainly affects an audience (such as your teachers, who might demand one-inch margins), other kinds of formats are important for digital writing, particularly file formats. If you want to deliver to a wide audience, you should select formats that are more universal. While many computers can open Microsoft Word documents, Adobe PDFs are more accessible, and the PDF reader can be downloaded for free. While your video might look better in a high definition format, this format might not be easily viewable if the intended audience doesn't have a fast download connection to the Internet. When preparing a document, research which file formats are most accessible, and consider what technological capabilities your audience will have. If you know they can view an HD video, then upload the larger file. However, if you're not sure, use a lower quality version or provide the option for either. If your audience can't download or view your file format, then your delivery will fail, and moreover, you'll probably frustrate your reader.

Although printed text primarily uses the colors black and white, arranged on 8.5" x 11" inch paper with 1-inch margins, the tools of digital word processors, combined with digital platforms such as photo editors, can help you add a variety of visual features to print-based assignments.

Color

Of these techniques, color becomes an important tool when trying to deliver a message through print. As discussed in Chapter 11, an audience often associates certain colors with particular meanings and emotions. For instance, white and black are often used to signify themes of good and evil (Figure B.1). The colors green and brown depict earthy, naturalistic feelings, while blue can be melancholic.

Figure B.1
Sony Playstation uses color to create a sense of good vs. evil. Do you see any problems with the use of color in this ad? Many consider the ad racist.

Although print doesn't typically use colors in these ways, it can still use colors rhetorically to help organize material for the reader, highlight important information, or emphasize a particular word, paragraph, or other graphical element. Just as an orator can change his or her tone, volume, or pitch when pronouncing a word, a writer—especially one using a computer's word processor—can think of the available graphical options as choices of delivery, choices for how one can augment the body of the page so that it best captures and holds the reader's attention.

Typography

Typography also plays a role in how an audience reads your document. Typography refers to how the individual letters are arranged in design, and the letter designs are called typefaces. Usually typefaces are created by professional type designers for specific purposes. The word we sometimes substitute for typeface—font—refers to a larger complex that not only includes the typeface, but also variables such as bold, italic, or underlined. Thus, Garamond is a typeface, while Garamond-bold-italic is a font (Figure B.2).

If you've ever used the font drop-down menu in a word editing program, you've noticed that you have hundreds of options when selecting a font. This section will provide some general guidelines to help you understand which fonts should be used in particular situations and allow you to filter through the many font options to select the one that's best for your particular project.

One of the basic differences between typefaces are those with serifs—which are the small lines that extend from letters (Figure B.3) such as the ones in this font—and san serif typefaces (without serif), which have no serifs, such as Arial or Nimbus Sans (Figure B.4). In general, choose serif typefaces for most of your large blocks of texts since the serifs help the audience by making reading easier, blending one letter into the next.

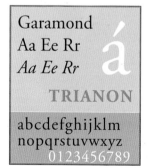

Figure B.2
Garamond

Figure B.3
Typefaces such as Garamond and Times New Roman have serifs, which are indicated in this diagram.

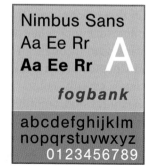

Figure B.4
Nimbus Sans is an example of a typeface without serifs.

Sans serif typefaces are better used for any text elements you want to stand out, such as headers or titles, since the letters are more distinct. These are just some guidelines, but when you do select a font, research the intended use for which it was designed. Some fonts display better on paper stock, while some are designed specifically for reading on a computer monitor. These details about a typeface may help confirm your choice or may give you pause to alter it. Either way, it will also provide some evidence if you have to justify your typeface choice to a client.

Point size simply refers to the size of the font, which is usually presented numerically, such as Arial 12, which indicates the typeface Arial at a 12 point size. For selecting a point size, consider how readable it will be for an audience and where it appears in a document. If the reader will be physically close to the document, such as a website or printed page, then 12-point font will probably be large enough. However, this same point size on a poster, or even something larger like a billboard, will probably be unreadable. For these genres, you should select a larger point size that can be read from a distance.

Point size should also change depending on the part of the document. While paragraphs of text can be set at 10-12 point, titles, headers, and other elements demand more emphasis; increasing the font size can make these features stand out from the rest of the page. Of course, other tools for emphasis such as bold-face and italics can do this as well.

You might find that the typefaces loaded into your word editor or photo editor don't have the best options for your project. By entering "font" into an Internet search engine, you will find many sites that offer free fonts, such as Dafont.com. Also, sites such as fontstruct.com allow you to design your own typeface for more custom applications (Figure B.5).

Credit: fontstruct

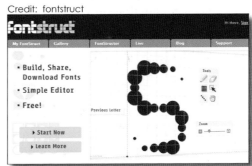

Figure B.5
Websites such as Fontstruct allow you to make your own typefaces.

Whitespace

You're probably already familiar with whitespace from writing your conventional academic papers. For example, you probably use one-inch margins on each page, place a line space between the title and the first paragraph, include space between major sections, or indent at each new paragraph. All of these features of a typed page create whitespace that helps separate the elements from each other so the audience can more easily read the page.

In creating visuals, whitespace (also called negative space) achieves the same goals. Whitespace is not simply empty space but space that helps to organize, balance, direct, and create an aesthetic effect. Whitespace separates, groups, arranges, and emphasizes the individual elements in the overall visual composition. Whitespace can be divided into two subcategories, micro and macro whitespace.

Micro whitespace

Micro whitespace refers to the smaller uses of whitespace you're probably most familiar with. Indenting a paragraph, inserting a break between a header and the section it identifies, the space between columns, the use of bulleted lists to off-set information, and even the spaces in-between individual words and letters all constitute micro levels of whitespace. Typically, this level of whitespace will determine how legible your text is to the reader. If letters and words are too close, then the text may be too hard to read. Alternatively, if the letters and words are spaced too far apart, then it may be difficult for the reader to easily scan the text, since large gaps between letters slow the pace of reading.

Micro whitespace may also include the whitespace within a group of elements separated by macro whitespace, such as an image and caption grouped together. Micro whitespace would be the amount of whitespace you use to separate the image and caption, or the title of the image, such as the space used in the examples in this text. You can also use whitespace instead of gridlines when designing a chart, table, or other graphic displaying information in column and row format.

Macro whitespace

Macro whitespace is used to separate larger elements, such as complete blocks of text, images, and any object that needs separation from the rest of the image. Macro whitespace can be a clean and simple way of highlighting or emphasizing elements. While one option might be to place a box, circle, or some other outline around such elements, these can become repetitive and clutter the overall design of the composition.

Macro whitespace can also be used to show relationships between multiple elements. Smaller areas of whitespace indicate that one element should be read in relation to another, while larger areas of whitespace create more distance and separation, showing what information belongs more closely with each other.

The homepage for Wikipedia (Figure B.6) uses a mixture of micro and macro whitespace. As you might notice, the logo in the center is separated from the language options, while the text itself is separated by smaller, micro whitespace. The text also uses macro whitespace in between some of the more important sections and margins as well as the links at the bottom. The micro whitespace on the page is subtle but important so like information is grouped together and separated from other kinds of information.

Credit: Wikipedia

Figure B.6
Wikipedia home page.

The medium you choose will dictate physical constraints that limit your overall design and therefore limit how much whitespace you can use. You can only fit so much information on a piece of paper, and even though a Web page can be limitless, you generally want a design to fit within typical monitor dimensions (typically 1280 x 768 pixels). In addition, you will have to include certain information on the medium, and doing so might take up every bit of space (consider a newspaper, for instance, which has much less whitespace compared with a magazine).

Finally, whitespace need not be "white" per se but any color devoid of text, images, or other information. Thus, sometimes white space is referred to as "negative space," or any space that is empty.

These visual features in print can help you organize a document, which helps you deliver by creating a positive design that affects your readers emotionally. Your audience would still be able to read your writing if you didn't include line breaks between paragraphs, margins, pages numbers, good choice of fonts, helpful use of color, boldface, italics, bulleted lists, and other textual choices. However, will they *want* to read such a document? In an oral context, if a particular speaker or actor is bad, the audience may stand up and leave. Likewise, even if an audience starts a text, they won't necessarily want to finish it if reading becomes too difficult. Even though the text's content might be stellar, what you deliver in the text may be undercut by how you deliver it.

Digital Techniques for Video

As mentioned throughout this book, alphabetic writing is still important in producing digital writing, but video and audio require physical and vocal skills to pull off whatever narration, dialogue, or scene descriptions are written. If you use live talent in your project—short of taking acting classes—you don't have much control over this aspect.

However, you can direct other visual facets of video. If you think of typographical and layout choices in print as influencing how the audience navigates and responds to your document, similar choices can affect how audiences respond to video. For instance, consider many of the editing techniques for video mentioned in Chapter 8. Although a dutch angle in a film isn't the same as a raised eyebrow by an orator giving a speech, the two offer aesthetic selections that affect how the audience interprets the content. To the extent that these choices draw in an audience, make them pay attention, and hopefully act in some desired way, stylistic choices are also useful delivery techniques.

Techniques of arrangement also influence how an audience uses your texts. Often, a document meant to be read live will include repetitive signposts that help the reader remember previous points, as well as cues to let the listeners know what the orator will speak about as a whole, what he is speaking about in the moment, and what he has just spoken about. Since a live audience member can't simply flip back to a previous page and reread what was just said, these reminders help orient the reader and keep them on-track with the speaker.

The arrangement of these cues becomes not just a delivery aid for the speaker—helping him or her navigate a speech—but also the audience member, so she can remember what has been said, where she is now, and where the orator will lead her. If these cues are improperly arranged, the audience may lose track of the argument, resulting in an ineffective delivery.

For example, consider Figure B.7, a transition to commer-

Credit: Fox Studios

04:52:27

Figure B.7
The television show 24 arranges multiple viewpoints to help create suspense and enhance delivery.
http://www.youtube.com/watch?v=ZFrl4Bw2kec

cial (or between major segments if watching on DVD) in the series *24*. In this transition, you should hear the beeping of a clock counting toward the end of the 24 hours, the length of time that a season of the series spans. During this transition, you also see several scenes simultaneously juxtaposed, arranged so you can see real-time action happening at once. This transition is a reminder of the various plot lines but also creates suspense as you see all the characters struggling to achieve their disparate goals. If the show simply faded to black from one of these many plot lines, you would not be as immersed in the real-time device of the show, and you would not be as aware of the time-sensitive nature under which the characters act. The show would not be as suspenseful, or as engaging. This arrangement affects the delivery of the show's emotional content to viewers.

You can also include textual cues in video, such as title sequences, color themes, or running headers to help viewers understand what they are looking at. As an example, identifying an interviewee through a textual graphic not only helps the audience understand who this person is, but also the reason why this person should be interviewed in the first place if you include her or his title or background; in other words, such textual information helps you establish *ethos*. Credits at the end of your video function like a Works Cited or References page to let the audience know where you acquired information and sources. Although your videos will primarily be visually driven, these techniques for integrating alphabetic text can help your reader make sense of the images they see.

Copyright and Reading Credits

Abramowitz, Rachel. "Johnny Depp Explains How He Picked His Poison with the Mad Hatter," from the *Los Angeles Times*, Dec. 24, 2009. Copyright © 2009 by the *Los Angeles Times*. Reprinted with permission. All rights reserved.

Allen, Erica Tyner. "The Kennedy-Nixon Presidential Debates, 1960," from The Museum of Broadcast Journalism. Reprinted with permission. All rights reserved.

August, John. "Why Email Addresses Matter," from *johnaugust.com*. All rights reserved.

Bennett, Clay. Cartoon copyright © by Clay Bennett. Reprinted with permission. All rights reserved.

Branson, Matthew. "How to Effectively Market with Memes (Without Forcing It)," from *BlueGrass Archive*. All rights reserved.

Brownlee, John. "Building a Better Radiation Symbol," from *Wired*, Feb. 20, 2007. Copyright © 2007 by Condé Nast. Reprinted with permission. All rights reserved.

Butts, Steve. "There and Not Quite Back Again," from *IGN.com*, Apr. 10, 2014. All rights reserved.

Evje, Mark. "*Top Gun* Boosting Service Signups," from *Los Angeles Times*, July 5, 1986. Copyright © 2016 by the *Los Angeles Times*. Reprinted with permission. All rights reserved.

Fricks, Keeli. "The Computer Keyboard" and "Augmented Reality Glasses and Blue Light Exposure." Student essays used with permission.

Friedman, Thomas L. "Why Putin Doesn't Respect Us," from *The New York Times*, Mar. 4, 2014. Copyright © 2014 by *The New York Times*. Reprinted with permission. All rights reserved.

Gaines, Brian. "Gangnam Style: Content and Rhetorical Analysis." Student essay used with permission.

Hall, Jonathan C. "Miles Away from Ordinary," from *creativedistraction.com*. Reprinted with permission. All rights reserved.

Hipwell, Kath. "Why 'Ethos Brands' like Ben & Jerry's and TOMS Shoes Need to Improve their Storytelling," from *Campaign Live*, May 28, 2014. Copyright © 2014 by Haymarket Media Group, Ltd. Reprinted with permission. All rights reserved.

Hoerling, Martin P. "Global Warming? Not Always," from *The New York Times,* Mar. 8, 2014. Copyright © 2014 by *The New York Times*. Reprinted with permission. All rights reserved.

Isaacson, Andy. "Are You Following a Bot?" from *The Atlantic*, May 2011. Reprinted with permission. All rights reserved.

Kendrick, James. "Texting in Business: Not a good Idea," from *zdnet.com*, Oct. 7, 2013. Reprinted with permission of The YGS Group. All rights reserved.

Lammers, Maura. "The Importance of Thoughtful Editing (Or Why I Tear Apart Manuscripts Like a Rabid Dog)," from *The Missouri Review,* July 13, 2012. Reprinted with permission. All rights reserved.

Lica, Mihaela. "How to Create the Right Avatar for You and Your Brand," from *siteprint.com*. All rights reserved.

Merica, Dan. "Atheist Group Targets Muslims, Jews with 'Myth' Billboards in Arabic and Hebrew," from *CNN*, May 1, 2012. Copyright © 2012 by Cable News Network, Turner Broadcasting System, Inc. Reprinted with permission. All rights reserved.

Morrison, Sara. "The Associated Press is Not *Vogue*, Fired Photoshopping Photographer Learns," from *The Wire*, Jan. 22, 2014. Reprinted with permission. All rights reserved.

Murray, Peter. "51 Percent of Total Online Traffic is Non-Human," from *Singularityhub.com*, Mar. 23, 2012. Reprinted with permission. All rights reserved.

Peel, Molly. "*Pathos* in Advertising," from Mause Media Group, June 13, 2014. Copyright © 2014 by Mause Media Group. Reprinted with permission. All rights reserved.

Quigley, Robert. "Cavaliers Owner Dan Gilbert Addresses Cleveland in Comic Sans: Why We Facepalm," from *themarysue.com*, July 7, 2010. All rights reserved.

Schaper, David. "Gang Signs and a Sticker: Chicago Pulls Teen's Dream," from *National Public Radio,* Feb. 9, 2012. Copyright © 2012 *NPR*. Reprinted with permission. All rights reserved.

Seigenthaler, John. "A False Wikipedia 'Biography," from *USA Today*, Nov. 29, 2005. Copyright © 2005 by *USA Today*, a division of Gannett Satellite Information Network, LLC. Reprinted with permission. All rights reserved.

Sweeney, Deborah. "How to Create a Great Hashtag to Advertise Your Business," from *Social Media Today,* Oct. 3, 2013. All rights reserved.

Temple, Emily. "Excerpts from 20 Great Writers on the Art of Revision," from *flavorwire.com*. All rights reserved.

Toos, Andrew. Cartoon copyright © Andrew Toos. Reprinted with permission. All rights reserved.

Index